Reading and Writing Short Arguments

Fourth Edition

WILLIAM VESTERMAN
Rutgers University

Mc
Graw
Hill

Boston   Burr Ridge, IL   Dubuque, IA   Madison, WI   New York
San Francisco   St. Louis   Bangkok   Bogotá   Caracas   Kuala Lumpur
Lisbon   London   Madrid   Mexico City   Milan   Montreal   New Delhi
Santiago   Seoul   Singapore   Sydney   Taipei   Toronto

McGraw-Hill Higher Education

A Division of The **McGraw-Hill** Companies

Reading and Writing Short Arguments

Published by McGraw-Hill, an imprint of The McGraw-Hill Companies, Inc., 1221 Avenue of the Americas, New York, NY 10020. Copyright © 2003, 2000, 1997, 1994 by McGraw-Hill. All rights reserved. No part of this publication may be reproduced or distributed in any form or by any means, or stored in a database or retrieval system, without the prior written consent of The McGraw-Hill Companies, Inc., including, but not limited to, in any network or other electronic storage or transmission, or broadcast for distance learning.

2 3 4 5 6 7 8 9 0 FGR FGR 0 9 8 7 6 5 4 3 2

Vice-president and Editor-in-chief: *Thalia Dorwick*
Executive editor: *Lisa Moore*
Senior developmental editor: *Renée Deljon*
Senior marketing manager: *David S. Patterson*
Designer: *Sharon Spurlock*
Senior production editor: *Christina Gimlin*
Senior production supervisor: *Pam Augspurger*
Senior supplements producer: *Louis Swaim*
Art editor: *Cristin Yancey*
Cover designer: *Lisa Buckley*
Cover art: *Gary Overacre*
Compositor: *G & S Typesetters*
Typeface: *Bembo*
Printer: *Quebecor World, Fairfield*

Library of Congress Cataloging-in-Publication Data

Reading and writing short arguments / [compiled by] William Vesterman.— 4th ed.
    p. cm.
  Includes bibliographical references and index.
  ISBN 0-07-255601-3 (alk. paper)
  1. English language—Rhetoric. 2. Persuasion (Rhetoric) 3. College readers.
  4. Report writing. I. Vesterman, William, 1942–
PE1431 .R43 2002
808'.0427—dc21

                                                    2002074333

www.mhhe.com

CONTENTS

Part I: Current Controversies from Three Points of View   *27*

Part IV: Moving to Longer Arguments *211*

Part V: A Minicasebook on Censoring Rock and Rap *239*

PREFACE

Reading and Writing Short Arguments offers substantial instruction, unique apparatus, and 71 reading selections that represent an exceptionally broad range of contemporary issues. Designed for courses that emphasize argument, it provides a complete introduction to critical reading, critical thinking, and argumentative writing. For three editions, teachers and students have praised the breadth and timeliness of this book's topics, as well as its diverse, balanced perspectives and accessible arguments.

ORGANIZATION AND PROVEN FEATURES

The opening section, **Introduction to Argument and Persuasion**, offers 25 pages of instruction on why and how we argue, what we do and don't argue about, types of appeals, the Toulmin system of logical analysis, kinds of arguments, fallacies, and how to read and write arguments. Following this introduction are 58 short, lively essays on controversial topics by authors with diverse perspectives—the heart of the book.

These 58 essays are organized in two parts: **Part I, Current Controversies from Three Points of View**, addresses each of 16 topics from diverse and opposing positions. The readings are followed by discussion questions that ask students to analyze the author's appeals to logic, character, and emotion. Further, in each controversy section, a major claim from one of the essays is presented as a Toulmin diagram, providing students with a visual model for analyzing claims. (The *Instructor's Manual* accompanying the text includes diagrams for the other two essays.) Each controversy section ends with questions that address the three readings as a group, and suggestions for writing. The goal throughout part I is to encourage critical thinking with prompts that help students begin the process of analysis.

For further flexibility in instruction and learning, **Part II, Single Essays on Controversial Topics**, consists of ten essays without accompanying questions and writing suggestions. Part II therefore gives students the chance to practice reading arguments and using the skills of analysis they have acquired without specific prompts.

The text's subsequent parts (III–VI) present additional arguments in three different formats, as well as a brief guide to writing research-based arguments. **Part III, Understanding Visual Arguments**, new to the fourth edition, gives students a chance to analyze and respond to types of arguments with which they are very familiar: advertisements and cartoons. For courses that include the study of longer arguments, **Part**

IV, Moving to Longer Arguments, offers three classic essays, ranging in length from six to thirteen pages, by Jonathan Swift, Elizabeth Cady Stanton, and Martin Luther King, Jr. Finally, **Part V, A Minicasebook on Censoring Rock and Rap**, and **Part VI, A Guide to Finding and Using Information**, offer a convenient selection of sources and a way of incorporating research into courses without having students buy another text.

HIGHLIGHTS OF THE FOURTH EDITION

The fourth edition of Reading and Writing Short Arguments offers many changes that ensure its currency and continuing ability to hold students' interest, among them:

- **Over 40 percent new readings.** In response to suggestions from reviewers who used the third edition, many successful essays have been retained, yet more than 40 percent of the essays are new. Many of the new selections appear in Part I, Current Controversies from Three Points of View, which includes six new issues: SUVs, cell phones, same-sex marriage, Internet censorship, reparations for slavery, and terrorism. Part II, Single Essays on Controversial Topics, includes six new arguments on issues such as Census 2000 and race classification, free music online, and distance learning. And Part IV, Moving to Longer Arguments, has one new selection, Elizabeth Cady Stanton's "Address to the National Woman Suffrage Convention."
- **Coverage of visual arguments**. The new part III, Understanding Visual Arguments, gives students a chance to analyze and write about familiar types of arguments. The part includes advertisements, and editorial and humorous cartoons.
- **Expanded and updated guide to research.** Part VI, A Guide to Finding and Using Information, includes increased coverage of two important topics: online research and plagiarism. Coverage of both the MLA and APA documentation styles has been increased to provide more models for electronic sources, and the APA section has been revised throughout to reflect the changes in the recently published fifth edition of the APA's Publication Manual (2001).
- **Web site to accompany** *Reading and Writing Short Arguments*, **Fourth Edition.** Offering abundant links relevant to the authors and issues presented in the book, and organized to follow the book's order, the site provides online resources for student projects, including research papers. The Web site's URL is <www.mhhe.com/vesterman>.

PRINT AND ELECTRONIC RESOURCES FOR INSTRUCTORS AND STUDENTS

In addition to the new Web site, *Reading and Writing Short Arguments,* Fourth Edition, is accompanied by an ***Instructor's Manual,*** available both in print and online. The manual includes the additional Toulmin diagrams for selections in Part I, as well as a general introduction to the text, sample syllabi for both semester- and quarter-length courses, discussions of how the reading selections' arguments work and the issues they represent, a brief discussion of the research guide and the sample student research paper, and a blank logic diagram. **Teaching Composition Faculty Listserv at <www.mhhe.com/tcomp>.** Moderated by Chris Anson at North Carolina State University and offered by McGraw-Hill as a service to the composition community, this listserv brings together senior members of the college composition community with newer members—junior faculty, adjuncts, and teaching assistants —in an online newsletter and accompanying discussion group to address issues of pedagogy, both in theory and in practice.

PageOut. McGraw-Hill's own PageOut service is available to help you get your course up and running online in a matter of hours—at no cost. Additional information about the service is available online at <http://www.pageout.net>.

AllWrite! Available online or on CD-ROM, *AllWrite* offers over 3,000 exercises for practice in basic grammar, usage, punctuation, spelling, and techniques for effective writing. The popular program is richly illustrated with graphics, animations, video, and Help screens.

ACKNOWLEDGMENTS

Many people have helped in the development of this book throughout its four editions. I wish now to thank the staff at McGraw-Hill who have helped with this edition, particularly Sharon Spurlock, Pam Augspurger, Megan Scully, Cristin Yancey, and Renée Deljon, my editor. I also thank Marty Granahan for securing permissions, Amy Marks for her truly outstanding copyediting, and Christina Gimlin at McGraw-Hill for her expert production management.

I also thank once again the reviewers of the first edition: Robert H. Bentley, Lansing Community College; Sue E. Cross, Mission College; Jean F. Goodine, Northern Virginia Community College; Edward McCarthy, Harrisburg Area Community College; Paul J. McVeigh, Northern Virginia Community College; Thomas A. Mozola, Macomb Community College; Joseph Nassar, Rochester Institute of Technology; Kathleen O'Shea, Monroe Community College; Teresa M. Purvis, Lansing Community College; and Richard J. Zbaracki, Iowa State University.

To their names I add, with thanks, the names of the reviewers who helped with advice on the second edition: Angela Berdahl, Portland

Community College; Curt Bobbitt, College of Great Falls; Susan Brodie, University of Wisconsin Center; Sue E. Cross, Mission College; Collett B. Dilworth, East Carolina University; Rose Gruber, Gloucester County College; Susan Hoyne, Centralia College; Jill Marie Karle, Piedmont Virginia Community College; Lutz Kramer, Rogue Community College; Colleen McGuigan, University of Wisconsin Center at Manitowoc; Nancy Montgomery, Sacred Heart University—Connecticut; Dan Pearce, Ricks College; Phoebe Reeves, San Francisco State University; Howard Sass, Roosevelt University; Greg Scholtz, Wartburg College; and James Strickland, Slippery Rock University.

My thanks as well go to those who thoughtfully reviewed the third edition: Kathryn E. Dobson, University of Maryland; Barry M. Maid, University of Arkansas at Little Rock; Patricia R. McClure, West Virginia State College; Marianne F. Pollack, Eastern New Mexico University; Michael W. Shurgot, South Puget Sound Community College; Stephen Wilhoit, University of Dayton; and William Zeiger, Slippery Rock University.

Finally, I thank the reviewers of the fourth edition: John Adams, University of Alabama at Birmingham; Cathryn Amdahl, Harrisburg Area Community College; Dr. Charles Franklyn Beach, Nyack College; Collett Dilworth, East Carolina University; Judith Dorn, St. Cloud State University; Robert P. Holtzclaw, Middle Tennessee State University; Peggy Jolly, University of Alabama at Birmingham; Steven R. Luebke, University of Wisconsin-River Falls; Barbara Gaal Lutz, University of Delaware; Janice Witherspoon Neuleib, Illinois State University; Stephen E. Severn, University of Maryland, College Park; Virginia Skinner-Linnenberg, Nazareth College of Rochester; and William Zeiger, Slippery Rock University.

William Vesterman,
New Brunswick, NJ

Introduction to Argument and Persuasion

MOTIVES AND METHODS OF ARGUMENT

Why Argue?

To human beings, forming opinions is as natural and necessary as breathing. Birds never have to decide what kind of nest to build, but humans decide how to build everything from a house to a society on the basis of thought and opinion. Because a diversity of opinion has always characterized human activities, listening to arguments and forming arguments of one's own are necessary ways of deciding among competing opinions.

We are not born with opinions but form them through our own mental and emotional lives and our interactions with the lives of others. At first we may receive most of our opinions unquestioningly, but very soon we begin to question even the views of our parents. The sounds of "Why?" and "Because!" echo throughout every childhood. However unsatisfactory that primitive dialogue may be (for both parties), those words present the basic structure of inquiry, and they begin to suggest some of the ways we form opinions. We want to know *why*—we want some reasons to follow the *because*—so that we can decide for ourselves whether we agree or disagree.

But our opinions are not just personal decisions. However confident we might have been of our views, and however inevitably convincing they might have seemed to us, "I wish that I had thought to say . . . !" is a common refrain when we find ourselves alone again after a dispute with other people. And merely announcing our views on a topic is seldom enough to convince anyone that we are right to think as we do. Dialogue rather than **assertion** is the basis of the process. If we want others to take our views seriously, let alone be persuaded by them, we have to argue our positions effectively and responsibly while finding answers to reasonable objections.

We don't change our minds unless we are persuaded by responsible arguments. Yet we don't need to be convinced to benefit from a dialogue. Though hearing other views and the arguments that support them may not change our minds, having to answer the arguments of others may clarify and strengthen our own opinions. As educated people we should never be satisfied to know what we already know, and we need all the clarity and mental strength we can get to face serious and complex issues. Clarification for ourselves and for others, rather than "winning," is a goal to which both parties in a dialogue can aspire.

Clarity and strength of opinion are necessary not only for education but also for the world of work and action. Thinking critically about problems and explaining suggested solutions are activities that play a large part in any business or profession. Even in a field as concerned with physical facts as engineering, for example, those who succeed are those who are able to explain to their superiors the importance of their work and to argue in support of the ideas they propose. The same skills are required at every level of government, from the smallest local committee to the largest national legislature. Public opinion ultimately controls democratic government, and effectively argued views ultimately control public opinion.

What We Don't Argue About

Argument is a term often incorrectly applied to quarrels, in which mere assertion and name-calling replace the rational presentation of opinion and the responsible meeting of opposing viewpoints. Quarrels can take place over any issue, but responsible and effective argument is impossible in certain areas:

- We can't argue about *facts*. For example, that the American Revolution occurred is beyond dispute; we are no longer ruled by Great Britain. Although it is possible to argue about the significance of facts or the probability that an assertion actually is a fact, verified matters are not matters of opinion.
- We can't argue about the *impossible*. For example, that men should be responsible for bearing children is not an arguable position.
- We can't argue about *preferences*. Preferences resemble opinions, but they are neither formed nor changed by logic. For example, that rap music is better than rock music, that baseball is more graceful than ballet, and that long hair is ugly on men are all matters of preference, not matters of rational debate.
- We can't argue about *beliefs* that lie beyond rational or empirical proof, such as religious faith.

What We Do Argue About

We argue about *opinions* because arguing is the process by which opinions are formed. For this reason, opinion is not the end of rational discussion but the beginning of a dialogue with others and with yourself. In fact, it is safe to say that the process of learning to argue in responsible and effective ways will expand, modify, and strengthen many of the opinions you have now.

Why Analyze the Arguments of Others?

Arguing is an activity requiring skill, and, as in most activities, you acquire skill by imitation as well as by instruction. As you read the essays in this book, the discussion questions following them will invite you to analyze how and why the writers' arguments work. Having done this, you should be able to imitate their methods to make your own arguments more effective. Simply having opinions is not enough. You must also decide how to organize and express them and how to counter your opponent's objections. The discussion questions will help you master this task by encouraging a dialogue between you and authors of short essays like those you will be asked to write.

The essays here have been chosen because they address a variety of current topics that you can discuss, preliminarily at least, without further research. Some of the essays in this book provide instances of what to *avoid* as an effective writer of arguments. These flawed essays may be just as useful as those better argued in stimulating the growth of your argumentative skills.

Argument and Persuasion

Since arguments offer reasons for taking a position on an issue, argument is often distinguished from **persuasion,** because we may be persuaded by means other than evidence or logic. These other means of persuasion are generally divided into (a) matters of *character*—the trustworthiness we may grant to the reputation, ethics, or clarity and strength of mind of the writer or speaker—and (b) matters of *feeling*—the emotional agreement we may come to feel with the speaker or writer. In ancient Greece, where these distinctions were first proposed, the appeal of the moral character of the arguer, or speaker, was called **ethos,** whereas **logos** referred to the powers of logic or reason in the argument, and **pathos** referred to the ways emotion persuaded the audience to agree. The Greeks called the study of persuasive argument **rhetoric** just as we do in English.

The following diagram, called the Rhetorical Triangle, may clarify the interaction of the three means of persuasion. To each point of the triangle have been added the terms of the **Toulmin system** of logic, to which you will shortly be introduced.

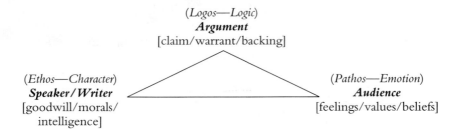

(Logos—Logic)
Argument
[claim/warrant/backing]

(Ethos—Character)
Speaker/Writer
[goodwill/morals/
intelligence]

(Pathos—Emotion)
Audience
[feelings/values/beliefs]

Argument is the first aspect of the Rhetorical Triangle that we will discuss. **Claim, warrant,** and **backing** are terms the Toulmin system uses to talk about this aspect of rhetoric.

THE WRITER AND LOGIC: APPEALS TO REASON

Logical is a word people often use informally to mean "reasonable." But the word *logic* also refers to formal systems of reasoning that depend on definite rules to determine the truth or falsity of an argument. In the West, formal logical theory began with the syllogism of Aristotle (see p. 7), and modern logicians have created various symbolic systems and techniques to meet needs for rigorous proof like those of mathematics. In ordinary verbal arguments, however, such strict proof is made extremely difficult not only by the complexity of life but also by the inherent ambiguities of language.

The Toulmin System of Logic

The feeling that logical theory was becoming too far removed from verbal arguments as they really took place among ordinary people caused British philosopher Stephen Toulmin to propose a new system of logic. Toulmin's method aimed not at the absolute truth of mathematical operations but at the kind of truth produced by argument within the legal system of English-speaking countries. In such legal argument a preponderance of evidence suggests a conclusion to a jury, and guilt needs to be proved, not beyond all conceivable doubt, but beyond a reasonable doubt. Legal argument, therefore, is close to the kind of argument used elsewhere in life. It depends for its persuasiveness on convincing an audience of the general strength of a case rather than on the rigorous but narrow standards of absolute proof used in mathematics or other formally constructed logical systems.

Toulmin's Terms

Let us look at Toulmin's names for the different parts of a logical argument before analyzing some examples to see how the parts go together. Toulmin breaks the structure of an argument into six parts:

- **Data:** what prompts you to make a claim, that is, the facts that lead you to believe your claim is true.
- **Claim:** what you believe your whole argument proves.
- **Qualifier:** the part of the argument that measures the strength or force of the claim. For example, is the claim *always* true? true *in the United States?* true *in modern times?*
- **Warrant:** an assumption that you expect your audience will share. The warrant supports the claim by connecting it to the data.
- **Backing:** any facts that give substance to the warrant. Not all arguments make use of explicit backing.
- **Rebuttal:** the part of an argument that allows for exceptions without having to give up the claim as generally true. The rebuttal does not so much refute your point as anticipate and answer attempts by someone else to refute it. For example, you could claim that most geese fly south for the winter while admitting that a few are still found in the north. The very fact that *few* are found helps to prove your general point that *most* migrate.

An Example of the Toulmin System

Let us put the terms to work and illustrate them by analyzing an example Toulmin himself uses. Suppose, he suggests, you find yourself forced to argue something you thought was fairly obvious. You claim in the course of conversation that a man mentioned in the newspaper, Sven Petersen, is probably not a Roman Catholic. In a friendly dialogue, someone doubts your claim, asking, "What makes you say that?" You reply, "I think Sven Petersen is almost certainly not a Roman Catholic, because he's Swedish and very few Swedes are Catholics." Sorted out, the elements of this simple argument are as follows:

- **Data:** Petersen is a Swede.
- **Claim:** Sven Petersen is not a Roman Catholic.
- **Qualifier:** almost certainly.
- **Warrant:** A Swede can generally be taken not to be a Roman Catholic.
- **Backing:** The proportion of Catholics in Sweden is very low. (If you researched the religious proportions of Sweden, you might find something like the following to use as backing: "According to Whittaker's Almanac, less than 2% of Swedes are Roman Catholic.")
- **Rebuttal:** unless Petersen is one of the 2%.

The Toulmin Diagram

The structure of the argument may be clearer in diagrammatic form:

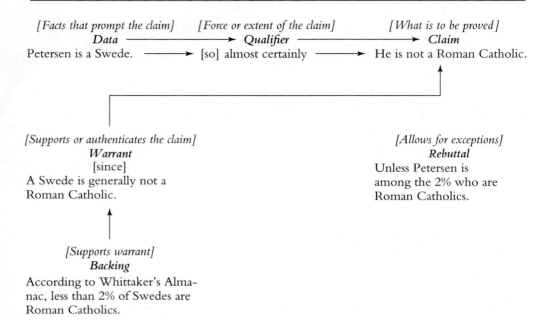

[Facts that prompt the claim]
Data
Petersen is a Swede. ⟶

[Force or extent of the claim]
Qualifier ⟶
[so] almost certainly ⟶

[What is to be proved]
Claim
He is not a Roman Catholic.

[Supports or authenticates the claim]
Warrant
[since]
A Swede is generally not a
Roman Catholic.

[Allows for exceptions]
Rebuttal
Unless Petersen is
among the 2% who are
Roman Catholics.

[Supports warrant]
Backing
According to Whittaker's Alma-
nac, less than 2% of Swedes are
Roman Catholics.

Of course not all arguments are so clear-cut. And most writers argue for several things in the course of a single essay. Further, one or more of the elements of an argument may be implicit or lacking altogether. For example, in analyzing an argument you may be unable to find the backing for one claim because the author took for granted that the warrant was so obvious as not to need further evidence. In the following passage, the qualifier is not explicitly stated, though it seems to have the force of something like "always."

The passage that follows is a single paragraph of "Government Is the Problem" by Walter E. Williams, an essay that appears in full later in this book (p. 195). In the course of arguing the main point suggested by his title, Williams devotes many single paragraphs to particular examples of what he sees as the general governmental "problem" Here is paragraph 6:

> Government control, such as the attempt to establish an official language, frequently leads to conflict, including wars and civil unrest, as we've seen in Quebec, Belgium, South Africa, Nigeria and other places. As our government creates bilingual legislation, we are seeing language become a focal point for conflict such as the ugly, racist-tainted "English Only" political campaigns in several states. The best state of affairs is to have no language laws at all.

Analyzed with the Toulmin system, the elements of Williams's argument are as follows:

- **Data:** As our government creates bilingual legislation, we are seeing language become a focal point for conflict such as the ugly, racist-tainted "English Only" political campaigns in several states.
- **Claim:** The best state of affairs is to have no language laws at all.
- **Qualifier:** always. [implied]
- **Warrant:** [since] Government control, such as the attempt to establish an official language, . . . leads to conflict. [implied warrant] And it is best to avoid conflict.
- **Backing:** as we've seen in Quebec, Belgium, South Africa, Nigeria and other places.
- **Rebuttal:** frequently.

Diagrammed, the argument looks like this:

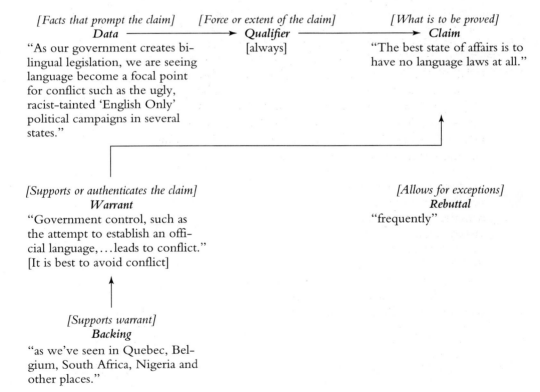

[Facts that prompt the claim]
Data ————————➤ *Qualifier* ————————➤ *Claim*
[Force or extent of the claim]
[What is to be proved]

"As our government creates bilingual legislation, we are seeing language become a focal point for conflict such as the ugly, racist-tainted 'English Only' political campaigns in several states."

[always]

"The best state of affairs is to have no language laws at all."

[Supports or authenticates the claim]
Warrant
"Government control, such as the attempt to establish an official language, . . . leads to conflict."
[It is best to avoid conflict]

[Allows for exceptions]
Rebuttal
"frequently"

[Supports warrant]
Backing
"as we've seen in Quebec, Belgium, South Africa, Nigeria and other places."

Aristotle's Syllogism

Let us illustrate Toulmin's system further by briefly comparing its methods with the ways in which the classical **syllogism** invented by

Aristotle might analyze the same argument. A syllogism is made up of three parts:

- **Major premise:** Conflict is bad.
- **Minor premise:** Government language laws create conflict.
- **Conclusion:** Therefore government language laws are bad.

Syllogistic reasoning assumes that if both premises are accepted as true, the conclusion must also be accepted as true. That is, if an entire class of facts is true, and if the case in question is a member of that class, the case in question must also be accepted as true, since what is true of a class must also be true of the members of that class.

You may notice that Williams's paragraph does not look like a syllogism and that the words used in the sample syllogism are sometimes not exactly his words. In fact, Aristotle says that most syllogisms are embedded in or implied by real-life arguments. He calls the implied syllogisms **enthymemes** (EN-thuh-meems). Teasing out the syllogisms from the enthymemes of a given argument is a skill that users of classical logic must acquire, just as arranging the writer's language and its implications into Toulmin's categories can often be a tricky matter at first and is always subject to differences of opinion on details.

Inductive and Deductive Reasoning

Whether analyzed by the Toulmin system or by Aristotelian logic, Williams's specific argument within the sample paragraph is an example of **deductive reasoning.** He deduces his conclusion about a specific problem from general premises. That is, his argument moves from a general proposition (conflict is bad) to a particular instance (government control of language is bad).

On the other hand, as you will see, Williams's essay as a whole is an example of **inductive reasoning**—the kind that scientists employ. Inductive arguments reason from particulars (government control of language is bad) to the general (government control is always bad). Williams gives example after example of the problems that he considers are caused by governmental interference; he expects us then to agree that government control makes a general "problem," one extending well beyond the examples he cites to all or most examples.

Inductive reasoning does not claim the strengths of absolute proof but seeks to establish a high degree of *probability* for the general truths it infers from the observation of particular facts. For instance, scientists have not examined every molecule of water to see whether they are all composed of hydrogen and oxygen, but since all the water molecules that *have* been examined show the same results, they conclude that all other water molecules would too.

Kinds of Arguments

Like Williams in "Government Is the Problem," many writers employ both the inductive and the deductive methods of reasoning at different times in the same essay. And whether analyzing arguments or forming them yourself, you will find that the arguments in an essay also tend to fall into some general categories. Because often several of the categories appear within a given essay, it will benefit you both as a reader and as a writer to understand the categories.

ARGUMENTS ABOUT THE NATURE OF SOMETHING—IS IT X? Arguments about the nature of something are based on definition. For example, in "Who's White? Who's Hispanic? Who Cares?" (p. 178), Jeff Jacoby questions the nature of *race* as a category. He asks if Hispanic is really a *racial* term.

Guidelines Definition usually plays a subordinate part in a larger argument, but it is important to develop a sense of when you need to define your terms and when you can take them for granted. In general you should always define terms that are new to you, ones you suspect will be new to your audience, ones you are conscious of using in a special sense, or ones you suspect an opponent will use to question your case. Imagining your opponent's potential questions in a fair-minded way will serve you well in this and other areas of argumentative discourse. In defining your own important terms, there are several reliable methods:

- *Dictionary definitions.* The most common (and perhaps the most overused) technique is simply to repeat what a dictionary says: for example, "According to *Webster's Third International Dictionary, Hispanic* is defined as. . . ."
- *Stipulative definitions.* A writer can simply state the particular sense in which he or she will be using a word. For example, in "What Should We Do about Tobacco?" (p. 139), Sally Chen provides a stipulative definition of *sophisticated* when she says that nonsmoking teenagers are "really sophisticated in the true sense of that word. They have a real 'knowledge of life and how to live in the world.'"
- *Definition by synonym.* You can define a word by means of synonyms. But choose carefully. *Home* is used by real estate agents as a synonym for *house,* but a poet tells us that "It takes a heap of livin' / To make a house a home."
- *Definitions by image or verbal picture.* For example, in one of the essays in the section "Animal Testing" (p. 85), medical researcher Ron Klien attempts to show what he understands *cruelty* to mean by describing the suffering of children he has known as patients. After doing so, he argues that such cruelty might be avoided by

medical advances based on a lesser degree of suffering undergone by animals in controlled experiments.

- *Definition by extended description.* For example, in "The Poor Have Enslaved the Rich" (p. 95), Paul Craig Roberts gives many examples and anecdotes to justify his use of the word *enslaved.*
- *Operational definition.* This is a kind of definition designed to make clear distinctions about terms based on actions that define what they mean. For example, in "Serving Time the Old-Fashioned Way" (p. 185), Dick Boland describes activities available to convicts that can hardly be defined as "punishment."

ARGUMENTS OF CAUSE AND EFFECT — HOW DID X COME TO BE?
If arguments of definition generally respond to the issue of "what?" arguments of cause and effect seek to answer the questions "how?" and "why?" Cause and effect can organize your argument in either direction:

- *From cause to effect.* For example, in "Needed: Techies Who Know Shakespeare" (p. 180), Ellen Ullman argues that a literary education makes people better technical workers.
- *From effect to cause.* For example, in "Public Servants Often Behave like Masters" (p. 159), Stephen Chapman argues that incivility in civil servants is an effect traceable to their status as workers in a public monopoly.
- *Antecedent and consequence.* This relation is useful in analyzing situations that may be deceptively similar to those involving cause and effect. Turning 18 does not cause you to become a voter: Acquisition of the right to vote is a consequence of that event but is not caused by it.

Guidelines Cause-and-effect reasoning is as tricky as it is important in forming effective and responsible arguments. Keep these general principles in mind:

- *An effect always follows a cause.* For example, thunder follows lightning, so the cause-and-effect relation must be that of "lightning-thunder" and never the other way round.
- *For repeated effects, the most likely cause is the common factor.* For example, if several children attending the same school become ill while their friends from other schools remain healthy, they most likely contracted the sickness at their school.
- *If the effect increases and decreases, you must find a cause that acts similarly.* If violent crime increases and decreases proportionally with the size of the male population 15–25 years old, you can make a good argument that connects characteristics of young males and violent crime.

ARGUMENTS OF EVALUATION—IS X BETTER OR WORSE THAN Y? Many larger arguments contain issues of evaluation that present special difficulties. Our senses of value go so deep that we tend to treat them as self-evident warrants. Yet the well-known saying "Everyone is entitled to his or her own opinion" need not end the discussion of values, which include beliefs about good/bad, right/wrong, and moral/immoral.

In the first place, differences of opinion are seldom so widespread that there is not a great deal of common ground. For example, most people come up with similar lists of the leading qualities that define good writing, and "clarity" is usually first on the list. In the second place, disagreements about values are often based on a lack of understanding about what the argument is about. Being clear about your own and others' bases of judgment (and understanding what is being judged) are basic requirements of discussion. In "On Reading Trash" (p. 151), for example, Bob Swift concedes the differences of quality in literature but argues that reading "bad" books is good for children because it leads to a love of reading that will later lead to a love of "classics."

Guidelines Some general philosophical principles are often evoked directly or indirectly as standards for judging value.

- The German philosopher Kant held in his "categorical imperative" that no human being should be used merely as a means to the ends of another.
- The British philosopher Bentham held that the greatest good for the greatest number should be the principle on which to judge actions.

Of course, more particular bases for judgment do exist, and you should be aware of distinctions among them.

- Naive egoism, for example—what's good for me is obviously good—is a poor basis for argument.
- In judging that something is bad, you should make clear the basis of your negative judgment. For example, is what you condemn bad because it is a sin, a wrong, or a crime—or is it some combination of these different categories? In the chapter on hate crimes and justice, for example, none of the writers is in favor of bigotry, but they do differ on whether bigotry changes the nature of a crime.

ARGUMENTS OF POLICY—SHOULD WE OR SHOULDN'T WE DO X? Arguments of policy are very common and are among the main modes of argument in almost all the selections in this book. As you will see, this kind of argument often makes use of the other kinds we have been reviewing, but you should be aware of some common checkpoints that will give additional help.

Guidelines Since arguments of policy generally respond to a "problem," your analysis in this regard needs to be thorough.

- Make sure you clearly designate the problem that the policy you recommend or reject addresses.
- Spell out the consequences that will ensue if the problem is not solved and any reasons that make the need for a solution especially pressing.
- Propose the solution and make specific recommendations of the procedures that will lead to the solution while explaining how they will do so.
- Consider opposing arguments and make sure you answer them.
- Support your proposal with solid backing and evidence, but don't neglect the moral and emotional supports for your policy and for the policies you reject.

Counterarguments

A part of most arguments is taken up not with advancing the reasons for your own views but with answering the reasoning of your opponents. In general you should seek to test opposing views on the same bases you use to test your own; the series of policy argument guidelines just given will be helpful in this regard as well.

Some Common Forms of Fallacious Reasoning

In the course of analyzing both your own arguments and those of others, you should be aware of some common errors of reasoning. You should be sure both to avoid these errors yourself and to point them out in the arguments of others when you make your counterarguments. It is important to note that fallacious reasoning does not necessarily make the claim wrong. That is a question you must decide by examining the whole issue for yourself.

FAULTY GENERALIZATION The error of faulty generalization comes from treating all members of a class or category as if they were defined by criteria that apply only to some members. For example, in "Whose Canon Is It, Anyway? It's Not Just Anglo-Saxon" (p. 153), Henry Louis Gates, Jr., argues that the list of "great books" has been formed by the tastes of only part of the reading population.

BEGGING THE QUESTION Users of the fallacy of **begging the question** try to take for granted the issues that need to be proved. They often use words and phrases like *obviously, of course,* and *simply* to preface unproved assertions. For example, in "Pecksniffs Can't Stop the

SUV" (p. 43), Brock Yates argues that to ask whether SUVs are safe is to beg the question, because Americans have already defined driving as an "acceptable risk."

FAULTY ANALOGY Comparing one issue to another is an effective and indispensable technique of argument, but an **analogy** is always open to question, and you should be sure that your comparisons are as solid as possible. For example, in "No More Jury Trials for Terrorists" (p. 31), Michelle Malkin argues that to treat acts of terror as crimes under the American judicial system is to act on the basis of a faulty analogy.

POST HOC, ERGO PROPTER HOC The Latin phrase **post hoc, ergo propter hoc** means roughly "after this, therefore because of this." The fallacy is a mainstay of superstitious reasoning that claims causal connection for events that merely succeed one another in time—seeing a black cat and experiencing misfortune, for example. But the issues are not always so clear-cut. In "On Reading Trash" (p. 151), for example, Bob Swift argues against the idea that reading "trashy" books when young leads to "trashy" tastes in adulthood.

ARGUMENT AD HOMINEM The Latin **ad hominem** means "to the man," and the fallacy involves attacking someone personally as a way of attacking that person's views. For example, the controversy over the performer called Ice-T that appears in the Minicasebook on Censoring Rock and Rap (pp. 239–91) revolves in part around the man himself.

ARGUMENT AD POPULUM An attempt to appeal "to the people" and their presumed common values and emotions may be another diversionary tactic designed to advance or oppose arguments unfairly. This tactic often uses what are called "God-words" (*pro-, help, family,* etc.) and "Devil-words" (*anti-, greed, mean-spirited,* etc.). In "Offering Euthanasia Can Be an Act of Love" (p. 129), Derek Humphry implies that opponents who compare mercy killing to Nazi exterminations are guilty of using both a faulty analogy and an argument **ad populum.**

RED HERRING The figure of speech that describes this fallacy comes from the fact that a **red herring** has a strong odor and can be dragged across the scent trail left by humans or animals to confuse pursuing dogs. For example, in "Shouting 'Fire!' in a Virtual Theater" (p. 68), Maureen Farsan argues that in claiming to defend free speech the defenders of pornography employ a red herring. They don't want to *speak* about pornography, she says, but to have access to it.

EQUIVOCATION To **equivocate** is to use terms in differing senses in an attempt to deceive. For example, in "Wartime Powers, but No War" (p. 34), Jim Mann says that the word *war* is used only figuratively in "the war on terrorism," which therefore should not be confused with a literal and legal war declared under the Constitution by Congress.

PROVING A NEGATIVE Arguments often take something like the following form: "If we do as you propose, what guarantees do we have that something awful will not occur as a result at some time in the future?" Negative propositions cannot be proved to an absolute degree because we can never know the future, or anything else, to an absolute degree. Recall Toulmin's example and remember that our system of logic is designed to prove only a preponderance of probability. One can argue the highly likely proposition that Sven Petersen is not a Roman Catholic without having to prove that it is impossible for him to be a member of that faith.

The foregoing examples of fallacious reasoning do not exhaust the category of logical fallacies, just as the brief introduction to logic itself is designed only to get you started. The next section looks beyond logic at other methods of presenting your views.

PERSUASION BY OTHER THAN LOGICAL MEANS

Let's look again at the Rhetorical Triangle to emphasize once more that, as important as logic is to human beings, reason is not the only attribute of human nature and therefore not the only means by which we express or respond to opinions.

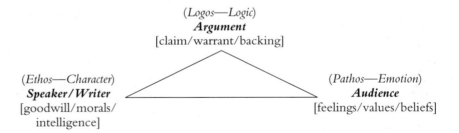

(Logos—Logic)
Argument
[claim/warrant/backing]

(Ethos—Character)
Speaker/Writer
[goodwill/morals/
intelligence]

(Pathos—Emotion)
Audience
[feelings/values/beliefs]

Character: The Writer's Personal Persuasion

As the diagram suggests, the strength of effective argumentation relies not only on reason but also on the credibility of the reasoner, and that credibility needs to be established with an **audience.** Establishing credentials is the function of the appeal to the writer's general character and personality. This "ethical appeal" acts with the appeals to logic and emotion to convince the reader that the writer's arguments are persuasive.

Classical rhetoric holds that writers and speakers should give their audiences an overall impression of a good character, including high intelligence, high moral standards, and an attitude of general goodwill. The audience gains its knowledge of these inward and spiritual virtues from the outward and visible signs of the writer's reputation and style and the format of the essay. Each of these elements in turn may make its ethical appeal by several means.

REPUTATION Intelligence and expertise can be shown through public credentials, which may strongly influence our responses one way or another. Most of the writers whose essays are included in this book are briefly identified in the Annotated Table of Contents, and you might try the following experiments to test the force of the ethical appeal. Open the book at any point and read an essay without referring to its author's description in the table of contents. Then read the brief biographical identification and rethink your response. As another experiment, simply remind yourself of the attitudes that new acquaintances seem to take toward you when you explain what your college major is or might be!

STYLE Even without elaborate public reputations, all writers can express character through their writing styles. Carefully formed sentences and paragraphs argue intelligence in general, but you must also adapt your tone of voice and manner of presentation to the occasion at hand. For example, consider how you automatically change your presentation of the same anecdote when recounting it to your grandmother and your close friends.

Adopting an appropriate style expresses not only your relation to your audience but also your respect and consideration for its time and attention. For example, how do you feel about a fellow student's argument, regardless of its rationale, when that speaker adopts a belligerent or blustering manner in class? To take another example: Public speakers are usually invited because they are presumed to know more about the topic in question than the audience they address, but many speakers begin their talks with a joke to display a character that does not consider itself above its listeners.

One final example of the ethical appeal through style can be seen in the Declaration of Independence. Signing that document meant death to its signers if the revolution failed, yet it ends with the pledge of "our lives, our fortunes, and our sacred honor." By putting *lives* in the least important position in the list and *honor* in the climactic place, the signers affirmed a hierarchy of values that shows high ethical standards as well as personal courage.

Your own stylistic choices should aim at establishing not only your intelligence but also your good faith, rationality, fair-mindedness, and benevolence. Without sounding like a know-it-all or a show-off, you should try both to connect your personal views to wider categories of public importance and to refer to publicly acknowledged **authorities** who agree with you. But you can achieve all the goals of the ethical appeal most easily if you write in a natural style rather than the artificial grandiosity often associated with "English papers." For example, few students have ever spoken the word *thus,* though many have written it.

FORMAT   The format and mechanical correctness of writing is also taken to express the character of its author. Neatness counts! And so does accuracy. Remember how widely ridiculed Vice President Quayle once was when he misspelled potato. If your essay is mechanically sloppy, your grammar careless, and your spelling poor, your **audience** will respond to those elements, whatever the strength of your reasoning might be.

Guidelines In checking your efforts to establish the impression of a character that includes intelligence and common sense, ask yourself these questions:

- Have I used arguments that I myself believe? Have I qualified or modified them for my audience as I would for myself?
- Have I overstated the case or used inappropriate language or **clichés?**
- Have I allowed for doubts and uncertainties and acknowledged the good faith of other viewpoints?
- In trying to establish good character and goodwill, have I made my own beliefs clear?
- Have I connected my views to other **authorities** and larger contexts?
- Have I shown consideration and respect for my audience?
- Have I reviewed any potential points of disagreement?
- Have I tried to show off?
- Have I avoided name-calling?
- Have I shown that I assume my audience's sincerity and common sense?
- Have I defined questionable terms and distinguished between my facts and the opinions they are to support?

Emotion: The Writer and Persuasive Feelings

In expressing their views, people often use the phrase "I feel that" as equivalent to "I think that"—and although thought and emotion may be separated for purposes of discussion, they are closely intertwined in an audience's response to your views. It may hardly need saying that emotions are not subject to logic, but they do have a rationale of their own. As Pascal says, "the heart has its reasons that reason knows not of." Here are some examples of the emotional appeal at work:

- In "Curbing the Sexploitation Industry" (p. 252), Tipper Gore attempts to **appeal** to the reader's sympathy for children as a way of answering those who accuse her of unconstitutional censorship.

- Very early in the modern debate on abortion, the sides ceased to describe themselves as *antiabortion* or *antiregulation* and began to use *prolife* and *prochoice* instead. The change was an acknowledgment of the greater force of positive terms in such an emotion-filled debate.
- Because freedom is a concept commonly applauded, whereas hatred is an attitude commonly disapproved of, the terms *free speech* and *hate speech* are often used by differing sides to describe the same phenomenon.

Emotions need not be so extreme or dramatically founded as some of the preceding examples to play an effective part in argumentative writing; many emotional appeals are more subtle. For example, absolute terms of assertion like *certainly* and *without a doubt* can evoke a mild annoyance in your readers that might lead them to hunt for minor exceptions to your argument. By avoiding such terms you may keep attention focused on the general strength of your case.

Avoiding negatively emotive words is only one side of a style formed to appeal to an audience's emotions. Figurative language is loaded with implied emotional appeals that can work positively—even if a term is negative in itself. For example, in "On 'Junk Food for the Soul': In Defense of Rock and Roll" (p. 247), Frank Zappa playfully admits the negative implication of "junk food" in his title, the better to express his confidence in his ability to act "In Defense of Rock and Roll."

In checking your emotional appeals, remember that emotions play a very strong part in the process of persuasion and that logical reasoning alone is seldom enough to stir an audience to action or deep conviction. As a reader of your own and others' arguments, try to sort out the emotional appeals from the logical reasoning. As a writer, remember that you cannot command the emotions of others. Let the **connotations** of the words you choose and the metaphors, images, and descriptions you employ speak for themselves.

Guidelines One set of discussion questions following each essay in Part I of this book examines the many ways in which the emotional appeal operates in persuasive writing. The idea is to gain as many effective techniques for your own writing as you can by carefully observing the techniques of professional writers. For general purposes, keep in mind this simple checklist:

- Ask yourself, "Have I given examples that might prompt positive or negative emotions such as pride or indignation?"
- Use images, figures of speech, and concrete examples to elicit the emotions in your audience. Avoid abstract words or direct assertions that *tell* your audience directly how to feel, such as "Every right-thinking person will be appalled at this state of affairs." *Show* your readers that the state of affairs in question is appalling and let them do the feeling for themselves. For example, in "The

Trials of Animals" (p. 83), Cleveland Amory tells us of experiments on laboratory monkeys in which "first nerves in their limbs were removed and then stimuli—including electric shocks and flames—were applied to see if they could still use their appendages." He doesn't need to tell us this is horrifying; we are horrified.

- Ask yourself, "Have I taken care not to insult my audience's values and assumptions?"
- Ask yourself, "Have I defined my position on the issues in a way that will appeal to my audience's general sense of fairness and justice?"

READING AND WRITING ARGUMENTATIVE ESSAYS

This introduction and the discussion questions that follow each essay in Part I are designed to foster your skills as both reader and writer. These skills are mutually supportive: By becoming a better reader of arguments made by others, you will learn how to form better arguments of your own. At the same time, the critical thinking you do in composing your own arguments will stimulate your analytical abilities as a reader. The discussion questions will invite you to write at least three kinds of essays prompted by your reading: (1) essays in which you critique the various appeals made by different writers on the same topic; (2) topical essays that you write without needing more information than the selections provide or you already know; and (3) essays that you write using information from outside sources such as the library. For any of these writing tasks, learning to be a better reader of arguments is a sensible first step.

Reading Arguments

The discussion questions will provide you with particular approaches to each topic, but some general advice for you as a reader of arguments is in order here. First of all, drop that highlighter, pick up a pencil, and open your dictionary! The arguments in this book are short enough to be read several times, and taking notes in the margin will be much more effective than reminding yourself to reread what you will reread anyway.

In your first reading, mark the words you don't know or are unsure of while you proceed rapidly through the essay. Next use your dictionary to make sure you understand the particular ways in which the writer uses his or her terms. Get in the habit of noting definitions in the margin and making other notes there as well.

Then read the essay carefully, several times if necessary, while making more elaborate notes. For example, translating a writer's arguments into summaries is worth a dozen rereadings, because you are reading the material actively. As an active reader, you will form, modify, and strengthen your own opinions on the topic as you participate in a mental dialogue with the writer.

Some other ways of improving your reading skills include what is sometimes called *prereading*—making notes (mental or written ones) on your own view of a given topic before reading the essays on that issue. This exercise will give you a firm basis for response and help you see more clearly how writers present and back up their positions. You can even prepare for prereading. Try keeping an idea log or journal as you read to note points of view or effective techniques. When you begin to write, you will have practice and material to depend on, and if you know your topic in advance, reading any other essay will suggest ways of meeting your particular task.

You may also try the technique of rereading an essay from a point of view opposite to yours. This should sharpen your sense of how firmly argued views include attention to answering opponents. Attending to all the differing points of view in each of the topical sections of this book will give you useful practice in this skill.

To sum up: Learning to be an active and effective reader in the ways suggested here is part of the initial process of learning to be an active and effective *writer* of your own arguments.

Reading with the Help of Discussion Questions

The discussion questions for each essay in Part I are designed to help you become a more active reader by prompting you to pay attention to the ways in which the essayist appeals to logic, character, and emotion in the course of arguing a case. All the questions fall into some general modes of inquiry that you can employ as a reader of any argument, while the questions for a given case attempt to lead you to more particular answers.

In general the questions on logic will ask you to focus on the following:

- What are the data that prompt the claim?
- What are the warrants for making the claim, and what backing is offered for the warrants?
- What provision is made for rebuttals or qualifiers?
- Has a writer used appropriate analogies and provided needed definitions?

Questions on character include the following:

- How does the writer attempt to establish his or her general competence for dealing with the issue?
- How do particular uses of language establish an impression of good character?
- What values, **assumptions,** and beliefs underlie the writer's position?

Some general questions on emotion are as follows:

- To what emotions in the audience does the writer appeal?
- What particular uses of language invite or evoke emotional responses, and how do they do so?

Finally, exercises at the end of each section will lead you to compare the approaches of different writers to the same topic. These exercises include the following questions:

- Where, how, and why do the writers agree and disagree?
- What are the values, assumptions, and beliefs that distinguish the positions taken?
- Does each writer imagine the same general audience?

Reading Visual Arguments

A new section in this edition contains examples of visual arguments from editorial cartoons, advertisements, and humorous cartoons. Exercises in that section of the book will help you practice how to analyze visual arguments in particular, but you will find that the methods and skills you have already practiced in responding to written arguments will make the transition to a new medium an easy one. In other words, understanding the analytical categories of logic, character, and emotion will help you just as much in "reading" arguments expressed in images as in reading arguments expressed in words.

Writing Arguments

Asking questions is the basis for writing, as it is for reading. Beginning the process of writing with questions rather than conclusions can also help you solve the problem of starting a writing task. Trying to state your views may seem like a sensible way to start writing, but it assumes that you already know everything you need to know, and that is seldom true. Even though your convictions on a topic are strongly felt, you may still end up staring at an otherwise blank page that looks like this:

I. Introduction
   a.

Such pages tend to remain blank. So don't try to express exactly what you think and feel about a topic until you have explored it fully by going through some other stages of the **writing process.**

The Writing Process: An Overview

You should think of writing as an activity that clarifies issues for yourself as well as for your audience. For most writers, that activity takes time. Remember, clear, well-organized thoughts do not flow out of a writer's mind onto paper as quickly and easily as they flow from the page into the reader's mind.

Many students think that they have a lot of trouble with writing because they have false expectations about the writing process: how easy it should be and how long it should take, for example. They believe in the myths about those legendary people for whom writing is a snap and conclude that it should be a snap for everyone. But most people find that they have to go through many stages to get to the final draft of a clear, well-organized, and complete essay. Not everything can be or need be said at once. If you divide up the many tasks involved in completing your essay, you won't have to think about everything at once, and no one stage will seem overwhelming.

In going through some or all of the exercises this section of the book suggests, you will use strategies that have proven successful for millions of beginning writers like yourself. Your ideas about your topic will become more varied in content and more forceful in expression. By examining the logic of your argument, you will discover weak points in your reasoning and be able to attend to them before your opponents do. You will discover in many instances how to use qualifiers to keep from stating your case in general or categorical terms that may unnecessarily irritate your reader.

By using the writing process to discover and explore your convictions, you will be doing a service not only to your reader but also to yourself as an educated person. Too often students turn in an unconvincing version of an essay that could have been made into an excellent one if its writer had taken it through a few more stages. Most of the errors teachers note in the margins of student essays could have been discovered and handled by the students themselves, alone or with some help from fellow students or collegiate resource centers. Similarly, matters of poor organization, such as rambling points and confused or missing transitions, are perfectly natural features of a good rough draft but are unacceptable in a final draft. Any essay must crawl before it stands up to run. The point is not to turn in the earlier stages of what could eventually be a fine essay, but to go back through the stages that will make your work suitable for public display.

Perhaps the first thing to remember is to start the writing process early enough to go through—or back through—the stages that prove useful or necessary. Some writers will need more time than others on early stages like note taking or the generation of ideas; others will need more time for later stages like revision to tighten and tune the draft. For most essays, you should try to have a first draft done at least a week before the essay is due. Such a schedule will allow you time for extensive revision, even if some of the earlier stages turn out to have taken up more time than you expected when you made your original plan. Remember that *revision* means "seeing again," and because that is what you are asking your audience to do when you address an issue with an argumentative essay, it is only fair that you be willing to look over your own work as many times as necessary. This means not only cleaning up difficulties in mechanical matters like spelling and punctuation but also revising your ideas as you discover more exactly what they entail through the process of putting them in writing.

Stages of the Writing Process

No two people go through exactly the same stages of the writing process, and a given individual may make more or less use of different stages in writing different essays. Your own sense of your strengths and weaknesses will determine how much attention you need to pay to any of the following stages or how often you need to pay conscious attention to the techniques employed in them. If you use them consciously, you may also find that you tend to skip forward to later stages or go back to earlier ones. Don't worry: Use the process the way it works best for you.

FIRST STAGE: GETTING STARTED For writers of argumentative essays, the beginning of the writing process is usually the discovery of an issue or a problem on which people disagree. You may already have taken sides, or you may think that you can contribute something to the debate that will clarify the issue or help solve the problem. Sometimes your point of view is already decided at this stage; sometimes it gets its focus later in the process.

Expressive Writing Expressive writing is talking to yourself on paper. It is useful to keep an idea log or journal as thoughts occur to you. If you have never done this sort of writing before, you will be pleasantly surprised at how much it clarifies your thinking. You needn't make entries every day as you would in an ordinary journal, but you should make entries when thoughts strike you for advancing a possible argument through appeals to character, emotion, or logic. Short entries of a sentence or two will add up to a comforting collection of things to work with as you begin an assignment.

You might do well to keep individual sections of your idea log under some headings commonly found useful for generating an inventory of issues:

- My friends and I tend to argue about . . .
- I think it's wrong that . . .
- I wish people could understand that they should . . .
- X believes . . . ; but I believe . . .
- Our college should definitely do something about . . .
- There ought to be a law that . . .

SECOND STAGE: EXPLORING AND REHEARSING This is the stage where you begin to assemble pertinent information on a given topic by recalling and jotting down your own experiences and views or by reading, interviewing, or undertaking other forms of research. At this stage you try to understand not only your own views but also the facts, values, assumptions, and beliefs about life that underlie all sides of the debate. This is the stage for prewriting and note taking or even for a rapidly written set of paragraphs on key points. Getting at least some of your thoughts down on paper, even though they may be revised later, makes you feel you are on your way.

Talking Try talking about ideas with a friend or a small group of classmates. Learning how others think will help turn your sense of an issue from a generalized subject into a collection of more particular views for and against various aspects of the issue. Often you'll find that what you thought could be taken for granted is hotly disputed by others and needs careful explanation on your part. Listen to any objections and try to get a feel for arguments that make sense to your friends on all sides of the issue. Generating ideas and gaining multiple perspectives like this are especially good ways to begin your writing, because you automatically maintains a clear sense of the argumentative essay not as a sermon but as a dialogue between the reader and the writer.

Notes In taking notes on what you read and discuss, get used to putting things under headings like *since* and *because* to form the habit of seeing facts in the explanatory or argumentative patterns you will need in your essay's drafts. The discussion questions and writing assignments in this book will encourage you to get into the questioning habit, but here is some general advice to begin with. Don't worry about where to begin with your notes. You needn't worry at first about organizing your perceptions and thoughts by claim, warrant, and data. Begin anywhere, and one thing will lead to another as you generate material that can be more fully organized or reorganized at a later stage. Use the following checklist for generating notes, along with any other questions a particular subject might suggest:

- Is there really a problem here?
- Would the proposed solution really solve it? Could the problem be solved more simply without disturbing related matters?
- Is the proposed solution really practical? Would there be any unforeseen consequences?

Once you have some preliminary notes, use the categories of logic for expanding and organizing your material. Get into the habit of sorting out the various claims, warrants, and data in the arguments you read so that you can more readily sort out the notes for your own essays. Like all skills, this analytical sorting may seem awkward at first, and there will be many instances when the proper category for a point is a debatable matter. Whether a statement should be seen as a claim or a warrant, for example, may depend on your point of view.

THIRD STAGE: WRITING A DISCOVERY DRAFT If you have already begun some writing beyond notes, this stage will blend into the second stage. A discovery draft is often messy and disorganized. It might seem chaotic to an outside reader, but this draft is meant only for you. Your efforts here should shift from gathering facts and views to putting them together. In writing this draft you will discover connections among your ideas, and rereading the draft when you're done will help you see how to reorganize what you have. Rearranging your points in a more effective order is much easier once you have expressed them in sentences and paragraphs, no matter how tentative.

Brainstorming To generate ideas and connections among them, you might try a technique sometimes called speed writing, brainstorming, or free writing. That is, write down sentences as fast as you can without worrying about whether they connect with one another. Keep going for 10 or 15 minutes, even if after the first few minutes you run out of your initial set of ideas. You will soon find that you are writing your way into a problem and discovering new views while you express some you already have.

FOURTH STAGE: REVISING OR "SEEING AGAIN" A discovery draft may have prompted you to go back to even earlier stages for further information or to rethink some aspect of the problem at hand. Revision is the stage for rethinking, and you may do several rewrites of your discovery draft until you are satisfied that you have made all your points, however roughly and awkwardly, and have placed these points in the order that seems most effective. As your argument becomes clearer in your own mind, you will begin to imagine your readers' reactions and will look into issues like unity, coherence, and flow more carefully. Try to imagine your essay as a conversation rather than a lecture, and you will write more naturally, fluently, and effectively.

Try imagining a classmate who may not agree with you but is well disposed and reasonable. Keeping such an audience clearly in mind will help you decide how much to define or explain and how much to take for granted. These questions are much harder to answer if you imagine yourself high on a podium talking down to a silent, respectful, and completely receptive public. Imagine your classmate as at first agreeable and then dubious, so that you will be better able not only to make your own points but also to meet any counterarguments. Imagine this classmate in class or in some other formal setting for your dialogue rather than in a place like the snack bar. This will help you avoid needless facetiousness or gratuitous remarks, two of the vices opposite but equal to the pomposity that can control your tone of voice when sermonizing from on high. Peer group discussions of your drafts are one of the best ways of making sure you have touched all the bases. Finally, don't be afraid to revise as many times as necessary, but concentrate on important points and leave the matters of detail to the next stage.

Revision Guidelines

- Keep your vocabulary at the natural level of educated readers and writers. Avoid unnecessary specialized words, and imagine your audience's response when weighing different choices.
- Make sure you have used examples to explain your general or abstract assertions.
- Avoid a belligerent or bossy tone of voice.
- As a rule avoid short paragraphs of one or two sentences. They may seem snappy in a journalistic text, but they suggest superficial or undeveloped thought in serious argument.
- Avoid repeating a point too often. Repetition makes you seem to underestimate your audience's abilities or attention.

FIFTH STAGE: EDITING At this stage you polish your draft until it shines like an essay. Carefully go over details of grammar and punctuation, and try to tighten up the structure of each sentence to make it as clear and forceful as possible. Avoid using too many sentences of the same form and length. Learn to combine some of your short sentences, and don't begin every sentence with *The*. Variety in sentence structure and length creates flow and pacing in your essay, and a variety of sentence openers will provide opportunities for connection and transition and keep your style from seeming plodding and dull. You can learn different ways to begin a sentence by observing how the professional writers represented in this book use their sentence openers to make transitions and signal their patterns of reasoning.

Finally, remember that while all these dos and don'ts add up to good general advice, you will learn the most about writing by actually writing and by critically reading other writers. When you find yourself admiring any aspect of a writer's method, analyze it and make it part of your own armory of stylistic resources.

Ready to Go

You are now ready to turn the theory you have learned in this introduction to practical advantage by analyzing the argumentative essays in the rest of the book and by writing essays yourself. You may of course come back to this introduction during the course of your studies to refresh your theoretical knowledge. You will understand better how to take advantage of its advice when you have engaged some of the problems of argument and persuasion yourself.

I   Current Controversies from Three Points of View

1. What Kind of Justice Do Terrorists Deserve?
2. Are SUVs Bad Sports?
3. Should We Regulate Cell Phones?
4. Should We Legalize Same-Sex Marriage?
5. Freedom and the Internet
6. Does America Owe Reparations for Slavery?
7. Animal Testing
8. The Rich—Saints or Sinners?
9. Hate Crimes and Justice
10. Toys for Tots
11. Should Flag Burning Be Made Unconstitutional?
12. Euthanasia
13. What Should We Do about Tobacco?
14. What Books Should Students Read?
15. Modern Manners
16. Should English Be the Official Language of the United States?

INTRODUCTION

In the section that follows, each of 16 controversial issues is addressed by three readings from divergent points of view. This arrangement should discourage any belief that simply choosing sides makes an appropriate method of either analyzing the arguments of others or forming one's own argument. Each reading is followed by discussion questions that invite the student to analyze the author's appeals to logic, character, and emotion. In each group of readings a major claim of one argument is analyzed in diagrammatic form according to the Toulmin system of logic. (The *Instructor's Manual* that accompanies the text includes diagrams for all other readings, along with additional material.) Each group ends with Intertextual Questions and Suggestions for Writing that invite students to move toward forming their own positions. The goal of all the critical apparatus in this part of the book is to make the reading and writing of arguments both easier and richer by encouraging habits of **analysis**—the breaking down of complex matters into simpler ones—and **demonstration**—the provision of reasons and evidence to support assertions.

1 What Kind of Justice Do Terrorists Deserve?

KANGAROO COURTS

William Safire

As soon as German U-boats put eight saboteurs on U.S. shores during World War II, one of the eight called the F.B.I. to betray the mission but was brushed off as a crackpot. Days later, he called again and managed to persuade the F.B.I. he was an authentic saboteur. Partly to keep this embarrassment of bungled enforcement from becoming known, the eight were secretly tried by a military court inside the F.B.I. headquarters.

Unexpectedly, a U.S. Army lawyer assigned to the Germans mounted a spirited defense. Col. Kenneth Royall, citing the landmark 1866 Supreme Court decision of Ex Parte Milligan—holding that martial law could not be applied where federal civil courts were in business—challenged the secret tribunal's legality.

F.D.R. told his attorney general, according to Francis Biddle's memoirs, that he would resist any Supreme Court decision to give the accused saboteurs a regular court trial: "I won't hand them over to any United States marshal armed with a writ of habeas corpus." Confrontation was averted when a cowed Supreme Court unanimously acknowledged the extra-judicial power of a president armed with a Congressional declaration of war. Six of the eight captives went to the electric chair; J. Edgar Hoover was awarded a medal of honor.

Now President Bush, with no such Congressional declaration, is using that Roosevelt mistake as precedent for his own dismaying departure from due process. Bush's latest self-justification is his claim to be protecting jurors (by doing away with juries). Worse, his gung-ho advisers have convinced him—as well as some gullible commentators—that the Star Chamber tribunals he has ordered are "implementations" of the lawful Uniform Code of Military Justice.

Military attorneys are silently seething because they know that to   5
be untrue. The U.C.M.J. demands a public trial, proof beyond reasonable doubt, an accused's voice in the selection of juries and right to choose

counsel, unanimity in death sentencing and above all appellate review by civilians confirmed by the Senate. Not one of those fundamental rights can be found in Bush's military order setting up kangaroo courts for people he designates before "trial" to be terrorists. Bush's fiat turns back the clock on all advances in military justice, through three wars, in the past half-century.

His advisers assured him that a fearful majority would cheer his assumption of dictatorial power to ignore our courts. They failed to warn him, however, that his denial of traditional American human rights to non-citizens would backfire and in practice actually weaken the war on terror.

Spain, which caught and charged eight men for complicity in the Sept. 11 attacks, last week balked at turning over the suspects to a U.S. tribunal ordered to ignore rights normally accorded alien defendants. Other members of the European Union holding suspects that might help us break Al Qaeda may also refuse extradition. Presumably Secretary of State Colin Powell was left out of the Ashcroft try-'em-and-fry-'em loop.

Thus has coalition-minded Bush undermined the antiterrorist coalition, ceding to nations overseas the high moral and legal ground long held by U.S. justice. And on what leg does the U.S. now stand when China sentences an American to death after a military trial devoid of counsel chosen by the defendant?

We in the tiny minority of editorialists on left and right who dare to point out such constitutional, moral and practical antiterrorist considerations are derided as "professional hysterics" akin to "antebellum Southern belles suffering the vapors." Buncha weepy sissies, we are. (Frankly, Scarlett, I don't give a damn—I've always been pro-bellum.)

The possibility of being accused, however, of showing insufficient   10 outrage at those suspected of a connection to terrorists shuts up most politicians. And a need to display patriotic fervor turns Bush's liberal critics into exemplars of evenhandedism. Careers can be wrecked by taking an unpopular stand.

But not always. Forty years ago, my political mentor introduced me to his senior partner, Ken Royall, who after World War II had been appointed by President Truman to be the last secretary of war. Royall, then head of a great New York law firm, considered the high point of his career his losing fight to get a group of reviled Nazi terrorists a fair American trial.

Questions for Analysis

Logic

1. According to Safire, how does the legal underpinning of President Roosevelt's decision on military tribunals differ logically from that of President Bush? What legal reasoning does he attribute to each case, and how do they differ?

2. Why, according to Safire, are military attorneys "silently seething" over [5] President Bush's decision to evoke the Uniform Code of Military Justice?   *Fundamental rights evoked*
3. How, according to Safire in paragraphs 6–9, has the antiterrorist coalition been "undermined" by President Bush's decision? Be sure to explain Spain's logic as reported by Safire.

Character
1. In paragraph 3 Safire describes the unanimous Supreme Court as "cowed." What sense of the Court's character does Safire create by doing so?
2. Where and how does Safire create a sense of his own character as not cowed?
3. Safire offers personal reminiscences in his last paragraph. What sense of his own character does Safire create here?

Emotion
1. Safire mentions in paragraph 3 the medal of honor awarded to J. Edgar Hoover. What emotions does Safire invite in his audience by doing so? Where and how does his earlier writing give an emotional context to what (in isolation) might seem only a simple declarative sentence?
2. In paragraph 4 Safire claims that President Bush is using a "Roosevelt mistake as precedent for his own dismaying departure from due process." What emotions are his readers invited to feel here? Would those emotions be different were Safire to have substituted "Supreme Court mistakes"? Explain your answer.
3. What emotions does Safire invite his *audience* to feel by his uses of language in paragraph 9? Explain your answer using examples.

————————

NO MORE JURY TRIALS
FOR TERRORISTS

Michelle Malkin

When American pacifists talk about seeking "justice" for terrorists, here is what they mean:

More than $7 million in U.S. taxpayer funds went to lawyers who defended Mohamed Rashed Daoud Al-'Owhali, Khalfan Khamis Mohamed, Mohamed Sadeek Odeh and Wadih El-Hage. Translation services alone totaled $1.4 million, according to a *New York Times* report earlier this summer. The paper found that our money even went to reimburse

El-Hage's lawyers for the cost of dry cleaning his "thobe, a traditional Arab garment that their client wore in court, and other clothes. The bill ran to $108."

Who are these people our money defended? They are the four murderous thugs who helped orchestrate and carry out the terrorist attacks on our embassies in Kenya and Tanzania in 1998. They killed 224 people, including 12 Americans. They had been obeying Osama bin Laden's "fatwa" to slaughter American soldiers and civilians around the world.

To the delight of American doves, then-President Clinton didn't respond by declaring war on terrorism. He had other things on his scandal-addled mind. Instead of turning to Delta Force to defeat the enemies, Clinton took bin Laden's bombers to federal court in Manhattan. And that's where they were last week, a stone's throw from the rubble of the Twin Towers toppled by their buddies—whom they reportedly cheered as they listened to radio news broadcasts of the 9-11 attacks from their jail cells.

All of the terrorists received life sentences. Two had faced the death   5
penalty, but were spared by a minority-dominated jury that swallowed the race-baiting of traitorous defense witness Ramsey Clark (the former U.S. attorney general under Lyndon Johnson). Clark testified that no member of a racial minority—African-American, Arab or other— could expect a fair trial in the U.S. He also blamed the Gulf War and U.S. sanctions on Iraq for creating the psychological "suffering" that led to the embassy attacks.

It's sickening to know that these four terrorist killers—aided in their publicly-funded defense by blame-America-firsters and race-card opportunists—are alive and well on our soil. It's an outrage to imagine them enjoying three square meals a day. Reading. Relaxing. Praying. Rejoicing for their conspirators around the world. Cursing our country with every unencumbered breath they draw.

This is the kind of "justice" the American apologists for terrorism seek. They believe all will be right with the world when Osama bin Laden is whistling behind bars, growing his beard to the floor, writing his memoirs, and breaking bread with kindred congressional visitors like Barbara Lee, Cynthia McKinney and Jim McDermott.

It doesn't have to be this way. Nearly six decades ago, America discovered terrorist schemers in the nation's midst and swiftly paid them in kind. In June 1942, two teams of Nazi German terrorists (analogous to bin Laden's "cells") hopped aboard submarines and landed on the shores of Amagansett Beach, Long Island, N.Y., and Ponte Verda Beach, Fla. Like bin Laden and his al Qaeda network, these Germans were highly trained, loaded with cash, and bent on hijacking the American way of life. They planned to inflict mass terror by bombing railroads, hydroelectric plants, factories and department stores across the country.

One of the eight plotters got cold feet and exposed the Nazi plans.

President Roosevelt refused to grant civilian jury trials to the belligerent saboteurs. Instead, he immediately appointed a secret military commission to try the cases. All eight were found guilty and sentenced to death. Six were executed on Aug. 8, 1942, in Washington, D.C. (The remaining two, both turncoats, won commutations and received life sentences.)

In dealing with terrorist masterminds, President Bush must follow   10
the Roosevelt precedent—not the intolerable Clinton cop-out. As the Supreme Court ruled unanimously when it upheld the secret military tribunals for the Nazi terrorists, an enemy "who without uniform comes secretly through the lines for the purpose of waging war by destruction of life or property" is an "unlawful combatant" who is not entitled to access our jury system.

The founding fathers' constitutional pledge to "provide for the common defense" was meant to protect liberty-loving Americans—not evil terrorists looking for victims to pay their legal expenses and clean their filthy, blood-stained robes.

Questions for Analysis

Logic
1. According to Malkin, what is the implied reasoning of her opponents in demanding jury trials for terrorists?
2. According to Malkin, what is wrong with that reasoning?
3. In paragraph 10 Malkin reports the Supreme Court's reasoning in the case of the Nazi terrorists that led it to deny them jury trials. What was the Court's reasoning?

Character
1. In paragraph 4 Malkin reports that the convicted terrorists cheered after hearing of the World Trade Center collapse. What sense of the terrorists' collective character does she create here?
2. Malkin calls her opponents "pacifists" and "doves" throughout the essay. What sense of her opponents' collective character does she create by doing so? Explain how her assumptions invite you to see *pacifists* and *doves* as negative terms.
3. In paragraph 4 Malkin describes her opponents as "delighted" by President Clinton's decision. What sense of her opponents' collective character does Malkin create by doing so? Explain how Malkin's own assumptions operate here.

Emotion
1. Malkin emphasizes money in paragraph 2. To what emotions does this emphasis appeal? Explain in your own words the process of feeling that Malkin seems to expect by listing the expenses large and small.
2. Malkin's essay contains an implied contrast between the physical and human destruction described in her early paragraphs and the

"psychological 'suffering'" reported in paragraph 5. What emotions does Malkin invite by making this contrast?

3. To what emotions does Malkin appeal in her last paragraph? Does she seem to you to feel those emotions herself or different ones? Explain your answer.

WARTIME POWERS, BUT NO WAR

Jim Mann

The main argument the Bush administration is using for its creation of military tribunals, its secret detentions and its other draconian crackdowns since Sept. 11 is that the United States is at war. Sure— except that we're not.

Our soldiers are fighting overseas. We feel as though we're at war at home. But we're not at war under the U.S. Constitution because Congress hasn't declared war.

And without a congressional declaration of war, the military tribunals and other extraordinary measures the Bush administration has adopted by executive order cannot be justified.

Earlier this year, when Attorney General John Ashcroft decided that the Second Amendment protects private gun ownership, he proclaimed his belief in strict construction of the Constitution and an examination of the "original intent" of the framers who drafted it.

Maybe Ashcroft should read again what the Constitution says about war: "The Congress shall have power . . . to declare war . . . and make rules concerning captures on land and water."

Ashcroft, it appears, talks about "strict construction" and "original intent" only when it suits him.

Of course, Congress hasn't formally declared war against anyone since World War II. Since that time, the United States has engaged in military conflicts in Korea, Vietnam, the Persian Gulf and elsewhere. Let's say for the sake of argument that it may be too late to insist the President needs a formal declaration of war before he sends U.S. troops into combat overseas. Yet none of the so-called "police actions" since World War II has been accompanied by the sort of measures we are now witnessing.

The one modern example the administration has repeatedly pointed to as justification for its actions was President Franklin D. Roosevelt's creation of special military courts to try Nazi saboteurs in the United States during World War II. But in that case, Roosevelt was acting with the benefit of a formal congressional declaration of war.

The Bush administration seems to realize the questionable nature of the way it uses war as the rationale for its executive actions. That's why its public statements are worded in such curious ways. "We're at war. The enemy has declared war on us," President Bush said last week.

In other words, he seemed to be saying, maybe we don't have to   *10* declare war, if someone else does.

Why not ask Congress for a declaration of war?

The argument is sometimes made that it's not clear what entity we should declare war against. Still, Congress could simply declare that a state of war exists, or it could declare war against the al Qaeda network. The Constitution doesn't specify that a declaration of war must be against a country. Or Congress could declare war against the Taliban regime for sheltering al Qaeda.

At the least, a formal congressional declaration of war would help to limit the damaging fallout at home and abroad caused by the Bush administration's actions. From now on, whenever American diplomats complain to, say, China about secret detentions or trials, China may answer that the United States has done likewise. Inside this country, whenever there is some egregious crime—a mass murder, for example—there could be public pressure to limit rights to a lawyer or to a public trial, just as the United States is doing in its anti-terrorist campaign.

We should be able to answer these claims by saying that these extraordinary infringements on individual rights cannot be justified without a formal declaration of war.

Congress is allowing the President to assume authority never envi-   *15* sioned in the Constitution.

The real culprits are the Republican leaders: House Speaker Dennis Hastert and Senate Minority Leader Trent Lott. They're the ones who should be standing up for Congress and making sure it plays its proper role.

The Democrats can't take the lead on this issue because their arguments would be dismissed as partisan.

The polls show that the public supports Bush's actions, at least so far. But on issues such as this, polls don't mean anything.

Ordinary people don't lose their jobs because of what they tell pollsters. Members of Congress, by contrast, can be held accountable. That's precisely why the Constitution gave Congress the power to declare war.

If the President is going to assume extraordinary domestic powers   *20* based upon a wartime rationale, then he should ask for a declaration of war. Congress ought to insist.

———

Questions for Analysis

Logic

1. According to Mann, what is wrong with Attorney General Ashcroft's logic?
2. Mann points out a problem with using President Roosevelt's creation

of special military courts as a precedent for President Bush's actions. What is that problem?

3. According to Mann, the lack of a congressional declaration of war might lead to "damaging fallout" [13]. Explain Mann's reasoning.

Character

1. In what ways does Mann invite his reader to see the character of Attorney General Ashcroft in paragraphs 4–6?
2. What qualities of character does Mann attribute to the Republican congressional leadership toward the end of his essay?
3. According to Mann, what qualities of character would keep the Democrat leadership from acting?

Emotion

1. Describe Mann's tone of voice and the emotions it expresses in the last sentence of paragraph 13. Explain how Mann's uses of language create your sense of him.
2. In paragraph 16 Mann attributes certain emotions to the Republican leadership. Describe these emotions in your own words.
3. Mann implies that people who support President Bush's actions, at least according to polls [19], feel certain emotions. Describe these emotions in your own words.

Mann

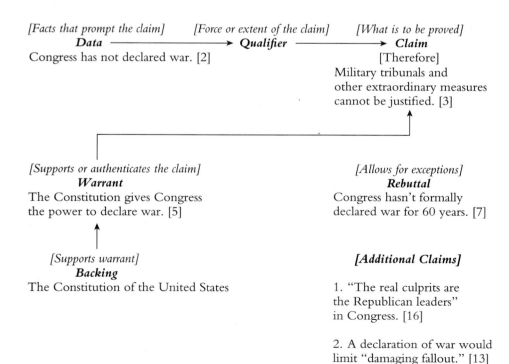

[Facts that prompt the claim]   *[Force or extent of the claim]*   *[What is to be proved]*
    Data ———————————→ **Qualifier** ———————————→ **Claim**
Congress has not declared war. [2]   [Therefore]
                                             Military tribunals and
                                             other extraordinary measures
                                             cannot be justified. [3]

[Supports or authenticates the claim]   *[Allows for exceptions]*
    Warrant   **Rebuttal**
The Constitution gives Congress   Congress hasn't formally
the power to declare war. [5]   declared war for 60 years. [7]

[Supports warrant]   **[Additional Claims]**
    Backing
The Constitution of the United States   1. "The real culprits are
                                       the Republican leaders"
                                       in Congress. [16]

                                       2. A declaration of war would
                                       limit "damaging fallout." [13]

EXERCISES: WHAT KIND OF JUSTICE DO TERRORISTS DESERVE?

Intertextual Questions

1. Where do the three authors stand on the issue of a congressional declaration of war? Would such a declaration, were it to take place, affect their arguments about justice? Explain your answer using examples.
2. All three writers refer to President Roosevelt's decision, yet they disagree about its meaning to some extent. How does each writer understand the meaning of the precedent?
3. Malkin seems to put the word *justice* in quotation marks to distinguish between mere legality and a higher and truer concept that the law is designed to serve but sometimes does not serve properly. Where do the other authors stand on this distinction? How do you think each might be expected to respond to Malkin on this issue?

Suggestions for Writing

1. Where do you stand on the legal rights of foreign nationals accused of crimes against the United States? Should they have the same rights as American citizens? Write an essay in which you explain and defend your position.
2. Are military tribunals (as opposed to jury trials) appropriate under any circumstances? Write an essay in which you explain and defend your position.
3. Do you support formal declarations of war by Congress in all cases of military force used by the United States? Write an essay in which you explain and defend your position.

2   Are SUVs Bad Sports?

ATTACKS ON SUV OWNERS ARE DRIVING ME UP THE WALL

Fran Wood

The first time my colleague, Paul Mulshine, attacked sport utility vehicles, I let it ride—even though I drive one. After all, he's a columnist, too, and he has as much right to be wrong as I do to be right.

For that reason, I also let it pass the second time Paul wrote about SUVs. And the third and fourth and fifth. If Paul wanted to add SUVs to his army of straw men, that was okay with me.

Besides, I like Paul. He is an engaging, standup guy with a terrific sense of humor and one of the quickest wits you'll ever encounter. He also has a kind heart and generous nature, so I tend to forgive him his misguided politics and obsessions.

Indeed, I didn't even know there was a line in the sand between us—until he crossed it with, by my count, his sixth attack on SUVs.

It takes a lot to get my Irish up, but this did it. The time had   5
come to defend SUV owners and crush him like a bug. Metaphorically speaking.

I don't have to defend my own SUV to Paul, by the way. He has told me more than once that I'm the only person he knows who is entitled to own one. That's because he's been to our house, whose long and steep driveway makes a winter ascent the equivalent of driving up the north face of Everest.

But Paul doesn't spend a lot of time in the northern hills of the state. If he did, he'd know many people couldn't get by without a four-wheel-drive vehicle in winter.

But wait, you say. The last three winters have been so mild that you've barely had to put up the top on your convertible. Correct. And you know why? Me and my SUV, that's why.

Remember those two awful back-to-back winters that preceded the three-year lull? Well, every time I couldn't make it up my driveway, I had to park a quarter-mile away and walk home. Pitch black, 9 o'clock in the freezing night, snow up to my hips, breaking trail. Trust me, it got old fast.

So in August 1996 I bought a used SUV, and we haven't had a bad 10 winter since. You may look on this as a coincidence. I look on it as having paid $18,000 for three years' worth of weather insurance for every motorist in New Jersey.

Indeed, Paul ought to be thanking me for making it possible for him to get to work every day for the last three winters. Because the one place he absolutely can't take his little red sports car in a serious snowstorm is out on the road.

Then, looking at the bigger picture, there's the contribution of all SUV owners: saving the American auto industry. Before Detroit started spitting out SUVs, this country's auto industry was practically on life support, having convincingly lost the small-car battle to the likes of Japan.

With SUVs, we regained our pre-eminent position—and the fact that we did it by being bigger and brawnier should hardly trouble an American traditionalist like Paul since that is the American tradition.

Let me also take a moment to defend the legion of responsible SUV drivers. Paul would have you believe the phrase is a contradiction in terms, but it's not. Most of the people I see driving SUVs obey the rules of the road.

In fact, I suspect owning sport utility vehicles has made us even bet- 15 ter drivers because their sheer size demands it. Sure, there are a few irresponsible SUV drivers. As long as there are other car makes and models, cell phones, parents in Little League bleachers and blue seats at Madison Square Garden, the world's quota of jerks will not be limited to SUV drivers.

As for Paul, he personally has one more reason to like SUVs. Whenever he's driving to work and he's stuck on an idea for a column, he can glance out his window, see our hubcaps and know his day's work is practically done.

Questions for Analysis

Logic

1. Paraphrase Wood's logic in paragraph 9. What reasoning made her conclude to buy an SUV? State her case as she sees it, using Toulmin's terms.

2. Explain Wood's reasoning in paragraphs 12 and 13 on "the bigger picture" of international competition.

3. According to Wood's logic, why do SUV owners become *better* drivers?

Character

1. Wood waits until the "sixth attack" [4] before responding to her opponent. What sense of her own character does she create by doing so?

2. The next-to-last sentence in paragraph 9 is not grammatically complete. How does its casual, colloquial style affect your response to
Wood's complaint? Try rewriting the sentence to get a sense of its
manner by contrast.
3. Wood jokes about "weather insurance" in paragraph 10. To what
sense of her character does this moment contribute?

Emotion
1. Wood creates a sense of exasperation (or mock exasperation) at the beginning of her essay. To what emotions does she appeal by doing so?
2. In what spirit does Wood treat her opponent? Is Mulshine treated as
an enemy, for example? A buffoon? What emotions does Wood invite her reader to feel toward Mulshine?
3. Does Wood's argument in paragraphs 12 and 13 appeal to the emotion of patriotism? Explain your reasoning.

FUEL ECONOMY LAWS BITE BACK

Paul Craig Roberts

Americans are experiencing increasing difficulty with nighttime
driving, especially in high traffic areas and on congested city streets. The
glare from oncoming headlights keeps automobile drivers in an almost
constant state of near blindness, and drivers of automobiles cannot see
the centerline or side of the road.

The experience is comparable to encountering an oncoming driver
on a two-lane highway who fails to dim his high beams. The difference
is that today's nighttime drivers experience the blinding glare as a constant rather than isolated occurrence.

The reason is sport utility vehicles, pickup trucks and vans. In
a short period of time these vehicles have jumped from a 20 percent
share of vehicle production to 42 percent. Moreover, the vehicles are no
longer used primarily by daytime businesses, farmers, and off-road en-
thusiasts. They have become substitutes for cars in personal and family
transportation.

These car substitutes sit high above the road. Their headlights are at
a car's windshield level—thus the blinding effect. As these car substitutes
comprise almost half of vehicular traffic, their blinding effect is nearly
continual.

The "utes" as they are called have other disadvantages for drivers of   5
mere cars. In a collision with a larger and heavier vehicle, car occupants

experience substantially higher fatalities and more severe injuries. More-over, the advantage that car substitutes have in weight and mass turns many owners into more aggressive drivers. Feeling safe sitting up high in a massive vehicle, drivers tend to throw their weight around.

One result is that people who were once content with a car are buying the larger vehicles for self-protection. As their numbers increase, no one will be able to drive at night without one—unless they have glare-proof eyes.

These car substitutes also make daytime driving problematic. It is impossible for car occupants to see around them. Drivers of cars are de-prived of "up-ahead" knowledge and must drive by the taillights of utes, pickups and vans.

Although many purchasers are choosing utes and pickups for safety reasons, in many ways these vehicles are less safe. They lack the stability and cornering power of a well-engineered car, and their high center of gravity makes them more prone to spin and to turn over.

The boom in car substitutes, which is making everyone less safe, is an unintended consequence of federal regulation, specifically the Corporate Average Fuel Economy Standard (CAFE). CAFE imposed miles per gallon requirements on gasoline vehicles. The requirement for cars was set higher, and has been raised faster, than the standard for car substitutes.

Manufacturers met the fuel economy standards by producing   10
smaller, lighter cars with less powerful engines. Consequently, fewer and fewer cars can be used for trailoring a boat, transporting a piece of fur-niture, or accommodating a family's sport and vacation luggage. As fed-eral regulations prevented the production of cars that met people's needs, people moved into car substitutes.

CAFE is the result of politicians and bureaucrats hyperventilating about "running out of oil." Two decades ago U.S. inflation forced oil prices up to $30 a barrel, and "experts" predicted the price would soar to $50 and $100. We wouldn't be able to cover our trade deficit. The world as we know it would come to an end.

The solution was to cure inflation, and President Reagan did. The price of a barrel of oil declined to today's low of $13. But we are stuck with the counterproductive CAFE standards. Thank your know-nothing government in Washington when you are forced to abandon your car and fork over $32,000 for a car substitute in order to continue nighttime driving and regain a sense of safety on the road.

Economists have long known of unintended consequences. Indeed, there are few government policies whose benefits outweigh the un-intended consequences. Now comes historian Edward Tenner who has written a spell-binder, *Why Things Bite Back,* about the unexpected

consequences of the things we do. Read it and become less susceptible to
the promises of experts and politicians.

———

Questions for Analysis

Logic
1. Roberts says that "utes" create less safe driving conditions for owners
   of ordinary cars under both day and night driving conditions. Explain
   his reasoning on the causes and effects involved in each case.
2. According to Roberts, why do "utes" tend to make their owners
   drive less safely?
3. Explain the ways in which fuel economy laws led to "utes," according to Roberts's reasoning.

Character
1. Roberts speaks at the beginning of his essay about "Americans'" experience of glare instead of speaking more specifically about his own.
   What sense of his own character does Roberts create by doing so?
2. What qualities of character does Roberts attribute to "manufacturers"
   [10] who met regulations by building smaller cars? Does he see them
   as villains, for example? Profiteers? Explain your answer.
3. At the end of the essay Roberts clearly aligns himself with "economists" as opposed to "experts and politicians." What qualities of character does he attribute to each group throughout the essay? Explain
   your answer using examples.

Emotion
1. Roberts calls SUVs, pickup trucks, and vans "car substitutes" throughout the essay. To what emotions does this phrasing seem intended to
   appeal?
2. In paragraph 11 Roberts says that CAFE is the result of "politicians
   and bureaucrats hyperventilating about 'running out of oil.'" To what
   emotions is the term *hyperventilating* designed to appeal?
3. At the end of his essay Roberts invites his readers to become "less susceptible." To what emotions is this phrasing designed to appeal?

Roberts

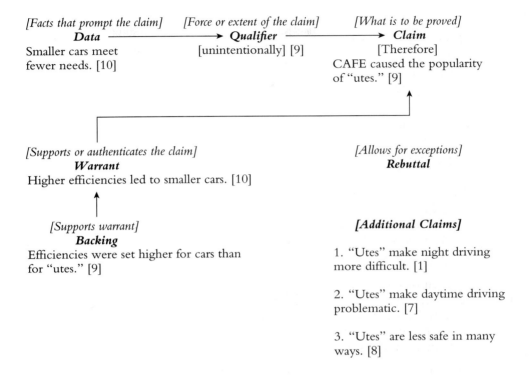

[Facts that prompt the claim]
Data
Smaller cars meet fewer needs. [10]

[Force or extent of the claim]
Qualifier
[unintentionally] [9]

[What is to be proved]
Claim
[Therefore]
CAFE caused the popularity of "utes." [9]

[Supports or authenticates the claim]
Warrant
Higher efficiencies led to smaller cars. [10]

[Allows for exceptions]
Rebuttal

[Supports warrant]
Backing
Efficiencies were set higher for cars than for "utes." [9]

[Additional Claims]

1. "Utes" make night driving more difficult. [1]

2. "Utes" make daytime driving problematic. [7]

3. "Utes" are less safe in many ways. [8]

PECKSNIFFS CAN'T STOP THE SUV

Brock Yates

With record profits to announce, you might have thought William Clay Ford Jr. had something to celebrate at his company's annual stockholders meeting last week. Instead he began blubbering about the intrinsic evil embodied in the 850,000 sport-utility vehicles and light trucks that Ford and Lincoln Mercury have produced so far this year. The young chairman seemed almost despondent that he had been responsible for the sale of these vehicles to thousands of customers who, pity them, seemed perfectly happy with their purchases.

Mr. Ford's bizarre mea culpa centered on the widely held notion that these machines, known simply as *SUVs,* are mechanical predators capable of pulverizing smaller vehicles in their path, swilling unconscionable quantities of gasoline, choking the atmosphere with acrid exhaust fumes, and flopping over without warning when turned quickly. He read from a 98-page "Corporate Citizenship Report" that sounded more like a screed from Friends of the Earth than the product of a proud, venerated company at the pinnacle of its power.

GUILT-RIDDEN RICH KID

Perhaps it was yet another example of the new public-relations ploy of universal contrition popularized by President Clinton, who has scored points by apologizing for everything except the Rape of Nanking and the crash of the Hindenburg. Whatever it was, it baffled stockholders, stunned Wall Street, angered dealers who were selling the scorned machines by the truckload, and left observers wondering if the latest Mr. Ford isn't yet another guilt-ridden rich kid, not a proud tycoon like those who preceded him.

It would have been strange enough for Mr. Ford to have excoriated his own company for producing a type of product that now accounts for 47.6% of the vehicles sold in the domestic market. But even more baffling than this act of penitence was Ford president and CEO Jacques Nasser's subsequent pledge to keep building the cursed machines because "our customers love them." Witnesses to Mr. Ford's statement, wherein he even quoted the Sierra Club's description of his own megaton Excursion as "a gas-guzzling rolling monument to environmental destruction," waited for some kind of a policy statement to correct the corporate sins—possibly the immediate cancellation of this lumbering soccer mom's answer to the Abrams tank. Or would he stop building the ground-pounders outright and plunge into the production of green machines powered by wheat germ and peanut oil?

Nothing of the sort was forthcoming. Aside from the report being 5 printed on 100% recycled fibers employing nontoxic soybean-based inks, and a few hazy promises to employ cleaner-emission engines and more recyclable parts, the statement seemed little more than a pre-emptive strike against the anticar guerillas whom Ford apparently believes pose the same kind of threat that has caused so much grief for tobacco companies.

Cynical public relations spin or nutball naiveté, the Ford statement elicited predictable huzzahs from the environmental lobby and the editors of certain elitist, big-city newspapers who wouldn't know an SUV from a BLT.

The SUV is a boxy amalgam of the pickup truck and the station wagon featuring a large cargo area, a comfortable interior and four-wheel drive. The machines trace their lineage back to 1935, when Chevrolet introduced its first Suburban, and to the late 1940s, when the Jeep and the British Land Rover came to market. The breakthrough arrived in the early 1990s when Ford's Explorer and Chrysler's Grand Cherokee added car-like luxury to the package. They seemed initially to attract only those living in stormy northern climes, but soon the appeal of the SUV became universal. They were especially embraced by women, who loved the security, the higher driving position, and the ease of loading and unloading kids and groceries from the tall, more commodious vehicles.

But the Pecksniffs now warn that the SUV's higher center of gravity might prompt rollovers, and that their extra weight can transform them into battering rams against smaller, lighter vehicles—an obvious result of Newtonian physics about which the drivers and passengers in SUVs, all of whom feel safer in a crash, give not a hoot.

Admittedly, because of their extra weight and lumpy aerodynamics, SUVs tend to produce highway efficiencies in the 14–18 miles-per-gallon range, or about 10 mpg less than conventional sedans. This means that over the span of 10,000 miles the owner of a Ford Explorer, Lexus LX470, GMC Yukon, Daimler Chrysler Grand Cherokee or Lincoln Navigator might consume 200 more gallons of gasoline—hardly akin to the Iraqi oil-well fires some environmental nuts claim as an equivalent waste.

SUVs do produce more exhaust emissions, but this is rapidly being   10
corrected. More efficient power plants and cleaner fuels are improving the situation at a rapid rate, and the automobile industry expects to clean up SUV and light-truck emissions well before the government-imposed deadline of model year 2004. As polluters, SUVs are minor offenders when compared to big-time felons like jet aircraft, diesel trucks and buses, lawnmowers, chainsaws, snowmobiles, farm equipment, stationary power generators, and scores of other internal-combustion engines that remain essentially unregulated.

As for the fear of an SUV tipping over in a corner like a drunk on a bar stool, there is little question that a taller vehicle tends to be less stable than one riding closer to the pavement (that's Newton again). But with proper tires and even a modicum of skill and sense, a modern sport utility can be driven with the same level of confidence and safety as a conventional automobile.

My wife, Pamela, whom I cherish, spends many hours a week at the wheel of our Grand Cherokee, and frankly it gives me an added feeling of confidence when she leaves the driveway in that rugged package. Neither she nor I fret over the possibility of her rolling some hapless victim in a Geo Metro into a wad of metal. If such fears haunt one, perhaps public transportation is the only solution.

In a world thankfully absent of a real crisis, and with the media cursed with endless months of low-octane news, the search continues for hot-button issues. In the world of automobiles, the shibboleth of "speed kills" has fizzled now that increased interstate velocities have produced lower accident rates, not the carnage predicted by the Chicken Littles. Air bags, which turned out to be less than the perfect solution despite the bloated claims of folks like Ralph Nader, have been made safer. Such issues as minivan door latches and pickup-truck fires gained traction only with the American Trial Lawyers Association.

ACCEPTABLE RISK

The reality is this: The American public, for the most part wise and prudent, considers travel by automobile an acceptable risk, regardless of the repeated attempts to instill fear and loathing by hysterical safety and

environmental lobbies with suspect motives and help from a bored national media. In the broad scheme of things, the SUV is a safe, responsible, functional device, and no amount of blather to the contrary will
convince Americans otherwise.

It is interesting to note that SUVs are not only beloved by the slob-   15
bering masses but by the elites of the nation—the well-educated, liberal-
leaning residents of such outposts of advanced civilization as Marin (Calif.)
and Fairfield (Conn.) counties. As of April, even Mr. Ford's megama-
chine, the much-despised 7,700-pound, 19-foot long, 310-horsepower,
$40,000 Excursion, had been scooped up by 15,838 customers. Demand
continues to exceed supply.

Why, in the face of all the fretting and hand-wringing by the mandarins in the media and overwrought greenies, does the SUV remain so
popular? In a word, it works. Its interior space, its boxy-but-functional
body style, its added traction and simple, Bauhaus theme appeal to a
vast number of clear-thinking, responsible American consumers, many
of whom are Ford Motor Co. customers and stockholders. In that regard, the remarks (and possibly the private sentiments) of Mr. Nasser in
Atlanta were more on target than those of his young boss.

Questions for Analysis

Logic
1. According to Yates, what reasonings do his opponents bring to their
   criticisms of the SUV?
2. Explain the reasoning Yates uses to explain William Clay Ford, Jr.'s,
   apparent acceptance of the criticism of those who oppose the SUV.
3. Explain Yates's own reasoning in support of SUVs.

Character
1. In paragraph 4 Yates calls the SUV "this lumbering soccer mom's answer to the Abrams tank." What sense of Yates's character does this
   joke create?
2. In paragraph 7 Yates provides a brief history of the SUV. What sense
   of his own character does he create by doing so?
3. In paragraph 12 Yates mentions his wife. How does his use of her experience as an example help to create a sense of his own character that
   supports his general argument?

Emotion
1. Mr. Pecksniff appears as a pompous, hypocritical, constantly moraliz-
   ing character in a novel by Charles Dickens. What emotional appeal
   does Yates's title seem intended to make to his readers?
2. Paragraph 6 begins with the phrase "cynical public relations spin or
   nutball naiveté." To what emotion does Yates appeal here?
3. What emotions does Yates consistently invite one to feel about the
   "clear-thinking, responsible American consumers" who are referred
   to throughout the essay as supporters of SUVs?

EXERCISES: ARE SUVS BAD SPORTS?

Intertextual Questions

1. Yates claims that SUVs are especially popular with women. Does his account of their reasoning square with that given and implied by Fran Wood? Provide evidence in support of your answer.
2. Roberts begins with the safety hazards caused by SUVs, whereas Wood and Yates emphasize the safety afforded to SUV owners. In your view, do they take into account and have answers to the position Roberts takes at the beginning of his essay? Explain your answer.
3. Both Roberts and Yates address the manufacturer's role in the story of the SUV. How and where are their views of that role similar? How and where do they differ?

Suggestions for Writing

1. Which writer gives the fullest account of the issues of safety raised by the popularity of SUVs? Write an essay in which you analyze the ways in which the writer of your choice more fairly treats both the hazards of SUVs and their advantages to safety.
2. The American consumer plays a part in the arguments of each writer. Write an essay in which you compare and contrast the authors' views of the power, rights, and needs of the American consumer.
3. Where do you stand on the issue? Write an essay in which you explain and defend your position on the SUV.

3   Should We Regulate Cell Phones?

END THE HANDS-OFF POLICY ON CELL PHONE USERS

Paul Mulshine

Not too long ago I was driving along minding my own business when the car next to me suddenly swerved into my lane. Not only was the jerk cutting me off, but he didn't even have the decency to signal.

I blew my horn just as the bozo was about to push me into the weeds. When he looked over, I realized why he hadn't signaled. His right hand was holding his cell phone. His left hand was dialing it. He would have needed a third hand to work the blinkers. If he'd had a fourth, it could have been usefully employed on the steering wheel.

This is among the reasons I fully support New York's ban on the use of cell phones while driving. I fervently hope New Jersey adopts such a ban as well. I would write into the law an exception for any Eastern deities who have driver's licenses, since some are said to have as many as six hands. But we two-handed mortals are not up to the task of using a telephone while driving.

This rather obvious point is lost on the many radio talk-show hosts and other self-proclaimed conservatives who have opposed cell phone bans in New York and in the New Jersey town of Marlboro on what they mistakenly believe to be principles of individual liberty. I consider myself something of a scholar on the question of liberty, and I can assure them that the principles they are citing do not exist.

The classic work on the subject is by John Stuart Mill. It is titled, appropriately enough, "On Liberty." Here is the relevant passage: "The individual is not accountable to society for his actions, in so far as these concern the interests of no person but himself."

Note the "but" in that sentence. You can yap all day on your home phone and you are affecting no one but yourself—and, of course, the person on the other end of the line, presumably a consenting adult.

But when you get into a 2-ton vehicle and direct it down a public road, your cell phone use concerns not just you but the thousands of other

5

drivers you will soon be menacing. Many of those drivers, *moi* for one, have not in any way consented to be run off the road so that your conversation can proceed more smoothly.

The cell phone defenders argue there is no evidence that using a cell phone while driving is any more dangerous than using the radio, drinking coffee or eating. Nonsense. As I've noted, we humans have but two hands. A minimum of one should always be on the steering wheel. If you wish to adjust your radio or sip your coffee, you can do so with your free hand at a time of your choosing, presumably a time when you are going down the road in a straight line. You set the schedule.

But if you have a cell phone, your schedule is being set by someone who is not in your car. Your phone can ring at a time when you should be using your turn signals, adjusting your wipers, turning on your headlights, concentrating on braking, or all of the above. And you have just a few seconds to answer it.

Once you start yapping, you have just one hand free for as long as you talk. Does the typical cell phone user say, "Excuse me, I have to put the phone down so I can employ my turn signal so Mulshine will know that I am about to dispatch him into the weeds"? If so, I've never seen it. In my experience, cell phone users have a harder time staying in their lanes than even drunks.

Any true conservative would see the cell phone as Mill would have seen it, a device that should be used sparingly for fear of causing offense or injury to others. That cell phones have changed driving behavior for the worse is obvious even if you accept for the sake of argument the mistaken contention that they are no worse than radios, coffee or screaming kids. All of those other distractions were there already. With the roads getting more crowded by the day, we don't need another distraction.

I think I can make that point best with this rather disturbing sight I encountered one day upon leaving Star-Ledger offices in Newark. A car came barreling through the intersection in front of the building. It is a corner packed with pedestrians and cars leaving the parking lots, but this clown sped right through without slowing down. As the car got closer, I saw the driver had a cell phone in his right hand. Was his left hand on the wheel? I fear not.

He was picking his nose.

10

Questions for Analysis

Logic

1. Explain John Stuart Mill's reasoning in the quotation from *On Liberty* [5].
2. Mulshine claims that banning cell phone use in cars will *not* violate individual liberty. Explain in your own words the reasoning behind Mulshine's claim.
3. According to Mulshine, cell phone defenders argue that using a cell

phone while driving is no different from drinking coffee or adjusting the radio while driving. Explain in your own words Mulshine's reasoning on the difference.

Character
1. In paragraphs 1 and 2 Mulshine uses the words *jerk* and *bozo* to characterize the man who cut him off. What sense of Mulshine's own character does he create by using such words?
2. Mulshine uses the term *self-proclaimed* in paragraph 4. What sense of his own character does Mulshine create by doing so?
3. Mulshine invokes the author John Stuart Mill and his book *On Liberty* in paragraph 5. What sense of his own character does Mulshine create by doing so?

Emotion
1. In paragraph 2 Mulshine apparently considers the blinkers of the car more important than the steering wheel. What emotions does Mulshine invite by doing so?
2. Mulshine uses the words *yap* [6] and *yapping* [10]. What emotions does Mulshine invite by doing so?
3. What emotion does Mulshine seem to feel in his last sentence? What emotion does he seem to invite you to feel?

——————

Mulshine

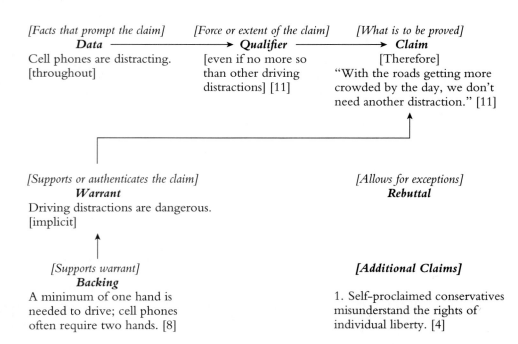

[Facts that prompt the claim]
Data ⟶
Cell phones are distracting. [throughout]

[Force or extent of the claim]
Qualifier ⟶
[even if no more so than other driving distractions] [11]

[What is to be proved]
Claim
[Therefore]
"With the roads getting more crowded by the day, we don't need another distraction." [11]

[Supports or authenticates the claim]
Warrant
Driving distractions are dangerous. [implicit]

[Allows for exceptions]
Rebuttal

[Supports warrant]
Backing
A minimum of one hand is needed to drive; cell phones often require two hands. [8]

[Additional Claims]

1. Self-proclaimed conservatives misunderstand the rights of individual liberty. [4]

2. Mill would approve of cell phone regulation. [11]

ALL I WANTED WAS TO CALL THE PIZZERIA

Kathleen O'Brien

When they first arrived on the scene, cell phones were bulky contrivances that looked like they were designed to be used by Robby the Robot in "Forbidden Planet."

They were luxury items, and use of them in public was a flamboyant declaration that the owner had money to burn. They didn't do much more than place and receive phone calls, and that they did only for a small, select group of people.

Technology moves on, so that now we have reached the next phase: Everyone has a cell phone.

And no one knows how to use them.   5

Sure, folks can make calls. And they can answer calls. But these new phones can do 97 other things that their owners either don't know about or don't care about. People stare bewilderingly at their cute little fashion-color phones and say, "It says I have two messages, but I don't know how to get them. Oh, well. If they really want to talk to me, they'll call back."

During my own recent "upgrade," I sprung for a cheapo model to replace the dead one I had. I thought that would be the surest way to get a no-frills kind that wasn't loaded with a lot of bells and whistles.

Of course, I was wrong. Let's put it this way: It would save time and paper if the instruction booklet simply listed what this phone *can't* do.

For all I know I can probably use it to cook a pork roast. Based on my ignorant fumbling with the keys this morning, I may be cooking a pork roast even as we speak.

Bells and whistles? It plays everything from Beethoven to Stephen   10
Foster, as if anticipating that vast legions of consumers would demand a phone that plays "Camptown Races."

It places and receives calls; places and receives voicemail; places and receives e-mail, and browses the Internet. I was tempted to joke that it can download the entire Encyclopaedia Brittanica, until I read this from the 51-page instruction booklet:

"You can download a phone book using the browser and store it in your phone." Of course, those numbers will be displayed in one of two settings: five lines of 7-point type; four lines of 8-point type. (The type you are now reading is about 11 point.)

The display window is the size of a postage stamp. So if I were to download a phone book—and believe me when I say the chances of that are extremely remote—not only would I need the hands-free headset, but the headset-mounted magnifying glass as well.

Considering that fully 80 percent of the calls I make from a cell phone are prompted by tardiness ("Hi, I'm running late . . ."), I don't see how I'll ever use any of these fancy features. I just want to be able to keep tabs on me and mine, and to be able to reach the pizzeria when necessary.

In anticipation of such routine conversations, my new phone has   *15* been pre-programmed with so-called "canned" messages, such as "Please call me back," "See you later" and "I'd like to order a large pie, half plain, half pepperoni."

(However, it failed to pre-program two frequently exchanged marital expressions: "What were you thinking?" and "Are you sure?")

Right now I'm in a race against time, trying to acquire enough knowledge about this phone's inner workings before history repeats itself and I lose the instruction booklet.

You see, technology may march on, but we humans need to stop now and then to catch our breath.

––––––––––

Questions for Analysis

Logic
1. According to O'Brien, what was the reasoning of people who purchased cell phones when they first became available?
2. What was the reasoning behind O'Brien's purchase of a "cheapo model" in the latest upgrade of her cell phone?
3. What seems to be the reasoning for new features of the "technology" that O'Brien says "moves on" [3] and describes as moving on throughout the essay?

Character
1. In what ways does O'Brien characterize her relation to technology in the essay? Give some examples of her language and explain how it creates a sense of her attitudes and abilities with regard to technology.
2. What sense of herself as a partner in a marriage does O'Brien create in paragraphs 14−16?
3. Does anything about O'Brien's style make you think her overmodest or joking about her level of technological competence? If you think so, explain the basis of your impression. If you think not, explain how a real scatterbrain could ever write paragraph 10.

Emotion
1. What emotions does O'Brien invite her readers to feel about her relation to technology?
2. What emotions does she invite her readers to feel about "everyone" [4], "folks" [6], "people" [6], and "humans" [18]?
3. Surely O'Brien invites her readers to laugh in paragraph 18. What are we invited to laugh at?

––––––––––

TOUGH CALL ON CELL PHONES

E. J. Dionne

No issue now under discussion offers a better opportunity for profound philosophical debate than the question of whether drivers should be barred from using hand-held cell phones.

I kid you not. This issue has everything.

You can ponder risk vs. security. You can think about whether individual rights trump the common good. You can argue about whether government is some horrible, meddlesome creature or whether one of its primary tasks is to protect human beings from human failure. As an individual, you can wonder whether your own personal convenience is worth the possibility that some distracted driver on his cell phone might smash into your car and perhaps even kill you.

There is a purity about the cell phone argument because it does not entail the profoundly difficult moral and religious principles raised by an issue like abortion. Wherever you stand on abortion, you can't deny that the moral status of the fetus is a huge deal.

Nobody has to have comparable worries about the cell phone, a   *5* marvelous invention but also an inert object that has no moral standing of its own. Because the cell phone issue is never likely to be a wedge issue, conservatives and liberals, libertarians and communitarians can argue peaceably and even come down on unexpected sides.

The core principle of libertarians, for example, is that government shouldn't legislate except to protect your life and your property. But the case against yakking on cell phones in cars is precisely that doing so threatens the life and property of other drivers.

As someone who regularly calls attention to the inconsistencies of politicians, I welcome this issue as a chance to face up to my own contradictions. I confess: I am a big-time user of my cell phone while driving. Worse: I love doing so.

Hard as I may try, I regularly fall behind in returning phone calls. Being able to put myself right with friends during drive time is a wonderful gift. It's also great to be able to set up interviews, confirm appointments and do a million other things during commuting hours that would otherwise be lost.

But cell phone users of the world, admit it: We all know that it's hard to dial someone up and maintain full and complete concentration on the road. We've all been angry at the driver who blows a red light while shooting the breeze. No matter how much we like our cell phones, we cannot for an instant pretend that they are not a distraction—even if we would all insist that we are oh, so careful in using them.

Thus, even avid vehicular cell users chuckle and occasionally cheer   *10* at the bumper sticker that declares: "Hang up and drive."

Politicians know this, which is why an anti–cell phone movement is building around the nation.

The New York Senate last week approved a bill that would bar the state's drivers from using hand-held cell phones. The National Conference of State Legislatures reports that 39 other states are considering such laws, according to the Associated Press. Many municipalities already have them.

"Finally, we will get the bird back in the cage," New York Assemblyman Felix Ortiz told the AP.

Ortiz noted that when he started campaigning for the ban five years ago, "people were making a lot of fun of me." No more.

"It eventually became not only an issue at the state level but on the national level," he said proudly. The Quinnipiac University Polling Institute found that 87 percent of New York voters favored the ban.

That number has to include not only those who never, ever use cell phones in their cars but also guilt-ridden users such as myself.

So where should we end up? My own contradictions on this are already obvious.

Personally, I would hate it if big government told me I could no longer use my cell phone in my car. But, also personally, I would hate it even more if my wife or my children were hurt by a driver who was so engaged in making phone calls that he forgot to remember he was driving. And, not to pretend to too much altruism, I wouldn't want that guy to hit me, either.

Thus a hunch: If enough studies show that cell phone users are indeed dangerous characters on the road, laws against them will pass all over the country. Ortiz will be able to claim prophetic powers. And we automotive cell users may, simultaneously, feel annoyed and relieved.

———————

Questions for Analysis

Logic
1. In paragraph 4 Dionne claims that "there is a purity about the cell phone argument." Explain in your own words the reasoning behind Dionne's claim.
2. In some respects Dionne opposes cell phone regulation. Explain the reasoning behind Dionne's opposition.
3. In concluding, Dionne explains that he favors regulation of cell phones. Explain in your own words the reasoning that leads Dionne to this conclusion.

Character
1. In paragraph 2 Dionne says, "I kid you not." But is he serious there? Explain the sense of his character created by taking paragraph 1 seriously. Then explain the sense of his character created by reading his words as ironic.

2. In paragraph 7 Dionne makes a "confession." What sense of his own character does this confession create?

3. What sense of Dionne's character does his last sentence create when it is taken in the context of the essay as a whole?

Emotion

1. Dionne's title is a punning one that uses the word *call* in two different senses. In the context of the essay as a whole, does his title invite his readers to laugh away the issue of cell phone regulation? Explain your answer.

2. At the end of paragraph 7 Dionne says, "Worse: I love doing so." Explain the emotions he invites his readers to feel about him at that moment.

3. At the end of the essay Dionne speculates that regulation might make him "simultaneously, feel annoyed and relieved." Are these the emotions the *reader* is invited to feel at the end of the essay? Explain your answer.

EXERCISES: SHOULD WE REGULATE CELL PHONES?

Intertextual Questions

1. Mulshine describes other people using cell phones, whereas both Dionne and O'Brien write from their own points of view as users themselves. In what ways if any do they confirm or refute Mulshine's arguments by their self-descriptions? Give examples with your answer.

2. O'Brien casts technology itself as her opponent and has nothing to say directly about regulating users of cell phones. With which of the other writers' positions would she align herself if forced to choose? Give evidence with your answer.

3. What would Mulshine be likely to say to Dionne about the position Dionne takes on regulation? What do you imagine Dionne might reply, based on your reading? Explain your reasons and provide evidence with your answers.

Suggestions for Writing

1. Dionne personally finds cell phones extremely useful, whereas O'Brien claims to have limited patience with or use for hers. But how would each author respond to Mulshine's clear-cut position on regulation? Write an essay in which you answer this question by analyzing evidence from all three essays.

2. All three writers use jokes in their titles, but which writer is the most consistently witty throughout? Write an essay in which you explain and defend your position.

3. Where do you stand on cell phone regulation? Write an essay in which you explain and defend your views. Be sure to take into account to some degree the authors in this section only to refute them.

4 Should We Legalize Same-Sex Marriage?

WHY FEAR SAME-SEX MARRIAGES?

William Raspberry

Vermont has passed a law giving homosexual couples the legal benefits of marriage. And there, says Gary Bauer, goes the institution.

Bauer may be more outspoken than some public figures, but he is not, on this issue, a member of the lunatic fringe. I dare say that if the proposition to extend the Vermont legislation to the entire country were put to national referendum—and almost certainly if the proposal were to allow gay and lesbian marriage—it would fail.

Why? What's the problem?

Bauer has no doubt on this score. "By approving same-sex marriage in everything but name," he said in a recent statement, "the Vermont Legislature has taken a major step toward radically redefining our most important social institution and overturning 4,000 years of Judeo-Christian moral teaching."

I agree. The Vermont law is prelude to a radical redefinition of marriage. It does fly in the face of the teachings of Judaism, Christianity and probably most organized religion.

The question for me is whether expanding the definition of marriage to include same-sex couples launches us on the path to perdition or merely heralds the shedding of another irrational prejudice.

Again Bauer is clear. "Granting same-sex unions the same moral and legal standing as marriage," he says, "is destructive of society's most important institution. At a time when Americans increasingly are concerned over the breakdown of the family, marriage and morality, this action is extremely damaging."

I don't get it.

I absolutely understand those whose religious beliefs disallow homosexual marriage because they disallow homosexual activity. You know: God created Adam and Eve, not Adam and Steve. What I don't understand is why, as a civil matter, we should be upset if Adam falls in love with Steve

5

or why it would threaten our marriages—or marriage in general—if they got married.

It's clear to me that a church might wish to withhold its blessing from   *10* a same-sex union. But why should the state withhold its legal sanction?

The lowering of the barriers against sex outside of marriage, as we countenance out-of-wedlock births, teenage sex and other formerly prohibited activities, threatens marriage. A lot of people want to have extramarital sex. Reducing the sanctions against something people want to do will lead more people to do it.

But in what way will letting homosexual couples marry tempt straight people into gay sex? Do we really believe that people are tempted into their sexual orientation? Or that they can catch homosexuality by exposure to gay couples?

Is our reaction, at least in part, esthetic? (I'm remembering the icky feeling I got the first time I saw two women kissing on a public street.) Does it have to do with our belief that homosexual activity is fundamentally immoral in a way that's different from heterosexual activity outside marriage? Are we afraid to sanction homosexual unions for the same reasons some of us are afraid to sanction needle exchange programs for drug addicts—not because we believe the exchange programs will tempt any nonuser into becoming a junkie but because we don't want to abet in any way behavior we think is wrong?

If we believe sexual orientation is something people choose, it might make sense to try to influence the choice in the direction of heterosexuality. But if we believe that sexual orientation is inborn and if we know that homosexuals are going to form unions, no matter what we do, shouldn't we encourage those who are so inclined to form monogamous and committed unions?

Isn't that the reason we have instituted marriage—civil and sacred—   *15* for the rest of us?

Questions for Analysis

Logic
1. According to Raspberry, what is Gary Bauer's reasoning in his opposition to same-sex marriage [1–4]?
2. Explain Raspberry's own reasoning in agreeing with Bauer's claim but disagreeing with what should be done about the issue.
3. Explain the logic behind the ways sanctions work or don't work, according to Raspberry [11–12].

Character
1. What sense of character does Raspberry establish for Gary Bauer in the beginning of the essay? Point to some of Raspberry's uses of language that create this sense.
2. What sense of his own character does Raspberry create by his treatment of Bauer's character (as opposed to his treatment of Bauer's logic)?

3. In your view, who is the "we" of the last paragraph? Describe the qualities of character that Raspberry attributes by implication to the "we."

Emotion

1. How would you characterize the emotions felt by Gary Bauer, as expressed by the statements that Raspberry quotes in the beginning of the essay?
2. How would you characterize the emotions felt by Raspberry himself in his account of Bauer's position? Does he seem to feel contempt, for example? Hatred? Point to the evidence that led you to your answer.
3. What seems to be the contribution of Raspberry's remembered "icky feeling" [13] to his final position on the issue? Is it a feeling he still has? Has he overcome it? Explain the basis of your answer.

Raspberry

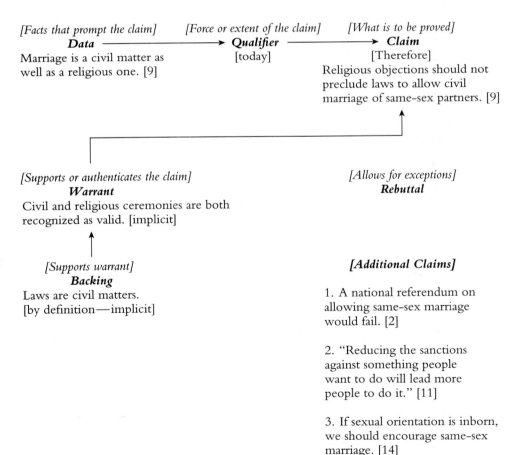

[Facts that prompt the claim]
Data ⟶ *[Force or extent of the claim]*
Qualifier ⟶ *[What is to be proved]*
Claim

Marriage is a civil matter as well as a religious one. [9]

[today]

[Therefore]
Religious objections should not preclude laws to allow civil marriage of same-sex partners. [9]

[Supports or authenticates the claim]
Warrant
Civil and religious ceremonies are both recognized as valid. [implicit]

[Allows for exceptions]
Rebuttal

[Supports warrant]
Backing
Laws are civil matters.
[by definition—implicit]

[Additional Claims]

1. A national referendum on allowing same-sex marriage would fail. [2]

2. "Reducing the sanctions against something people want to do will lead more people to do it." [11]

3. If sexual orientation is inborn, we should encourage same-sex marriage. [14]

IT'S THE FINAL STEP IN KILLING MARRIAGE

Maggie Gallagher

After the Rev. Walter Fauntroy, a black civil-rights leader, joined an interfaith, multicultural coalition supporting a federal marriage amendment that would block court-imposed gay marriage, Rick Rosendall, vice president of the Gay and Lesbian Activist Alliance, circulated the following e-mail:

"I wish to thank Mark Thompson, chair of the NAACP-DC Police Task Force, who called Rev. Fauntroy to convey my objections to Fauntroy's participation in such an attack on the gay community. Mark reports that Fauntroy expressed strong feelings about marriage and is immovable on the subject. So Fauntroy wraps himself in democracy and the civil-rights movement while seeking to disenfranchise a group of Americans. Truly obscene.

"Call Rev. Fauntroy . . . and register your objection to his alliance with anti-gay bigots. Tell him how offensive it is that he—a civil-rights veteran, of all people—would deny to others freedoms that he himself enjoys."

Here's the question: Will these kinds of uncivil, name-calling harassment tactics, demonizing those who disagree, ultimately succeed?

If decent people permit these tactics to be used against a man called   5
a "civil-rights legend," who is safe?

Marriage is neither a conservative nor a liberal issue; it is a universal human institution, guaranteeing children fathers, and pointing men and women toward a special kind of socially as well as personally fruitful sexual relationship.

Gay marriage is the final step down a long road America has already traveled toward deinstitutionalizing, denuding and privatizing marriage. It would set in legal stone some of the most destructive ideas of the sexual revolution: There are no differences between men and women that matter, marriage has nothing to do with procreation, children do not really need mothers and fathers, the diverse family forms adults choose are all equally good for children.

Increasingly, gay activists are the self-righteous zealots, stigmatizing any disagreement with their point of view, no matter how reasoned and civil, as bigotry, hate speech and discrimination.

I don't know what to call a group that feels free to dub a civil-rights legend a bigot because he does not support same-sex marriage, and to circulate his home phone number over an Internet list so broad that one of them even ended up in *my* mailbox.

Tolerant isn't the word that comes to mind.   10

Questions for Analysis

Logic

1. Explain in your own words Rick Rosendall's apparent reasoning as expressed by his language quoted in paragraphs 2–3.
2. What does Gallagher object to in what she quotes? Explain her reasoning.
3. In paragraph 7 Gallagher refers to the "deinstitutionalizing" of marriage. Explain Gallagher's apparent reasoning.

Character

1. By what techniques does Gallagher establish a sense of the Reverend Walter Fauntroy's character?
2. By what techniques does Gallagher establish a sense of Rick Rosendall's character?
3. By what techniques does Gallagher establish a sense of her own character?

Emotion

1. In paragraph 4 Gallagher calls the tactics of her opponents "uncivil." She also says there that they are "demonizing those who disagree." Explain the difference between the two emotional appeals she makes here.
2. In paragraph 6 Gallagher says that "marriage is neither a conservative nor a liberal issue." What emotions does this claim seek to arouse or dispel?
3. In paragraph 9 Gallagher says that she doesn't know what to call her opponents. What emotions does that claim suggest that she feels? What emotions does she invite her readers to feel?

———

COMMITTED COUPLES WOULD STABILIZE SOCIETY

Andrew Sullivan

It's been almost exactly a year since civil unions debuted, and social collapse doesn't seem imminent.

Perhaps panicked by this nonevent, the social right last month launched a Federal Marriage Amendment, which would bar any state from enacting same-sex marriage, forbid any arrangement designed to give gays equal marriage benefits, and destroy any conceivable claim that conservatives truly believe in states' rights.

For Stanley Kurtz and other cultural conservatives, the deepest issue is sex and sexual difference. "Marriage," Kurtz argues in National Review Online, "springs directly from the ethos of heterosexual sex. Once marriage loses its connection to the differences between men and women, it can only start to resemble a glorified and slightly less temporary version of hooking up."

But isn't this backward? Surely the world of no-strings heterosexual hook-ups and 50 percent divorce rates preceded gay marriage. It was heterosexuals in the 1970s who changed marriage into something more like a partnership between equals, with both partners often working and sex roles less rigid than in the past. All homosexuals are saying, three decades later, is that, under the current definition, there's no reason to exclude us.

The deeper worry is that gay men simply can't hack monogamy and   5
that any weakening of fidelity in the Clinton-Condit era is too big a risk to take with a vital social institution. One big problem with this argument is that it completely ignores lesbians.

So far in Vermont there have been almost twice as many lesbian civil unions as gay males ones—even though most surveys show that gay men outnumber lesbians about two to one.

So if you accept the premise that women are far more monogamous than men, and that, therefore, lesbian marriages are more likely to be monogamous than even heterosexual ones, the net result of lesbian marriage rights is clearly a gain in monogamy, not a loss. For social conservatives, what's not to like?

But the conservatives are wrong when it comes to gay men as well. Gay men—not because they're gay, but because they are men in an all-male subculture—are almost certainly more sexually active with more partners than most straight men. Many gay men value this sexual freedom more than the stresses and strains of monogamous marriage (and I don't blame them). But this is not true of all gay men. Many actually yearn for social stability, for anchors for their relationships, for the family support and financial security that come with marriage.

I guess the catch would be if those gay male couples interpret marriage as something in which monogamy is optional. But given the enormous step in gay culture that marriage represents, and given that marriage is entirely voluntary, I see no reason why gay male marriages shouldn't be at least as monogamous as straight ones.

Perhaps those of us in the marriage movement need to stress the   10
link between gay marriage and monogamy more clearly. We need to show how renunciation of sexual freedom in an all-male world can be an even greater statement of commitment than among straights.

In Denmark, where de facto gay marriage has existed for some time, the rate of marriage among gays is far lower than among straights, but, perhaps as a result, the gay divorce rate is just over one-fifth that of heterosexuals. And, during the first six years in which gay marriage was legal, scholar Darren Spedale has found, the rate of straight marriages rose 10 percent, and the rate of straight divorces decreased by 12 percent.

In the only country where we have real data on the impact of gay marriage, the net result has clearly been a conservative one.

Within gay subculture, marriage would not be taken for granted. It's likely to attract older, more mainstream gay couples, its stabilizing ripples spreading through both the subculture and the wider society.

Because such marriages would integrate a long-isolated group of people into the world of love and family, they would also help heal the psychic wounds that scar so many gay people and their families.

Far from weakening heterosexual marriage, gay marriage would, I   15
bet, help strengthen it, as the culture of marriage finally embraces all citizens. How sad that some conservatives still cannot see that. How encouraging that, in such a short time, so many others have begun to understand.

————

Questions for Analysis

Logic
1. Explain in your own words the logic in paragraph 3 of Sullivan's opponent Stanley Kurtz.
2. In paragraph 7 Sullivan claims that "a gain in monogamy" would be the result of legalizing marriage for lesbians. Explain in your own words the logic Sullivan uses in making this claim.
3. In paragraph 10 Sullivan claims that "renunciation of sexual freedom in an all-male world can be an even greater statement of commitment than among straights." Explain in your own words the apparent reasoning behind this claim.

Character
1. In paragraph 2 Sullivan uses the word *panicked* when referring to the social right. What sense of his own character does Sullivan create by doing so?
2. In paragraph 9 Sullivan speculates about monogamy. What sense of his own character does Sullivan create by the ways he does so?
3. In paragraph 15 Sullivan uses the phrase "how sad" when referring to the inability of conservatives to see gay marriage as helping to strengthen heterosexual marriage. What sense of his own character does Sullivan create by his tone here?

Emotion
1. What emotions does Sullivan invite by using the word *panicked* in paragraph 2?
2. Does Sullivan's use of the word *conservative* in paragraph 12 make an emotional appeal apart from its logical function at that point? Explain your answer.
3. What emotions does Sullivan invite by using the phrase "the world of love and family" in paragraph 14?

EXERCISES: SHOULD WE LEGALIZE SAME-SEX MARRIAGE?

Intertextual Questions
1. Raspberry discusses the institution of marriage both as a social and as a civil matter. Do the other writers explicitly or implicitly view marriage in these ways? Explain how their arguments do or do not take into account Raspberry's distinction. Give and analyze examples from their essays.
2. Gallagher says that "marriage is neither a conservative nor a liberal issue." Do the other writers explicitly or implicitly view marriage in this way? Explain how their arguments do or do not take into account Gallagher's distinction. Give and analyze examples from their essays.
3. Sullivan discusses the issue of same-sex marriage from the points of view of both gay men and lesbians. Do the other writers explicitly or implicitly take into account his distinction? Explain how their arguments do or do not. Give and analyze examples from their essays.

Suggestions for Writing
1. Do you find the distinction between the religious and the civil aspects of marriage to be a crucial one for you in deciding on this issue? Write an essay in which you explain and defend your position.
2. Do you find the distinction between liberal and conservative a crucial one for you in deciding on this issue? Write an essay in which you explain and defend your position.
3. Taking all the arguments of the writers in this section into account, where do you stand on the issue of legalizing same-sex marriage? Write an essay in which you explain and defend your position.

5   *Freedom and the Internet*

G-MEN AND E-MAIL
FBI's Internet Surveillance
Plan Should Worry Us

Duncan Levin

The FBI recently revealed a startling new government surveillance program for the Internet that should alarm all of us who care about the privacy of our e-mail.

This newest wiretapping system, originally dubbed Carnivore, is designed to sift through every e-mail of a suspect's Internet service provider, capturing all incoming and outgoing communications.

The name conjured up so many unflattering images of flesh-eating animals that the FBI decided to rename the controversial Internet surveillance tool. Now it's known as DCS1000, an alpha-numeric name that doesn't generate any images because it's meaningless.

DCS1000 raises immediate and grave constitutional concerns, and Congress, now considering the fate of this new surveillance mechanism, should be keenly aware of the delicate balance between justifiable national security concerns and the protection of individual privacy.

Without strict new standards for this program, for every legitimate   5
e-mail that DCS1000 captures, there will be many e-mails unrelated to any criminal investigation that the government will read—including yours and mine. Indeed, without adequate safeguards, the system may also be programmed to pick up the use of particular words or phrases written by anyone on the Internet.

Clearly, the law should permit and encourage the FBI to conduct reasonable criminal investigations and should not allow the Internet's expansive connectivity to hamper such efforts. But the FBI cannot be permitted to use the technology to add to its already exponentially increasing surveillance power if it means a concomitant decrease in individual privacy.

As if the DCS1000 program were not enough, witness the FBI's unfolding plans to conduct investigations over the World Wide Web.

The bureau, it was recently discovered, is developing a method to listen in on the increasing number of voice telephone calls placed over the Internet and to monitor live online discussions on a system known as Internet Relay Chat. Those stark revelations were made public through Freedom of Information Act documents obtained by the Electronic Privacy Information Center, a technology civil liberties group in Washington.

Further tipping the balance away from individual privacy, according to a Philadelphia Inquirer report, the FBI in 1999 planted in the keyboard of an organized crime suspect a newfangled device that stored everything the suspect typed into his computer, including the password for the encryption program that guarded the files on his hard drive.

The FBI's attitude to the outcry over the DCS1000 program, as reported by the New York Times, is extremely troubling, to say the least.   10

"The public," an FBI spokesman told the newspaper, "should be concerned about the criminals out there abusing this stuff and not the good guys."

Not the good guys? Not ordinary Americans' private communications?

This outlook is evidence enough that safeguards are needed to ensure that the FBI does indeed concern itself with the "good guys."

Congress, which is debating these issues, should establish strict standards for the FBI's new Internet surveillance programs, beginning with its DCS1000 program.

The FBI says DCS1000 is more protective of individual privacy   15 than typical phone-tapping tools because the system can be programmed to filter out e-mails that investigators should not see.

It equates the system to "pen registers" and "trap and trace" devices, which record the phone numbers of calls that suspects place and receive. DCS1000, it claims, can be programmed in much the same way to yield only communications to and from a particular suspect.

However, comparing DCS1000 to a traditional phone tap is problematic: The technology hugely widens the scope of intercepted communications, capturing thousands of e-mail conversations at the same time. Because of that, even if some sort of electronic filtering is applied to the e-mails, scores of irrelevant and private communications will be read by government investigators.

Furthermore, unlike a phone tap, DCS1000 must be specifically programmed to be restrictive in its searches for communications.

Congress should implement clear legal standards for the electronic programming of such searches, with the intention of minimizing privacy invasion.

It used to be that the federal government was hampered in its sur- *20*
veillance efforts not only by the basic constitutional guarantees of the
Fourth Amendment—which offers protection from unreasonable search
and seizure—but also by its technological incapacity to engage in widespread surveillance of communications.

Now, with the advent of global communications, the government's
power is increasing exponentially.

As the FBI pours out proposals for new surveillance technologies,
we must all ensure that its necessary national security function does not
greatly whittle away our individual privacy.

Questions for Analysis

Logic
1. Explain in your own words the reasoning by which, beginning in
   paragraph 10, the FBI justifies the DCS1000 program.
2. Explain in your own words the reasoning by which Levin attempts to
   refute the FBI's claims.
3. Why, according to Levin, is it unreasonable to compare the DCS1000
   to a phone tap?

Character
1. In paragraph 6 Levin comes out in favor of some electronic surveillance. What sense of his own character does he create by doing so?
2. In paragraph 11 Levin quotes the FBI. What sense of the FBI's collective character does this quoted language seem designed to create?
3. In his last paragraph Levin uses the word *pours* when referring to
   the FBI's proposals for new surveillance technology. What sense of the
   FBI's collective character does Levin's use of this word create?

Emotion
1. In paragraph 1 the FBI is said to have itself revealed the DCS1000,
   but its phone tap technology for the Internet was revealed only by
   the efforts of an outside group. What emotions does Levin invite his
   readers to feel by the order of these two points? Suppose they had
   been reversed: Would readers tend to feel the same emotions about
   the FBI?
2. "Carnivore" was the initial name of the DCS1000. What emotions
   do the implications of this name create? What might you imagine was
   the FBI's initial emotional attraction to the name? What kind of response might people who share Levin's view have to this name?
3. What emotions does Levin invite his readers to feel by his language
   in paragraph 21?

SHOUTING "FIRE!" IN A VIRTUAL THEATER

Maureen Farsan

Way back in the olden times before the Internet, Chief Justice Oliver Wendell Holmes made the classical distinction between the constitutionally protected American right of free speech and the criminal abuse of that right when he wrote that falsely shouting "Fire!" in a crowded theater was *not* free speech. Today in the Computer Age some 28 million children have both parents working or their only parent at work. These children, like the rest of American youngsters, seem to pick up more computer skills at a younger age than ever before. These skills allow them easy access to the sleezy virtual theater of the Internet which is crowded with salacious material and the electronic presence of people seeking that material—and more.

Is there anyone who can seriously deny that such material is completely unfit for the consumption of young children? Moreover, through the Internet function of email, any adult of whatever sexual obsession is free to communicate with children who have computer access and perhaps seduce them. Surely the seduction of minors is not free speech, but a criminal act well known to exist on the law books. In order to enforce the law the federal government should expand, not curtail, its technological monitoring of email and prosecute anyone trying to ruin a child's emotional life forever in order to satisfy his or her perverted desires. Further, these stalkers usually begin by directing their prey to sexually explicit sites. No children should be allowed access to these sites and if the technology does not yet exist to protect our children, those sites should be banned until it does. Salacious material by definition seeks to inflame the passions. These flames should not be allowed to spread and consume our children.

The obvious cost/benefit analysis comes to an obvious conclusion. Unlimited so-called free speech does more harm to children than any so-called censorship hurts any perverted or oversexed adult. Of course, if such people really want to make a *speech* about pornography, they are perfectly free to do so—only keep it clean.

Questions for Analysis

Logic

1. Explain the implicit logic behind Justice Holmes's distinction between the constitutional right of free speech and unlawful speech [1].
2. Explain the apparent logic behind Farsan's connection of the Holmes example and her own view of the Internet.
3. Explain the logic behind Farsan's use of irony in the last paragraph, where she refers to her opponents making a speech.

Character
1. To what sense of her own character does Farsan's knowledge of Justice Holmes and his legal decision seem designed to contribute?
2. Farsan uses the word *seriously* at the beginning of paragraph 2. What sense of her own character do you get from her use of this word? Try reading the sentence aloud with and without the word, and then compare the effects of each version.
3. What sense of her opponents' character does Farsan attempt to create in paragraph 2? Explain how you reached your conclusion.

Emotion
1. What emotions does Farsan seem to feel throughout the essay toward salacious material? Find some examples, and explain how her use of language creates your sense of her feelings.
2. What emotions does Farsan seem to feel throughout the essay toward those who would defend unlimited free speech on the Internet? Find some examples, and explain how her use of language creates your sense of her feelings.
3. Does Farsan's emotional temperature rise or cool off during her brief essay? Or does it remain more or less the same? Analyze examples of her language to support your answer.

Farsan

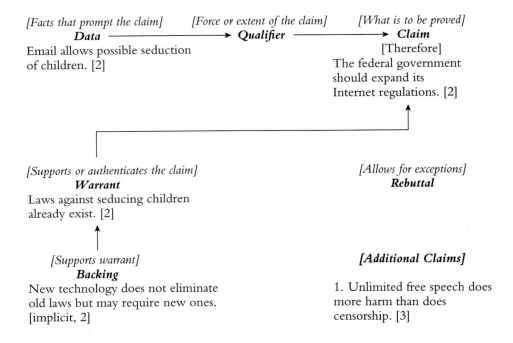

[Facts that prompt the claim]   *[Force or extent of the claim]*   *[What is to be proved]*
    Data ⟶ **Qualifier** ⟶ **Claim**
Email allows possible seduction   [Therefore]
of children. [2]   The federal government
    should expand its
    Internet regulations. [2]

[Supports or authenticates the claim]   *[Allows for exceptions]*
    Warrant   **Rebuttal**
Laws against seducing children
already exist. [2]

[Supports warrant]   ***[Additional Claims]***
    Backing
New technology does not eliminate   1. Unlimited free speech does
old laws but may require new ones.   more harm than does
[implicit, 2]   censorship. [3]

SCREEN SAVIORS

Wendy Kaminer

Protecting civil liberties is an exercise in déjà vu. On March 20, 2001, for the third time in five years, the American Civil Liberties Union filed suit in the Third Circuit Court of Appeals in Philadelphia seeking to enjoin a federal law aimed at protecting children from the ravages of the Internet.

First, the ACLU successfully challenged the Communications Decency Act of 1996, which prohibited "indecency" in cyberspace and was struck down by a nearly unanimous Supreme Court. Then Congress enacted the Child Online Protection Act (COPA), criminalizing the commercial dissemination of speech deemed "harmful to minors"; the ACLU went back to the Third Circuit, which invalidated COPA (in a decision that may also be reviewed by the Supremes). Now, along with the American Library Association, the ACLU is challenging the Children's Internet Protection Act (CHIPA), which conditions federal support for the nation's public schools and libraries on the installation of blocking software on computers. Supporters of CHIPA sometimes argue that the use of censorware represents an ordinary exercise of discretion by librarians and school administrators, who regularly edit material available to kids (devising a curriculum is partly a process of elimination). But in fact, the use of blocking software delegates discretion to the anonymous employees of publicly unaccountable companies like Cyber Patrol and Net Nanny, who decide which sites will be blocked. Parents who take comfort from these programs might as well randomly select a group of people from the subway to monitor their children's reading habits.

The problems with CHIPA are as obvious as the limitations of blocking software, which have been frequently chronicled. (See Geoffrey Nunberg, "The Internet Filter Farce," *TAP*, January 1–15, 2001, or the March 2001 issue of *Consumer Reports,* which confirms the software's unreliability.) Filtering programs are blunt instruments that censor a range of Web sites unquestionably protected by the First Amendment— Web sites of organizations ranging from Planned Parenthood to the U.S. Army Corps of Engineers; even a map of Disney World has fallen prey to the whims of cybercensors. Almost everyone's ox is likely to be gored. One former Republican candidate for Congress has joined the ACLU suit because Cyber Patrol blocked his campaign Web site, which broadcast his positions on numerous issues, including the use of blocking software (he was for it).

Congress engages in self-parody when it passes legislation like CHIPA. But the consequences of this stupid law will not be funny. Critics have charged that it will widen the digital divide: If CHIPA is effectively enforced, it will arbitrarily limit the pool of information and ideas available to children from low-income homes, who must depend on school and library computers in order to access the Internet.

But fear of the Web and other media is stronger than appreciation of their benefits, especially with regard to kids, who are supposedly endangered by popular culture. You can't control culture without controlling speech, as many are hungry to do in the belief that they would be regulating behavior or harm, not expression. People often assume that speech they deem offensive causes serious harm; or they believe that offensiveness itself constitutes harm. ("It's not about censorship; it's about harassment," the politically correct are apt to say.)

There is, however, little question that the Constitution—not to mention a regard for free speech in general—requires proof that speech causes actual harm before it can be prohibited. In March the estimable Judge Richard Posner of the Seventh Circuit Court of Appeals reaffirmed this principle in an opinion enjoining enforcement of an Indianapolis, Indiana, ordinance that would limit minors' access to violent video games. In *American Amusement Machine Association v. Kendrick,* Posner stressed that the government's claim that violent video games incite violence was entirely unsubstantiated. The few studies cited by the city did not show that "video games have ever caused anyone to commit a violent act, as opposed to feeling aggressive, or have caused the average level of violence to increase anywhere."

Conventional wisdom about the harm of violent video games and other media often persuades legislators to prohibit unpopular speech, but it is not evidence in a court of law. "The grounds [for suppressing speech] must be compelling and not merely plausible," Judge Posner observed. Besides, he suggested, the harm of censorship is as plausible as the harm of violent speech.

People are unlikely to become well-functioning, independent-minded adults and responsible citizens if they are raised in an intellectual bubble. No doubt the City would concede this point if the question were whether to forbid children to read without the presence of an adult *The Odyssey,* with its graphic descriptions of Odysseus's grinding out the eye of Polyphemus with a heated, sharpened stake, killing the suitors, or hanging the treacherous maidservants.

I wish I had so much faith in government officials. School administrators regularly censor respected works of literature (like *Huckleberry Finn*) to mollify angry parents; sometimes all it takes to ban a book is one or two complaints. "It's not about censorship, it's about protecting children," the censors will say. But depriving kids of access to information, ideas, and their choice of literary pleasures seems more like punishment than protection to me. Once, the juvenile courts deprived children of due process rights in order to protect them. I'm often suspicious of child savers.

Questions for Analysis

Logic

1. In paragraph 2 Kaminer refutes those who claim that "censorware represents an ordinary exercise of discretion by librarians and school administrators." Explain in your own words the logic behind her refutation.
2. In paragraph 5 Kaminer sketches out the logical relations of "speech" and "culture." Explain her sense of these relations in your own words.
3. In the last two paragraphs Kaminer makes an analogy between the censorship of books and the censorship of other media. Explain in your own words the logic of her analogy.

Character

1. In the first three paragraphs Kaminer goes over several historical facts related to her subject. What sense of her character does that aspect of her argument create?
2. Beginning in paragraph 6 Kaminer expresses her admiration for Judge Richard Posner. What is Kaminer's sense of his character, and how does she create that sense through her writing?
3. In paragraphs 8 and 9 Kaminer alludes to *The Odyssey* and *Huckleberry Finn*. What sense of her own character does she create by doing so?

Emotion

1. What emotions does Kaminer seem to express in her first paragraph? Resignation? Exasperation? Sorrow? Give the emotions a name or names, and explain how her use of language creates your sense of her feeling.
2. In paragraph 3 Kaminer calls filtering programs "blunt instruments." What emotions does that phrase seem to invite? Explain how and why the phrase operates as you feel it does.
3. In paragraph 5 Kaminer says that "many are hungry" to control speech and culture. What emotions does she suggest these opponents feel, and what emotions does she invite you to feel about them by her use of this phrase?

EXERCISES: FREEDOM AND THE INTERNET

Intertextual Questions

1. All three writers talk about the government as well as about freedom and the Internet. What do the authors seem to feel about government? Where do they agree and where do they disagree about the proper role of government? Which *branch* of government does each find most reassuring? Which most threatening? Give examples with your answers.

2. Kaminer says in paragraph 8 that "people are unlikely to become well-functioning, independent-minded adults and responsible citizens if they are raised in an intellectual bubble." How do you think the other writers would respond to this claim? Give evidence with your answers.

3. All three writers admit explicitly or implicitly that the issues they face are matters of judging between costs and benefits. Which of the writers makes this judgment most convincingly? Which least? Give examples in support of your answers.

Suggestions for Writing

1. Two of the authors explicitly address particular problems of children and the Internet. Which writer seems most convincing to you? Write an essay in which you explain and defend your position.

2. Each author uses techniques of argument other than logical ones. Which author best makes his or her case through appeals to character and emotion? Write an essay in which you explain and defend your choice.

3. Where do you stand with regard to the cost-benefit analysis of Internet regulation? Write an essay in which you explain and defend your position.

6   Does America Owe Reparations for Slavery?

AN IDEA WHOSE TIME HAS COME . . .
Whites Have an Obligation to
Recognize Slavery's Legacy

Manning Marable

In 1854 my great-grandfather, Morris Marable, was sold on an auction block in Georgia for $500. For his white slave master, the sale was just "business as usual." But to Morris Marable and his heirs, slavery was a crime against our humanity. This pattern of human-rights violations against enslaved African-Americans continued under Jim Crow segregation for nearly another century.

The fundamental problem of American democracy in the 21st century is the problem of "structural racism": the deep patterns of socio-economic inequality and accumulated disadvantage that are coded by race, and constantly justified in public discourse by both racist stereotypes and white indifference. Do Americans have the capacity and vision to dismantle these structural barriers that deny democratic rights and opportunities to millions of their fellow citizens?

This country has previously witnessed two great struggles to achieve a truly multicultural democracy.

The First Reconstruction (1865–1877) ended slavery and briefly gave black men voting rights, but gave no meaningful compensation for two centuries of unpaid labor. The promise of "40 acres and a mule" was for most blacks a dream deferred.

The Second Reconstruction (1954–1968), or the modern civil-rights movement, outlawed legal segregation in public accommodations and gave blacks voting rights. But these successes paradoxically obscure the tremendous human costs of historically accumulated disadvantage that remain central to black Americans' lives.

The disproportionate wealth that most whites enjoy today was first constructed from centuries of unpaid black labor. Many white institutions, including Ivy League universities, insurance companies and banks, profited from slavery. This pattern of white privilege and black inequality continues today.

Demanding reparations is not just about compensation for slavery and segregation. It is, more important, an educational campaign to highlight the contemporary reality of "racial deficits" of all kinds, the unequal conditions that impact blacks regardless of class. Structural racism's barriers include "equity inequity," the absence of black capital formation that is a direct consequence of America's history. One third of all black households actually have negative net wealth. In 1998 the typical black family's net wealth was $16,400, less than one fifth that of white families. Black families are denied home loans at twice the rate of whites.

Blacks remain the last hired and first fired during recessions. During the 1990–91 recession, African-Americans suffered disproportionately. At Coca-Cola, 42 percent of employees who lost their jobs were blacks. At Sears, 54 percent were black. Blacks have significantly shorter life expectancies, in part due to racism in the health establishment. Blacks are statistically less likely than whites to be referred for kidney transplants or early-stage cancer surgery.

In criminal justice, African-Americans constitute only one seventh of all drug users. Yet we account for 35 percent of all drug arrests, 55 percent of drug convictions and 75 percent of prison admissions for drug offenses.

White Americans today aren't guilty of carrying out slavery and   *10* segregation. But whites have a moral and political responsibility to acknowledge the continuing burden of history's structural racism.

A reparations trust fund could be established, with the goal of closing the socioeconomic gaps between blacks and whites. Funds would be targeted specifically toward poor, disadvantaged communities with the greatest need, not to individuals. Let's eliminate the racial unfairness in capital markets that perpetuates black poverty. A national commitment to expand black homeownership, full employment and quality health care would benefit all Americans, regardless of race.

Reparations could begin America's Third Reconstruction, the final chapter in the 400-year struggle to abolish slavery and its destructive consequences. As Malcolm X said in 1961, hundreds of years of racism and labor exploitation are "worth more than a cup of coffee at a white café. We are here to collect back wages."

Questions for Analysis

Logic

1. In paragraph 2 Marable claims that "the fundamental problem of American democracy in the 21st century is the problem of 'structural

racism.'" Explain in your own words the reasoning Marable uses to support his claim.
2. Explain in your own words the reasoning that leads Marable to conclude that reparations will overcome "the fundamental problem."
3. Explain in your own words the reasoning that leads Marable to conclude that his proposals might be adopted.

Character
1. Marable alludes to his great-grandfather in paragraph 1. What sense of his own character does Marable establish by doing so?
2. Throughout his essay Marable mentions many historical dates. What sense of his own character does Marable establish by doing so?
3. Does it change your sense of the character expressed through Marable's writing to know that he is the director of African American Studies at Columbia University?

Emotion
1. At the end of paragraph 2 Marable raises a question. To what emotions does Marable appeal by raising this question?
2. In paragraph 7 Marable focuses on an "educational campaign." To what emotions does Marable appeal by doing so?
3. To what emotions do Malcolm X's words (quoted in the last paragraph) seem to have been intended to appeal? Does Marable intend the same appeal to his audience in quoting the words? Explain your answer.

REPARATIONS QUESTION WON'T GO AWAY

Mona Charen

The reparations question will not go away. Black congressional leaders are criticizing the Bush administration for not taking a larger role in the upcoming World Conference Against Racism, which will take up the question of reparations.

A group of black lawyers, including Johnnie Cochran, has announced plans to sue large corporations they claim have benefited from slavery, as well as the federal government. And on college campuses across America, David Horowitz has caused a ruckus by publishing—or vainly attempting to publish in college newspapers—an advertisement listing 10 reasons to oppose reparations.

The idea will not die because many parts of the black community are sunk in what Prof. James McWhorter calls the "cult of victimology." But the truth is that family structure is a far better predictor of success in America today than race, or the condition of servitude of one's ancestors.

Black intact families enjoy incomes and standards of living indistinguishable from whites. But only 30 percent of black children are born to married couples today. Is this family disintegration itself a legacy of slavery? Doubtful. As economist Walter Williams writes, "In 1880, in Philadelphia, two-parent family structure was: black, 75.2 percent; Irish, 82.2 percent; German, 84.5 percent; native white American, 73.1 percent."

Slavery was a crime and a sin. The Founders knew it. Jefferson said, "I tremble for my country when I reflect that God is just."   5

But no one alive today was ever a slave or the son of slaves, neither is anyone alive today a slaveowner or son of a slaveowner. The intervening generations have swelled the population with immigrants, so that a majority of whites living in America today have no ancestors who lived in America at the time of slavery. Only one third of the citizens of the Confederacy (and, believe it or not, 12,000 free Southern blacks) owned slaves.

If we were to attempt to categorize Americans as oppressors or victims based on their skin color, we will sink into an impossible morass. Millions of Americans are of mixed racial ancestry—many due to the widespread practice of slaveowners raping or taking slaves as unofficial concubines, but many others the product of mixed marriages in the generations since. How should these people be counted? And what about those, like Tiger Woods, who have four or five races in their family tree? Shall they pay with one hand and receive with the other?

Just since the 1950s, American taxpayers have spent, according to Williams' calculations, roughly $6.1 trillion on the war on poverty, education, housing and medical care—all aimed mostly at relieving the poverty and hopelessness so prevalent in the black slums. Since the 1960s, the U.S. government and virtually the entire private sector have maintained a system of racial preferences and reduced standards in employment and education aimed at eradicating the "legacy of slavery."

But of course, that legacy has not prevented blacks from excelling in sports, entertainment and music. Eighty percent of blacks are now in the middle and upper classes. Surely the idea of Oprah Winfrey and Michael Jordan receiving reparations checks must give pause.

To end slavery, the United States undertook the greatest and most   10
devastating war of our history. More Americans were killed in the Civil War than in all of the rest of the wars we've fought put together. Those 620,000 dead represent the ultimate reparation for slavery. Lincoln saw

it in those terms. In his Second Inaugural Address, he said: "Fondly do we hope, fervently do we pray, that this great scourge of war may speedily pass away. Yet, if God wills that it continue until all the wealth piled by the bondsman's 250 years of unrequited toil shall be sunk, and until every drop of blood drawn by the lash shall be paid by another drawn with the sword, as was said 3,000 years ago, so still it must be said, 'The judgments of the Lord are true and righteous altogether.'"

Just one month later, Lincoln paid for those sentiments with his own life.

Human history is sadly littered with crimes and cruelty. But historical crimes cannot be avenged. Many black criminals have blighted the lives of other Americans. It is justice to make other blacks pay reparations to other whites for that? Of course not. Only the actual criminal can be punished and only the actual victim can be compensated. Anything else is dangerous nonsense.

Questions for Analysis

Logic
1. In your own words explain the logic of Charen's historical reasoning in paragraph 6.
2. In your own words explain the logic of Charen's racial reasoning in paragraph 7.
3. In your own words explain Charen's logic in her last paragraph, where she distinguishes between groups and individuals.

Character
1. Consider the title of Charen's essay and her explanation of the title in the essay's first three paragraphs. What sense of her own character does Charen establish through the title and her explanation? Explain your answer.
2. In paragraphs 10 and 11 Charen refers to the Civil War and President Lincoln. What sense of her own character does Charen establish through these references?
3. Does it change your sense of the character Charen establishes through her writing to know that she is a longtime, nationally syndicated columnist?

Emotion
1. Professor James McWhorter is quoted in paragraph 3 on the "cult of victimology." To what emotions does he appeal by his use of the word *cult?*
2. President Jefferson is quoted in paragraph 5. To what emotions does he appeal? Does Charen make the same appeal by quoting him? Explain your answer.
3. To what emotion does Charen appeal by her reference to President Lincoln in paragraph 11? Explain your answer.

Charen

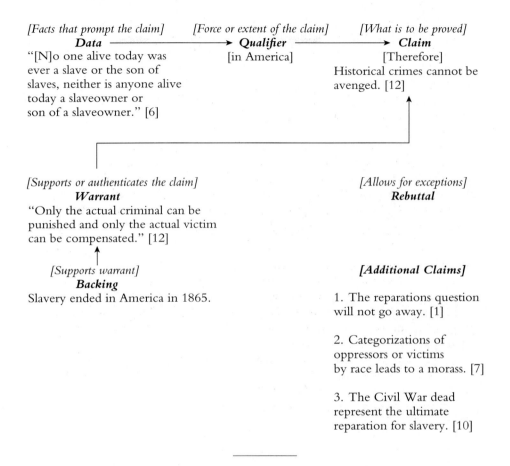

[Facts that prompt the claim]
Data ────→ *[Force or extent of the claim]*
Qualifier ────→ *[What is to be proved]*
Claim

"[N]o one alive today was
ever a slave or the son of
slaves, neither is anyone alive
today a slaveowner or
son of a slaveowner." [6]

[in America]

[Therefore]
Historical crimes cannot be
avenged. [12]

[Supports or authenticates the claim]
Warrant
"Only the actual criminal can be
punished and only the actual victim
can be compensated." [12]

[Allows for exceptions]
Rebuttal

[Supports warrant]
Backing
Slavery ended in America in 1865.

[Additional Claims]

1. The reparations question
will not go away. [1]

2. Categorizations of
oppressors or victims
by race leads to a morass. [7]

3. The Civil War dead
represent the ultimate
reparation for slavery. [10]

SLAVERY REPARATIONS CREATE BLACK VICTIMS

Thomas Sowell

Blacks have already been the first victims of the campaign to get reparations for slavery. The longer this futile campaign goes on, the more additional blacks will be victimized.

How have blacks been victimized thus far? Some have been asked to supply identifying information, so they can get their individual shares of the reparations. Those who complied and supplied this information have since discovered that it was being used to steal their identities and saddle them with debts run up by con men.

The most important thing to keep in mind about reparations is that it is never going to happen. No Congress is going to pass, and no president is going to sign, a bill that takes money from the great majority of American voters to pay a debt that they don't feel they owe.

You are never going to convince people whose ancestors arrived in America after the Civil War that they owe anybody anything for what happened in the antebellum South. You are never going to convince people outside the South that they owe something for what happened in the South. And you are never going to convince the descendants of the majority of white Southerners, whose ancestors were too poor to buy slaves if they wanted to, that they owe anybody anything.

It doesn't matter what rhetoric or whines or threats there are, no   5
elected body is going to take money from millions of voters who resent the suggestion that they owe it. So the real question is: What are blacks going to gain—and lose—from the continuation of this fruitless effort?

Those who promote the reparations campaign will gain publicity, book sales and the political support of some blacks and a few whites. Ideologues will gain self-righteous satisfaction from denouncing other people. But these "leaders" and shouters are a minority within a minority.

The great majority of blacks will gain nothing. Among the things they will lose is the good will of the rest of the society—a society in which they are not even the largest minority any more. In that vulnerable position, blacks can ill afford to come across as people who are constantly trying to get something without earning it.

That negative—and false—impression has already been created by such things as racial preferences and quotas. Despite much of what has been said by both black "leaders" and white critics of affirmative action, most blacks worked their way out of poverty themselves. The greatest reduction of poverty among blacks occurred before the civil rights revolution of the 1960s or the affirmative action policies of the 1970s.

Black politicians and activists have taken credit for obtaining from whites what blacks achieved on their own. This in turn has added to resentments from whites, who are offended by racial double standards and the relatively small percentage of the black population who have been able to take advantage of them.

Those who ask why blacks cannot lift themselves up by their own   10
bootstraps, as other minorities have done, usually have no idea that this is what most blacks have done. Worse yet, decades of propaganda from black "leaders" have also convinced many—if not most—blacks that their advancement has been due to political activism and that an end to racial preferences and quotas would mean an end to their progress.

Blacks lose most of all by the diversion of their efforts and energies from many economic opportunities that pay off a lot bigger. Getting in on the computer revolution offers far more bang for the buck than complaining about history. Being a race hustler is a very lucrative business for people like Jesse Jackson and Al Sharpton. But such people can extort money and power from white business and political leaders precisely because it is easier to pay off a relative handful of noise makers than to be bothered fighting them. But tens of millions of blacks cannot duplicate what a small band of extortionists do.

Chasing a will o' the wisp like reparations cannot produce what blacks most want—respect, including the self-respect that comes ultimately from one's own achievements. This is something that whites could not give blacks if they wanted to. And it is something too important to be forfeited by a futile attempt to get reparations.

Questions for Analysis

Logic
1. In paragraph 1 Sowell claims that the campaign for reparations victimizes blacks. Explain in your own words the reasoning Sowell uses to support his claim.
2. In paragraph 3 Sowell claims that no reparations bill will ever be passed by Congress and signed by a president. Explain in your own words the logic behind Sowell's claim.
3. Explain in your own words Sowell's reasoning in his last paragraph.

Character
1. In paragraph 6 Sowell puts the word *leaders* in quotation marks. What sense of his opponents' character does Sowell create by doing so?
2. What sense of his own character does Sowell create in his next-to-last sentence? Explain your answer.
3. Does it change your sense of the character Sowell expresses through his writing to know that he is an African American economist?

Emotion
1. Consider the title Sowell gives his essay. To what emotions does he appeal by choosing this title? Explain your answer.
2. To what emotions does Sowell appeal in the first sentence of paragraph 9?
3. Sowell uses the terms *race hustler* and *extortionists* when referring to his opponents. To what emotions does Sowell appeal by doing so?

EXERCISES: DOES AMERICA OWE REPARATIONS FOR SLAVERY?

Intertextual Questions

1. How do the three authors understand the term *black* in similar and different ways? Give examples from each essay to support your answer.
2. How do the three authors use the term *Americans* in similar and different ways? Give examples from each essay to support your answer.
3. In what different and similar ways do the three authors understand the effects of slavery on blacks living in America today? Give examples from each essay to support your answer.

Suggestions for Writing

1. Which writer has the best understanding of American history with regard to the question of reparations? Write an essay in which you explain and defend your position.
2. Which writer has the best understanding of today's African Americans with regard to the question of reparations? Write an essay in which you explain and defend your position.
3. Where do you stand on the issue of reparations for slavery? Write an essay in which you explain and defend your position.

7   Animal Testing

THE TRIALS OF ANIMALS

Cleveland Amory

Ask an experimenter about the animals in his laboratory. Nine times out of ten he will tell you that they are well cared for and that he abides by the Animal Welfare Act passed by Congress in 1966.

What he will not say is that both he and his colleagues fought the act and the amendments to it every step of the way; that, under the act, his laboratory is inspected at most (if at all) once a year; that when his animals are under experimentation, the act doesn't apply. Nor will he say that many laboratories ignore the act's most important amendment, passed in 1986, which mandates that at least one member of the public vote on the laboratory's animal-care committee.

Your experimenter is not a scofflaw. Having been for so long sole judge and jury of what he does, he believes that he is above the law. A prime example is that of the monkeys in Silver Spring, Maryland.

The monkeys were used in experiments in which, first, nerves in their limbs were removed and then stimuli—including electrical shocks and flames—were applied to see if they could still use their appendages.

Dr. Edward Taub, who ran the laboratory, was eventually tried and   5
found guilty, not of cruelty to animals but of maintaining a filthy lab. Maryland is one of many states that exempts federally funded experiments from cruelty charges.

Dr. Taub is today a free man. His monkeys, however, are not. They are still in a laboratory under the jurisdiction of the National Institutes of Health, which first funded these cruel experiments. Three hundred members of Congress have asked the NIH to release the monkeys; the NIH says it does not want them; two animal sanctuaries have offered to take them. Why can't they live what remains of their lives receiving the first evidence of human kindness they have ever known?

In the overcrowded field of cat experimentation, researchers at Louisiana State University, under an eight-year, $2 million Department of Defense contract, put cats in vises, remove part of their skulls, and then shoot them in the head.

More than two hundred doctors and Senator Daniel Inouye, chairman of the Defense Appropriations Subcommittee, have protested this cruelty. The experimenters say that their purpose is to find a way to return brain-wounded soldiers to active duty.

"Basic training for an Army infantryman costs $9,000," one experimenter argued. "If our research allows only 170 additional men to return to active duty . . . it will have paid for itself." But Dr. Donald Doll of Truman Veterans Hospital in Columbia, Missouri, said of these experiments: "I can find nothing which supports applying any of this data to humans."

At the University of Oregon, under a seventeen-year, $1.5 million *10* grant, psychologists surgically rotated the eyes of kittens, implanted electrodes in their brains, and forced them to jump onto a block in a pan of water to test their equilibrium. These experiments resulted in a famous laboratory break-in in 1986, and the subsequent trial and conviction of one of the animals' liberators.

During the trial, experimenters were unable to cite a single case in which their research had benefited humans. Additional testimony revealed instances of cats being inadequately anesthetized while having their eye muscles cut, untrained and unlicensed personnel performing the surgery, and mother cats suffering such stress that they ate their babies.

The trial judge, Edwin Allen, stated that the testimony was "disturbing to me as a citizen of this state and as a graduate of the University of Oregon. It would be highly appropriate to have these facilities opened to the public."

It would, indeed—and a judge is just what is needed. A judge first, then a jury. The experimenters have been both long enough.

Questions for Analysis

Logic
1. Is there anything puzzling to you about the logic of paragraph 6? Give an example of some facts or reasons that could be added to the paragraph to help clear up any problems or sharpen the reasoning there.
2. Two acknowledged experts testify in paragraph 9. In what ways does Amory work here and in the surrounding paragraphs to influence your view of the testimonies?
3. Throughout the essay Amory supports public scrutiny, and his own essay may be seen as a means toward allowing that scrutiny. Explain in your own words Amory's apparent reasoning on the benefits of greater public scrutiny.

Character
1. What qualities of character does the beginning of the essay seek to establish in its author? How do the implications about the element of character in his opponents' arguments contribute here to your sense of Amory's own character?

2. Some of the people who figure in the essay are named and some are not. What differences of effect does Amory's choice in naming create for your sense of the characters involved?
3. Amory uses selected and edited quotations in his essay. In what differing ways do the differences among the quotations contribute to your senses of their speakers? How, for example, does the emphasis on costs in paragraph 9 affect your sense of the speaker?

Emotion
1. After you have read the essay, what two senses does the word *trials* in the essay's title come to have for you? Briefly describe the emotional appeal made in the essay by each sense of the word.
2. Two legal trials resulting in convictions are described in the course of the essay [5—6, 10]. What emotional appeals does Amory make in each case?
3. How would you describe the general tone of voice that Amory uses in the essay? Formal and scholarly? Breezy and amused? Controlled outrage? Point to some examples and show how particular uses of language create the tone you hear.

A SCIENTIST: "I AM THE ENEMY"

Ron Kline

I am the enemy! One of those vilified, inhumane physician-scientists involved in animal research. How strange, for I have never thought of myself as an evil person. I became a pediatrician because of my love for children and my desire to keep them healthy. During medical school and residency, however, I saw many children die of leukemia, prematurity and traumatic injury—circumstances against which medicine has made tremendous progress, but still has far to go. More important, I also saw children, alive and healthy, thanks to advances in medical science such as infant respirators, potent antibiotics, new surgical techniques and the entire field of organ transplantation. My desire to tip the scales in favor of the healthy, happy children drew me to medical research.

My accusers claim that I inflict torture on animals for the sole purpose of career advancement. My experiments supposedly have no relevance to medicine and are easily replaced by computer simulation. Meanwhile, an apathetic public barely watches, convinced that the issue has no significance, and publicity-conscious politicians increasingly give way to the demands of the activists.

We in medical research have also been unconscionably apathetic. We have allowed the most extreme animal-rights protesters to seize the initiative and frame the issue as one of "animal fraud." We have been complacent in our belief that a knowledgeable public would sense the importance of animal research to the public health. Perhaps we have been mistaken in not responding to the emotional tone of the argument created by those sad posters of animals by waving equally sad posters of children dying of leukemia or cystic fibrosis.

Much is made of the pain inflicted on these animals in the name of medical science. The animal-rights activists contend that this is evidence of our malevolent and sadistic nature. A more reasonable argument, however, can be advanced in our defense. Life is often cruel, both to animals and human beings. Teenagers get thrown from the back of a pickup truck and suffer severe head injuries. Toddlers, barely able to walk, find themselves at the bottom of a swimming pool while a parent checks the mail. Physicians hoping to alleviate the pain and suffering these tragedies cause have but three choices: create an animal model of the injury or disease and use that model to understand the process and test new therapies; experiment on human beings—some experiments will succeed, most will fail—or finally, leave medical knowledge static, hoping that accidental discoveries will lead us to the advances.

Some animal-rights activists would suggest a fourth choice, claiming that computer models can simulate animal experiments, thus making the actual experiments unnecessary. Computers can simulate, reasonably well, the effects of well-understood principles on complex systems, as in the application of the laws of physics to airplane and automobile design. However, when the principles themselves are in question, as is the case with the complex biological systems under study, computer modeling alone is of little value.

One of the terrifying effects of the effort to restrict the use of animals in medical research is that the impact will not be felt for years and decades: drugs that might have been discovered will not be, surgical techniques that might have been developed will not be, and fundamental biological processes that might have been understood will remain mysteries. There is the danger that politically expedient solutions will be found to placate a vocal minority, while the consequences of those decisions will not be apparent until long after the decisions are made and the decision making forgotten.

Fortunately, most of us enjoy good health, and the trauma of watching one's child die has become a rare experience. Yet our good fortune should not make us unappreciative of the health we enjoy or the advances that make it possible. Vaccines, antibiotics, insulin and drugs to treat heart disease, hypertension and stroke are all based on animal research. Most complex surgical procedures, such as coronary-artery bypass and organ transplantation, are initially developed in animals. Presently undergoing animal studies are techniques to insert genes in humans in order to replace the defective ones found to be the cause of so much disease. These studies will effectively end if animal research is severely restricted.

In America today, death has become an event isolated from our daily existence—out of the sight and thoughts of most of us. As a doctor who has watched many children die, and their parents grieve, I am particularly angered by people capable of so much compassion for a dog or a cat, but with seemingly so little for a dying human being. These people seem so insulated from the reality of human life and death and what it means.

Make no mistake, however: I am not advocating the needlessly cruel treatment of animals. To the extent that the animal–rights movement has made us more aware of the needs of these animals, and made us search harder for suitable alternatives, they have made a significant contribution. But if the more radical members of this movement are successful in limiting further research, their efforts will bring about a tragedy that will cost many lives. The real question is whether an apathetic majority can be aroused to protect its future against a vocal, but misdirected, minority.

Questions for Analysis

Logic
1. How does the metaphor of "scales" in paragraph 1 represent the reasoning as a whole in Kline's support for animal experimentation?
2. In paragraphs 4 and 5 Kline lists the choices he sees as available on the issue of experiment and medical advance. In your own words, explain the implied logic of the support these paragraphs create for his own choice.
3. In what ways during the essay does the author acknowledge and concede well-made points of argument to his opponents?

Character
1. How does the essay as a whole work to refute the self-styled negative characterization of Kline's first two sentences?
2. How does Kline establish a sense of character that includes compassion? Does his compassion extend to the point of view that his essay opposes? Explain.
3. Kline attributes apathy on the issue of experimentation to the general public. Does he seem to include his readers in that characterization? Explain. How does he work to overcome apathy in the essay?

Emotion
1. Kline is a pediatrician, and his examples focus on children. Explain the operation of the emotional appeal created by that focus.
2. In paragraph 4 Kline examines some emotional appeals of his opponents and makes some emotional appeals of his own. Explain why he thinks his own arguments in this regard "more reasonable."
3. What is the emotional appeal of the "computer model" discussed in paragraph 5? In what ways does Kline seek to refute this emotional appeal?

Kline

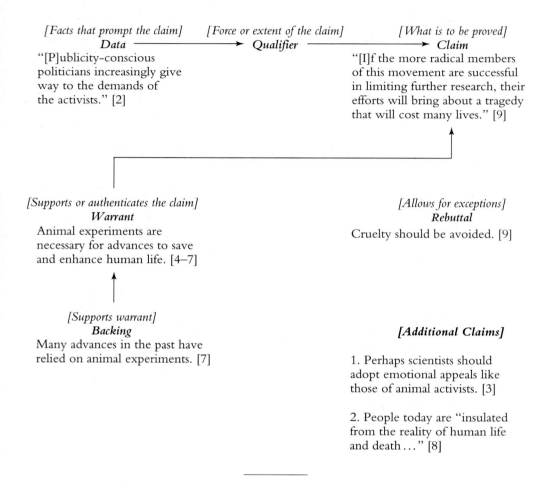

[Facts that prompt the claim]
Data

[Force or extent of the claim]
Qualifier

[What is to be proved]
Claim

"[P]ublicity-conscious politicians increasingly give way to the demands of the activists." [2]

"[I]f the more radical members of this movement are successful in limiting further research, their efforts will bring about a tragedy that will cost many lives." [9]

[Supports or authenticates the claim]
Warrant
Animal experiments are necessary for advances to save and enhance human life. [4–7]

[Allows for exceptions]
Rebuttal
Cruelty should be avoided. [9]

[Supports warrant]
Backing
Many advances in the past have relied on animal experiments. [7]

[Additional Claims]

1. Perhaps scientists should adopt emotional appeals like those of animal activists. [3]

2. People today are "insulated from the reality of human life and death..." [8]

IN DEFENSE OF THE ANIMALS

Meg Greenfield

I might as well come right out with it: Contrary to some of my most cherished prejudices, the animal-rights people have begun to get to me. I think that in some part of what they say they are right.

I never thought it would come to this. As distinct from the old-style animal rescue, protection, and shelter organizations, the more aggressive newcomers, with their "liberation" of laboratory animals and periodic championship of the claims of animal well-being over human well-being when a choice must be made, have earned a reputation in the world I live in as fanatics and just plain kooks. And even with my own recently (relatively) raised consciousness, there remains a good deal in both their critique and their prescription for the virtuous life that I reject, being not just a practicing carnivore, a wearer of shoe leather, and so forth, but also a supporter of certain indisputably agonizing procedures visited upon innocent animals in the furtherance of human welfare, especially experiments undertaken to improve human health.

So, viewed from the pure position, I am probably only marginally better than the worst of my kind, if that: I don't buy the complete "speciesist" analysis or even the fundamental language of animal "rights" and continue to find a large part of what is done in the name of that cause harmful and extreme. But I also think, patronizing as it must sound, that the zealots are required early on in any movement if it is to succeed in altering the sensibility of the leaden masses, such as me. Eventually they get your attention. And eventually you at least feel obliged to weigh their arguments and think about whether there may not be something there.

It is true that this end has often been achieved—as in my case—by means of vivid, cringe-inducing photographs, not by an appeal to reason or values so much as by an assault on squeamishness. From the famous 1970s photo of the newly skinned baby seal to the videos of animals being raised in the most dark, miserable, stunting environment as they are readied for their life's sole fulfillment as frozen patties and cutlets, these sights have had their effect. But we live in a world where the animal protein we eat comes discreetly prebutchered and prepacked so the original beast and his slaughtering are remote from our consideration, just as our furs come on coat hangers in salons, not on their original proprietors; and I see nothing wrong with our having to contemplate the often unsettling reality of how we came by the animal products we make use of. Then we can choose what we want to do.

The objection to our being confronted with these dramatic, disturbing pictures is first that they tend to provoke a misplaced, uncritical, and highly emotional concern for animal life at the direct expense of a more suitable concern for human suffering. What goes into the animals' account, the reasoning goes, necessarily comes out of ours. But I think it is possible to remain stalwart in your view that the human claim comes first and in your acceptance of the use of animals for human betterment and *still* to believe that there are some human interests that should not take precedence. For we have become far too self-indulgent, hardened, careless, and cruel in the pain we routinely inflict upon these creatures for the most frivolous, unworthy purposes. And I also think that the more justifiable purposes, such as medical research, are shamelessly used as cover for other activities that are wanton.

For instance, not all of the painful and crippling experimentation that is undertaken in the lab is being conducted for the sake of medical

5

knowledge or other purposes related to basic human well-being and health. Much of it is being conducted for the sake of superrefinements in the cosmetic and other frill industries, the noble goal being to contrive yet another fragrance or hair tint or commercially competitive variation on all the daft, fizzy, multicolored "personal care" products for the medicine cabinet and dressing table, a firmer-holding hair spray, that sort of thing. In other words, the conscripted, immobilized rabbits and other terrified creatures, who have been locked in boxes from the neck down, only their heads on view, are being sprayed in the eyes with different burning, stinging substances for the sake of adding to our already obscene store of luxuries and utterly superfluous vanity items.

PHONY KINSHIP

Oddly, we tend to be very sentimental about animals in their idealized, fictional form and largely indifferent to them in realms where our lives actually touch. From time immemorial, humans have romantically attributed to animals their own sensibilities—from Balaam's biblical ass who providently could speak and who got his owner out of harm's way right down to Lassie and the other Hollywood pups who would invariably tip off the good guys that the bad guys were up to something. So we simulate phony cross-species kinship, pretty well drown in the cuteness of it all—Mickey and Minnie and Porky—and ignore, if we don't actually countenance, the brutish things done in the name of Almighty Hair Spray.

This strikes me as decadent. My problem is that it also causes me to reach a position that is, on its face, philosophically vulnerable, if not absurd—the muddled, middling, inconsistent place where finally you are saying it's all right to kill them for some purposes, but not to hurt them gratuitously in doing it or to make them suffer horribly for one's own trivial whims.

I would feel more humiliated to have fetched up on this exposed rock, if I didn't suspect I had so much company. When you see pictures of people laboriously trying to clean the Exxon gunk off of sea otters even knowing that they will only be able to help out a very few, you see this same outlook in action. And I think it *can* be defended. For to me the biggest cop-out is the one that says that if you don't buy the whole absolutist, extreme position it is pointless and even hypocritical to concern yourself with lesser mercies and ameliorations. The pressure of the animal-protection groups has already had some impact in improving the way various creatures are treated by researchers, trainers, and food producers. There is much more in this vein to be done. We are talking about rejecting wanton, pointless cruelty here. The position may be philosophically absurd, but the outcome is the right one.

Questions for Analysis

Logic

1. In paragraph 4 Greenfield says that the ends of animal-rights activists have "often been achieved—as in my case—by means of vivid, cringe-inducing photographs, not by an appeal to reason or values so much as by an assault on squeamishness." In your view, have the non-logical means by which Greenfield herself has been persuaded affected the logic of her argument? Explain.
2. In your view, have the nonlogical means of Greenfield's own persuasion affected the organization of her argument?
3. On what basis does Greenfield fault the "philosophical" logic of her own position? Explain in your own words with examples.

Character

1. What aspects of her own character does Greenfield seek to establish in paragraph 1? Pick another place in the essay where she seeks to establish similar qualities and analyze the ways in which she does so.
2. In paragraph 2 Greenfield says that she rejects "a good deal" of the animal-rights activists' "prescription for the virtuous life." What elements in her own implied definition of the virtuous life does she seek to establish by this rejection?
3. What does Greenfield define in her last paragraph as "the biggest cop-out"? What elements of her own character does she seek to establish by her definition here?

Emotion

1. Greenfield says she is embarrassed by her new position on the issue. In your own words explain (a) the source of her embarrassment and (b) the ways in which she uses this embarrassment as an emotional appeal to her reader.
2. In paragraph 6 Greenfield argues against experiments for purposes other than those related to "basic human well-being and health." In your own words analyze the ways in which she creates her emotional appeal within this paragraph.
3. In paragraph 7 Greenfield argues against human sentimentality about animals. In your own words analyze the ways in which she creates her emotional appeal in this paragraph.

EXERCISES: ANIMAL TESTING

Intertextual Questions

1. All three authors may be said to oppose "needless" cruelty. Compare the differing ways in which you understand each author to define implicitly or explicitly this key term.
2. In your view, which of the writers best counters the position of those opposed to the writer's own opinions? Explain your answer using particular examples.
3. Another writer has said: "All other animals are always cruel. Human beings are the only animals who *don't* treat animals like animals." Discuss the ways in which you think each of the three authors in this section would respond to this statement.

Suggestions for Writing

1. In your opinion, which argument makes the most effective emotional appeal, whether or not you agree with its conclusion? Write an essay in which you analyze the strength of the essay's emotional appeal by comparing it to the emotional appeals of the other essays.
2. Another writer has said: "The sufferings of animals take place in the present, while the benefits to human beings are only imagined for the future—this is the strength of the claims to animal rights." Write an essay on animal experimentation in which you examine and discuss the theme of time as it affects differing points of view on the topic.
3. Another writer has said: "Almost all animals used in experiments are bred only for that purpose. If life is a good, they are rewarded by existence. If their lives include suffering and end in death, they are no different from other lives." Write an essay that begins with your response to this proposition and goes on to argue for your further views on animal experimentation.

8   *The Rich—Saints or Sinners?*

DOWNSIZING THE MIDDLE CLASS
Rhonda Burns

It used to be that people were proud to work for the same company for the whole of their working lives. They'd get a gold watch at the end of their productive years and a dinner featuring speeches by their bosses praising their loyalty. But today's rich capitalists have regressed to the "survival of the fittest" ideas of the nineteenth-century Robber Barons and their loyalty extends not to their workers or even to their stockholders but only to themselves. Instead of giving out gold watches worth a hundred or so dollars for forty or so years of work, they give themselves "golden parachutes" worth tens and even hundreds of millions of dollars as they sell down the river the company they may have been with for only a few years. Some other corporation is the purchaser and this new "player" (other people's lives are only a game to them) immediately announces new profits and "growth" to be had through downsizing (i.e., firing the people whose loyalty created the company's worth at time of sale) and outsourcing (i.e., shipping the jobs of loyal Americans overseas to low-paid foreigners).

The new rich selfishly act on their own to unfairly grab the wealth that the country as a whole has produced. The top 1 percent of the population now has wealth equal to the whole bottom 95 percent and they want more. Their selfishness is most shamelessly expressed in downsizing and outsourcing because these business maneuvers don't act to create new jobs as the founders of new industries used to do, but only to cut out jobs while keeping the money value of what those jobs produced for themselves.

To keep the money machine working smoothly the rich have bought all the politicians from the top down. The president himself is constantly leaving Washington and the business of the nation because he is summoned to "fundraising dinners" where fat cats pay a thousand or so dollars a plate to worm their way into government not through service but through donations of vast amounts of money. Once on the inside they have both political parties busily tearing up all the regulations that protect the rest of us from the greed of the rich—regulations that took the whole of the twentieth century to create and that are now being destroyed overnight.

The middle class used to be loyal to the free enterprise system and throughout the Cold War with Russia it had nothing but laughter to give in response to Communist propaganda that urged it to hate the rich. In those days the people of the middle class mostly thought they'd be rich themselves someday or have a good shot at becoming rich, so why poison the well? But nowadays income is being distributed more and more unevenly and corporate loyalty is a thing of the past. The middle class may also wake up to forget its loyalty to the so-called free enterprise system altogether and the government which governs only the rest of us while letting the corporations do what they please with our jobs. As things stand, if somebody doesn't wake up, the middle class is on a path to being downsized all the way to the bottom of society.

―――――――

Questions for Analysis

Logic
1. Burns argues that politicians are "bought." What evidence does she bring in support of this claim? Explain your judgment of the importance of evidence in this and similar instances.
2. According to Burns, what was the reasoning of the middle class with regard to the rich throughout the Cold War? What does she suggest may be the new middle-class reasoning with regard to the rich?
3. Burns claims that the rich are loyal only to themselves. What evidence or data does she bring in support of this claim?

Character
1. In the course of her argument Burns speaks of the past, the present, and the future. How old do you imagine her to be, and what aspects of her writing create a sense of her character as a woman of experience?
2. How would you characterize the tone of voice in which Burns makes her points? Aggrieved? Offended? Outraged? Describe her tone as clearly as you can, and point to some of the ways in which her use of language works to create it.
3. Burns seems to have a low opinion not only of business leaders but also of politicians. Point to some of the ways in which she creates a sense of the character of politicians through her uses of language.

Emotion
1. Throughout her argument Burns values loyalty as a means of creating social cohesion. Make a list of the actions that seem to her to define acts of *disloyalty* and explain how their presentation is designed to appeal to the reader's emotions.

2. In paragraph 1 Burns redefines several terms in her own way. Pick two of these terms, and explain how the redefinitions appeal to the reader's emotions.

3. Burns uses the term *downsizing* in her last sentence in a different sense from the one she employs earlier in the essay. Explain what is added to the negative emotional appeal of the term by this new twist.

THE POOR HAVE ENSLAVED THE RICH

Paul Craig Roberts

According to the latest information released by the Internal Revenue Service, the top 1 percent of income earners in the United States paid 30.4 percent of the personal income tax revenues collected in 1995, the latest year for which the information is available. The top 5 percent of income earners paid almost 50 percent of the income tax collected, and the top 25 percent paid over 80 percent. The top half of income earners paid over 95 percent of the income tax, leaving the bottom 50 percent to bear less than 5 percent of the tax burden.

If that's not the rich paying taxes, I don't know what is.

Is it fair? Absolutely not. Anyone in the top 1 percent is paying the government amounts ranging from hundreds of thousands to millions of dollars annually. In exchange, they are permitted to stay out of prison but get very little else for their money. They don't use public housing, food stamps, Medicaid, subsidized public transportation or public schools. In the United States today, the rich are the equivalent of slaves in the 19th century. The only real difference is that they are owned by the government instead of by private owners.

In a democracy, the people are the government, and what we have done is to put the rich in chains and make them work for the rest of us. They are publicly owned slaves. This system works because our slaves are such productive people that governments at all levels can take away more than half of their incomes and they are still rich after-tax. But nonetheless slaves.

Once we perverted our democracy in 1913 with a constitutional amendment permitting an income tax, we set about enslaving our most productive citizens. Historically, slaves were exploited to the extent of about half of their labor. The other half was necessary to support their own lives and reproduction. In the United States today, only about the top 2 percent of income earners meet the historical definition of a slave, but many of the rest of us are partial slaves. With the top half of income earners paying more than 95 percent of the income tax, they are at least the partial property of the other half and of the governments that run the plantation.

Many Americans do not understand their slave status. They think they are free because they travel to and from work, change jobs and generally move about impeded only by traffic in contrast to their 19th century counterparts, who labored directly on the property of their owners. If 19th century slave owners had possessed the equivalent of the IRS, social security numbers and payroll withholding, their slaves could have been put out to work for wages instead of toiling directly in the fields. Indeed, some slaves did work for wages, which they shared with their owners. Some even saved enough from their earnings to purchase their freedom, something we cannot do from the IRS.

Any American who imagines he is free can put it to a test by trying to hold on to all of his income. The jerk on the chain from the IRS will quickly cure the illusion.

Income tax apologists try to muddy the issue by claiming (falsely) that whereas the rich pay 30 percent of the taxes, they receive 30 percent or more of the income, so there is no disproportion. According to the IRS, this is definitely not the case. In 1995 the rich paid over 30 percent of the total income tax but earned less than 15 percent of the total income. The top 5 percent paid almost half of the income tax but earned only 28 percent of the total income.

Thus, extreme disproportion does exist. Like 19th century slaves, the rich own no more than half of their own labor. The rest of their labor pays for the upkeep of others. The only difference between the income tax and prior forms of slavery is that the poor have enslaved the rich rather than vice versa.

This is not what our country was supposed to be. Unless we get rid   10
of the income tax, we won't return to the path of freedom on which citizens receive the full fruit of their labors and are responsible for themselves and their families.

Questions for Analysis

Logic
1. Explain in your own words the reasoning that Roberts brings to justify his title.
2. In paragraph 7 Roberts expands his argument to include "any American." Explain why, according to Roberts, any American is like the rich.
3. In paragraph 8 Roberts refutes what he sees as the false reasoning of "income tax apologists." According to him, what is that reasoning, and why is it false?

Character

1. *Slavery* is a highly charged emotional word. What sense of Roberts's character is created for you by the way he uses that term strictly as an economic one, as opposed to, say, a moral or a racial one?
2. In paragraph 3 Roberts speaks of fairness. In the essay as a whole, does he present himself in your view as possessing the quality of fairness in his character? Explain your answer with evidence.
3. In paragraph 4 Roberts speaks of "the rest of us" in contrast to the rich. Explain the sense of his character created by claiming to argue as he does from such a position in society.

Emotion

1. Roberts acts throughout as a demythologizer of conventional wisdom. To what emotions does a demythologizer attempt to appeal? What response does he risk? Explain your answers.
2. In paragraph 7 Roberts speaks of a "jerk on the chain." Make a list of other images of slavery used throughout the essay to create emotional appeals.
3. What is the emotional appeal of "the path of freedom" in paragraph 10? Is the reference here purely an economic one? Explain your answer.

KING'S RANSOM

Dan Moran

The Doctor tells Stephen King he has six months to live. King says "I want a second opinion." Doctor: "Alright, you're the King of Horror."

Complaining about celebrity salaries has become such a national pastime that Stephen King's decision last week to end his 20-year relationship with Viking Books seemed like, well, if not the World Series, at least Scott Hamilton's triumphant return to the ice.

There is certainly plenty to complain about in the notion of King, whose multimedia and licensing deals constitute an empire as vast and sprawling as Diamond Jim Brady's, turning up his nose at his longtime publisher's offer of "almost" $15 million. When you consider that an M.A.-equipped entry-level Viking editor makes $18,000 a year, the discrepancy between Barry Bonds' salary and the peanut vendor's begins to look as equitable as communism by comparison.

Right now, King is "shopping around" different publishing houses to see who gets to release his latest novel, *Bag of Bones*. And how can he lose? He is a writer so popular that he can release two 800 page books on the same day (last year's *The Regulators* and *Desperation*)—retailing in the neighborhood of $25 each—and see both make it to the top of the best-seller list (the "Richard Bachman" alias he used on *Regulators* was originally intended to help King avoid flooding the market—but it's now mainly a marketing gimmick). It's a wonder they don't call him the Hughes of Horror instead.

Writer? And money? For shame! Isn't it offensive enough that we live in a nation where John Grisham is now contractually entitled to have his name included in all future film adaptations of his books (e.g., "John Grisham's The Pesky Prosecutor") while not one of Charles Portis' books is in print, and Thomas Berger (or even Joseph Hergesheimer) is remembered mainly for being forgotten? Where American poetry is long dead, and the short story is limited to a few column inches in the *New Yorker* and a few other literary petri dishes? We should be wounded to the heart that *The Dead Zone* outsells *Moby Dick,* and more people have seen *Maximum Overdrive* than Branagh's *Hamlet*. King's empire, you could argue, is everything that's wrong with publishing as well as the reading public.

Well, you have to agree with some of this, and as an English teacher, I know that at least part of my job is to loiter in the school library and make sure the kids are reading *Ivanhoe* or *Two Years before the Mast* instead of *Salem's Lot* or *The Stand*. I'm supposed to tell students that their time would be better spent reading Franklin's autobiography than *Christine*. And if a kid tries to tell me how much he liked reading *The Shining,* I may be patient, and even encouraging (this is almost the twenty-first century, after all), but must always remind him that if he doesn't move on to deciphering the courtly double entendres in *Love's Labour's Lost* he will end up wearing a name tag and hairnet for his entire working life.

But if we assume that getting people to read is a worthy end, it's hard to see the King of Horror's empire as anything other than a good thing. In fact, I'll stake my reputation as a fuddy-duddy and say that reading his first eight or nine books were instrumental in making me a dedicated reader.

I can already hear my audience muttering, "Who cares about this guy's reputation? Who the hell is he?" The answer is, of course, nobody—just another fan who's full of beans. But I've seen too many kids introduced to nose-in-the-book reading because they were wowed by the history of the Overlook Hotel, or the flat-out coolness of Trashcan Man's blowing up oil tanks to be completely appalled at King's imperial delusions. If you ever went through your King period, you'll know there's nothing as drop-dead scary (at the time, anyway) as Barlow, the vampire (or should I say "vampyre"?), floating in front of kids' windows, or as satisfying as Carrie's dropping a psychic neutron bomb on the bullies who have doused her in pig's blood! Nothing comes close. And if you get hooked on these things it matters little if, in ten years, you grow tired of reading parenthetical remarks in midsentence, or realize that Kubrick's movie of *The Shining* is better and smarter than the book. No—the point is that this goofy literary industrialist manipulated you into loving books—and who can fault him for that?

And if he gets rich as King Farouq for doing it, why do we complain? It's part of our old mistrustful love affairs with both money and learning. We lament the nation's preference for smart bombs to smart children, then object when a writer gets rich by actually getting kids to read. We tuttut at the still mostly male literary world, then sneer at the writers (most of them women) whose careers have soared after having their books chosen for Oprah's Book Club.

With King, there is the added benefit that he is, by any reasonable   10 standard, a good writer. His companions in the club of most-read fiction authors include the objectionable Grisham, turgid weapons pornographer Tom Clancy (whose books are popular with male adolescents aged 25 to 55), masters of false elegance like Nicholas Evans and David Guterson, "H Is for Heebyjeebies" assembly line Sue Grafton, and so on. Stephen King looks like Dickens in this company, and his recent elevation to Author of Literature status (signified by a glowing Roger Angell review and the inevitable appearance in the *New Yorker*) justifies his lifelong devotion to superbly purple prose and detailed (if often shockingly lazy) plot construction.

Whether you think the Maine book machine has given a false brilliance to the bestseller list or contributed to the delinquency of American letters, don't ignore the testimony of 12-year-old andrew__c__d @hotmail.com, who posted a review to Amazon that called *Desperation* "an awesome book," and one of his "favorite books of all time."

Maybe Andrew is the kind of geek who would have become a book junky even without Stephen King's assistance. But this year, thousands of kids will read *Bag of Bones* and tell themselves that it is The Best Book Ever. With any luck, 0.05% of them may go on to chuckle at the trilingual puns in *Ulysses,* or just to better books generally. Perhaps they'll even grow up to be misshapen bookworms like me. Whatever happens, they'll most likely grow up, like all of us, to be serfs. And like all serfs, they'll be secretly happy to know their King is rich.

Questions for Analysis

Logic

1. In paragraph 3 Moran claims that "there is certainly plenty to complain about" with regard to King's refusal of a $15 million contract. Explain in your own words the rationale behind Moran's complaint.
2. In paragraph 5 Moran says that "King's empire, you could argue, is everything that's wrong with publishing as well as the reading public."

What *are* the arguments for what's wrong? Does Moran himself make or imply them? Give evidence in support of your answers.

3. In paragraph 7 Moran argues for seeing King's "empire" as a good thing. Explain the rationale of this argument, and point to the language of the text that supports it.

Character

1. In paragraph 6 Moran jokes about the different career paths open to those who read Shakespeare and those who don't. What aspects of character are created for Moran by the joke? What for the hypothetical student? Explain in your own words how these aspects are suggested by Moran's writing.

2. In paragraph 7 Moran offers to "stake my reputation as a fuddy-duddy." Does the character he creates for himself through his writing in general seem to you like that of a fuddy-duddy? Support your answer with evidence.

3. Throughout the essay Moran puns on King's name and calls him by other titles such as "the Maine book machine" in paragraph 11. How do these mock-heroic titles work to create a sense of Moran's estimation of King's character as a writer?

Emotion

1. In paragraph 2 what are the emotions that Moran suggests are involved in "complaining about celebrity salaries"? What is the effect of his implied comparison of King with baseball players in qualifying these emotions? Does the comparison invite a stronger feeling about King or a weaker one? Explain.

2. Paragraph 5 introduces the issue of "shame." According to Moran, who should feel shame and why? Even if you see the phrase "for shame" as a joke, try to explain the values and assumptions that make the emotional basis of the joke.

3. At the end of his essay Moran suggests that "serfs" are "secretly happy to know their King is rich." In what does Moran imply that the happiness is assumed to reside, and why is it secret? If you agree with him, explain the basis of your own feelings. If you disagree, explain the emotions you do feel and explain their bases.

Moran

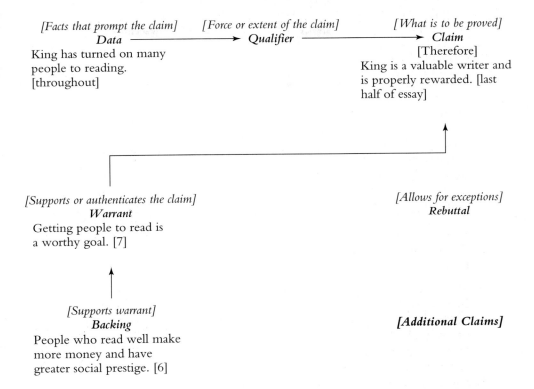

[Facts that prompt the claim]
Data ——————————→
King has turned on many
people to reading.
[throughout]

[Force or extent of the claim]
Qualifier ——————————→

[What is to be proved]
Claim
[Therefore]
King is a valuable writer and
is properly rewarded. [last
half of essay]

[Supports or authenticates the claim]
Warrant
Getting people to read is
a worthy goal. [7]

[Allows for exceptions]
Rebuttal

[Supports warrant]
Backing
People who read well make
more money and have
greater social prestige. [6]

[Additional Claims]

EXERCISES: THE RICH—
SAINTS OR SINNERS?

Intertextual Questions

1. The management theorist P. Owen Hatteras has written that "those excluded from the great American pastime of wealth like to speak of 'fairness' because that magic word—like abracadabra or Open, Sesame!—instantly transforms the speaker from humble spectator to all-powerful umpire." In your view where does each writer stand on the issue of "fairness" with regard to money? Would any of them agree with Hatteras? Disagree? Explain your judgments.
2. Burns and Roberts use similar statistics to reach opposite conclusions. Explain the differing ways in which each interprets the numbers.
3. The topic of money can raise powerful emotions, including envy and greed. In what differing ways do the authors in this section take into account those emotions in themselves and in their readers? First, identify particular uses of language that seem to you to express or invite greed or envy; then show how the language works emotionally.

Suggestions for Writing

1. *Rich, middle class, poor, serfs,* and *slaves* are some of the emotion-laden terms of economic status used by the writers in this section, but how are they defined? Pick any one of the key terms used by two writers and write an essay showing how each works to define it.
2. Waiving the issue of their definition, which of the writers in your view best uses the emotion-laden terms of economic status to advance his or her argument through appeals to emotion? Write an essay that analyzes the methods of the writer of your choice.
3. Which of the writers in the section best represents your views on "the rich"? Write an essay in which you advance and defend your views, taking into account those expressed by the writers here.

9   *Hate Crimes and Justice*

HATE CRIME LAWS ARE A BAD IDEA
Charley Reese

Passing "hate crime" laws is a step toward totalitarianism. There are several reasons why such legislation is a bad idea.

First, to make a distinction between crimes based on motive is nonsense and an injustice. People who are victims of violence, vandalism or arson are equally injured, whether the criminal's motives are greed, general malice or prejudice.

To punish a crime of prejudice more than an otherwise identical crime of greed or general malice is a slap in the face to the victims of ordinary criminals.

Second, so-called hate crimes are a minor percentage of crime, and the government shouldn't be wasting its time trying to make the problem larger than it is.

Third, hate crime legislation is just laying the groundwork for hate   *5* speech legislation, which, indeed, is already on the books in some states. This is the step toward totalitarianism. This is a direct assault on free speech and should be vigorously opposed.

The First Amendment of the Constitution was not designed to protect safe or uncontroversial or politically correct speech or government-approved speech. Such speech needs no protection. You can speak of trivia and government-approved topics in a government-approved manner in any dictatorship in the world, present or past.

Remember that old Cold War joke, when an American in Moscow tells a Russian, "Look, I can stand out in front of the White House and call the president a warmonger and nothing will happen to me. That's how free my country is."

"So what? So can I," said the Russian, and to prove it, he shouted, "The American president is a warmonger."

No matter how obnoxious or offensive we find certain speech, we must never consent to allowing the government to police it, for to police speech is to police thought, and that is the essence of the totalitarian philosophy.

And we have plenty of would-be totalitarians who are eager to   *10*
brand as hate speech any speech that criticizes them or their sacred cows or just meets with their disapproval. In Canada and Germany it is considered hate speech to question even the details of the Holocaust; people in Germany have ended up in prison for doing nothing more than that. Since when does a fact of history need the police power of the state to protect it? No one who values liberty should ever allow a government to make it a crime to be wrong or to question the orthodox version of events.

Truth is often arrived at by argument and debate. Even genuine historians are continuously revising their histories as more information becomes available. As one wag put it, God cannot rewrite history, but historians can and do all the time.

Some people in this country seem to want to enjoy the privileges of the communist party as it was in the Soviet Union—to be completely immune from criticism and to make sure none of their ideas or policies, no matter how cockamamie, are questioned. Hence the eagerness to brand all their critics, legitimate or otherwise, as peddlers of hate speech and to push the government into criminalizing it.

A free society, if it's to remain free, must leave even genuine bigoted speech free to be combatted by reason and education. The alternative is to move toward totalitarianism, in which thinking the wrong thoughts can land you in prison or before a firing squad.

There may not be [a] dime's worth of difference between Republicans and Democrats, but there is a gap light years wide between those who believe in freedom and those who believe in totalitarianism. If you find freedom offensive, perhaps you ought to emigrate.

Questions for Analysis

Logic
1. In paragraph 2 Reese claims that "to make a distinction between crimes based on motive is nonsense." Explain his reasoning on this point in your own words.
2. In the same paragraph Reese also says that the distinction creates an "injustice." Explain his reasoning on this point in your own words.
3. Explain in your own words the reasoning behind Reese's claim that the punishment of hate crimes will lead to the punishment of free thought and free speech.

Character
1. What qualities of character does Reese seem to seek to establish by means of the joke in paragraphs 7–8?

2. What qualities of character does Reese attribute to "some people" in paragraph 12?
3. What sense of his own character does Reese seem to seek to establish by his suggestion in the last paragraph that "there may not be [a] dime's worth of difference between Republicans and Democrats"?

Emotion
1. To what emotions does Reese appeal by his use of the phrase "slap in the face" in paragraph 3? Explain your answer.
2. You have been asked a question about the sense of character established by Reese's Cold War joke in paragraphs 7–8. To what emotion or emotions in his reader does this joke seem designed to appeal? Explain your analysis.
3. You have been asked a question about the character Reese attributes to "some people" in paragraph 12. To what emotion or emotions in his reader does he seem to appeal by his attempt to characterize "some people"?

Reese

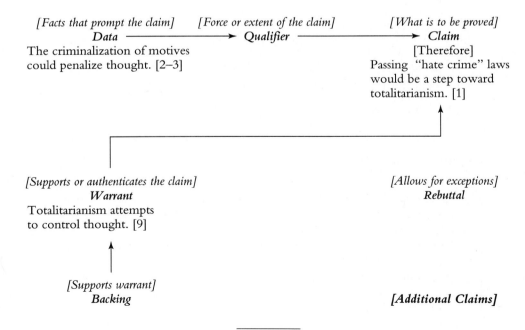

SPECIAL CRIMES NEED SPECIAL LAWS

Helen Dodge

It's over two hundred years since the American Constitution was adopted to protect and govern all the people of the thirteen diverse colonies that became the first thirteen states. Yet those people were mostly of English origin, except for the African slaves who had no protection at all. As the twenty-first century approaches America is more diverse than ever before in terms of race, religion, national origin, and sexual orientation. And great progress has been made over the centuries: Slavery has been abolished, Eurocentric immigration laws are gone, and people are now ashamed to admit it publicly if they privately try to keep minorities out of their clubs and organizations.

Yet hate crimes are on the increase and these crimes strike at the heart of the American dream itself. They strike at its diversity and the need for all its people to live in harmony with one another. *E pluribus unum*— from many one—that is the motto of the United States and it is a motto that calls for the union not only of state but of people. It calls for making of one nation out of diverse races, creeds, and sexual orientations.

Those who oppose the goals of the United States are traitors to its ideals. They attack someone not just to rob him or her and gain money, they beat people up not just because they are sadistic. No, they do these things in the case of hate crimes because they hate the victim. They don't just want money or freaky pleasures; they want to express their hatred as well. Because there are therefore really two crimes involved, the ordinary laws against robbery and assault are not enough. We need special hate crime laws because hate crimes are special and they work to destroy what is special about America.

Hate crime laws would focus on the hatred behind the crime and not just on the crime itself. Opponents say that extra laws will not provide extra protection and for once I agree with them. Those bent on violence ignore the law and even delight in breaking it all the time. But the law serves to punish them when they do and in the case of hate crimes it sends them a message in advance about where we stand as a nation. Special crimes need special laws and those laws will serve to unite the rest of us and give public and legal expression to our union. The haters are the only things worth hating and the rest of us should unite against them. *E pluribus unum!*

Questions for Analysis

Logic

1. Explain in your own words the facts that prompt Dodge's claim in paragraph 1 that "great progress has been made."

2. In paragraph 2 Dodge claims that hate crimes "strike at the heart of the American dream itself." Explain her reasoning in your own words.
3. On what basis does Dodge attempt to refute those opponents who claim that no special laws are needed for hate crimes?

Character
1. Point to and explain some of the ways in which Dodge attempts to establish a sense of her own character as a patriotic one.
2. What senses of her character besides that of patriotism does the author's knowledge of the Latin motto tend to create?
3. In paragraph 4 Dodge says that in one instance she agrees with her opponents. What sense of character does that acknowledgment tend to create?

Emotion
1. In paragraph 3 Dodge calls those who commit hate crimes "traitors." To what emotions in her reader does she appeal by using this word?
2. In paragraph 3 Dodge attributes the desire for "freaky pleasures" to those who commit hate crimes. To what emotion in her reader does she appeal by using this phrase?
3. To what emotions in her reader does Dodge appeal by ending her assignment with the words *E pluribus unum?* Name more than one emotion, and explain your answers.

"HATE CRIME" LAWS
CHANGE THE LAW

Samuel Francis

The Economist, a British-based but globally circulated news magazine of the proper progressive tint, is not exactly a hate-sheet of the racialist right, but even it is having problems with the very concept of "hate crimes." Acknowledging that the murder in Jasper—where three white men, ex-convicts, tied a black man to the bumper of their pickup truck and dragged him to death, dismembering his body—was one of particular "horror," the editorial nevertheless proceeds to argue that "the notion of 'hate crimes' is flawed."

Had the black victim in Jasper, James Byrd, been white and had he been killed in the same way by the same men, the magazine asks, would the crime have been any less a horror? Had the killers been motivated by perverse sexual drives, by psychopathic delusions, or simply by mercenary reasons, to swipe the change in Mr. Byrd's pockets, would the killing merit the additional punishment that state and federal law reserve only for crimes motivated by race?

Put in that context, the answer ought to be obvious. Murder is murder, and to say that some are motivated by "hate" and others aren't strikes most normal folk as at best a bizarre usage of the word. Sadists who dismember children for pleasure and jilted husbands who beat their wives to a pulp are at least as driven by "hate" in any normal usage as white hoodlums who murder a black man for the fun of it. Yet, the editorial concludes, hate crime laws imply that murders for other motives are "less awful" than those motivated by race.

It also notes that "Once race—or religion, or gender—is introduced into the equation, this naturally colours the motive for the crime in the eyes of the criminal justice system." In effect, the law criminalizes the motives, as it does not do for any other kind of crime.

But the "white supremacist" opinions and the Nazi paraphernalia 5 supposedly left at the scene of the crime are not in themselves against the law. Hence, "The notion of 'hate crime' may be, in effect, an extra penalty imposed on people whose views are offensive, as well as their actions. Ironically, it makes the justice system pick on them simply because they are different."

The editorial implies an important point, namely, that hate crime laws come very close to outlawing certain opinions, ideas and attitudes simply because they're offensive to most people. On the same grounds, the law could plausibly penalize perverse sexuality and even jealousy and greed at least as much as it currently punishes "hate."

Yet the editorial could go a bit further. Anglo-American law does not traditionally criminalize motive, no matter how offensive, and the distinction between "motive" and "intent" (which is criminalized in law) used to be quite clear.

If I rob a bank to help my family and my accomplice robs the bank to pad his pockets, we each have a different motive—but we both had the same intent: to rob the bank. "In law," found a leading court case on the issue, People v. Weiss, "there is a clear distinction between" "motive" and "intent." "'Motive' is the moving power which impels to action for a definite result. Intent is the purpose to use a particular means to effect such result."

"Intent," of course, is the element in law that creates the crime itself. A homicide without intent is not murder but manslaughter, and carries a lesser penalty. "Motive," on the other hand, is largely irrelevant to the criminal act and to the punishment the act receives.

No one seems to doubt that the suspects in Jasper "intended" to 10 commit murder, and if the prosecution can prove that intent, their road to the death house will be expedited. But if their crime is tried as one of "hate," not only their intent to kill but also their reasons for killing will have to be proved in court.

That may or may not add to the burdens of the prosecution, but there's no reason to think it will enhance whatever justice is eventually dispensed—and there's every reason to believe that other ideas and the motives they create sooner or later may also become criminal acts.

———————

Questions for Analysis

Logic

1. Beginning in paragraph 5 Francis argues that "hate crime" laws may end up being used to penalize people with views that those in power might find offensive. Explain his reasoning in your own words.
2. Beginning in paragraph 6 Francis argues that "hate crime" laws may end up penalizing other emotions such as jealousy. Explain his reasoning in your own words.
3. Beginning in paragraph 8 Francis addresses the traditional legal distinction between *intent* and *motive*. Explain the logic of his distinction in your own words.

Character

1. Francis begins by emphasizing that *The Economist* is a "progressive" and a foreign publication. What sense of his character does this emphasis seem designed to create?
2. In paragraph 3 Francis uses the phrase "normal folk." What sense of his character does this phrase seem designed to create?
3. According to Francis, what should be the place in criminal prosecution for arguments about the character of the accused? Explain your answer.

Emotion

1. Francis puts the phrase "hate crime" within quotation marks when he uses it for the first time, though later these marks are omitted. What seems to be the emotional appeal created by the initial use of quotation marks?
2. Does the word *ex-convicts* in paragraph 1 make an emotional appeal to the reader? If you think it does, explain the appeal and how it works to support the author's argument as a whole. If you think it does not, explain how you came to your opinion.
3. To what emotions does the example of robbing a bank "to help my family" appeal in paragraph 8? What might be an example of "different motives"? Explain the emotional appeal of the example you invent.

EXERCISES: HATE CRIMES AND JUSTICE

Intertextual Questions

1. Using only four paragraphs Dodge writes the shortest of the three short arguments here. In your opinion, does her restricted length keep her from addressing all the arguments of the other writers? What if anything do they include that she leaves out?
2. Francis brings up the question of a difference between motive and intent that is not explicitly addressed by the other writers. What do you imagine Dodge and Reese would have to say about this distinction? Explain the reasoning behind your answer.
3. Dodge and Reese both refer to specifically American traditions, whereas Francis quotes a British magazine. In your opinion, is the issue of hate crimes a particularly American one? Explain your answer.

Suggestions for Writing

1. Francis supports *The Economist*'s position that the legal system must maintain the traditional distinction between motive and intent. Write an essay in which you attack, defend, or modify this position.
2. Dodge claims that the need for hate crime laws is a particularly American one and even that those who commit hate crimes are "traitors." Reese, by contrast, claims that hate crime laws would be so un-American as to foster totalitarianism. Write an essay in which you argue for or against one or the other view.
3. What are your own views on the need for hate crime laws? Write an essay in which you make your own case, being careful to take into account the views of the writers in this section.

10   *Toys for Tots*

SEX AND THE SINGLE DOLL

Yona Zeldis McDonough

Now that my son is six and inextricably linked to the grade school social circuit, he gets invited to birthday parties. Lots of them. Whenever I telephone to say he's coming, I always ask for hints on what might be a particularly coveted gift for the birthday child. And whenever that child is a girl, I secretly hope that the answer will be the dirty little word I am longing to hear: *Barbie*.

No such luck. In the liberal Brooklyn neighborhood where we live, there is a definite bias against the poor doll, a veritable Barbie backlash. "My daughter loves her, but I can't stand her," laments one mother. "I won't let her in the house," asserts another. "Oh, please!" sniffs a third.

But I love Barbie. I loved her in 1963, when she first made her entrance into my life. She was blond, with a Jackie Kennedy bouffant hairdo. Her thickly painted lids (carved out of plastic) and pouty, un-smiling mouth gave her a look both knowing and sullen. She belonged to a grown-up world of cocktail dresses, cigarette smoke, and perfume. I loved her in the years that followed, too, when she developed bendable joints; a twist-and-turn waist; long, silky ash-blond hair; and feathery, lifelike eyelashes. I never stopped loving her. I never will.

I've heard all the arguments against her: She's a bimbo and an air-head; she's an insatiable consumer—for tarty clothes, a dream house filled with garish pink furniture, a pink Barbie-mobile—who teaches little girls that there is nothing in life quite so exciting as shopping. Her body, with its buoyant breasts, wasplike waist, and endless legs defies all human proportion. But at six, I inchoately understood Barbie's appeal: pure sex. My other dolls were either babies or little girls, with flat chests and chubby legs. Even the other so-called fashion dolls—Tammy, in her aqua-and-white playsuit, and Tressy, with that useless hank of hair, couldn't compete. Barbie was clearly a woman doll, and a woman was what I longed to be.

When I was eight, and had just learned about menstruation, I fash-   5
ioned a small sanitary napkin for her out of neatly folded tissues. Rubber
bands held it in place. "Oh, look," said my bemused mother, "Barbie's
got her little period. Now she can have a baby." I was disappointed, but
my girlfriends all snickered in a much more satisfying way. You see, I
wanted Barbie to be, well, dirty. We all did.

Our Barbies had sex, at least our childish version of it. They hugged
and kissed the few available boy dolls we had—clean-cut and oh-so-
square Ken, the more relaxed and sexy Allan. They also danced, pranced,
and strutted, but mostly they stripped, showing off their amazing, no-
way-in-the-world human bodies. An adult friend tells me how she used
to put her Barbie's low-backed bathing suit on backwards so the doll's
breasts were exposed. I liked dressing mine in her pink-and-white candy-
striped baby-sitter's apron—and nothing else.

I've also heard that Barbie is a poor role model for little girls. Is
there such widespread contempt for the intelligence of children that we
really imagine they are stupid enough to be shaped by a doll? Girls learn
how to be women not from their dolls but from the women around
them. Most often this means Mom. My own was a march-to-a-different-
drummer bohemian in the early sixties. She eschewed the beauty parlor,
cards, and mahjongg that the other moms in the neighborhood favored.
Instead, she wore her long black hair loose, her earrings big and dan-
gling, and her lipstick dark. She made me a Paris bistro birthday party
with candles stuck in old wine bottles, red-and-white-checked table-
cloths for decorations; she read the poetry of T. S. Eliot to the assembled
group of enchanted ten-year-olds. She was, in those years, an aspiring
painter, and her work graced not only the walls of our apartment, but
also the shower curtain, bathroom mirror, and a chest of drawers in my
room. She—not an eleven-and-a-half-inch doll—was the most powerful female role model in my life. What she thought of Barbie I really don't
know, but she had the good sense to back off and let me use the doll in
my own way.

Barbie has become more politically correct over the years. She
no longer looks so vixenish, and has traded the sultry expression I remember for one that is more wholesome and less covert. She now exists
in a variety of "serious" incarnations: teacher, Olympic athlete, dentist.
And Mattel recently introduced the Really Rad Barbie, a doll whose
breasts and hips are smaller and whose waist is thicker, thus reflecting a
more real (as if children wanted their toys to be real) female body. None
of this matters one iota. Girls will still know the real reason they love
her—and it has nothing to do with new professions or a subtly amended
figure.

Fortunately, my Barbie love will no longer have to content itself
with buying gifts for my son's friends and the daughters of my own. I
have a daughter now, and although she is just two, she already has half a
dozen Barbies.

They are, along with various articles of clothing, furniture, and   *10*
other essential accoutrements, packed away like so many sleeping prin-
cesses in translucent pink plastic boxes that line my basement shelves. But
the magic for which they wait is no longer the prince's gentle kiss. Instead, it is the heart and mind of my little girl as she picks them up and
begins to play. I can hardly wait.

Questions for Analysis

Logic
1. On the basis of the essay as a whole, fill out more completely the implied logic of "the arguments against Barbie" in paragraph 4.
2. Explain the ways in which McDonough explicitly and implicitly answers the objections of the opponents of Barbie.
3. Explain McDonough's reasoning in paragraph 7 about the role of role
   models.

Character
1. McDonough claims that there was a serious side to her playing with
   dolls. Does her character as a writer display both seriousness and play-
   fulness? Explain your answer with evidence.
2. What qualities of character does the author attribute to Barbie's opponents? How does she create for her reader her sense of these qualities? Analyze some examples.
3. What qualities do Barbie's opponents attribute to the doll? What aspects of her "style" are said to create those qualities? In what ways has
   Barbie's remake addressed those criticisms?

Emotion
1. To what emotion does the word *dirty* in paragraph 1 seem to appeal?
   How is that appeal modified or changed by the writer's choice of the
   word *bias* in paragraph 2. What sense does the word *dirty* have for the
   reader of the essay as a whole?
2. What emotions and emotional attitudes are created for the reader by
   the narrative attributions of *laments, asserts,* and *sniffs* in paragraph 2?
3. To what emotions in her reader does McDonough appeal in her last
   paragraph? In what ways might these appeals, if successful, be expected to support her argument as a whole?

McDonough

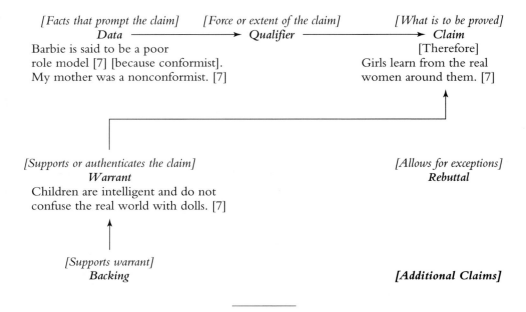

[Facts that prompt the claim]
Data
Barbie is said to be a poor
role model [7] [because conformist].
My mother was a nonconformist. [7]

[Force or extent of the claim]
Qualifier

[What is to be proved]
Claim
[Therefore]
Girls learn from the real
women around them. [7]

[Supports or authenticates the claim]
Warrant
Children are intelligent and do not
confuse the real world with dolls. [7]

[Allows for exceptions]
Rebuttal

[Supports warrant]
Backing

[Additional Claims]

A MEDITATION ON BARBIE DOLLS

Robert Atwan

> *When nature has work to be done, she creates a genius to do it.*
> Ralph Waldo Emerson

Our daughter has always displayed an aversion to dolls. This never bothered me, but it disappointed my wife who for years kept trying to interest Emily in an endless parade of Barbies, with their cute costumes and flashy accessories. I recently found the Barbies, about forty of them, stuffed into a plastic laundry basket in the basement. The dolls had been violently ripped apart, their arms and legs detached from their nubile torsos, strands of shiny hair scissored off, smiling heads removed. Their little skirts and jackets and shoes had disappeared. Emily hadn't been playing with her Barbies over the years, she had been submitting them to torture. No wonder she never watched Sesame Street.

As I carted the mutilated dolls to the town dumpster, along with what was left of an expensive, two-story doll house my wife had also op-timistically purchased, I amused myself by reflecting on one of today's favorite "issues": toys and gender. Are boys and girls inherently different, or do we shape their development to encourage certain masculine and feminine characteristics? Do girls play with dolls because they are gentle, nurturing creatures or simply because they have been taught—or, as some would say, "conditioned"—to prefer dolls. Do boys go gun-crazy because they're naturally violent predators or because our culture encourages them to relish gun play?

I realized right off that my daughter's case raises a problem, what philosophers would call a "counterexample." If girls are instinctively drawn to dolls, then how do I explain Emily's apparent rage against the Barbies? If a preference for dolls is really a result of exposure and environment, then why didn't she simply learn to appreciate the dolls lavished upon her? Something was wrong with the equation. Emily's antidoll behavior could not be the result of Na (Nature) or Nu (Nurture), nor even Na + Nu. What was missing? Was my ten-year-old daughter a complete anomaly? Should I worry about a little girl who savaged her Barbie dolls? Should I be concerned that she harbors in her room a water gun the size of an AK 47 and that her favorite video—the one she knows by heart— is *The Great Escape?*

When I got to the dump, I tossed out the doll house first. It was hard to tell what she had done with it, but the wood was cracked in so many places that it looked like it had been used as a climbing toy— which is probably what she had wanted in the first place. I then reached for the dolls. Emily herself had—being told to clean her closet—thrown all the butchered Barbies into the laundry basket. Arms and legs stuck out all over. I worried that a neighbor might see the Barbies and think I was responsible for the carnage.

The stuffed basket mesmerized me. It was shocking, almost porno- 5 graphic, but at the same time comical. I imagined that if I surreptitiously piled the dolls into a corner of an art museum the grotesque assemblage could very easily be accepted as a work of contemporary art, most likely profeminist. "*Nature v. Nurture,* Emily Atwan 1996"

As I stared in fascination at the Barbies, the answer to my question slowly edged its way forward. The truth is we're all counterexamples in one way or another, every one of us, all of the time. Variation rules; not predictability. This heap of massacred dolls represented neither Nature nor Nurture—what could be more artificial than these capitalized dichotomies?—but something else, something not so easily labeled and polarized for discussion groups or news magazine cover stories. Emily isn't a bundle of instincts nor a sponge prepared to absorb whatever messages "society" or "culture" sends her. Like any of us, her behavior can't be explained by genes or environment, or some convenient combination of both. There's another powerful factor at play—the unique, complex, independent, emerging consciousness that is Emily and Emily alone. We are shaped, to be sure, by what we inherit and by the world around us. But that's not the sum of the human story. We also do a lion's share of the shaping—or, in some cases, the unshaping. And the messages travel both ways. Emily's message was loud and clear. It read: "Watch out, world!"

She saw those Barbies and *chose* to destroy them. "A perfectly rational response," I thought, as I tossed her artistic creation into the dumpster and watched the ravenous gulls circle overhead.

––––––––

Questions for Analysis

Logic

1. According to Atwan, what is the logic of the claims made by the "nature" side of the debate over toys and gender?
2. According to Atwan, what is the logic of the claims made by the "nurture" side of the debate over toys and gender?
3. In the context of the essay as a whole, explain the rationale of the "perfectly rational response" mentioned in the last paragraph.

Character

1. As you begin the essay, what sense of the writer's character is created for you by his choice of an epigraph from Emerson?
2. After you have read the essay as a whole, what aspects of the writer's character are created for you by his having chosen the epigraph by Emerson?
3. What senses of character in father and in daughter are suggested by the image of the gulls at the end of the essay?

Emotion

1. In paragraph 2 what is the difference between the emotional appeals of the words *taught* and *conditioned*? What sense of human nature does each imply?
2. *Destruction* and *creation* are words with very different emotional appeals. What appeals to the reader's emotions does Atwan create by describing a destruction as a creation in paragraph 5 and again at the end of the essay? Do you think the paradox supports Atwan's argument as a whole? Explain your answer.
3. What emotions in Emily are suggested by her implied "message" to the world in the next-to-last paragraph? What does Emily seem to warn the world about?

––––––––

THE Q GENE

Sara Bird

I suppose the moment of maximum political incorrectness came last Saturday at that commercial shrine to all that is right-thinking and green, the Nature Company, when my 4-year-old son, Gabriel, strafed the baby dolphins in the computer-generated video with his toy Uzi.

A woman standing behind us pulled her own children away as the frolicking Flippers ate hot lead. I imagine that this woman was probably the sort of mother who had a bumper sticker like the one I had scraped off the back of my own car when Gabriel was 18 months old: "Don't Encourage Violence. Don't Buy War Toys." I imagine that she was the sort of mother who had successfully banned all implements of destruction from her house. You know the sort of mother I mean. The mother of daughters. Or the mother of a son who obsesses about Thomas the Tank Engine rather than battle-axes, nunchuks, hand grenades and catapults.

My boy, however, came hard-wired for weaponry. His first two-syllable word, right after momma, dadda and backhoe, was scabbard. Scabbard at 18 months? Why did I ever bother resisting?

Why? Because in college, in the sixties, I started Damsels in Dissent, which counseled draft candidates to eat balls of tinfoil and put laundry soap in their armpits to fool induction center doctors. Because I believed that wars were a manifestation of testosterone run amok, much like the purchase of bad toupees and red Miata convertibles. Because I believed that white sugar, commercial television and guns were afflictions of a sick society and that any child could be immunized against them *if only he had the right mother* to pass along her more highly evolved antibodies.

Parents do not, indeed, live by bread alone. We feast daily on banquets of our own words. My child has never seen an adult touch another adult in anger; he has never been spanked; he has never even watched a Ninja Turtle cartoon—yet he is as bloodthirsty as Quentin Tarantino. 5

In his toy bin are half a dozen Ninja Silent Warrior Assassin Swords, two scimitars, three buccaneer blades, two six-shooters, four Laser Fazer stun guns, a Captain Hook flintlock, the aforementioned Uzi and a silo full of items he manufactures himself. This inventory is by no means complete. I have lost friends over this arsenal. They cannot allow their children to be exposed to such untrammeled barbarism. Friends? I have lost an entire self-image and my deep Jeffersonian faith in the infinite perfectibility of man.

I resisted at first, certain that if only I stayed the course I would end up with a gentle little boy who named his stuffed animals and found Beatrix Potter a bit brutish. And I was holding the line rather well, too, till he started sleeping with a shoe. Though never one to question too closely anything that encourages slumber, I did finally ask, why a shoe? He answered, clutching the tip of the shoelace, "So that when the bad things come in my dreams I can shoot them away."

". . . when the bad things come in my dreams."

Zen monks could contemplate their koans for years and not come close to the transformation I experienced when my child aimed his shoelace at me. Children are small and weak. The world is big and scary. Gabriel's need to feel safe so outweighed my own need to feel morally

correct that the contest ended. From that night, we began building the
armory until we achieved the overwhelming first-strike capability we
have today.

I know what drives this war machine. It's a discovery of my own   10
that I call the Q gene. The Q gene is that chromosomal imperative that
compels little boys to pick up sticks and hair dryers; to chew their organ-
ically grown, wholegrain sandwiches into the shape of guns; to use whatever they can lay their murderous hands on, take aim and commence
firing: "Kyew. Kyew. Kyew." The Q gene.

And here is my awful confession. I passed the Q gene on to my son.
As in male pattern baldness, I displayed none of the symptoms myself but
carried it from both of my parents. My father an Air Force officer, my
mother an Army nurse—I am the daughter of two warriors. I reflect on
this heritage as my son stands beside a helicopter at nearby Camp Mabry.
We have already examined the tanks and fighter jets parked on either side.
Compared relative firepower. Discussed how each would fare in a battle
with Tyrannosaurus rex. But my son pats the shark's grin painted on the
helicopter and announces: "This is the one, Mom. This one is the best."

Watching him calls to mind a photograph of my father taken in
the late fifties. He stands before a plane with a shark's smile painted on
it, just beneath the inscription: 6091st Reconnaissance Squadron. My
family lived in Japan then, conquerors grinning into the last minutes of
a doomed colonialism. The crew with my father have their arms thrown
around each other's shoulders, as heedless and glamorous as movie stars,
frat boys, R.A.F. pilots, any gang of young men who know they will
never grow old, never die.

Thirty years were to pass before I learned what it was my father did
when he left us for weeks at a time. He and his smiling buddies would
fly their "birds" over Russia and wait to be chased back into American
airspace to test Soviet response time. That was when I understood why
my mother, alone with six children, would burst into tears whenever an
officer in uniform came to our front door.

I watch my son stroke the shark's grin and I want to whisper to
him: "It is evil. All these machines are evil. You must never think about
them again." But it can never be that simple.

I hear myself sometimes, times like this one right now. I see myself   15
the way the mother shielding her children from the sight of my son
opening up on the baby dolphins must have seen me, and I feel like a shill
for the N.R.A. My position is indefensible, illogical, inconsistent. But
love makes intellectual pretzels of us all. It's just that I know, long before
I would like, there will come a moment when I can do nothing to chase
away the bad things in my son's dreams. Until then, if I can give him a
shoelace's worth of security I guess I will.

O.K., so I caved in on the white sugar, the TV, the war toys. There
is, however, one moral issue that I have not wavered, have not wobbled,

have not waffled on. I swore before my child was born that I would never buy a certain particularly insidious toy, and I am happy to report that I have held that line. There has never been, nor will ever be, a Barbie doll in my house.

———————

Questions for Analysis

Logic
1. Bird claims in paragraph 6 that "I have lost an entire self-image and my deep Jeffersonian faith in the infinite perfectibility of man." Explain in your own words the rationale that Bird has lost. In particular what was the logic of her reasoning that man could be perfected with regard to the evils of violence?
2. Explain in your own words the logic of Bird's son with regard to his attitude toward means of violence.
3. Explain in your own words the rationale of Bird's claim in paragraph 5 that "we feast daily on banquets of our own words."

Character
1. Bird begins her essay with a mock confession and ends with a mock boast, both on the theme of "political correctness." What sense of her character does this aspect of her essay's organization tend to create? Explain the process that leads you to your conclusion.
2. In paragraph 2 we are told that "the frolicking Flippers ate hot lead." What point of view on the scene is implied by the style here? What quality of character is expressed in that point of view? Is it the same quality of character perceived by the mother who pulls her children away? Explain your answers.
3. Explain the sense of her character created by Bird's claim in paragraph 15 that "love makes intellectual pretzels of us all." Do you find her character in the essay as a whole to be that of an intellectual pretzel? Explain your answer.

Emotion
1. To what emotions in her reader does Bird appeal by her claim in paragraph 15 that "love makes intellectual pretzels of us all"? In what ways might this emotional appeal be expected to help her argument as a whole?
2. In paragraph 9 Bird claims to have experienced a transformation. Explain the emotional aspects of this transformation in your own words.
3. In paragraph 15 Bird says she sometimes sees herself as the woman in paragraph 2 must have seen her. To what emotions in her reader does this claim appeal? How might that appeal be expected to support her argument as a whole?

EXERCISES: TOYS FOR TOTS

Intertextual Questions

1. In paragraph 8 of her essay McDonough implies that children don't want their toys to be what they "really" are. According to her, what do they want their toys to be? Are her views shared by the other writers in the section? Support your answer with evidence.

2. In the last two essays each parent seems eager to understand his or her child. In what different ways is that sense of parental concern expressed in the writing? Find and analyze some examples.

3. The writer Cosimo Konstantine has said that "all literature is about love and death—of the innumerable subjects in reality only those stimulate the literary imagination." Are all *toys* about love and death, according to the authors in the section? Support your answers with evidence.

Suggestions for Writing

1. Barbie is a figure that appears in every essay. But is it the same Barbie? Write an essay in which you discuss the different senses of Barbie expressed by the writers in this section.

2. What were your own favorite toys as a child, and what were the bases of their appeal to you? Write an essay in which you argue for the value of your favorite toys.

3. If you were to become a parent what would your toy policy be? Write an essay in which you explain and defend your views.

11 Should Flag Burning Be Made Unconstitutional?

BURNED UP OVER FLAG BURNING

Cal Thomas

Watching the Fourth of July festivities in Washington (and around the country on television) showed the depth of love most Americans have for this country. That is why a constitutional amendment to ban the burning of the American flag is so silly, stupid and unnecessary.

No one forced the millions of people waving flags—who respect and honor the republic for which it stands—to love America. They exhibited a spontaneity no law can impose.

When the House last month passed a constitutional amendment that would, should the Senate and states concur, outlaw flag burning, it continued a game politicians have been playing with public school prayer. The rules of the game are that the social problems confronting America can be fixed from the top—a kind of "trickle-down" morality.

Politicians love this because they have done much to promote such a view, which advances their careers and preserves their jobs. Many others hold this belief because it absolves them of responsibility for fixing what is wrong with their own priorities and transfers it to government. And when government increasingly reveals its inability to repair social damage, we blame not ourselves but government and politicians, deepening the cynicism against institutions and those who work in them.

There hasn't been a lot of flag burning since the Vietnam War. Sen. Howell Heflin (D-Ala.) says that's why now, when the heat of passion is reduced, is the best time to ban it.

But any time is a bad time for such a ban. First, what constitutes a "flag"? Is it only the cloth that waves from a flagpole or can be stapled to a wooden stick and held in the hand? Is the reproduction of the Stars and Stripes on a napkin, patch or coffee cup considered a flag? Some flags are

5

made in Taiwan or in other nations. Would they count as American flags? I saw a chair upholstered in a flag. If the chair was thrown on a bonfire during a protest rally, would that violate the proposed constitutional amendment? And why is burning being singled out for prohibition? Isn't stomping, spitting or pouring paint on the flag also desecration?

Those who would ban flag burning have placed the American flag in a category and context that is idolatrous. Idolatry is defined as "the worship of a physical object as a god; immoderate attachment or devotion to something." While we don't worship or devote ourselves to the flag as we might a religious symbol or being, the attachment some would force on the rest of us comes pretty close to resembling that definition.

The Fourth of July overwhelms us all with the number of displayed and waved American flags. As with speech, the best way to overcome the ugly variety is with more and more beautiful speech, along with a common rejection of the ugly speaker and his words. When a flag is burned, it is the protester, not the flag, who is demeaned. He reveals his base ingratitude when he burns a symbol of a nation great enough even to allow him to indulge in moronic behavior.

Banning flag burning will increase the probability flags will be burned. Allowing it removes the political stinger.

Questions for Analysis

Logic
1. Thomas says in his first paragraph that an amendment is "silly, stupid and unnecessary." In your opinion, does the logic of his essay address all three criteria? Explain your answer using examples.
2. Explain Thomas's reasoning when he claims in paragraph 4 that "politicians" love what he calls in paragraph 3 "'trickle-down' morality."
3. Explain Thomas's reasoning in his last paragraph. Do you think he logically connects politicians and flag burners earlier in ways sufficient to earn this claim? Explain your answer.

Character
1. Describe the ways in which Thomas attempts to establish his character as containing "patriotism."
2. Describe the ways in which Thomas attempts to establish his character as containing "objectivity."
3. Describe the ways in which Thomas attempts to establish the characters of his opponents as "silly."

Emotion
1. Thomas's title claims he is "burned up." What is he burned up over, and how does he attempt to convince you he feels that emotion?

2. Explain the appeal to emotion used by Senator Heflin as reported in paragraph 5.
3. How does the word *desecration,* which ends paragraph 6, serve as a transition to the theme of paragraph 7?

MY FLAG—BURN IT AND BURN

Maria Hernandez

If anyone is ever foolish enough to try to sexually harass me at work, he (or she) will be out of a job in a hurry. If anybody insults me in print, I'll make sure he (or she) is hit with a libel suit right away. If anyone trys to trash my home, I'll call the police and have him (or her) sent directly to jail without stopping to pass go. Put some graffiti on my car, and it's bye bye birdbrain.

Every individual in this great country has the same rights I do because so many people have fought and struggled for those rights in battle and through representative democracy. Our flag is the great symbol of this struggle, and it belongs to each and every American. Now why in God's name shouldn't each of us have our flag protected just as we are protected by law in every other way?

Some people say that the Constitution guarantees free speech in the First Amendment of the Bill of Rights and that everyone should have the right to protest government by burning or otherwise desecrating our flag. What nonsense! Everyone agrees that sexual harassment and libel aren't free speech, that trashing my house is not the way to disagree with me, and that graffiti is not only ugly and insulting but illegal. If you want to protest the government's actions, write to your representatives or senators or the president—you elected them. You are the government. If the representatives and senators or president don't do anything, talk to your neighbors or anyone who will listen about electing people who will. That's real free speech and real democracy.

All this is so obvious that we have never had to have a particular law before to protect the flag that is our common property and common dignity. It's too bad that nowadays there are some who take advantage of this loophole to show off by trashing everyone's flag without fear of being punished. But luckily since we live in a democracy there is something we can do about those cowards who insult the brave soldiers who died for the flag and the rest of us as well. We need to pass a constitutional amendment to ban the desecration of our flag so that we all can be protected against common insults just as we are already protected against individual insults.

———

Questions for Analysis

Logic
1. Hernandez makes several analogies in the first paragraph. How does the logic of each analogy serve as an attempt to refute the logic of the "free speech" argument of her opponents in paragraph 3?
2. Hernandez sees both "battle" and "representative democracy" as parts of the same "struggle." Explain the logic by which she attempts to connect acts of war and acts of peace.
3. In her last paragraph, Hernandez speaks of a "loophole," but her own claim is that no law protecting the flag exists. How could there be a loophole in a law when there is no law? How do you imagine she would respond to this objection to her logic?

Character
1. What are the principal features of character that Hernandez seeks to create through her writing? In what ways does each feature further her argument? Explain your answer using examples.
2. What are the principal features of character to which Hernandez appeals in her audience? Are they necessarily the same as those she projects? Explain your answer.
3. What are the principal features of character with which Hernandez seeks to create a sense of her opponents? Explain your answer using examples.

Emotion
1. In what ways, if any, do the analogies of the first paragraph appeal to the same emotions in the audience? In what ways, if any, does each analogy appeal to a different emotion? Explain your answer.
2. Would it be fair to say that Hernandez appeals to her audience to re-spect its government? Explain your answer.
3. In her last paragraph Hernandez asserts that the flag is our "common dignity." Where else in the essay do you find the issue of dignity as a theme?

Hernandez

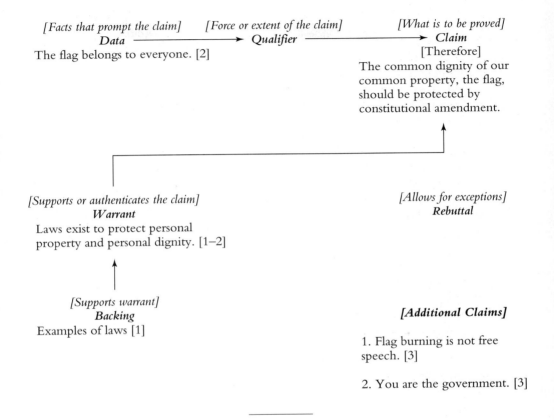

AN AMENDMENT IS NOT THE WAY TO HONOR THE FLAG

Don Feder

Concerning the constitutional amendment to ban flag desecration, which passed in the House of Representatives by a resounding 312–120 vote last week, my heart tells me to go one way, my head the other.

My heart says, "Yeah, punish the bastards. The flag is our highest national symbol, and symbols deserve protection."

My heart swells at the words of Rep. Henry Hyde (R-Ill.), chairman of the House Judiciary Committee, who told his colleagues during the floor debate: "Too many men have marched behind the flag, too many have returned in a wooden box with the flag as their only blanket . . . not to honor and revere that flag."

And I do, believe me, I do. I understand what a blessing America has been in a benighted world, how much that star-spangled banner represents our yearnings and all we hold dear—freedom, compassion, virtue and brotherhood. Even its devices, the stars of heaven's field, allude to the eternal.

For me, the flag provokes a thousand unspoken emotions—all of them poignant. 5

If I only listened to my heart, I would be in the vanguard of proponents of this amendment. But my head says: "Hold on a minute. Vile and reprehensible as flag burning is, it's also an authentic form of political expression. Do we want to start limiting the First Amendment?"

Now, I happen to be an iconoclast of First Amendment law. Much of what the Supreme Court has said regarding the Bill of Rights in the past 50 years is the most pluperfect nonsense.

In rulings on the First Amendment's free-speech clause, the words of the founding fathers have been perverted beyond recognition. Not in their wildest imagining did those gentlemen ever suppose the amendment would be used to protect porn shops, obscenities on T-shirts or the lewd gyrations of exotic dancers.

The First Amendment was intended to shield political dissent, period—including protest of every shape and hue. Sadly, flag burning falls within these very broad parameters.

In its 1989 case, the Supreme Court asked if flag burning is intended to convey a message and if there is a likelihood that the communication would be understood. To both, they answered in the affirmative. 10

The message of flag burners is utter contempt for our nation and its institutions. That's the intent; that's the interpretation. "America, the red, white and blue, we spit on you," chanted the scummy savages in the Texas case that prompted the 1989 decision.

Disgusting? Yes. But it was just such disgusting, obnoxious, loathsome advocacy (words repellent to the majority) that James Madison and his associates had in mind when they erected the great bar to governmental infringement of political speech.

After all of the Fourth of July rhetoric is done, the anti-flag-burning amendment is really about safeguarding the sensibilities of veterans and other patriotic Americans.

But isn't this exactly what the politically correct crowd is doing on the college campuses with their totalitarian speech codes, which punish people for "hurtful words" and aggravate and agitate various minorities? How ironic that conservatives have fallen into their own form of political correctness.

Once we begin limiting symbolic speech that causes emotional trauma, where do we stop? When a Holocaust survivor sees a swastika arm band, does he feel more or less psychic pain than the war veteran at a flag burning? Should we ban Nazi paraphernalia? 15

African Americans are outraged by cross-burnings. How many of their people have been beaten or lynched by the diabolical light of the Ku Klux Klan's satanic emblem? Ban them too?

It hurts me to see my nation's flag dishonored. But the flag itself feels no pain, unlike the 1.5 million unborn children grimly reaped in our annual abortion harvest. The child in the womb is in far greater need of protection than a piece of cloth, however splendid the ideals it represents.

Our national government is sorely in need of reform. A balanced-budget amendment would avert the looming debt crisis. A term-limitation amendment would save the republic from the cancerous growth of career politics by re-establishing a citizen legislature.

An anti-flag-burning amendment would achieve nothing substantive. Given the mind-set of the Kunstler clients who engage in such odious acts, it will do little to stop flag desecration. Its sole effect will be to comfort the majority (with the knowledge that flag-burners can be punished) and, in the process, compromise free-speech rights.

Perhaps the best rebuke to flag burners is for those of us who love   20
America to respect the flag more—to honor it by our devotion instead of passing laws that give inane protesters the attention they so desperately crave.

———

Questions for Analysis

Logic
1. Feder argues in general that with regard to the proposed amendment his head is more important than his heart. In your opinion, does Feder make a logical case for this preference or is his argument basically an appeal to the assumption that we should be cautious of emotion? Explain your answer.
2. Explain Feder's reasoning on the "perversion" of the First Amendment [7–12].
3. Explain the parallels Feder draws between the logic of the amendment's proposers and the logic of "political correctness" [13–16].

Character
1. Describe the ways in which Feder works to establish "patriotism" as a part of his character.
2. Describe how Feder works to establish "feeling" as a part of his character. In other words, how does he come to seem more than a cold-hearted rationalist?
3. What aspect of character does Feder attempt to express by his attack on and support of flag burners [11–12]?

Emotion
1. In paragraph 2 do you find "yeah" a more or less appropriate expression than "yes"? Explain your answer.
2. In paragraph 5 Feder says that "the flag provokes a thousand unspoken emotions." What are some emotions that are expressed verbally

in the essay? Name some and explain how they are expressed through language.

3. Compare the emotional temperature of paragraphs 10 and 11. In a way they make the same point. Explain how the difference in emotion is achieved, paying particular attention to the cooler tone of paragraph 10.

EXERCISES: SHOULD FLAG BURNING BE MADE UNCONSTITUTIONAL?

Intertextual Questions

1. In your opinion, which essay in this section makes the strongest logical case? Support your answer by explaining the strengths of your choice and the weaknesses of the other essays with regard to logic.

2. In your opinion, which author in this section makes the strongest appeal to emotion? Support your answer by explaining the strengths of your choice and the weaknesses of the other essays in their appeals to emotion.

3. Representatives of government are mentioned in each essay. Which writer seems to have the most respect for his or her political representatives and which the least? Explain your answer using examples.

Suggestions for Writing

1. Feder suggests that banning flag burning would lead to attempts to ban an impossibly long and disputed series of symbols. Do you agree? Write an essay in which you address the unintended consequences of the proposed amendment, whether or not you find them serious.

2. All three writers use religious terms at some point, terms like *desecrate* and *idolatry*. Write an essay in which you attack or support the proposition that the dispute over flag burning is essentially a religious dispute. Be sure in your essay to take a position on the proposed amendment.

3. All three writers appeal to the emotion of patriotism. In your opinion, who does the best job in this regard? Write an essay in which you support your answer using examples from all three essays.

12 Euthanasia

OFFERING EUTHANASIA CAN BE AN ACT OF LOVE

Derek Humphry

The American Medical Association's decision to recognize that artificial feeding is a life-support mechanism and can be disconnected from hopelessly comatose patients is a welcome, if tardy, acceptance of the inevitable.

Courts in California and New Jersey have already ruled this way, and although a Massachusetts court recently ruled in an opposite manner, this is being appealed to a higher court.

The AMA's pronouncement is all the more welcome because it comes at a time when the benefits of some of our modern medical technologies are in danger of being ignored because of the public's fear that to be on life-support machinery can create problems.

People dread having their loved ones put on such equipment if it means they are never likely to be removed if that proves later to be the more sensible course. As medical ethicist and lawyer George Annas has said, "People have rights, not technologies."

The argument by the pro-life lobby that food is a gift from God, no matter how it is introduced, and thus to deprive a comatose person of pipeline food is murder, is fallacious. A pipe is a manufactured item; the skill to introduce it into the body and maintain it there is a medical technology. Without the pipeline, the person would die. Food is common to all humans, but taking it through a pipeline is a technique carried out because the person has sustained an injury or suffers an illness which prevents normal feeding. 5

The pro-life lobby also harks back to Nazi excesses of the 1930s and 1940s as part of its argument for continued pipeline feeding. True, Nazi Germany murdered about one hundred thousand Aryan Germans who were mentally or physically defective because it considered them "useless eaters," detracting from the purity of the German race.

But neither the views of the victims nor their relatives were ever sought: they were murdered en masse in secret fashion and untruths concocted to cover the crimes.

No terminally ill or comatose person was ever helped to die by the Nazis. Moreover, their barbarous killing spree took in 6 million Jews and 10 million noncombatant Russians, Slavs, and gypsies. Life was cheapened by the Nazis to an appalling degree. What connection is there between the Nazis then and the carefully considered euthanasia today of a permanently comatose person who might, as Karen Quinlan did, lie curled up for ten years without any signs of what most of us consider life?

Helping another to die in carefully considered circumstances is part of good medicine and also demonstrates a caring society that offers euthanasia to hopelessly sick persons as an act of love.

Questions for Analysis

Logic
1. Where does Humphry suggest a definition of the "carefully considered circumstances" of his last paragraph?
2. Explain the logic of Humphry's distinction between the Nazi murder of "useless eaters" and his own position on artificial feeding.
3. What in your view would be gained or lost for Humphry's argument if the essay were reorganized with the last paragraph made the second paragraph?

Character
1. What does the separation of the medical and legal issues in paragraphs 1 and 2 contribute to your sense of the author's character?
2. What attempts does Humphry make through his word choice to avoid a possible accusation of unfeeling brutality?
3. What sense of Humphry's character is created by the fact that almost all his sentences are declarative in their grammatical form?

Emotion
1. The phrase "acceptance of the inevitable" in paragraph 1 is one often used to describe dying. Do you think Humphry is making a joke here about the AMA? Explain your answer.
2. To what emotions does Humphry appeal in his characterization of his opponents as "the pro-life lobby" in paragraphs 5 and 6?
3. To what emotions does Humphry appeal by using the word *helping* in reference to euthanasia?

EUTHANASIA IS NOT THE ANSWER

Matthew E. Conolly

From the moment of our conception, each of us is engaged in a personal battle that we must fight alone, a battle whose final outcome is never in any doubt, for, naked, and all too often alone, sooner or later we *all* must die.

We do not all make life's pilgrimage on equal terms. For some the path is strewn with roses, and after a long and healthy life, death comes swiftly and easily, for others it is not so. The bed of roses is supplanted by a bed of nails, with poverty, rejection, deformity, and humiliation the only lasting companions they ever know.

I know that many people here today carry this problem of pain in a personal way, or else it has been the lot of someone close to you. Otherwise you would not be here. So let me say right at the outset, that those of us who have not had to carry such a burden dare not criticize those who have, if they should plead with us for an early end to their dismal sojourn in this world.

HARD CASES MAKE BAD LAWS

Society in general, and the medical profession in particular, cannot just turn away. We must do *something;* the question is—what?

The "what" we are being asked to consider today, of course, is voluntary euthanasia. So that there be no confusion, let me make it quite clear that to be opposed to the active taking of life, one does not have to be determined to keep the heart beating at all costs.

I believe I speak for all responsible physicians when I say that there clearly comes a time when death can no longer be held at bay, and when we must sue for peace on the enemy's terms. At such a time, attending to the patient's comfort in body, mind, and soul becomes paramount. There is no obligation, indeed no justification, for pressing on at such a time with so-called life-sustaining measures, be they respirators, intravenous fluids, CPR, or whatever. I believe that there is no obligation to continue a treatment once it has been started, if it becomes apparent that it is doing no good. Also, withholding useless treatment and letting nature take its course is *not* equivalent to active euthanasia. Some people have attempted to blur this distinction by creating the term "passive euthanasia." The least unkind thing that can be said about this term is that it is very confusing.

Today's discussion really boils down to the question—do hard and tragic cases warrant legalization of euthanasia? There can be no doubt that hard and tragic cases do occur. However, the very natural tendency to want to alleviate human tragedy by legislative change is fraught with hazard, and I firmly believe that every would–be lawmaker should have tattooed on his or her face, where it can be seen in the mirror each morning, the adage that HARD CASES MAKE BAD LAWS.

If we take the superficially humane step of tailoring the law to the supposed wishes of an Elizabeth Bouvia (who, incidentally, later changed her mind), we will not only bring a hornet's nest of woes about our own ears, but, at a stroke, we will deny many relatives much good that we could have salvaged from a sad situation, while at the same time giving many *more* grief and guilt to contend with. Even worse, we will have denied our patients the best that could have been offered. Worst of all, that soaring of the human spirit to heights of inspiration and courage which only adversity makes possible will be denied, and we will all, from that, grow weaker, and less able to deal with the crisis of tomorrow.

UNLEASHING EUTHANASIA

Let's look at these problems one by one. The first problem is that once we unleash euthanasia, once we take to ourselves the right actively to terminate a human life, we will have no means of controlling it. Adolf Hitler showed with startling clarity that once the dam is breached, the principle somewhere compromised, death in the end comes to be administered equally to all—to the unwanted fetus, to the deformed, the mentally defective, the old and the unproductive, and thence to the politically inconvenient, and finally to the ethnically unacceptable. There is no logical place to stop.

The founders of Hemlock no doubt mean euthanasia only for those *10* who feel they can take no more, but if it is available for one it must be available for all. Then what about those precious people who even to the end put others before themselves? They will now have laid upon them the new and horrible thought that perhaps they ought to do away with themselves to spare their relatives more trouble or expense. What will they feel as they see their 210 days of Medicare hospice payments run out, and still they are alive. Not long ago, Governor Lamm of Colorado suggested that the old and incurable have a *duty* to get out of the way of the next generation. And can you not see where these pressures will be the greatest? It will be amongst the poor and dispossessed. Watts will have sunk in a sea of euthanasia long before the first ripple laps the shore of Brentwood. Is that what we mean to happen? Is that what we want? Is there nobility of purpose there?

It matters to me that my patients trust me. If they do so, it is because they believe that I will always act in their best interests. How could such trust survive if they could never be sure each time I approached the bed that I had not come to administer some coup de grace when they were not in a state to define their own wishes?

Those whose relatives have committed more conventional forms of suicide are often afterwards assailed by feelings of guilt and remorse.

It would be unwise to think that euthanasia would bring any less in its wake.

A BETTER WAY

Speaking as a physician, I assert that unrelieved suffering need never occur, and I want to turn to this important area. Proponents of euthanasia make much of the pain and anguish so often linked in people's minds with cancer. I would not dare to pretend that the care we offer is not sometimes abysmal, whether because of the inappropriate use of aggressive technological medicine, the niggardly use of analgesics, some irrational fear of addiction in a dying patient, or a lack of compassion.

However, for many, the process of dying is more a case of gradually loosing life's moorings and slipping way. Oftentimes the anguish of dying is felt not by the patient but by the relatives: just as real, just as much in need of compassionate support, but hardly a reason for killing the patient!

But let us consider the patients who do have severe pain, turmoil, and distress, who find their helplessness or incontinence humiliating, for it is these who most engage our sympathies. It is wrong to assert that they must make a stark choice between suicide or suffering.

There is another way.

Experience with hospice care in England and the United States has shown repeatedly that in *every* case, pain and suffering can be overwhelmingly reduced. In many cases it can be abolished altogether. This care, which may (and for financial reasons perhaps must) include home care, is not easy. It demands infinite love and compassion. It must include the latest scientific knowledge of analgesic drugs, nerve blocks, antinausea medication, and so on. But it can be done, it can be done, it can be done!

LIFE IS SPECIAL

Time and again our patients have shown us that life, even a deformed, curtailed, and, to us, who are whole, an unimaginable life, can be made noble and worth living. Look at Joni Earickson—paraplegic from the age of seventeen—now a most positive, vibrant and inspirational person who has become world famous for her triumph over adversity. Time and time again, once symptoms are relieved, patients and relatives share quality time together, when forgiveness can be sought and given— for many a time of great healing.

Man, made in the image of his Creator, is *different* from all other animals. For this reason, his life is special and may not be taken at will.

We do not know why suffering is allowed, but Old and New Testament alike are full of reassurances that we have not been, and will not ever be, abandoned by our God. "Yea, though I walk through the valley of the shadow of death, I will fear no evil *for thou art with me.*"

CALL TO CHANGE DIRECTION

Our modern tragedy is that man has turned his back on God, who alone can help, and has set himself up as the measure of all things. Gone then is the absolute importance of man, gone the sanctity of his life, and the meaning of it. Gone too the motivation for loving care which is our responsible duty to the sick and dying. Goodbye love. Hello indifference.

With our finite minds, we cannot know fully the meaning of life, but though at times the storms of doubt may rage, I stake my life on the belief that to God we are special, that with Him, murder is unacceptable, and suicide (whatever you call it) becomes unnecessary.

Abandon God, and yes, you can have euthanasia. But a *good* death it can never be, and no subterfuge of law like that before us today can ever make it so.

My plea to the Hemlock Society is: Give up your goal of self-destruction. Instead, lend your energy, your anger, your indignation, your influence and creativity to work with us in the building of such a system of hospice care that death, however it come, need no longer be feared. Is not this a nobler cause? Is not this a better way?

Questions for Analysis

Logic
1. How and where does Conolly separate the medical, legal, and religious implications of his argument? How and where are they combined?
2. What seems to be the reasoning behind Conolly's claim that with euthanasia "there is no logical place to stop"? [9]
3. Explain Conolly's reasoning at the end of his essay when he distinguishes between the idea of "good" and what he calls a "subterfuge of law." [23]

Character
1. Conolly's argument is taken from a speech he delivered to the Hemlock Society—a group that favors euthanasia. What does this fact contribute to your sense of Conolly's character?
2. Conolly talks as a doctor, but what other personal attributes does he imply as defining characteristics of his identity?
3. Do you find the first sentence of paragraph 9—"Let's look at these problems one by one"—is representative of Conolly's style in general? Explain why or why not.

Emotion
1. To what emotions does Conolly appeal in paragraph 3?
2. To what emotions does Conolly appeal by using the term *unleash* in paragraph 9?
3. To what emotions does Conolly appeal by discussing his patients' trust in paragraph 11?

Conolly

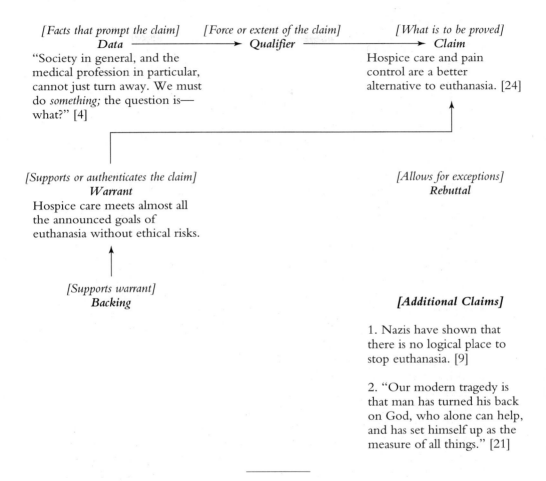

[Facts that prompt the claim]
Data ⟶ *[Force or extent of the claim]* **Qualifier** ⟶ *[What is to be proved]* **Claim**

"Society in general, and the medical profession in particular, cannot just turn away. We must do *something;* the question is— what?" [4]

Hospice care and pain control are a better alternative to euthanasia. [24]

[Supports or authenticates the claim]
Warrant
Hospice care meets almost all the announced goals of euthanasia without ethical risks.

[Allows for exceptions]
Rebuttal

[Supports warrant]
Backing

[Additional Claims]

1. Nazis have shown that there is no logical place to stop euthanasia. [9]

2. "Our modern tragedy is that man has turned his back on God, who alone can help, and has set himself up as the measure of all things." [21]

MUST THEY TINKER WITH THE DYING?

Nancy M. Lederman

My grandmother, Freda Weinstein, was hospitalized for more than four weeks after she was hit by a little girl riding a bicycle in a New York playground. The unwary girl knocked her over, breaking her hip. It was a bad fracture, the surgeon said. A week later, another surgeon said my 90-year-old grandmother had a perforated ulcer, and it was immediately repaired. Then she had internal bleeding and a heart attack.

In hospital jargon, these are "events." The older the patient, the more likely a hospital stay will trigger a succession of events leading to one final event.

My grandmother's strength was impressive. She was tied to her bed to keep her from pulling out the catheter and intravenous lines that supplied fluids, pain-killer and sedation. Despite the restraints, she pulled out the ventilator tube that helped her breathe. Fighting the restraints, she developed blisters on her forearms. She also had a gastro-nasal tube in her nose.

The doctors wanted desperately to save her; that's what doctors are programmed to do. To deal with the bleeding, they performed an endoscopy, trailing another tube down her throat to her stomach. When that didn't work, they wanted to do another. I said, enough. They wanted to operate to stanch the bleeding, or do an angiogram, or both. Enough. The prognosis kept changing. One doctor said, "I.C.U. psychosis." Another said, "How can you let her bleed to death?"

The odds were she would wind up where she most dreaded, in a   5
nursing home. At the least, she would need 24-hour care for a long time. She would be "walker-dependent"—if she could walk at all. These things, I knew, she emphatically did not want. I had her health care proxy. I had drafted it. Although she had no living will, we discussed her wishes many times. But we had not anticipated this.

She wasn't terminal. Once on the ventilator, she would stay there as long as she needed it to breathe. Her body was fighting to live, as if she was programmed to survive. Her mind was fighting, too. When I squeezed her hand, she squeezed back. Hard.

If she could fully wake, what would she tell me? Would she say, Let me die? In her pocketbook, I found speeches she had written, to be delivered to her senior center. I had a "eulogy" she had prepared months before, to be read at her funeral. It was a letter to her family and friends telling them not to grieve: she had lived a full life.

They say our ethics have yet to catch up to our technology. Medical advances are prolonging life for more and more people. Longer lives are not necessarily better ones.

They say you must have a living will or a health care proxy. Preferably both. Only then can you be assured that you or your chosen surrogate will be able to make critical health care decisions for you. They don't tell you what it's like to make those decisions for someone else—to play the odds with someone else's life.

My grandmother's "case" was used by the hospital ethicist on train-   10
ing rounds. Interns, nurses, and physicians' assistants discussed options. One resident said he couldn't understand why I refused the angiogram, why I had signed a "do not resuscitate" order if I was continuing to permit blood transfusions.

As the doctors kept offering me interventions to save her, I began looking for a way out. I wanted her off that ventilator, sooner rather than later. Once she was off, I could refuse to let her back on.

How can you let her bleed to death? How could I not? I wasn't brave. But she was, and I had her proxy.

She died on Nov. 19. I wasn't there. I don't know what killed her. Respiratory failure, kidney failure, heart failure—it didn't matter. No experiments, she had said. None, I promised her. I kept my promise.

Questions for Analysis

Logic
1. Lederman's essay is organized partly by chronology. Do you see any other organizing principles at work? Explain your answer.
2. A large part of Lederman's appeal to reason takes place in the final paragraph. What elements in the reasoning there also appear elsewhere in the essay?
3. In what explicit and/or implicit ways does Lederman attempt to refute the arguments of her grandmother's doctors?

Character
1. Lederman is a lawyer by profession. In what ways do you think she does or does not attempt to express that aspect of her character in the essay?
2. In what ways does Lederman express the intensity of her concern for her grandmother? Point to specific uses of language that work to create this aspect of her character as expressed in the essay.
3. In what ways does Lederman create a sense of her grandmother's character? How does this sense of character support her argument?

Emotion
1. Explain the ways in which the word *tinker* in the essay's title appeals to the reader's emotions. Does Lederman appeal to the same emotions elsewhere in the essay? Explain.
2. How would you describe the emotions expressed by the general style of the essay and the tone of voice it creates? Point to some examples in explaining your answer.
3. What emotions does Lederman suggest were expressed by the doctors in charge of her grandmother? How does she suggest them? Point to some particular moments, and explain the operations of the specific language involved.

EXERCISES: EUTHANASIA

Intertextual Questions
1. Compare the uses that Humphry and Conolly make of the example of Nazi Germany in their arguments.
2. With what, if anything, would Humphry and Lederman take issue in Conolly's paragraph 6? Explain your answer.
3. Compare the roles that the writers see for love in what they consider to be the proper response to suffering.

Suggestions for Writing
1. Write an essay that compares the views of all the writers on the issue of personal versus medical responsibility in euthanasia.
2. Write a letter to the author with whom you most disagree and argue for your own views while answering his or hers.
3. Write an essay that analyzes the ways in which each writer attempts to bring an appropriate dignity of style to the great issues of life and death.

13   What Should We Do about Tobacco?

SMOKING IS BAD FOR EVERYONE SO IT SHOULD BE ILLEGAL

Sally Chen

It breaks my heart to see all the high school kids standing on one foot outside school property and puffing away furtively and defiantly on their cigarettes. They've learned from movies and advertising that smoking makes them more mature and sophisticated. They are more mature in one sense—they're all much further along on their way to horrible deaths and early graves than their friends who have enough sense not to start. And those friends are the ones who are really sophisticated in the true sense of that word. They have a real "knowledge of life and how to live in the world." They know that cigarettes are dangerous and that one of the dangers is how hard it is to stop once you've started.

But none of this fazes the big tobacco corporations like Phillip Morris with their rich executives who make their living by making other people die. And none of this fazes government at any level either. What is more, governments are even more hypocritical than the tobacco companies or the movie big shots who say they are only "portraying the way society really is."

Governments love to "regulate" tobacco through taxes and ineffectual laws that supposedly protect minors. First of all, politicians love to raise taxes of any kind so they can have more money to spend on their favorite programs, which are designed to attract more voters, which allows them to remain in office so that they can raise taxes again. It's a merry-go-round for them and a vicious circle for the rest of us.

But while the voters love programs that benefit them individually, they also hate having their taxes raised generally. Taxing tobacco is the perfect solution: it allows the politicians to feel good about themselves that they are "doing something" about the dangers of smoking. But the taxes on cigarettes are hidden and seem to be a part of the price

of the pack, so no one blames the politician. The cigarette smokers themselves are (rightly) too ashamed to protest as they would about a rise in
their income taxes that they could see in their paychecks. But what kid
ever stopped smoking because it was expensive? That's part of the prestige for them. And those "no one under eighteen" signs—who are they
kidding? There is no teenager in the world who can't figure a way around
that one.

The only thing to do is to outlaw tobacco entirely. It's an addictive   5
drug that not only harms the user but everyone else through secondary
smoke. Since cigarettes are a problem for everyone in this country, cigarettes are a federal problem and we need a constitutional amendment.
Petty regulations and more and more taxes have made no dent. We need
to stop killing our own citizens and allow everyone the right to life, liberty, and the pursuit of happiness in a world without nicotine.

———————

Questions for Analysis

Logic
1. According to Chen, what is the logic of young smokers who wish to
   be perceived as "sophisticated"? What is the logic of Chen's **refutation,** or rebuttal?
2. What is the logic of Chen's opposition to higher taxes as a way of
   curbing smoking?
3. According to Chen, why should smoking be attacked at the constitutional level?

Character
1. What sense of her own character does Chen create in the opening
   paragraph? Is that sense of character sustained throughout the essay?
   Explain your answer using evidence.
2. According to Chen, how are the character flaws of tobacco companies and politicians alike? How do they differ? Give evidence for your
   answers.
3. What sense of character in smokers does Chen create in her last paragraph by calling tobacco "an addictive drug"?

Emotion
1. How does Chen use adjectives and adverbs in her first paragraph to
   create appeals to her readers' emotions? Account for as many modi-
   fiers as you can by explaining their implicit appeals.
2. How does Chen appeal to emotion in her phrase "make their living
   by making other people die" in paragraph 2?
3. According to Chen, is smoking a sin, a wrong, a crime, or a combination? Explain your answer using examples.

Chen

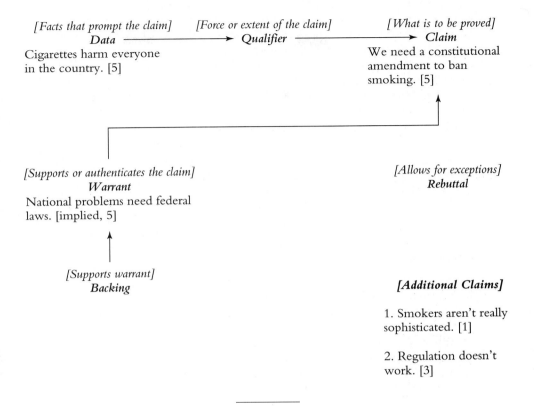

[Facts that prompt the claim]
Data ──────────→
Cigarettes harm everyone
in the country. [5]

[Force or extent of the claim]
Qualifier ──────────→

[What is to be proved]
Claim
We need a constitutional
amendment to ban
smoking. [5]

[Supports or authenticates the claim]
Warrant
National problems need federal
laws. [implied, 5]

[Supports warrant]
Backing

[Allows for exceptions]
Rebuttal

[Additional Claims]

1. Smokers aren't really
sophisticated. [1]

2. Regulation doesn't
work. [3]

BIG BROTHER'S TWO-MINUTE HATE

Linda Bowles

Eric Fromm, internationally acclaimed social philosopher and psychologist, viewed the novel *1984* by George Orwell as a warning "that
unless the course of history changes, men all over the world will lose their
most human qualities, will become soulless automatons, and will not even
be aware of it."

George Orwell's story takes place in a futuristic society where the
minds, emotions and bodies of citizens are under the tyrannical control
of Big Brother. One of the techniques of mind management used by
this totalitarian state is to fabricate a loathsome threat to the national well
being—and then have Big Brother step forward to protect the people
from it.

Every day, workers are required to gather in groups to participate in a Two-Minute Hate. The face of a hideous enemy, known only as Goldstein, is projected onto a huge screen. Goldstein is the epitome of evil: he is "the primal traitor, the earliest defiler of the Party's purity."

These Two-Minute Hate periods are orgies of screaming emotional outbursts. People curse and rail and throw things at the leering image of Goldstein. Then, at a moment when the rage and fear have reached a climax, Big Brother appears on the screen, speaking words of encouragement and reassurance. His powerful presence wipes away the threat of the enemy.

A typical reaction is that of a woman in the audience who cries aloud, "My savior!" and extends her arms toward the screen. All is well once again. Big Brother has made it so.   5

Orwell's description of government deceit and manipulation in the future is background for a discussion of government deceit and manipulation in the present.

The subject is tobacco. For purposes of this discussion, substitute "Joe Camel" for Goldstein and "Big Bubba" for Big Brother.

Before continuing, let's get the usual obligatory disclaimers out of the way. Tobacco products are harmful. Those who smoke tobacco should stop. Those who do not smoke should never start. We need to do something to prevent our children from ever lighting up that first cigarette. The people in the tobacco industry who have committed crimes should be indicted and tried.

Having agreed on these points and principles, it's time to talk plainly and think realistically about the implications of our government's approach to solving the problem of smoking.

What we have in view are proposals that have very little to do with curing the ills of tobacco. What we see is a scheme by government autocrats to take over a private industry, plunder its wealth, raise taxes—and look like heroes in the process.   10

It is a scam. For the scam to work, tobacco executives must be demonized. It must be repeated over and over again that every dirty dollar they own came from selling death-dealing, addictive drugs to hapless adults and innocent children.

These cold-hearted tobacco moguls don't deserve what they have and being stripped of it is pure justice.

It is a format for the advancement of tyranny. Where will Big Bubba next focus our hate? Will it be on those responsible for secondhand exhaust fumes from oversized autos and trucks? Will it be on parents who smoke in homes where children are present? And how about those filthy meat packers, greedy pharmaceutical houses and liquor barons? How about Ronald McDonald as a target?

The opportunities for the government to further intrude into our lives, with our enthusiastic consent, are boundless.

It is frightening that for the scam to work we the people have to view   *15*
ourselves as victims, needy and powerless, and convinced that the true
causes of our problems are out there somewhere, not inside ourselves.

This sense of helplessness impels us to exchange our freedoms for
security. We have given politicians and bureaucrats a mandate to pass laws
and institute programs premised upon our helplessness, our dependency
and our incompetence.

Eric Fromm wrote a book called *Escape From Freedom,* in which he
takes exception to the conventional view that mankind always struggles
to be free.

He points out that freedom carries with it the considerable risks and
substantial burdens of self-responsibility. Many people, he says, perhaps
most, are desperately searching—not for independence but for some person, institution or government willing to take care of them, assume their
burdens, make their decisions and give them packaged answers to life's
questions.

How lucky we are that Big Bubba stands ready to answer our prayers,
assume our burdens and take crib-to-tomb responsibility not only for
ourselves but for our children and our parents, as well.

How long will it be before our gratitude is such that at the very   *20*
sight of the beneficent Big Bubba, we will be unable to resist extending
our arms and crying out, "My savior!"

Questions for Analysis

Logic

1. Bowles argues in part by analogy. Summarize that analogy as con-
   cisely as you can. Begin your summary as follows: "Just as in Orwell's
   1984. . . ."
2. According to Bowles in paragraph 13, what is the implied reasoning
   that could lead to governmental opposition to Ronald McDonald?
3. Bowles begins paragraph 8 by saying "Before continuing, let's get the
   usual obligatory disclaimers out of the way." Would her overall argument be strengthened or weakened by placing the disclaimers at the
   end of the essay? Explain your reasoning.

Character

1. Bowles begins by referring to two famous authors. What sense of herself as an author do these literary references create for you? Would
   your sense be changed if she had referred only to George Orwell? Explain your answers.
2. Bowles refers to "a feeling of helplessness" as one of the keys to understanding public behavior. Does it seem to you from the manner of her
   writing that *she* feels helpless? Explain your answer using examples.

3. According to Bowles her opponents encourage hatred of their opponents. How would you characterize the sense Bowles creates of her feelings toward "Big Bubba"? Justify your characterization with evidence from the text.

Emotion

1. In paragraph 4 Bowles characterizes the responses to Goldstein as composed of both rage and fear. According to her, how are the two emotions combined in reactions to the tobacco problem?
2. Bowles calls the proposals of her opponents a "scheme" in paragraph 10 and a "scam" in paragraph 11. What is the emotional appeal made by each word, and how do they differ?
3. The imagined threats of paragraph 13 end with "How about Ronald McDonald as a target?" Name the emotions Bowles invites her readers to feel at this point, and explain how they might be expected to advance her overall argument.

THE TYRANNY OF THE MAJORITY
Walter E. Williams

Whenever Mom told my sister and me to share the last piece of pie or cake, or divide a pot of oatmeal that we both hated, she'd tell one of us to do the cutting or spooning, and the other had the first choice.

That rule gave whoever was the cutter or spooner uncanny incentive to be fair. For example, if I cut the cake unevenly, I'd lose because my sister had first choice and would choose the larger piece of cake (or the smaller bowl of oatmeal). Mom's strategy should be the basis for all societal rules. Good laws (rules) are those written as though our worst enemy had the power to enforce them.

Let's apply this idea to laws about speech and ask: If we seek fairness, what kind of laws should there be about speech? How about a law that says people are permitted to speak freely so long as they don't say something that offends another? Or, how about a law that mandates the nation's official language be English?

Some people might agree, pointing out they would promote sensitivity toward the feelings of others and strengthen the common culture. But what if your worst enemies win control of Congress and the White House? Then, if you said to a young lady, "Those jeans are really fitting you well," you might be fined or jailed for speech that the majority power deems offensive. If you're for making English the official language, a future majority might make the official language Spanish or French.

We don't have a lot to worry about with speech because the Framers   5
anticipated Mom's rule, saying: "Congress shall make no law . . . abridg-
ing the freedom of speech." If there's respect for that rule, even if our
worst enemies take over Congress and the White House, no sweat.

There are a bunch of Momlike rules in our Bill of Rights, containing distrustful and highly negative language like: "shall not be infringed,"
"shall not be violated," "shall not be required," and "nor be deprived."

Mom's rules would never be seen in heaven—they'd be an insulting insinuation that God cannot be trusted with power and that God is
not a just God. However, if you are unfortunate enough to end up in the
other place, you'd surely want Mom's rules, as you can't trust the Devil
to do right.

We Americans have forgotten the warnings of James Madison and
Thomas Jefferson about the tyranny of the majority. We think that because there's a majority vote of support, that fact alone confers legiti-
macy on laws passed by Congress. If you think a majority consensus is
fair, how would you like enactment of the following law: Congress shall
have the power to ban, regulate or tax out of existence any product found
to have no nutritional necessity but [to be] costly to the nation's health-
care system?

While most Americans support what Congress is now doing to
cigarette smokers, I'd be willing to bet my bank account they wouldn't
support those actions as a general rule. For example, there's absolutely no
nutritional reason for adding salt to food, or consuming beer, whiskey,
butter, potato chips and candy—but consumption of these goods raises
health-care costs.

Why would Americans support cigarette control and not a general   10
rule allowing Congress to ban or control consumption of other products
deemed harmful to our health? Most of the answer is cigarettes are the
other guy's vice, and a majority has the power to be arbitrary. For me,
I'll take Mom's rule any day—until I have the power to impose my values on others.

Questions for Analysis

Logic
1. Explain in your own words the reasoning behind "Mom's rule."
2. According to Williams, is the rationale of the negative language in the
   Bill of Rights Momlike?
3. Explain how, according to Williams, the rationale of the hypothetical
   law proposed in paragraph 8 is *not* Momlike.

Character
1. In the context of the essay as a whole, how do you take Williams's last
   sentence? As a menacing confession? A joke? Explain your answer.
2. As implied by the beginning of the essay, how does Mom view the

characters of her children? Suppose she viewed them differently. Give a rule for cutting the cake that would imply a different assumption about her children's characters.

3. Does Williams present himself as being like his mother in the character implied in him as the author of this essay? Does he view the "majority" as she views her children? Explain your answer using evidence.

Emotion

1. What are the usual associations of the words *tyranny* and *majority?* Write some sentences on the topic of government using these words separately. Does the title of Williams's essay invoke a kind of emotional paradox for you? Explain the emotional appeal of the title as clearly as you can.

2. "Mom and apple pie" is a phrase commonly used to sneer at sentimental appeals to an audience's emotions. Would it be fair to use this phrase to characterize Williams's use of his mother in his argument? Explain your answer using examples.

3. In the last sentence of paragraph 5 Williams is rather casual in his grammar and **diction** levels. What attitudes does this aspect of his style express toward the threats to freedom that are the implied subject of the paragraph? Explain your reasoning.

EXERCISES: WHAT SHOULD WE DO ABOUT TOBACCO?

Intertextual Questions

1. On which aspect of governmental regulation do Chen and Bowles agree? On which do they disagree?

2. Both Bowles and Williams are suspicious of singling out the tobacco industry for regulation. Do they come to this common conclusion for the same reasons? Explain your answer using evidence.

3. Which of the other two writers most agrees with the values and assumptions that underlie Williams's "Mom's rule"?

Suggestions for Writing

1. Taking into account the arguments of all three writers, write an essay that argues for your own views on the proper relations of individual and group rights with regard to the problem of tobacco.

2. Taking into account the arguments of all three writers, write an essay that argues for your own views on the propriety of governmental regulation with regard to the problem of tobacco.

3. Both Bowles and Williams are concerned with questions of tyranny that go beyond the issue of tobacco. Write an essay in which you analyze and compare their views of the broader threat of tyranny inherent in the tobacco controversy.

14   *What Books Should Students Read?*

PREFACE TO
THE GREAT CONVERSATION
Robert M. Hutchins

Until lately the West has regarded it as self-evident that the road to education lay through great books. No man was educated unless he was acquainted with the masterpieces of his tradition. There never was very much doubt in anybody's mind about which the masterpieces were. They were the books that had endured and that the common voice of mankind called the finest creations, in writing, of the Western mind.

In the course of history, from epoch to epoch, new books have been written that have won their place in the list. Books once thought entitled to belong to it have been superseded; and this process of change will continue as long as men can think and write. It is the task of every generation to reassess the tradition in which it lives, to discard what it cannot use, and to bring into context with the distant and intermediate past the most recent contributions to the Great Conversation. This set of books is the result of an attempt to reappraise and re-embody the tradition of the West for our generation.

The Editors do not believe that any of the social and political changes that have taken place in the last fifty years, or any that now seem imminent, have invalidated or can invalidate the tradition or make it irrelevant for modern men. On the contrary, they are convinced that the West needs to recapture and re-emphasize and bring to bear upon its present problems the wisdom that lies in the works of its greatest thinkers and in the discussion that they have carried on.

This set of books is offered in no antiquarian spirit. We have not seen our task as that of taking tourists on a visit to ancient ruins or to the quaint productions of primitive peoples. We have not thought of providing our readers with hours of relaxation or with an escape from the dreadful cares that are the lot of every man in the second half of the twentieth century after Christ. We are as concerned as anybody else at the headlong plunge into the abyss that Western civilization seems to be taking.

We believe that the voices that may recall the West to sanity are those which have taken part in the Great Conversation. We want them to be heard again—not because we want to go back to antiquity, or the Middle Ages, or the Renaissance, or the Eighteenth Century. We are quite aware that we do not live in any time but the present, and, distressing as the present is, we would not care to live in any other time if we could. We want the voices of the Great Conversation to be heard again because we think they may help us to learn to live better now.

We believe that in the passage of time the neglect of these books in the twentieth century will be regarded as an aberration, and not, as it is sometimes called today, a sign of progress. We think that progress, and progress in education in particular, depends on the incorporation of the ideas and images included in this set in the daily lives of all of us, from childhood through old age. In this view the disappearance of great books from education and from the reading of adults constitutes a calamity. In this view education in the West has been steadily deteriorating; the rising generation has been deprived of its birthright; the mess of pottage it has received in exchange has not been nutritious; adults have come to lead lives comparatively rich in material comforts and very poor in moral, intellectual, and spiritual tone.

We do not think that these books will solve all our problems. We do not think that they are the only books worth reading. We think that these books shed some light on all our basic problems, and that it is folly to do without any light we can get. We think that these books show the origins of many of our most serious difficulties. We think that the spirit they represent and the habit of mind they teach are more necessary today than ever before. We think that the reader who does his best to understand these books will find himself led to read and helped to understand other books. We think that reading and understanding great books will give him a standard by which to judge all other books.

We believe that the reduction of the citizen to an object of propaganda, private and public, is one of the greatest dangers to democracy. A prevalent notion is that the great mass of the people cannot understand and cannot form an independent judgment upon any matter; they cannot be educated, in the sense of developing their intellectual powers, but they can be bamboozled. The reiteration of slogans, the distortion of the news, the great storm of propaganda that beats upon the citizen twenty-four hours a day all his life long mean either that democracy must fall prey to the loudest and most persistent propagandists or that the people must save themselves by strengthening their minds so that they can appraise the issues for themselves.

Great books alone will not do the trick; for the people must have the information on which to base a judgment as well as the ability to make one. In order to understand inflation, for example, and to have an intelligent opinion as to what can be done about it, the economic facts in a given country at a given time have to be available. Great books cannot help us there. But they can help us to that grasp of history, politics, morals, and economics and to that habit of mind which are needed to form a valid judgment on the issue. Great books may even help us to know what information we should demand. If we knew what information to demand we might have a better chance of getting it.

Though we do not recommend great books as a panacea for our ills, we must admit that we have an exceedingly high opinion of them as an educational instrument. We think of them as the best educational instrument for young people and adults today. By this we do not mean that this particular set is the last word that can be said on the subject. We may have made errors of selection. We hope that this collection may some day be revised in the light of the criticism it will receive. But the idea that liberal education is the education that everybody ought to have, and that the best way to a liberal education in the West is through the greatest works the West has produced, is still, in our view, the best educational idea there is.

Questions for Analysis

Logic

1. Many of Hutchins's arguments have to do with refuting objections to the selections recommended by the series of books his essay introduces. Pick an example of this activity, and explain the reasoning of his refutation.

2. Hutchins implies that his key term, *greatness,* is not defined as an eternal quality that is necessarily part of the nature of a book in itself. Explain the author's reasoning on the topics of "change" [2] and "progress" [5] in the selection of great books.

3. Explain Hutchins's reasoning on the difference between a great book and one that embodies only "propaganda" [7].

Character

1. "Greatness" is a lofty subject. Exemplify and explain the ways in which you think Hutchins's style does or does not suggest qualities of character that would make him a proper judge of greatness in writing. Do you think, for example, that he adopts a suitably lofty point of view?

2. Does Hutchins seem to suggest a character that includes prejudice against traditions other than those of the West? Explain your answer using examples.

3. To what qualities of the imagined reader's character does Hutchins appeal? Analyze an example of an appeal to the reader's character, and explain its operation by referring to particular uses of language.

Emotion

1. What emotions are appealed to by the claim in the first paragraph, that until recently the main point the author argues has been "self-evident"?

2. Describe and explain the emotional appeal Hutchins makes in paragraph 4 on the issue of "sanity."
3. Hutchins does not hesitate to make judgments of value. To what emotions does this quality appeal? Explain your answer using particular examples.

Hutchins

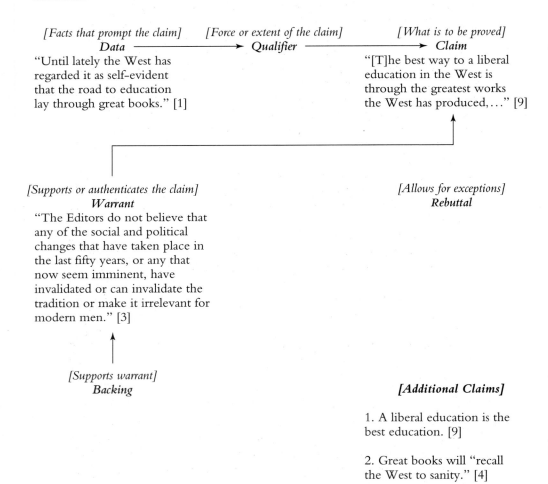

[Facts that prompt the claim]
Data ⟶

"Until lately the West has regarded it as self-evident that the road to education lay through great books." [1]

[Force or extent of the claim]
Qualifier ⟶

[What is to be proved]
Claim

"[T]he best way to a liberal education in the West is through the greatest works the West has produced,..." [9]

[Supports or authenticates the claim]
Warrant

"The Editors do not believe that any of the social and political changes that have taken place in the last fifty years, or any that now seem imminent, have invalidated or can invalidate the tradition or make it irrelevant for modern men." [3]

[Allows for exceptions]
Rebuttal

[Supports warrant]
Backing

[Additional Claims]

1. A liberal education is the best education. [9]

2. Great books will "recall the West to sanity." [4]

3. "[U]nderstanding great books" will lead to reading, understanding, and better judging other books. [6]

ON READING TRASH

Bob Swift

If you want kids to become omnivorous readers, let them read trash. That's my philosophy, and I speak from experience.

I don't disagree with The National Endowment for the Humanities, which says every high school graduate should have read 30 great works of literature, including the Bible, Plato, Shakespeare, Hawthorne, the Declaration of Independence, "Catcher in the Rye," "Crime and Punishment" and "Moby Dick."

It's a fine list. Kids should read them all, and more. But they'll be better readers if they start off on trash. Trash? What I mean is what some might call "popular" fiction. My theory is, if you get kids interested in reading books—no matter what sort—they will eventually go on to the grander literature all by themselves.

In the third grade I read my first novel, a mystic adventure set in India. I still recall the sheer excitement at discovering how much fun reading could be.

When we moved within walking distance of the public library a   *5* whole new world opened. In the library I found that wonder of wonders, the series. What a thrill, to find a favorite author had written a dozen or more other titles.

I read a series about frontiersmen, learning about Indian tribes, beef jerky and tepees. A Civil War series alternated young heroes from the Blue and the Gray, and I learned about Grant and Lee and the Rock of Chickamauga.

One summer, in Grandpa Barrow's attic, I discovered the Mother Lode, scores of dusty books detailing the adventures of Tom Swift, The Rover Boys, The Submarine Boys, The Motorcycle Boys and Bomba the Jungle Boy. It didn't matter that some were written in 1919; any book you haven't read is brand new.

Another summer I discovered Edgar Rice Burroughs. I swung through jungles with Tarzan, fought green Martians with John Carter, explored Pellucidar at the Earth's core, flew through the steamy air of Venus with Carson Napier. Then I came across Sax Rohmer and, for book after book, prowled opium dens with Nayland Smith, in pursuit of the insidious Fu Manchu.

In the seventh grade, I ran across Booth Tarkington's hilarious Penrod books and read them over and over.

My cousin went off to war in 1942 and gave me his pulp magazines.   *10* I became hooked on Doc Savage, The Shadow, G8 and His Battle Aces, The Spider, Amazing Stories. My folks wisely did not object to them as trash. I began to look in second-hand book shops for past issues, and found a Blue Book Magazine, with an adventure story by Talbot Mundy. It led me back to the library, for more of Mundy's Far East thrillers. From

Mundy, my path led to A. Conan Doyle's "The Lost World," Rudyard Kipling's "Kim," Jules Verne, H. G. Wells and Jack London.

Before long I was whaling with Herman Melville, affixing scarlet letters with Hawthorne and descending into the maelstrom with Poe. In due course came Hemingway, Dos Passos, "Hamlet," "The Odyssey," "The Iliad," "Crime and Punishment." I had discovered "real" literature by following the trail of popular fiction.

When our kids were small, we read aloud to them from Doctor Dolittle and Winnie the Pooh. Soon they learned to read, and favored the "Frog and Toad" and "Freddie the Pig" series.

When the old Doc Savage and Conan the Barbarian pulps were re-issued as paperbacks, I brought them home. The kids devoured them, sometimes hiding them behind textbooks at school, just as I had. They read my old Tarzan and Penrod books along with Nancy Drew and The Black Stallion.

Now they're big kids. Each kid's room is lined with bookshelves, on which are stacked, in an eclectic mix, Doc Savage, Plato, Louis L'Amour westerns, Thomas Mann, Gothic romances, Agatha Christie, Sartre, Edgar Allen Poe, science-fiction, Saul Bellow, Shakespeare, Pogo, Greek tragedies, Hemingway, Kipling, Tarzan, Zen and the Art of Motorcycle Maintenance, F. Scott Fitzgerald, Bomba the Jungle Boy, Nietzsche, the Iliad, Dr. Dolittle, Joseph Conrad, Fu Manchu, Hawthorne, Penrod, Dostoevsky, Ray Bradbury, Herman Melville, Conan the Barbarian . . . more. Some great literature, some trash, but all good reading.

Questions for Analysis

Logic

1. In your view, is Swift's whole appeal to reason essentially contained in his first paragraph? If you think so, explain what the rest of the essay contributes to his appeal to reason within the categories of Toulmin's model of logic. For example, does the rest of the essay expand on the data? The claim? The warrant? The backing? If you don't think all the logical parts of the argument are essentially contained in the first paragraph, show where they are exemplified in the rest of the essay.
2. By what means does Swift organize his essay? Explain how the organization does or does not support his major point.
3. Explain some of the criteria by which Swift creates throughout the essay a sense of the "eclectic mix" mentioned in his last paragraph.

Character

1. How would you characterize the general tone of voice Swift employs in the essay? Dignified? Chatty? Boasting? Describe what you hear in more than a word or two, and explain the qualities of character that Swift's tone seems designed to express.
2. What sense of character is created for you by Swift's mentioning different family members throughout the essay?

3. What sense of character is created for you by the self-proclaimed eclecticism of the many lists of authors and books that Swift gives throughout the essay?

Emotion
1. What emotions are evoked in general by Swift's use of the term *trash* to describe many of the books he mentions? Do you see any advantages for his use of that term rather than *popular fiction* [3]?
2. To what emotions does Swift appeal when he says that "any book you haven't read is brand new" [7]?
3. To what emotions does Swift appeal by his account of his children's reading habits? In what ways does the account advance his argument?

WHOSE CANON IS IT, ANYWAY? IT'S NOT JUST ANGLO-SAXON

Henry Louis Gates, Jr.

I recently asked the dean of a prestigious liberal arts college if his school would ever have, as Berkeley has, a 70 percent nonwhite enrollment. "Never," he replied. "That would completely alter our identity as a center of the liberal arts."

The assumption that there is a deep connection between the shape of a college's curriculum and the ethnic composition of its students reflects a disquieting trend in education. Political representation has been confused with the "representation" of various ethnic identities in the curriculum.

The cultural right wing, threatened by demographic changes and the ensuing demands for curricular change, has retreated to intellectual protectionism, arguing for a great and inviolable "Western tradition," which contains the seeds, fruit and flowers of the very best thought ever uttered in history. (Typically, Mortimer Adler has ventured that blacks "wrote no good books.") Meanwhile, the cultural left demands changes to accord with population shifts in gender and ethnicity. Both are wrongheaded.

I am just as concerned that so many of my colleagues feel that the rationale for a diverse curriculum depends on the latest Census Bureau report as I am that those opposed see pluralism as forestalling the possibilities of a communal "American" identity. To them, the study of our diverse cultures must lead to "tribalism" and "fragmentation."

The cultural diversity movement arose partly because of the fragmentation of society by ethnicity, class and gender. To make it the culprit

5

for this fragmentation is to mistake effect for cause. A curriculum that reflects the achievement of the world's great cultures, not merely the West's, is not "politicized"; rather it situates the West as one of a community of civilizations. After all, culture is always a conversation among different voices.

To insist that we "master our own culture" before learning others—as Arthur Schlesinger Jr. has proposed—only defers the vexed question: What gets to count as "our" culture? What has passed as "common culture" has been an Anglo-American regional culture, masking itself as universal. Significantly different cultures sought refuge underground.

Writing in 1903, W. E. B. Du Bois expressed his dream of a high culture that would transcend the color line: "I sit with Shakespeare and he winces not." But the dream was not open to all. "Is this the life you grudge us," he concluded, "O knightly America?" For him, the humanities were a conduit into a republic of letters enabling escape from racism and ethnic chauvinism. Yet no one played a more crucial role than he in excavating the long buried heritage of Africans and African Americans.

The fact of one's ethnicity, for any American of color, is never neutral: One's public treatment, and public behavior, are shaped in large part by one's perceived ethnic identity just as by one's gender. To demand that Americans shuck their cultural heritages and homogenize themselves into a "universal" WASP culture is to dream of an America in cultural white face, and that just won't do.

So it's only when we're free to explore the complexities of our hyphenated culture that we can discover what a genuinely common American culture might actually look like.

Is multiculturalism un-American? Herman Melville didn't think so. *10* As he wrote: "We are not a narrow tribe, no . . . We are not a nation, so much as a world." We're all ethnics; the challenge of transcending ethnic chauvinism is one we all face.

We've entrusted our schools with the fashioning and refashioning of a democratic policy. That's why schooling has always been a matter of political judgment. But in a nation that has theorized itself as plural from its inception, schools have a very special task.

Our society won't survive without the values of tolerance, and cultural tolerance comes to nothing without cultural understanding. The challenge facing America will be the shaping of a truly common public culture, one responsive to the long-silenced cultures of color. If we relinquish the ideal of America as a plural nation, we've abandoned the very experiment America represents. And that is too great a price to pay.

———

Questions for Analysis

Logic

1. The word *canon* in Gates's title refers to the books that a given culture considers its most valuable literary works. According to Gates, what

is the reasoning of the "cultural right wing," and what arguments does he bring to refute that reasoning?

2. According to Gates, what is the reasoning of the cultural left wing, and what arguments does he bring to refute that reasoning?

3. Explain Gates's own reasoning on the meaning of the key term *tolerance*.

Character

1. What qualities of Gates's character are suggested by the anecdote with which he begins the essay?

2. What qualities of Gates's character are suggested by the ways in which he responds to opposing viewpoints? Explain your answer using particular examples.

3. In what ways does Gates seek to align his views with those of publicly acknowledged authorities? Explain your answer using particular examples.

Emotion

1. Gates refers to the "West," and to "Anglo-Saxon," and "Anglo-American" culture. What are the emotional appeals of each term? What is the emotional effect of using them interchangeably?

2. What is the emotional appeal created by the use of the term *white face* in paragraph 8?

3. To what emotions does Gates appeal in paragraph 12 when he says that "society won't survive without the values of tolerance"?

EXERCISES: WHAT BOOKS SHOULD STUDENTS READ?

Intertextual Questions

1. Compare the ways in which each author takes into account the factor of historical change in his essay.
2. Both Hutchins and Gates use the metaphor of conversation to describe literary culture. Compare the ways in which each author understands and uses the implications of conversation in his argument.
3. Both Hutchins and Gates see the proper selection of books as a way of solving problems. Compare the ways in which each author understands the criteria for choosing books as a matter of problems and solutions.

Suggestions for Writing

1. Write an essay on the ways in which each author uses evidence as a means of supporting his claims for the ideas about books that he advances.
2. Literature is often said to combine delight and instruction. Write an essay in which you analyze the ways in which each author addresses the issues suggested by this dual definition.
3. Each writer imagines literature in some way as a "heritage." Write an essay that analyzes the ways in which this metaphor is used implicitly or explicitly to create appeals to emotion. Who or what, for example, would *literally* be the one to give you an inheritance? What implications would there be for you in your receiving an inheritance? For refusing to accept one? For not caring to know whether it exists? Compare these implications to the simple act of refusing to read or not caring to know about a book that someone else recommends.

15　Modern Manners

RUDENESS CAN BE LETHAL

Miss Manners

One of the leading causes of modern crime, Miss Manners gathers from paying attention to the news reports, is senselessness.

"Another senseless shooting," they keep announcing.

"A senseless stabbing . . . a senseless murder . . ."

We used to have such sensible crime.

Miss Manners can't help wondering what went wrong.　　　　　　　　5

Sensible crimes were ones committed for love or money. When neither revenue nor revenge is involved, the modern crime seems to strike people as unreasonable.

But Miss Manners has also been paying attention to what the criminals themselves give as their motives, and they make a certain deplorable sense to her. People are now killing over—you're going to have a hard time believing this one—etiquette.

One of our leading causes of murder is a perceived lack of respect. Respect is a basic concept of manners, which features such principles as dignity and compassion, rather than strict justice, which it leaves to the law. Being treated respectfully is not one of our rights, nor is treating others respectfully a legal obligation. Only manners require it.

Yet "dissin' "—showing real or apparent disrespect—is cited as the motive in an amazing number of murders.

As a Washington, D.C., high-school football player said when discussing the shootings of members of his team—one dead, three wounded　　10
last summer alone—"The biggest thing everybody is looking for is respect in the streets. It isn't money. They are just trying to make sure you respect them. People are just pushing each other to the maximum to get respect. And the maximum is death."

Remember what all those 18th-century Frenchmen in lace cuffs did when they got fussed about people looking at them cross-eyed? The chief difference now is that the duel has lost some of its frills, such as gloves, seconds and allowing both participants to shoot at the same time.

In keeping with modern practicality, the idea caught on that it is more effective to shoot when your victim isn't looking.

Failure to provide road courtesies is given as the motivation for the new sport of car-to-car shootings. Law is supposed to regulate the highway, but traffic law does not cover such courtesies as letting others pass, not playing a car radio so loudly that it annoys people in other cars, and not going slowly in a fast lane. So highway murderers seem to think of themselves as encouraging drivers' etiquette.

Fairness is a concept that manners shares with law, but only etiquette requires it in such informal situations as waiting in line. Some months ago, there was a stabbing in a Bethesda, Maryland, grocery store over the fact that someone had broken into the checkout line out of turn.

Does all this sound as if Miss Manners is on the side of the criminals? She is, after all, devoted to stamping out rudeness, just as these people have claimed to be.

But she has her limits about how it can be done. And she makes a   15
strict division between the jurisdictions of the law and of manners. Crime is not merely lethal rudeness.

Without even squabbling, she and Miss Justice managed to divide the task of regulating social behavior so that the law, with its fierce sanctions, agreed to punish behavior that is seriously threatening to life, limb or property, while gentle Miss Manners tries to persuade people to avoid the kind of behavior that leads to such unpleasantness.

But when poor old etiquette fails, the law must take over. It was a humiliating defeat for manners when both smokers and nonsmokers refused to curb their rudeness toward one another, and the law had to take over what used to be in the jurisdiction of manners.

Miss Manners' point about the new etiquette-motivated crime is that when there is no recognition of the need to observe courtesies, everyone finds life unbearable. Asking the law to regulate petty conduct would trespass on our basic rights, but allowing individual impulses to go totally unrestrained leads to mayhem.

There is no use telling Miss Manners that no one cares about etiquette any more. Even outlaws are outraged when others do not follow its rules.

Questions for Analysis

Logic

1. Explain in your own words what Miss Manners takes to be the sense behind some "senseless" crimes.
2. Explain in your own words the rationale of "respect" explained in paragraphs 9 and 10.
3. Explain in your own words the distinction Miss Manners makes beginning in paragraph 15 between her own relationship to rudeness and that of criminals.

Character
1. What techniques of writing does Miss Manners employ to create a sense of her own character as a well-mannered one? Cite and analyze two examples.
2. What differences in character does Miss Manners attribute to duelists and drive-by shooters in paragraph 11? What uses of language create your sense of those differences?
3. What sense of character does Miss Manners create for Miss Justice in paragraph 16? What uses of language create this sense?

Emotion
1. Miss Manners speaks of herself always in the third person. What effect does this technique create with regard to the emotional range of feelings her essay expresses? Is the range a constrained one? Explain your answer.
2. In the analysis in paragraph 10, the football player uses the word *just* twice. Read the sentences aloud with and without the word. What effect on the emotional content of his sentences does this word create?
3. To what emotions does Miss Manners appeal in her discussion of smoking regulations in paragraph 17? Explain how her uses of language create the appeal.

PUBLIC SERVANTS OFTEN BEHAVE LIKE MASTERS

Stephen Chapman

The other day, I arrived at the bus stop, where my bus was waiting, and walked up to the door behind two other commuters. They got on, but before I could board, a Chicago Transit Authority fare collector abruptly stepped in front of me, blocked the door, told the driver to close it and drive on, and then, when I asked for an explanation, strode away without a word, even though he apparently had nothing else to do.

The bus was half-empty during rush hour, there was no other bus in sight, and I was not holding things up. But for some strange reason, the guy in the CTA uniform decided he just had to prevent me from spending my money for the benefit of his employer.

When I called the agency's customer service line to report his badge number, the lady who took the information was perfectly polite, and she actually managed to sound surprised by my account. But if you have ever had the pleasure of dealing with urban transit workers, the idea of being abused for no conceivable purpose will strike you as perfectly normal.

The CTA, I am happy to report, has a lot of workers who do their jobs competently and helpfully. Probably a majority, I suspect. It also has many who think of mass transit patrons as an intolerable nuisance that keeps them from getting their paychecks with the least possible exertion.

It's a good day when a driver will advise you which stop you want   *5* or a fare collector will tell you where a bus goes. A friend of mine, new to town, ventured into an L station and approached a CTA employee. "Excuse me," he said politely, "I'm trying to get to State and Randolph." Came the reply: "Buddy, who the hell's stopping you?"

The government takes all sorts of antitrust actions to prevent private companies from acquiring monopolies, but the only monopoly truly worth fearing is the one exercised by the government itself. In a democracy, public employees are supposed to be accountable to the people. In fact, their privileged status, safe from competing alternatives, often allows them to be indifferent to, and even contemptuous of, those they theoretically work for.

Our helpful fare collector is a good example. Can you imagine an employee at a movie theater, a hardware store or a fast-food restaurant physically preventing an unoffending customer from entering the establishment during normal business hours to make a purchase? Private companies offering goods and services for sale can't survive if they go out of their way to alienate consumers. Buyers can always go elsewhere.

In the public sector, workers are shielded from that horrid prospect. If you want to take a plane from O'Hare to New York or Dallas or Los Angeles, you have plenty of airlines to choose from. But if you want to take a bus across town, there's only one supplier. And if you don't like it, your local transit provider can get along just fine without you: It gets a subsidy extracted forcibly from the taxpayer at large.

A colleague of mine was recently reminded of the bleak realities of dealing with the public servants whose salaries she helps pay. Her 15-year-old son needed to take a written test for his learner's driving permit. But the licensing office is open only during the hours when she and her husband are unable to get there because of their jobs—with the sole exception of Saturday morning. So she and her son had to go on Saturday and wait two and a half hours for him to take a 20-minute test. The wait was necessitated solely by the refusal of public employees to make themselves available at times convenient to their patrons.

That's how most government offices function. You can get a pizza   *10* delivered at 3 a.m., most commodities can be bought in well-appointed stores seven days a week, and computer help lines operate round the clock. You can complete many transactions without ever leaving your home. But federal, state and municipal offices make few of the elementary concessions needed to accommodate ordinary people.

Of course, a lot of people who work in the private sector would also prefer to have their evenings and weekends free. But the nature of competition in the free market is that the consumer is sovereign—and the seller has to serve the consumer's needs or perish.

Government workers claim to serve the public, too, but in too many cases, their actions speak louder. Democracy, we are told, forces the government to respond to the bidding of the people. But it is not the nature of government, democratic or otherwise, to do that on a day-to-day basis. The imbalance of power is too large and too secure. Next time you're dealing with a sullen public employee, you should have no trouble figuring out who is the servant.

Questions for Analysis

Logic
1. According to Chapman, what reasons make it more pleasant to deal with workers in the private sector?
2. In paragraph 6 Chapman claims that "the only monopoly truly worth fearing is the one exercised by the government itself." Explain in your own words two ways in which he supports this claim logically.
3. Chapman does not argue explicitly for a solution to the problem of rudeness on the part of public employees. In your own words describe any implicit arguments he makes in this regard. Does he imply, for example, that we should change our form of government from democracy to something else to achieve better manners?

Character
1. Chapman argues that public employees are often ill mannered. What techniques of writing does he employ to create a sense of his own character as well mannered? Point to and analyze two examples.
2. In paragraph 4 Chapman allows that perhaps a majority of public employees act properly. What sense of Chapman's own character does this claim help to create?
3. In paragraph 9 Chapman speaks of working hours as the result of a "refusal"; in paragraph 11 he speaks of them in terms of preference. How does his choice of words help to create a sense of differing characters for workers in the public and private sectors?

Emotion
1. Point to three words in paragraph 1 that Chapman uses to create the sense of rudeness on the part of the fare conductor, and explain their implications.
2. In paragraph 3 Chapman says that the customer service representative "actually managed to sound surprised." What does Chapman imply are her real emotions, and how does he use language to make this implication?
3. In paragraph 5 what emotions are expressed by the employee's remarks? Explain in particular how his use of the word *Buddy* helps to express them.

Chapman

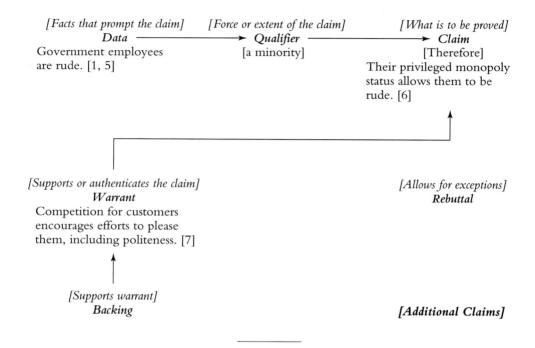

[Facts that prompt the claim]
Data
Government employees
are rude. [1, 5]

[Force or extent of the claim]
Qualifier
[a minority]

[What is to be proved]
Claim
[Therefore]
Their privileged monopoly
status allows them to be
rude. [6]

[Supports or authenticates the claim]
Warrant
Competition for customers
encourages efforts to please
them, including politeness. [7]

[Allows for exceptions]
Rebuttal

[Supports warrant]
Backing

[Additional Claims]

WHO'S HARASSING WHOM?

Marianne M. Jennings

Nearly 30 years in the workplace, and not once have I been sexually harassed. I suppose I'm grateful, but given the action other working women seem to be getting, a part of me wonders: Exactly what's wrong with me? It's not as if I haven't been in high-risk environments. I began my legal career as an intern for the federal government. Yet I haven't had so much as a comment from a male coworker since the Reagan administration. After the Anita Hill spectacle in 1991, I noticed men averting their eyes.

But what I resent more than the lack of attention is the assumption underlying the rules and court decisions governing sexual harassment: that I am incapable of handling unwanted sexual suggestion. My employer trusts me with budgeting, lobbying, fund-raising and shaping the minds of the next generation, but is forced by the Equal Employment Opportunity Commission and the courts to conclude that I can't handle the advances of knuckleheads.

I resent the women who bring sexual harassment suits and convince courts that we are as helpless and victimized as Melanie Wilkes in "Gone With the Wind." I come from a long line of unharassed women who taught me that the best defense against offensive male behavior is a good offense. The female arm has an appendage created for dealing with cads. Women in the 1940s used said appendage quite effectively to administer a slap in the face and thereby deter drunken sailors. And yet working women today can't handle a boor in wing tips and bifocals without the help of the Supreme Court?

The court's recent rulings on harassment make it easier to win damages against a company even if it is unaware that a supervisor is harassing an employee, and even if the plaintiff suffered no career damage. The likely result: Companies will redouble their already vigorous efforts aimed at preventing harassment.

But who's harassing whom when I'm forced to attend "sensitivity training" seminars and reveal my personal feelings to coworkers with whom I don't even exchange recipes? At one Fortune 500 company, a sensitivity consultant instructed employees to conduct the following "group exercise": "I want all of the men to sit down on the floor in the center of the room. You are not allowed to speak while sitting down. The women are to stand around the men in a circle and begin to whistle and make sexist comments about the appearance and anatomy of the men." What if I don't *want* to talk about my colleagues' anatomy?

How innocent are the victims of harassment anyway? "Dateline NBC" recently ran a story on women who claimed they were harassed while working on the production lines at a Ford plant in Chicago. They tearfully told of sleeping with supervisors to keep their jobs and of being hospitalized for stress. These women defined their ethical dilemma as most people who make poor decisions do: Either I stay here and get harassed, or I leave and take another job for less pay but keep my sanity and virtue. To put it another way, the supervisors' brutish behavior was awful, but for $22 an hour the employees were willing to put up with it. Similarly, if you believe Anita Hill's story, she tolerated Clarence Thomas's misbehavior for years because riding to a career pinnacle on the tails of a shooting star was worth it.

Like tenants who claim "constructive eviction" due to horrible living conditions yet remain on the leased premises, the legal claim of women that their working environment is hostile doesn't jibe with their own decision to remain. Women define what's repulsive, stay in it and then file and win multimillion-dollar verdicts, which in many cases exceed the amounts awarded to children crippled in horrific accidents. The courtroom playing field reflects academic theories such as the following, touted in the Journal of Business Ethics: "Sexual harassment signifies to women that their presence is threatening to the dominant patriarchal order, that they are unwelcome, and works to maintain gender stratification." The guys at the Ford plant were interested in "gender stratification"? Sounds to me like they were just after a roll in the hay.

The most damaging result of sexual-harassment law is the chilling effect it has on men in the workplace. Mentoring, which I had from decent and honorable men and without which I would not have survived 30 years ago, is a lost art. Men who hold the keys and skills for advancement hesitate to involve themselves in one-on-one counseling of female employees. Men fear closing the office door during meetings with women. At the University of Nebraska, a graduate student was even ordered to remove a picture of his bikini-clad wife from his desk after two colleagues complained.

I see a fear in my male colleagues' eyes that they will unwittingly offend someone and will be the subject of a career-derailing investigation. The fear is justified. An accused rapist, after all, receives better treatment than an accused harasser. The rape defendant is entitled to due process, the presumption of innocence and his day in court. When a man is charged with sexual harassment, the employer's response will be swift, decisive and one-sided.

I resent that men in my office feel they must cast their eyes down- *10* ward. It's not their sexual appetites they're holding back. It's candor. It's friendliness. It's lunch together. They're certainly not harassers, but they can no longer risk being my friends or mentors. Feminists claimed victory with these latest decisions because liability for sexual harassment now rests squarely with those responsible—employers. That's wrong. Employers don't cause sexual harassment. Women have defined it, capitalized on it and exacerbated it. We also possess the tools for handling it, without a federal judge or bureaucracy. Dear sisters, we have met the enemy and she is us.

Questions for Analysis

Logic
1. Which of her opponents' assumptions about ways to deal with sexual harassment does Jennings most question? On what assumption does she rest her own argument?
2. Explain in your own words Jennings's objections to the logic of "innocent victims" beginning in paragraph 6.
3. Explain in your own words Jennings's reasoning on the subject of mentoring in the workplace.

Character
1. Jennings claims to be able to handle herself in the event of any harassment. Point to some uses of language that create a sense of self-reliance in her character.

2. What are Jennings's feelings about "personal feelings" in paragraph 5? What sense of her character is created by her objections here?
3. What qualities of character does Jennings attribute to the female auto workers? What to their supervisors? Explain your answers.

Emotion
1. Jennings claims several times to feel resentment. Besides the use of the word itself, what techniques of writing work to express this emotion? Point to and analyze two examples.
2. In paragraph 6 what are the emotions appealed to by the female workers? What emotions does Jennings herself invite us to feel about them? Analyze the techniques in each case.
3. In paragraph 7 what emotions are the readers invited to feel by the contrast between the levels of diction in "gender stratification" and "roll in the hay"? How might these two emotions be expected to gain support for Jennings's argument?

EXERCISES: MODERN MANNERS

Intertextual Questions

1. In paragraph 3 Chapman invites his readers to agree that "being abused for no conceivable purpose" is "normal" for those dealing with public employees. He locates the problem in economics in the form of public monopolies. Discuss the ways in which the other two writers do or do not provide alternative ways of understanding the kind of rudeness that prompted Chapman's claim.
2. In paragraph 10 Miss Manners reports an analysis of "dissin.'" Discuss the ways in which this analysis does or does not illuminate the difficulties of manners that are the subjects of the other two essays.
3. The political philosopher Hannah Arendt claims that one of the defining features of modern life has been "the conquest of society by the state." Discuss the ways in which the three authors in this section view the interaction between "society," where personal relations are controlled by convention, and "government," where personal relations are controlled by law.

Suggestions for Writing

1. The writer Roberta Conde has said, "Lord Acton didn't go far enough. While it is true that power corrupts and that absolute power corrupts absolutely, it is also true that petty power corrupts in petty ways." Write an essay in which you draw on your own experiences to attack, defend, or modify this claim as a way of understanding public and private rudeness.
2. Write an essay in the form of a letter addressed to someone who has been rude to you, in which you argue that the action was not only wrong in itself but also symptomatic of the larger social problem of modern manners.
3. Marianne Jennings rejects lawsuits and sensitivity training as proper responses to sexual harassment. Taking her position into account—whether to attack, modify, or defend it—write an essay in which you argue for the proper response to sexual harassment in school and the workplace.

16   Should English Be the Official Language of the United States?

IN SUPPORT OF OUR COMMON LANGUAGE . . .

U.S. English

ENGLISH, OUR COMMON BOND

Throughout its history, the United States has been enriched by the cultural contributions of immigrants from many traditions, but blessed with one common language that has united a diverse nation and fostered harmony among its people.

As much by accident as by design, that language is English. Given our country's history of immigration and the geography of immigrant settlements, it might have been Dutch, or Spanish, or German; or it might have been two languages, as is the case in Canada, our neighbor to the north.

But English prevailed, and it has served us well. Its eloquence shines in our Declaration of Independence and in our Constitution. It is the living carrier of our democratic ideals.

English is a world language which we share with many other nations. It is the most popular medium of international communication.

THE SPREAD OF LANGUAGE SEGREGATION

The United States has been spared the bitter conflicts that plague so many countries whose citizens do not share a common tongue. Historic forces made English the language of all Americans, though nothing in our laws designated it the official language of the nation.

But now English is under attack, and we must take affirmative steps to guarantee that it continues to be our common heritage. Failure to do so may well lead to institutionalized language segregation and a gradual loss of national unity.

The erosion of English and the rise of other languages in public life have several causes:

- Some spokesmen for ethnic groups reject the "melting pot" ideal; they label assimilation a betrayal of their native cultures and demand government funding to maintain separate ethnic institutions.
- Well-intentioned but unproven theories have led to extensive government-funded bilingual education programs, ranging from preschool through college.
- New civil-rights assertions have yielded bilingual and multilingual ballots, voting instructions, election site counselors, and government-funded voter registration campaigns aimed solely at speakers of foreign languages.
- Record immigration, concentrated in fewer language groups, is reinforcing language segregation and retarding language assimilation.
- The availability of foreign language electronic media, with a full range of news and entertainment, is a new disincentive to the learning of English.

U.S. ENGLISH: A TIMELY PUBLIC RESPONSE

In 1981, Senator S. I. Hayakawa, himself an immigrant and distinguished scholar of semantics, proposed a constitutional amendment designating English as the official language of the United States. Senator Hayakawa helped found U.S. ENGLISH in 1983 to organize and support a citizens' movement to maintain our common linguistic heritage.

U.S. ENGLISH is committed to promoting the use of English in the political, economic, and intellectual life of the nation. It operates squarely within the American political mainstream and rejects all manifestations of cultural or linguistic chauvinism.

OUR GUIDING PRINCIPLES

Our goal is to maintain the blessing of a common language—   *10*
English—for the people of the United States.

These principles guide us:

- In a pluralistic nation such as ours, government should foster the similarities that unite us rather than the differences that separate us.
- The nation's public schools have a special responsibility to help students who don't speak English to learn the language as quickly as possible.

- Quality teaching of English should be part of every student's curriculum, at every academic level.
- The study of foreign languages should be strongly encouraged, both as an academic discipline and for practical, economic, and foreign-policy considerations.
- *All* candidates for U.S. citizenship should be required to demonstrate the ability to understand, speak, read, and write simple English, and demonstrate basic understanding of our system of government.
- The rights of individuals and groups to use other languages and to establish *privately funded* institutions for the maintenance of diverse languages and cultures must be respected in a pluralistic society.

OUR ACTION PROGRAM

U.S. ENGLISH actively works to reverse the spread of foreign language usage in the nation's official life. Our program calls for:

- Adoption of a constitutional amendment to establish English as the official language of the United States.
- Repeal of laws mandating multilingual ballots and voting materials.
- Restriction of government funding for bilingual education to short-term transitional programs only.
- Universal enforcement of the English language and civics requirement for naturalization.
- Expansion of opportunities for learning English.

Toward these ends, U.S. ENGLISH serves as a national center for consultation and cooperation on ways to defend English as the sole official language of the United States. It directs its efforts to leading a public discussion on the best language policies for our multiethnic society; educating opinion leaders on the long-term implications of language segregation; encouraging research on improved methods of teaching English; and promoting effective programs of English language instruction.

WE NEED YOUR HELP

U.S. ENGLISH welcomes to membership all who are concerned about the prospect of entrenched language segregation and the possibility of losing our strongest national bond.

We hope that you will join us and defend our common language *15* against misguided policies that threaten our national unity.

Questions for Analysis

Logic

1. Where in the essay do you find an attempt to meet the counter-arguments of opponents? Can you think of objections that have not been met?
2. Explain in your own words the logic of the claim in paragraph 6 that failure to defend English will lead to "language segregation."
3. In what ways does the document seek to avoid the objection that it is prejudiced? What reasons are mentioned that might seek to counter this charge?

Character

1. "In Support of Our Common Language . . ." was modified or approved by more than one author. Do you see any evidence of multiple authorship in any aspect of the document's style? Explain your answer using examples.
2. What does the phrase "as much by accident as by design" in paragraph 2 contribute to the sense of character U.S. English projects? What motivations or rationales might be anticipated and rejected by the implications of the phrase?
3. What contribution does paragraph 4 make to the sense of character projected? What values and assumptions seem to underlie the statement? How does it expand the meaning of *our* in the subhead title "Our Guiding Principles" on page 168?

Emotion

1. What emotions are appealed to by the examples given in paragraph 3? Can you point to evidence for the same emotional appeal elsewhere in the document?
2. What emotional response seems invited by the example of Senator Hayakawa in paragraph 8?
3. The word *serve* appears in paragraphs 3 and 13. What are the emotional implications of the word, and what does it invite the audience to feel in each case? Does it act differently in each case? Explain your answer.

U.S. English

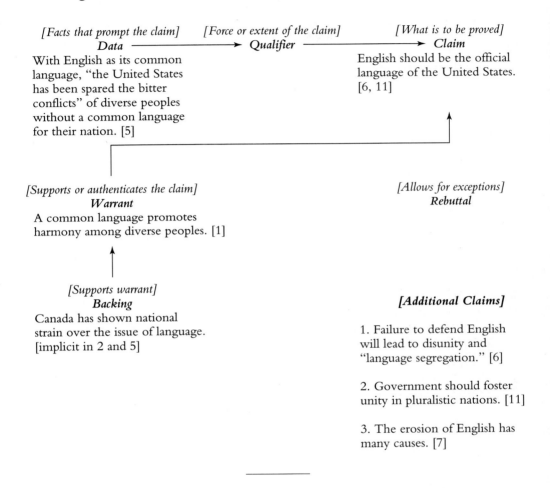

[Facts that prompt the claim]
Data ——————→ *Qualifier*

[Force or extent of the claim]
——————→

[What is to be proved]
Claim

With English as its common language, "the United States has been spared the bitter conflicts" of diverse peoples without a common language for their nation. [5]

English should be the official language of the United States. [6, 11]

[Supports or authenticates the claim]
Warrant
A common language promotes harmony among diverse peoples. [1]

[Allows for exceptions]
Rebuttal

[Supports warrant]
Backing
Canada has shown national strain over the issue of language. [implicit in 2 and 5]

[Additional Claims]

1. Failure to defend English will lead to disunity and "language segregation." [6]

2. Government should foster unity in pluralistic nations. [11]

3. The erosion of English has many causes. [7]

GAINS AND LOSSES

Richard Rodriguez

My *mother!* My *father!* After English became my primary language, I no longer knew what words to use in addressing my parents. The old Spanish words (those tender accents of sound) I had used earlier—*mamá* and *papá*—I couldn't use anymore. They would have been too painful reminders of how much had changed in my life. On the other hand, the words I heard neighborhood kids call *their* parents seemed equally unsatisfactory. *Mother* and *Father; Ma, Papa, Pa, Dad, Pop* (how I hated the all-American sound of that last word especially)—all these terms I felt were unsuitable, not really terms of address for *my* parents. As a result, I never used them at home. Whenever I'd speak to my parents, I would try to get their attention with eye contact alone. In public conversations, I'd refer to "my parents" or "my mother and father."

My mother and father, for their part, responded differently, as their children spoke to them less. She grew restless, seemed troubled and anxious at the scarcity of words exchanged in the house. It was she who would question me about my day when I came home from school. She smiled at small talk. She pried at the edges of my sentences to get me to say something more. (What?) She'd join conversations she overheard, but her intrusions often stopped her children's talking. By contrast, my father seemed reconciled to the new quiet. Though his English improved somewhat, he retired into silence. At dinner he spoke very little. One night his children and even his wife helplessly giggled at his garbled English pronunciation of the Catholic Grace before Meals. Thereafter he made his wife recite the prayer at the start of each meal, even on formal occasions, when there were guests in the house. Hers became the public voice of the family. On official business, it was she, not my father, one would usually hear on the phone or in stores, talking to strangers. His children grew so accustomed to his silence that, years later, they would speak routinely of his shyness. (My mother would often try to explain: Both his parents died when he was eight. He was raised by an uncle who treated him like little more than a menial servant. He was never encouraged to speak. He grew up alone. A man of few words.) But my father was not shy, I realized, when I'd watch him speaking Spanish with relatives. Using Spanish, he was quickly effusive. Especially when talking with other men, his voice would spark, flicker, flare alive with sounds. In Spanish, he expressed ideas and feelings he rarely revealed in English. With firm Spanish sounds, he conveyed confidence and authority English would never allow him.

The silence at home, however, was finally more than a literal silence. Fewer words passed between parent and child, but more profound was the silence that resulted from my inattention to sounds. At about the time I no longer bothered to listen with care to the sounds of English in public, I grew careless about listening to the sounds family members made when they spoke. Most of the time I heard someone speaking at home and didn't distinguish his sounds from the words people uttered in public. I didn't even pay much attention to my parents' accented and ungrammatical speech. At least not at home. Only when I was with them in public would I grow alert to their accents. Though, even then, their sounds caused me less and less concern. For I was increasingly confident of my own public identity.

I would have been happier about my public success had I not sometimes recalled what it had been like earlier, when my family had conveyed its intimacy through a set of conveniently private sounds. Sometimes in public, hearing a stranger, I'd hark back to my past. A Mexican farmworker approached me downtown to ask directions to somewhere. "¿Hijito . . . ?" he said. And his voice summoned deep longing. Another time, standing beside my mother in the visiting room of a Carmelite convent, before the dense screen which rendered the nuns shadowy figures, I heard several Spanish-speaking nuns—their busy, singsong overlapping voices—assure us that yes, yes, we were remembered, all our family was remembered in their prayers. (Their voices echoed faraway family sounds.) Another day, a dark-faced old woman—her hand light on my shoulder—steadied herself against me as she boarded a bus. She murmured something I couldn't quite comprehend. Her Spanish voice came near, like the face of a never-before-seen relative in the instant before I was kissed. Her voice, like so many of the Spanish voices I'd hear in public, recalled the golden age of my youth. Hearing Spanish then, I continued to be a careful, if sad, listener to sounds. Hearing a Spanish-speaking family walking behind me, I turned to look. I smiled for an instant, before my glance found the Hispanic-looking faces of strangers in the crowd going by.

Questions for Analysis

Logic
1. Make a list of the stated or implied reasons that English was a loss for Rodriguez in his private life.
2. Make a list of the stated or implied reasons that English was a gain for Rodriguez in his public life.
3. In your own words summarize Rodriguez's reasoning on the difference between literal and figurative silence.

Character
1. Does Rodriguez project a sense of character that seems fair-minded? Analyze some examples that support your answer.
2. Does Rodriguez project a sense of character that seems intelligent and reasonable? Analyze some examples.
3. Does the character suggested by the essay's style seem to be founded on moral and ethical principles? Analyze the evidence that leads you to your response.

Emotion
1. In the narrative of the reactions of his family, compare the emotions Rodriguez suggests that he felt with those he seems to invite his audience to feel.

2. Of his mother Rodriguez says in paragraph 2 that "she pried at the edges of my sentences." What emotions in his mother does the author's metaphor dramatize?
3. What differing emotions in his father does Rodriguez dramatize in paragraph 2 when he describes him speaking first in English and then in Spanish?

HOW NOT TO GET THE INFIDEL TO TALK THE KING'S TALK

Ishmael Reed

"How will we eradicate Black English?" Dick Cavett, public television's resident Anglo-lover, asked a group of linguists and John Simon. "You'd have to eradicate the black people," a linguist answered. Chilling thought, considering that there are historical precedents for people being exterminated because they didn't speak and write the way others thought they should.

When his arguments failed to convince the linguists of the existence of a "standard English," guest John Simon said that blacks should speak "'standard English' in order to get ahead," or as William Prashker wrote in the *New York Times* magazine section, "Black culture doesn't mean zip" when you're trying to impress "the man downtown." The Man downtown.

Of course, neither Prashker nor Simon and Cavett could explain the successes of Gerald Ford, or of New York City's Mayor Ed Koch, who confuses "each other" with "one another." Nor did they explain the triumphs of Dwight Eisenhower, who introduced the word "finalize" and whose press conference transcripts do not obey the rules of grammar.

Nelson Rockefeller, the late governor of New York, was a wealthy man, yet this man thought that the word "horrendous" was a word of praise. Really. The former President of the United States says "fahm" for what we call "farm." I was appalled to learn, in *The Brethren,* that Chief Justice Burger's decisions are so illiterate that the law clerk has to correct them so that they won't embarrass the Court.

If people who make these errors are "idiots," as Simon says, then 5 many of our elected officials, industrialists, and writers are idiots: *As I Lay Dying* is filled with "errors" by Faulkner.

Did the powerful people who "rule" America—all white males according to the April 16, 1979, issue of *U.S. News and World Report*—"get ahead" by speaking like characters in a Henry James novel? Did oilmen? Did Teamster presidents? I doubt it.

You not gone make me give up Black English. When you ask me to give up my Black English you askin me to give up my soul. But for reasons of commerce, transportation–hassleless mobility in everyday life, I will talk to 411 in a language both the operator and I can understand. I will answer the highway patrolman who stops me, for having a broken rear light, in words he and I both know. The highway patrolman, who grew up on Elvis Presley, might speak Black English at home, because Black English has influenced not only blacks but whites too.

So when trying to get the infidel to talk so that the British Tea Company can keep an eye on the infidel, the missionaries should be aware that appeals to "getting ahead" will be seen through by the millions of Black English followers both overt and covert. The phantom legions.

Don't blame the mass defections from "standard English" on them; their rulers were the first to surrender.

The ironies don't end there. During an appearance before the   *10* English–Speaking Union in San Francisco, John Simon spoke of reprimanding a young woman for saying "between Bill and I" instead of "Bill and me." He went on to say he didn't have the "foggiest notion who Bill or the woman speaking or the woman behind the counter *were*." As reporter Charles Haas pointed out in the December 17, 1979, issue of *New West* magazine, Simon should have said "was."

Questions for Analysis

Logic

1. What are the logical parallels of cause and effect that Reed implies between British rule of the American colonies and standard English on the one hand and the Boston Tea Party and Black English on the other?
2. What are Reed's stated and implied reasons for wanting to keep Black English?
3. What are Reed's stated and implied reasons for wanting to keep a command of standard English?

Character

1. What does Reed's sentence structure, as exemplified in paragraph 3, contribute to our sense of his character? What does the relation between the sentences contribute to the structure of the paragraph and a further sense of Reed's character?
2. Reed could have pointed out the error mentioned in paragraph 10 himself or could have referred to a general grammar book. What does his having given credit to Charles Haas contribute to our sense of his character?

3. What does Reed's use of Black English in paragraph 7 contribute to our sense of his character? How is that style affected by the stylistic context of the rest of the essay?

Emotion

1. What emotions does Reed's use of Black English in paragraph 7 evoke in his audience? If Reed were to imagine that audience as composed of speakers of both standard English and Black English, what emotions might be expected of each group?
2. What emotions does Reed invite by his emphasis on the word *eradicate* in paragraph 1? Are those emotions like the ones invited by his emphasis on *man/Man* in paragraph 2? Explain.
3. Do you understand the joke made by calling Dick Cavett an "Anglolover" in paragraph 1? If you do not, note carefully the differences it makes in your emotional relation to the paragraph when the joke is explained.

EXERCISES: SHOULD ENGLISH BE THE OFFICIAL LANGUAGE OF AMERICA?

Intertextual Questions

1. Do the three essays in this section seem to operate on a common understanding of the definition of standard English? Explain your answer using examples.
2. The three essays may be seen as not directly opposing one another's positions. Pick examples of areas that overlap, and explain some similarities in the positions taken.
3. What differences exist among the three essays in any area they all address? Explain your answer using examples.

Suggestions for Writing

1. Write a letter as though it were written by either Rodriguez or Reed to U.S. English, and explain the degree of support or opposition that you think the writer would express regarding the principles of the organization.
2. Write a letter from U.S. English to either Reed or Rodriguez that responds to the letter suggested in suggestion 1.
3. Write a short essay that argues for your own position on whether standard English should be a national goal.

II   *Single Essays on Controversial Topics*

INTRODUCTION

All the earlier issues have been represented by multiple points of view and accompanied by extensive analytic apparatus. The idea of the following section is for you to practice the skills you have acquired by asking your own questions about the ways the authors argue through logic, character, and emotion and forming (if necessary) your own alternative opinions to those represented here. The range of topics includes many of those currently most controversial, and you will no doubt already have formed opinions on many of them. But whether you agree or disagree with the stance taken by these writers, you should be prepared both to analyze the ways in which their arguments operate and to respond to those arguments with supporting or opposing arguments of your own.

This section provides material for you to use in expanding and honing your analysis and argumentative writing skills without the help (or interference) of the editorial apparatus provided in the previous section. The selections have been made with the idea of giving one of the most controversial positions taken on controversial issues, so that you will have plenty of room to disagree with, modify, or support the author's point of view. Remember to pay attention to all sides of the Rhetorical Triangle whether analyzing the essays or responding to them with essays of your own.

WHO'S WHITE? WHO'S HISPANIC? WHO CARES?

Jeff Jacoby

It was big news earlier this year: New census data showed that Hispanics were on the verge of surpassing blacks as the largest minority group in the nation. This occasioned a good deal of comment, some of it worried, some of it celebratory. At around the same time came word that in many parts of the country, whites were dwindling to a minority group themselves—if, indeed, they hadn't become one already.

"Boston became a majority minority city in the 1990s for the first time," the *Boston Globe* reported in March, "as Latinos, Asians, and blacks arrived and as tens of thousands of whites left." A continent away, the *Los Angeles Times* put the story on Page 1: "For the first time ever, no racial or ethnic group forms a majority in California."

But pull up the Census Bureau data yourself and you discover something interesting about these dramatic changes: They didn't happen.

Of the 281 million people enumerated in the 2000 census, 34.7 million gave their race as black. Respondents were allowed to check more than one racial category, and another 1.7 million identified themselves as black and something else. Total black (or partly-black) population: 36.4 million. The comparable number for whites was 217 million; for Asians, 11.9 million; for American Indians, 4.1 million; for native Hawaiians/Pacific Islanders, 0.9 million; and for those choosing "other," 18.5 million.

But there is no comparable number for Hispanics, because the Census Bureau doesn't treat "Hispanic" as a race. Last year's questionnaire asked respondents whether they identified themselves as "Spanish/

5

Hispanic/Latino," and 35.3 million said yes. On the separate race question, some of those 35.3 million Hispanics said they were white (48 percent), some said black (2 percent), some marked multiple races (6 percent), and some—presumably those who *do* identify their race as
Hispanic—marked the box labeled "other" (42 percent).

Hispanics, in other words, come in all colors—just like Catholics,
or veterans, or the elderly. Asking whether Hispanics or blacks constitute
the nation's largest minority is as meaningless as asking whether the book
industry publishes more paperbacks or more mysteries. They are overlapping categories.

It is clear that some activists are eager for "Hispanic" to acquire
the status of a full-fledged racial category. It's hardly a mystery why:
Racial minority status confers political clout and a share of the affirmative action pie. But it is also pretty clear that most Hispanics don't buy
into that agenda. More than half, after all, consider themselves white or
multiracial.

Which is why you can safely tune out those stories about California
and Boston and so many other venues no longer having white majorities.
"No racial or ethnic group forms a majority in California," the *L.A. Times*
said, but the Census Bureau begs to differ. Of California's 33.9 million
residents, 20.1 million—59 percent—identified themselves last year
as white. Likewise Boston. In 2000, 589,000 people lived in the city;
321,000 of them—54.5 percent—were white.

The nation as a whole remains overwhelmingly white—75.1 percent, the census found. "The suggestion that the white population of
America is fast on the way to becoming a minority," writes Orlando Patterson, the noted sociologist, "is a gross distortion."

So where did the stories about The Incredible Shrinking White   10
Majority come from? From manipulating the data so that white Hispanics are not counted as white. But whose opinion should we be relying
on? The children and grandchildren of Latin American immigrants who
say they are white? Or the Hispanic journalists and pressure groups who
tell them they aren't?

For 250 years, the American melting pot has been turning ethnic
groups once thought to be racially distinct (and socially indigestible) into
undifferentiated—which has usually meant white—Americans. In 1896,
Senator Henry Cabot Lodge bemoaned the influx of "races with which
the English-speaking people have never hitherto assimilated, and who are
most alien to the great body of the people of the United States." He was
talking about Russians, Poles, and Greeks. Early in the 20th century, Ital-
ians, Jews, and the Irish were classified as separate races by federal immigration authorities.

Today, it is strange to think that Irish or Russian immigrants were
once deemed "nonwhite." Fifty years from now, it will seem just as odd
that Mexicans and Cubans were once regarded the same way.

But let us hope that by then we will have abandoned the fable that racial categories have concrete meaning in the first place. How useful is the term "white," after all, if its definition is so mutable? Isn't race, as the confusion over "Hispanic" suggests, ultimately a matter of personal choice? In a nation where millions of people fall in love and raise children without regard to the color line, isn't it time the government stopped counting by race altogether?

———————

NEEDED: TECHIES WHO KNOW SHAKESPEARE

Ellen Ullman

High-technology companies are so desperate for programmers, according to recent reports, that they are luring students out of the classroom with well-paying jobs. It's the schools' fault, say people in the industry and some computer-science professors. Students aren't being taught the skills they need and therefore don't see the point of getting a degree.

But critics are forgetting that the very idea of the computer science degree is a relatively recent point on the short time line of the computer industry. Historically, most programmers had plenty of education, but little of it came from computer science departments. The problem is not the technical curriculum, but the undergraduate–computer science degree itself.

Computer programming has always been a self-taught, maverick occupation. Except for a brief moment in the late 1980s and early 1990s— what I think of as the Dilbert era—no one thought that programming was something you should learn in college.

Prospective programmers spent a great deal of time in school, but they typically studied something other than computers. Aside from a few famous dropouts—like Bill Gates, Steven Jobs and Stephen Wozniak— the profession has always attracted the very well-schooled.

Physicists and mathematicians created the industry just after World War II and became the first programmers. As the need for such skills grew in the 1970s, business and government had to look beyond people with doctorates.

Fortunately, that demand coincided with the end of the 1960s, when all sorts of overeducated people were on the loose, looking for a way to earn a living.

That's where I came in: I'm a member of the generation that came to computing as a second, third or fourth vocation. My first boss had two master's degrees in social science and had spent years as a Sufi dancing disciple. My next boss, a former bartender, had a master's degree in library science. The head of technical services at the same company had a Ph.D. in anthropology, and she hired people who had completed all but their dissertations in linguistics, archeology and classics. In this crowd, I felt like the dunce with my undergraduate degree in English.

We had all taught ourselves computing. For us, it was just one more difficult subject to learn. No one was intimidated by learning another computer language — or anything else for that matter. What we knew was how to learn, which is all that one can hang on to in a profession in which change is relentless.

The generation of programmers who followed us were, well, disappointing. They had engineering and computer science degrees, and none of them seemed to have read anything but technical textbooks. They stood mute among us when we said the occasional phrase in French. They looked confused when we alluded to Shakespeare or Proust. If today's would-be programmers are fleeing the sort of education that these people received, well, that's wonderful.

A good friend of mine finished engineering school in the late 1980s. *10* He managed to get his degree without having studied much of what some still call Western civilization.

Poignantly, he knows he's missed something. He is now a principal of a startup company developing E-mail services for the World Wide Web. My friend is building connections around the planet, and he is ashamed that he has never even studied a foreign language.

I don't mean for these stories to persuade aspiring programmers to drop out of school. Quite the contrary, I hope it might make students and professors realize that programming instruction can take place in a few classes, and students can spend the rest of their time studying foreign language, literature, linguistics, philosophy and history of science.

Schools might as well give up on teaching the latest skills, since those skills will soon become obsolete anyway. Instead, they might stress subjects that foster a flexible and open mind. Programmers seem to be changing the world. It would be a relief, for them and for all of us, if they knew something about it.

"FREE" MUSIC CAN FREE THE ARTIST

Chuck D

Unlike many of my fellow artists, I support the sharing of music files on the Internet. The Recording Industry Association of America has sued Napster, an Internet application that helps people find, copy and share songs free of charge on the Web, arguing that it encourages users to violate copyright laws. Some artists have spoken out against Napster as a threat to their livelihoods, and most recently Dr. Dre and the band Metallica have become involved in lawsuits against the service.

But I believe that artists should welcome Napster. We should think of it as a new kind of radio—a promotional tool that can help artists who don't have the opportunity to get their music played on mainstream radio or on MTV.

As someone who has been connected to hip-hop and rap music for 22 years, I've seen how difficult it has become for the majority of artists, songwriters, producers and independent labels to get their music to the fans directly, without signing with a major label and subjecting themselves to rules that are in the best interest of the label.

Beginning in the late 1980's when video hit the scene, record companies upped the ante on what it took to promote and market a song, totally squeezing the small, independent entrepreneur out of the distribution game. Now, with most radio stations playing popular favorites and with the high cost of making and distributing music videos, it is almost impossible for an independent record producer or an artist to get music to fans.

I believe this structure has hurt the artist more than someone passing a song around free of charge.   *5*

Not that most artists ever have much say about how their work is marketed and sold anyhow. Most contracts only guarantee artists a few cents in royalties from each record sold. And if a song doesn't become a hit, the label can cease selling it but still own rights to it forever.

The major labels have also benefited from being a step ahead on the technology that allows the listener to hear and keep music. As the technology progressed from phonograph to stereo hi-fis, eight-track, cassettes and CD's, record companies have been the only ones able to repackage the music they own to fit the new format. And in fact, when companies like Sony bought record companies, they gained control of the music to add to their control of the device needed to hear it.

The last straw was the CD period, when labels increased their markup without raising artists' royalties in kind. At the same time, record companies created the concept of a disposable artist; with jacked-up marketing and promotional costs, record companies stopped nurturing career artists. They have been able to fatten profits by flipping small batches of artists in and out.

That is today's music industry.

Well, Napster has been a thorn in that bull's side. By exposing people   *10* to music, companies like Napster are creating new fan interest and establishing a new infrastructure for unknown artists to attract an audience—a new radio for the new millennium.

But the question remains: Will the corporations that dominate concede to sharing the musical marketplace? We'll see. Until then we will slowly see formations of new rules and regulations that will eventually support many more artists than the record companies of yesterday. The Internet has created a new planet for musicians to explore, and I'm with that.

———————

END THE WAR ON DRUGS

Joanne Jacobs

President Clinton has inherited two costly, nasty and never-ending wars from George Bush. I don't know what he should do about the war against Saddam Hussein, but I think he should end the war on drugs.

Bush drew a line in the snow, so to speak, and fought hard to make the hawkish supply-side strategies work. Drug war spending quadrupled, to nearly $13 billion a year for the federal effort alone, and Bush put 70 percent of the money into interdiction and enforcement.

The prison population doubled in the past 10 years, in large part due to more hawkish enforcement and long mandatory sentences for drug offenses.

"In California, the number of persons sent to prison for drug offenses tripled between 1980 and 1985, and tripled again in the following five years, rising from less than 1,000 to more than 10,000 over the decade," reports the Rand Research Review. No wonder the state is broke.

The result of this multibillion-dollar war: Less occasional drug use,   5
as much or more hard-core abuse. By one measure—emergency-room admissions for cocaine and heroin overdoses—things are considerably worse.

Meanwhile, the murder rate has gone up in step with the drug-war budget. This is not a coincidence, observes Peter Reuter, a Rand drug-policy analyst. "Frequent harassment of street drug sellers increases the incentives to use violence to maintain market share."

Furthermore, our civil liberties have suffered collateral damage, as all Americans—but especially minorities—are subjected to drug tests, warrantless searches and long-distance snooping.

On the campaign trail, Clinton promised a "national crusade" that will spend more on treatment and prevention. He also pledged to provide federal funds for local police to suppress drugs.

A crusade is better than a war, but not much. Clinton's wording still implies a one-shot campaign leading to total victory, or perhaps total redemption.

The president has an opportunity for leadership toward some of that   10
change we've been hearing about: He can recast drug policy as a public-health issue.

After all, Clinton's half-brother is one of those drug criminals we've heard so much about. He served 15 months in federal prison for selling cocaine in 1984. Clinton participated in family therapy to aid his brother's treatment for addiction. He knows Roger Clinton Jr.'s criminal substance abuse is closely related to Roger Clinton Sr.'s legal substance abuse.

Perhaps Clinton guesses that if his brother had come from a poorer family—with no family friends to provide a job and no money to pay for therapy—his drug conviction would have ended his chances to find honest work or live a drug-free life.

The president of the Arkansas Senate was criticized this week for commuting two sentences while serving as acting governor: One was a murderer's life sentence; the other was a 50-year prison term for transporting cocaine. The drug carrier had served five years, and would not have been eligible for parole for another 18 years.

The foot-soldiers in the drug war are ready to change. Police chiefs and cops, probation officers, judges and prosecutors know that what they've been doing doesn't do any good. Most now advocate the pragmatic approach called "harm minimization." (Some favor decriminalization, but that much change isn't going to happen.)

What can Clinton do?   15

Stop promising a "drug free" America, and drop the military rhetoric. Announce that drug abuse will be treated like alcohol abuse, a serious public-health problem causing harm to innocent victims as well as to abusers.

Cut the drug czar's bloated office—which in the past has been filled with political hacks—and transfer it to Health and Human Services.

Fund treatment programs with a record of success and rehabilitation programs for prisoners. Currently, there are enough federally funded treatment slots for fewer than one out of three serious drug abusers.

Don't put more money into prevention programs without evidence of effectiveness. Kids don't need more antidrug education. What they need is education to prepare for a future in which they'll have better choices than using or selling drugs.

(My sixth-grader just attended a school assembly featuring a guy   20
who demonstrated jumping rope and ventriloquism—including the singing of "Hava Nagila" for "our Jewish-American friends"—and led students in hope-not-dope and self-esteem chants. She threatened to start using drugs if forced to listen to one more antidrug spiel.)

Fund those cops on the beat to make neighborhoods safer for decent people. Sure, patrolling mean streets is not a federal responsibility, but as long as we're going to ignore that, make sure the money goes for community policing, not task forces and SWAT teams.

The money can come from eliminating the Drug Enforcement Administration. We've got the FBI; we don't need multiple agencies tripping over each other.

Take every dollar spent trying to interdict drug supplies and use it to pay for education, job training and drug treatment for inner-city kids.

Eliminate mandatory sentences that put first-time drug offenders behind bars for years longer than murderers and rapists, and fill jails with petty drug users. Some states are forced to release violent criminals early in order to make room for nonviolent drug offenders serving no-parole sentences.

Use the billions saved by reducing sentences to pay for locking up   25 violent criminals, for in-prison drug programs, for probation officers and for boarding schools (boot camps, if you prefer) for kids who get in trouble.

Finally, stop confiscating property unless there's proof it was bought with criminal proceeds. In some cases, cars, boats and homes have been seized without a criminal conviction, or with no evidence against the owner. This is the sort of arbitrary government power the Constitution is supposed to protect Americans against. The Supreme Court just agreed to hear a test case.

President Clinton is the first president to have smoked marijuana, even if he didn't inhale. I'd guess that almost all the Friends of Bill, and half his Cabinet, were drug criminals once.

U.S. drug policy casts millions of Americans as the enemy on whom war must be waged. It's time for a change.

———————

SERVING TIME THE OLD-FASHIONED WAY

Dick Boland

When it comes to correcting some of the ills that have plagued our nation for years, we should once again look to California for guidance. Gov. Pete Wilson is moving to eliminate many of the privileges inmates enjoy in California prisons.

He wants to remove weight-training equipment and enforce personal hygiene. These changes will not be popular with those who feel punishment should be confined to raising self-esteem. If you are laying out any of your hard-earned cash to go down to the health spa and lift weights, you will probably side with the governor.

He also wants to remove the law books from the prison library. Inmates use law books to challenge the courts that put them there. We have a system that is turning out musclebound paralegals. The prisoners complain that their rights are being violated. These are the people who killed and raped and committed all kinds of heinous crimes and now demand to be treated with dignity.

Prison officials are enforcing new grooming standards that require men's hair to be closely cropped. As a result, 100 inmates at Folsom Prison staged a hunger strike. This is good news for taxpayers, who have to feed these morons. Let's hope hunger strikes catch on. Prisoners will also be undergoing random drug tests and packages being sent directly to inmates will be examined. It appears that we are going to start treating inmates like they can't be trusted. Let's hope they can stand up under the pressure.

Of course, we have prisoners' rights advocates who claim these   5
measures are punitive. Imagine, punishing convicts. Everyone knows how well rehabilitation works. How do you rehabilitate a murderer? Would you care to have a rehabilitated murderer working for you or living next door? Only in the United States can a murderer be put to death on the one hand or spend his life lifting weights and watching TV on the other. I would say it is time for some prison reform.

Prison guards also object to any reduction in privileges in our overcrowded prisons, and you have to sympathize with them. The answer is to build more prisons or hire more guards. Surely if we can support thousands of prisoners for a good part of their lives, we can come up with the bucks to have an adequate guard force to do the job. Perhaps we should have a prisoner-exchange program with a country like Turkey, or even Mexico. Returning prisoners can explain how fortunate they are to have committed a crime in the United States.

The correctional system we have now does not hinder crime, nor will it ever until such time as being imprisoned becomes so unpleasant that one will think twice before taking a chance on going there. Prisoners should have minimal rights. Weight-lifting, television, telephone, free mail and law libraries should be removed from our penitentiaries.

If not, we should start calling prisons rest homes. How come I have to pay for all of the things the convict gets for nothing?

WOMEN, SEX, AND RAPE
Have Some Feminists Exaggerated the Problem?

Cathy Young

The vast majority of Americans, women or men, undoubtedly take a positive view of changes the women's movement has brought about in attitudes toward rape. It is now widely accepted that a woman does not have to be a paragon of chastity to prove she has been raped; that her sexual history should not be put on trial; that even if she has been having drinks with a man or invited him in, he has no right to force sex on her. These advances, however, may be undermined by the efforts of some feminists to so enlarge the concept of rape as to demonize men, patronize women and offend the common sense of the majority of both sexes.

A recent example of this extremism was provided by the panel discussion on an ABC News special, "Men, Sex and Rape." Men and women in the audience as well as the panel were seated separately, implicitly reinforcing the message that *every man is a potential rapist.*

Five of the six women panelists, among them legal scholar Catherine MacKinnon and "Backlash" author Susan Faludi, backed the view that rape, far from being a pathology, reflects the norm in male-female relations in our society. As proof, MacKinnon asserted that 47 percent of all American women have been sexually assaulted and 25 percent raped. When a male panelist questioned these numbers, she retorted, "That means you don't believe women. It's not cooked, it's interviews with women by people who believed them when they said it."

But not all researchers on the topic do believe their female respondents. University of Arizona psychologist Mary Koss, whose studies in the field are among the most frequently cited, herself wrote in a 1988 article that of those women whom the researchers classified as victims of rape by nonromantic acquaintances, only 27 percent considered themselves rape victims. In situations involving dating partners, only 18 percent of the researcher-classified victims thought they had been raped. (In surveys that directly ask women about forced intercourse, fewer than 10 percent report such experiences.)

Do these feminists believe women, or do they believe that women   5
need expert guidance to know when they've been raped?

The reason for this startling "credibility gap" becomes clear when one looks at how the concept of rape has been broadened by the radical feminists. In their redefinition, physical force or threat of injury are no longer required.

In a recent volume of the *Journal of Social Issues,* for example, University of Kansas professor Charlene Muehlenhard and three coauthors cite the finding that "the most common method men used to have sexual intercourse with unwilling women was ignoring their refusals *without using physical force* [emphasis mine]. . . . The prevalence of rape found in these studies would have been much lower if the definition had required physical force."

A couple is necking, and at some point she says, "Please don't," and perhaps pulls back a little; he keeps trying and she eventually goes along rather than push him away or repeat her refusal more forcefully. Is this rape? Yes, say the hardliners: She does not resist because of fear. Even if the man does not threaten her, his size and muscle implicitly do.

But many people, myself included, will find it hard to believe that most women are afraid their dates will beat them up if they resist. Indeed, many who are attacked by strangers and have far stronger reasons to fear injury still fight back or scream.

Women have sex after initial reluctance for a number of reasons,   10
and fear of being beaten up by their dates is rarely reported as one of them. Some may be ambivalent or confused; they may believe that they

shouldn't want sex, and feel less guilty if they are "overpowered." Sometimes both the man and the woman are drunk, which adds to the confusion and miscommunication. Some women may change their mind, perhaps because they get sexually excited by the man's attentions. Others may be genuinely unwilling but concerned about displeasing the man or hurting his feelings. As one student, prodded by a campus presentation on date rape to conclude that she was a victim, explained to a journalist, "I thought, 'Well, he's my friend . . . whatever happens, it's not going to be that bad' . . . no big deal."

Is it unfortunate that many women are brought up to be so anxious not to offend, to be liked? Yes. But the answer should be to encourage assertiveness, not make excuses for doormat behavior.

The redefinition of rape also includes "psychological coercion" such as "continual arguments." Muehlenhard and her coauthors suggest that if lack of resistance cannot be regarded as consent when a woman is threatened with being shot, it might be no different if she is threatened with being dumped. The old "If you loved me, you'd do it" line becomes a felony.

To the cutting-edge anti-date-rape activists, even a "no" is no longer necessary for a finding of coercion; the absence of an explicit "yes" will suffice. In the January/February issue of Ms., a scene of clearly consensual (but wordless) rough sex from "Basic Instinct" is described as one in which "a woman experiences date rape and then kisses the perp."

All these definitional shenanigans might be funny if they didn't have serious practical consequences. Young men on college campuses are now being told in rape prevention workshops (mandatory for male freshmen at some schools) that they may have raped some of their seemingly willing sexual partners; and young women are being encouraged to abdicate responsibility for their sexual behavior by labeling unsatisfactory experiences as coercive. Harvard's Date Rape Task Force recently issued a report recommending that university policy define rape as "any act of sexual intercourse that occurs without the expressed consent of the person," as well as sex with someone impaired by "intake of alcohol or drugs."

Of course, in the enterprise of redefining rape, there is no reason   15
to stop at requiring verbal agreement. If a woman's failure to object to unwanted sex can be attributed to intimidation, so can explicit consent. Inevitably, on the outer limits, this patronizing line of thinking reaches the conclusion that in our oppressive society, *there can be no consensual sex.* Even if a woman thinks she wants it, that's only because her desire has been "constructed" by the patriarchy.

People have a right to the wackiest of ideas, but it is disturbing that some proponents of this theory are being treated as mainstream feminists. MacKinnon, who has emerged as a leading spokeswoman on sexual harassment and rape, has written such things as: "The similarity between the patterns, rhythms, roles and emotions, not to mention acts, which make

up rape on one hand and intercourse on the other . . . makes it difficult to sustain the customary distinctions between violence and sex. . . .
The issue is less whether there was force and more whether consent is a
meaningful concept." When she appears on television or is quoted in the
press, this (one would think) very relevant aspect of her beliefs is tactfully
omitted.

So anxious are they to extend the concept of rape, these crusaders
become almost annoyed when discussions focus too much on violent attacks by strangers or near-strangers. They want to hammer in the point
that the greatest danger to women comes from male friends, lovers, husbands. (University of Washington professor Marilyn Friedman has compared Rhett Butler sweeping up Scarlett O'Hara and carrying her upstairs
to mass murderer Richard Speck.) They insist that rape at knifepoint in
a parking lot is not different from an ambiguous encounter in which a
woman is pushed further sexually than she wanted to go, and further,
that women have no responsibility whatsoever to avert situations of the
latter sort.

On the ABC panel, Naomi Wolf (author of *The Beauty Myth*)
complained that "in this culture we tend to trivialize the harm that rape
does to women." But if anything, much of the effort to broaden the
definition of rape trivializes the horror of real sexual violence (by strangers or acquaintances).

The same program included footage of a treatment program for
jailed sexual offenders, who were made to listen to a recording of a woman
calling 911 just as a rapist breaks into her house. The terrified woman
gasps, "He's here! He's here!" before her voice dissolves into screams and
whimpers. One would have to be utterly removed from the real world
to insist this is comparable to the experience of a woman who yields because she's tired of pushing away her date's roving hands.

A friend of mine, although acknowledging that some feminist   20
rhetoric is excessive, believes that expanding the definition of rape to
include noncoercive experiences is useful because it sensitizes the society to the pain that sexual pressure and manipulation often cause. But
pressure and manipulation are not a one-way street; women can apply
them too. Besides, the law is not there to ensure we have trauma-free
relationships.

Trying to relabel insensitive behavior as illegal can only backfire:
When a cad is accused of being a rapist, the unfairness of the charges may
make him an object of sympathy, leading people to overlook his moral
flaws.

While I, personally, do not think that "no-maybe-yes" games are the
stuff of romance, or that the vanishing of feminine coyness would be a
great loss, to replace those rituals with new ones based on suspiciousness,
calculation and consent forms in triplicate would hardly be a gain.

CAN YOU BE EDUCATED FROM A DISTANCE?

James Barszcz

By almost any measure, there is a boom in Internet-based instruction. In just a few years, thirty-four percent of American colleges and universities have begun offering some form of what's called "distance learning" (DL), and among the larger schools, it's closer to ninety percent. If you doubt the popularity of the trend, you probably haven't heard of the University of Phoenix. It grants degrees entirely on the basis of online instruction. It enrolls 90,000 students, a statistic used to support its claim to be the largest private university in the country.

While the kinds of instruction offered in these programs will differ, DL usually signifies a course in which the instructors post syllabi, reading assignments, and schedules on Web sites, and students send in their written assignments by e-mail. Other forms of communication often come into play, such as threaded messaging, which allows for posting questions and comments that are publicly viewable, as a bulletin board would, as well as chat rooms for real-time interchanges. Generally speaking, face-to-face communication with an instructor is minimized or eliminated altogether.

The attraction for students might at first seem obvious. Primarily, there's the convenience promised by courses on the Net: you can do the work, as they say, in your pajamas. But figures indicate that the reduced effort results in a reduced commitment to the course. While attrition rates for all freshmen at American universities is around twenty percent, the rate for online students is thirty-five percent. Students themselves seem to understand the weaknesses inherent in the setup. In a survey conducted for eCornell, the DL division of Cornell University, less than a third of the respondents expected the quality of the online course to be as good as the classroom course.

Clearly, from the schools' perspective, there's a lot of money to be saved. Although some of the more ambitious programs require new investments in servers and networks to support collaborative software, most DL courses can run on existing or minimally upgraded systems. The more students who enroll in a course but don't come to campus, the more the school saves on keeping the lights on in the classrooms, paying custodians, and maintaining parking lots. And, while there's evidence that instructors must work harder to run a DL course for a variety of reasons, they won't be paid any more, and might well be paid less.

But as a rule, those who champion distance learning don't base their arguments on convenience or cost savings. More often, they claim DL signals an advance in the effectiveness of education. Consider the vigor- 5 ous case made by Farleigh Dickinson University (FDU), in Madison, New Jersey, where students—regardless of their expectations or desires—are now required to take one DL course per year. By setting this requirement, they say, FDU recognizes the Internet as "a premier learning tool" of the current technological age. Skill in using online resources "prepares our students, more than others, for life-long learning—for their jobs, their careers, and their personal growth." Moreover, Internet-based courses will connect FDU students to a "global virtual faculty," a group of "world-class scholars, experts, artists, politicians, and business leaders around the world."

Sounds pretty good. But do the claims make much sense? First, it should be noted that students today and in the future might well use the Internet with at least as much facility as the faculty. It's not at all clear that they need to be taught such skills. More to the point, how much time and effort do you suppose "world-class scholars" (much less politicians and business leaders) will expend for the benefit of students they never meet or even see? Probably a lot less than they're devoting to the books, journal articles, and position papers that are already available to anyone with access to a library.

Another justification comes from those who see distance learning as the next step in society's progress toward meritocracy. A recent article in *Forbes* magazine cites Professor Roger Schank of Northwestern University, who predicts that soon "students will be able to shop around, taking a course from any institution that offers a good one. . . . Quality education will be available to all. Students will learn what they want to learn rather than what some faculty committee decided was the best practical compromise." In sum, says Professor Schank, who is also chairman of a distance-learning enterprise called CognitiveArts, "Education will be measured by what you know rather than by whose name appears on your diploma."

Statements like these assume education consists in acquiring information ("what you know"). Accept that and it's hard to disagree with the conclusions. After all, what does it matter how, or through what medium, you get the information? But few truly educated people hold such a mechanistic view. Indeed, traditionally, education was aimed at cultivating intellectual and moral values, and the "information" you picked up was decidedly secondary. It was commonplace for those giving commencement speeches to note that, based on etymology, education is a drawing out, not a putting in. That is, a true education *educes,* or draws out, from within a person qualities of intellect and character that would otherwise have remained hidden or dormant.

Exactly how this kind of educing happens is hard to pin down. Only in part does it come from watching professors in the classroom present material and respond to student questions, the elements of education that can be translated to the Net with reasonable fidelity. Other educational experiences include things like watching how professors joke with each other (or not!) in the hallways, seeing what kinds of pictures are framed in a professor's office, or going out for coffee after class with people in your dorm. Such experiences, and countless others, are sometimes labeled (and dismissed) as "social life on campus." But they also contribute invaluably to education. Through them, you learn a style, in the noblest sense of that term, a way of regarding the information you acquire and the society you find yourself in. This is what the philosopher Alfred North Whitehead meant when he called style the ultimate acquisition of a cultivated mind. And it's the mysterious ways of cultivating that style that the poet Robert Frost meant when he said that all that a college education requires is that you "hang around until you catch on." Hanging around, that is, on campus, not lurking on the Net.

LIVING TOGETHER: TEST RUN FOR LONELINESS

Mona Charen

With the brave exception of Dr. Laura Schlesinger, no one uses the term "shacking up" anymore. Living together without benefit of marriage now raises only the most sensitive of eyebrows. Is the widespread acceptance of cohabitation a good idea? Most people have accepted the new dispensation uncritically.

But the National Marriage Project, a privately funded research program affiliated with Rutgers University (www.smartmarriages.com/ cohabit.html), wants you to know that the track record of "living together" is not so great—particularly if the goal is a long and happy marriage.

Living together is seen by many people, particularly the young, as a sort of test drive for marriage. Let's move in together, they reason, and find out if we're compatible. Sixty percent of high school seniors in a recent survey endorsed the practice. But according to the available data, living together before marriage not only does not contribute to marital happiness, it may actually increase the likelihood of eventual divorce.

A 1992 study concluded that "prior cohabitors" had a 46 percent greater hazard of divorce than non-cohabitors.

That's easy to explain, some have said, it's self-selection. People who choose to cohabit are less conventional, less religious and accordingly more likely than other kinds of people to get divorced. That's logical enough. But even when the researchers controlled for the free-spirit factor, a statistically significant gap still remained between those who had lived together before marriage and those who hadn't. (These data do not apply to those couples who move in together during their engagement period or just prior to the wedding.)

It is difficult to pin down exactly how cohabitation contributes to later marital instability. The researchers affiliated with the National Marriage Project speculate that the non-marital living arrangement tends to generate its own dynamic. It may resemble a marriage, but both partners are highly aware that it is far more than the lack of a "piece of paper" that separates them from married couples. Each member of the pair places greater value on his own autonomy than on the durability of the relationship.

Such habits of mind appear to become ingrained over time. People who experience serial cohabitations before marriage have much higher divorce rates than those who lived with only one person. Having lived through the dissolution of one or many relationships increases one's tolerance for heartbreak and instability, and perhaps hardens people in their idiosyncrasies. Rather than proving a test run for marriage, living together instead can prove a test run for eventual loneliness.

My own guess is that cohabitation leeches a good deal of the romance out of marriage. The breathless excitement a young married couple feels about setting up house together and sleeping in the same bed is one of the great joys of life. Looking back on it later cements the sense that marriage is something sacred and precious. But if the male/female living arrangement becomes a matter of convenience rather than commitment, if crossing a threshold is not accompanied by thrown rice and silver gift packages, it does become more hollow and more brittle.

Unsurprisingly, the National Marriage Project data show that cohabitation is most harmful for children. In 1997, 36 percent of these households included children, up from only 21 percent 10 years before. There are estimates that half of America's children will spend some time in a cohabiting household before the age of 16, and three-quarters of these children will see their parents split up. (Only one-third of children born to married couples will endure a divorce.)

The high split rate among cohabitors means that the children are nearly certain to live with a non-biological parent (mom's boyfriend) for some time. The rates of child abuse in such settings are far higher than in married-couple families. A British study found that children living with mom and her boyfriend were 33 times more likely to be abused physically and sexually than children living with both biological parents.

As with so many of the cultural changes of the past three decades, the trend toward cohabitation—even leaving morality to one side—turns out to be unsatisfying for adults and terrible for children.

10

SCIENTISTS KEEP CROSSING THE LINE ON CLONING

Linda Chavez

It barely made news last week, but a hundred years from now, the big story out of 2001 may not be the attack on America or the war in Afghanistan but what happened in a petri dish in Worcester, Mass. For a few hours, three human embryos that had been created from single human cells taken from an adult man and infused into human eggs survived.

The cloning of human beings has begun.

Although the scientists who conducted this experiment claim their intention was not to create a human life but to create human embryonic stem cells, which could then be used for therapeutic purposes, the distinction will become meaningless. Does anyone doubt that others will follow in their footsteps and implant some future laboratory-cloned human embryos into a human womb? And there is nothing to stop them from doing so—the process is perfectly legal, at least for now.

Although the House of Representatives passed a ban on human cloning in August, the Senate never acted. Several senators have now called the human cloning experiment troubling, including Sen. Patrick Leahy (D-Vt.), chairman of the Judiciary Committee. But it remains to be seen whether they will act to try to stop further experiments. It is already illegal to use federal funds to clone human embryos. But will Congress take the next step and ban the procedure altogether?

The scientists at Advanced Cell Technology who created the Worcester clones say that they want to grow a human embryo only to the point when stem cells can be extracted—which requires an embryo of at least a few hundred cells. This is supposed to given us moral reassurance. After all, these folks aren't trying to create some *Brave New World* of human baby factories or some real-life imitation of *The Boys From Brazil,* a 1978 film about a Nazi scientist who cloned dozens of young Adolf Hitlers.

Maybe not. But they are talking about creating human life in order to harvest body parts—and then destroying it. And the moral justification they use is that greater good would come from their experiments than whatever harm they might cause—a kind of utilitarian ethics.

At the moment, scientists don't know whether stem cells taken from human embryos will help cure devastating diseases such as Parkinson's or help those who have been paralyzed from spinal cord injuries. Whatever stem cells scientists harvest now will be used solely for experiments—which might or might not lead to such medical advances.

But for the sake of argument, let's assume research produces the ability to use human embryos for this purpose. Are we willing to sacrifice one life in order to save or improve perhaps hundreds of others? If that is our criteria, why stop at using only stem cells harvested for that purpose?

Why not allow cloned embryos to develop until their organs can be harvested for transplant? If a cloned fetus could save or improve the lives of, say, a dozen others, why not sacrifice its heart, lungs, kidneys, liver, corneas, bone marrow and whatever else we can use?

And who should make the choice? The cell or egg donor? The *10* Worcester scientists used cow eggs for some of their early human embryo experiments—would that make it easier to use the body parts we needed without seeking permission?

If we're willing to use cloned human embryos to save lives, why shouldn't we consider sacrificing other human beings whose lives may be about to end anyway or who live in a permanent vegetative state? Should we be able to shave off a few hours or days from a terminally ill patient's life in order to save someone else's? China reportedly harvests organs from prisoners on death row. Should we?

Once we start down the road to creating life for utilitarian purposes, there is no bright line that separates the permissible from the unthinkable.

GOVERNMENT IS THE PROBLEM

Walter E. Williams

Which is more important, eyeglasses, books or schools? It's hard to tell. If you need eyeglasses, and don't have them, what good are books and schools? Eyeglasses and books are important for education, and we're doing well without much government control, doing so well that it never crossed your mind. Schools are completely controlled by government, and we have all sorts of customer dissatisfaction. Could there be a relationship between the level of government involvement and customer satisfaction?

Which is more important—marriage or work? Did you say marriage? If that's so, how come we have anti-discriminatory and equal-opportunity laws when it comes to work but not when it comes to marriage? Take me. Thirty-two years ago, when interviewing prospective spouses, I engaged in open discrimination. No interviews were offered to Oriental, Hispanic or white women, and men of any race. Moreover, there was no consideration of women given to intemperate drinking habits, foul language and criminal behavior. I'm sure my interview procedure violated all Equal Employment Opportunity Commission (EEOC) regulations for negotiating contracts, not to mention the Americans with Disabilities Act. Probably most men and women engage in similar grossly discriminatory behavior. But no sweat. Anybody who wants to be married tends to get married, even those that many consider undesirable. How is this happy outcome possible without government regulation?

How about language? Language is mankind's most important tool. Who discovered language? Who governs its use, deciding which words become part of the language and which get discarded from ordinary use? Nobody. Our language just evolved over time, adjusting itself to human uses, conditions and tastes; there were no government rules and dictates. Unlike the arrogant French, we anglicize anybody's word and make it a part of our vocabulary. That's one of the reasons why English is the world's most efficient language (efficiency measured as the number of bits of information conveyed per character).

All of these are examples of Williams' law: On balance, the less government is involved in something, the fewer the problems, the greater the level of satisfaction and the cheaper the cost.

Imagine that the decision of what kind of eyeglasses and books were   5
to be produced, and delivered to whom at what time, was determined by Congress or state legislators. The resultant cruelty is unthinkable. Those who wanted paperback books would be in political conflict with those who wanted hardback. Similarly, those who wanted plastic lenses would be fighting those who wanted glass. It would resemble the fights between those who want prayers, the teaching of creationism and no sex education in school, and those who take the opposite view. Government allocation of resources always enhances the potential for human conflict.

Government control, such as the attempt to establish an official language, frequently leads to conflict, including wars and civil unrest, as we've seen in Quebec, Belgium, South Africa, Nigeria and other places. As our government creates bilingual legislation, we are seeing language become a focal point for conflict such as the ugly, racist-tainted "English Only" political campaigns in several states. The best state of affairs is to have no language laws at all.

Finally, there's the animal rights people. I'm wondering how they got the right to speak for animals and protect them from cruelty: Did the animals vote them in? Who's to say that animals don't like cruelty anyway? After all, cruelty seems to be a way of life among animals. When's the last time you saw cats and rats, lions and zebras, or birds and worms respect each other's rights? Only humans don't treat animals like animals.

III   *Understanding Visual Arguments*

INTRODUCTION

We have been examining arguments expressed verbally, but visual images also make arguments designed to influence feeling and action. Everyone knows what it is like to be moved by a picture—to excitement, to amusement, to annoyance, or to a sense of conviction and resolve. However, most people are no more used to talking about that kind of experience than they are about the ways arguments in words work as appeals to logic, character, and emotion. At this point you have mastered to some degree a vocabulary of analysis to bring to your experiences of verbal arguments and have had some practice in understanding how their claims are made.

Yet what good is this vocabulary for dealing with pictures? Aren't words and pictures incompatible, or at least at odds? How can an analysis of essays that use words and sentences be helpful in dealing with images that use lines and shapes? Isn't it proverbially true that a picture is worth a thousand words? The short answer is, try saying *that* in a picture! The fact is that images make a form of human expression just as words do, and there is no reason to expect that human beings are incapable of communicating about any of their means of communication.

Let's take an example—the cover of this book. You see a balance with an apple on one end and an orange on the other. The images arrest the attention, a fact to which thousands of readers of three previous editions can attest. Why do the images catch the eye? How do they express arguments graphically, and how might those arguments be analyzed?

One thing that makes the design striking is its placement of two proverbial images in opposition to one another. The first such image is that of the balance, a traditional symbol for the process of objective human reasoning. It is an outward and visible sign for an inward and mental activity particularly associated with human justice, because it is especially true that in matters of justice, arguments and evidence must be fairly and

impartially "weighed." The juxtaposed fruits represent another proverbial truth: "You can't compare apples and oranges." The reasoning behind this proverb is based on the fact that of two things, one is not necessarily right and the other wrong, nor need one be superior and the
other inferior, one good and one bad. Rather, the two things may have
different qualities, so that each of them may be good in its own way. The
proverb often comes up, of course, when someone tries to point out that
a disagreement may be the result of an argument at cross-purposes.

So on the cover we apparently see a balance, which is proverbially
used to compare things justly, being employed for things that proverbially cannot be justly compared! It is in part this paradox that arrests the
attention, especially in the context created by the words of the book's title.
But the visual paradox simultaneously expresses its own solution: Different things *can* be compared if one can find the proper means of comparing them—in this case, weight. Both apples and oranges have weight,
and so analyzing them from this point of view does not do an injustice
to their proper particularities.

There is much more to be said about the images, but it ought to be
clear already that to talk in this way is to talk about the logic implicit in
visual images. It also should be clear that such logic could be expressed in
Toulmin's terms (though of course it needn't be): The *data* involved are
the two things to be weighed, one *claim* of the balance is to impartiality,
the claim's *warrant* is the law of gravity with *backing* from one's experience of simple mechanics, and so on. The emotional appeals and the appeals to character involved in the expression of short arguments by visual
means may also be analyzed in similar ways using Toulmin's vocabulary.
In this part of the book we will ask you to make such analyses.

The first section involves editorial cartoons, which use the most obviously argumentative of visual images. The next section, on advertising,
is also obviously associated with attempts at persuasion. The last section,
on humorous cartoons, may seem to contain less obvious examples of
visual argument, but you will quickly come to see that such visual jokes
have a logic of their own along with appeals to character and emotion.

Each section first provides some analysis of an example and then asks
you to do some visual analysis of your own on an image in the text. Finally,
you will be asked to find an example for analysis from outside the book.
In an environment saturated with images from editorials, advertising,
and entertainment, examples are easy to find and any problems you have
will be in selecting an example from all the interesting possibilities.

EDITORIAL CARTOONS

Editorial cartoons have been a feature of newspapers since at least
the nineteenth century and have ancestors in graphic political satire that
go back even further. As a combination of the verbal and the visual fo-

cused on a controversial topic, they provide a means of transition from the purely verbal topical arguments you have been examining.

The values and assumptions of a veteran editorial cartoonist are summarized in the following short argument by Drew Sheneman of the Newark, NJ, *Star-Ledger* and are illustrated through drawings by Sheneman and colleagues from other newspapers.

Sheneman made his claims during a crucial and testing time for his profession. He wrote only one month after the attacks on New York City of September 11, 2001, and the extraordinary facts of that historical moment provided a test case for the principles of editorial cartooning that he announces as his own and that he claims his colleagues share. Notice how in the course of his essay he touches on the relations among opinion, emotion, and character as they are expressed through both verbal and visual means.

CARTOONING ISN'T FUNNY BUSINESS
Times like These Call for Something More Than a Comic Touch

Drew Sheneman

I've had the following conversation no less than six times in the last three weeks. It varies occasionally in structure, but usually it's some variation of the following.

"Wow, your job must be really hard right now with all that's going on. How do you go in every day and try to be funny?" Then I explain how I've had so much to say in the last three weeks that I can't draw every idea. And as far as trying to be funny, I haven't done that yet.

Cartoonists around the country have had a difficult time with the World Trade Center tragedy, but the problem is saying everything you want and saying it at the right time.

A good editorial cartoon is not a daily gag. Editorial cartooning has a unique ancestry all its own that predates our relatives on the comics pages. To the trained viewer, the relationship between a comic strip and an editorial cartoon is like the link between birds and dinosaurs. Some of the basic physiology is the same, but they're two different animals.

An editorial cartoon is essentially an illustrated opinion column.   5
It trades the luxury of words for the impact of pictures. While many

cartoonists, myself included, choose to work with humor, it is only a means to convey a point. In a good editorial cartoon, humor is a tool and not an obligation.

Editorial cartoonists are usually perceived, I'll admit, as the class clowns of newspapers, but the job isn't that one-dimensional. We try to give credit where it's due and deflate an oversized ego when necessary.

Past criticism of Mayor Rudolph Giuliani doesn't change the overwhelming sense of gratitude for the job he's done. And the drawings have reflected that. Giuliani has received a cartoon makeover. Gone are the images of him slugging it out with his wife on the Jumbotron in Times Square. Now he's drawn receiving a warm embrace of thanks from the Statue of Liberty. Both images are well-suited and well-deserved at that moment.

That begs the question of what is appropriate and when.

The cartoons in the days following the attack expressed the only thing they could: sorrow and disbelief. As time went on and the country digested what had happened, the commentary changed. The next logical step was anger at the terrorists. Then pride, and gratitude watching the rescue workers. You can read the time line of the tragedy through the cartoons. As the story progressed, the cartoons progressed with it. Each one felt right at the time it was drawn.

Different topics within the same story demand different approaches.   10
There is a surprising amount of room for humor and sarcasm when talking about certain aspects of the tragedy. It's okay to take potshots at the Taliban. It's perfectly acceptable to show frustration at the state of airport security. It's your right as an American to be baffled by the failure of the Central Intelligence Agency and U.S. intelligence organizations. And it's always open season on bigotry.

The nation's editorial cartoonists have been drawing cartoons about the attack for three straight weeks now. It's hard to draw heartbreaking images of firefighters searching through rubble. I wish they could go back to drawing trenchant observations about computer viruses and ATM fees. But this tragedy isn't something that is ever going to go away. We can't impeach it or vote it out of office. It is now part of our lives. As such, the country's cartoonists and commentators will have something to say about it every step of the way. In this space is some of what they've said so far.

––––––––––

Sheneman argues that an editorial cartoon is "essentially an illustrated opinion column," and that although there is plenty of "room for humor and sarcasm," many different things can be expressed through the medium. He refers to an example showing Mayor Giuliani and the Statue of Liberty. Let's begin with that drawing and take notes on some of its aspects arranged in the form we have been following all along.

NOTES

Though many more things might be added to each category, perhaps we can agree at least on the following points:

Data: Smoke comes from the left of the picture; the statue embraces the mayor.

The Twin Towers were near the southern tip of Manhattan and the Statue of Liberty still farther south in New York Harbor, so we see the scene from the point of view of the rest of the United States looking eastward toward the Atlantic Ocean and New York City. Symbolically the smoke expresses the ongoing tragedy of destruction and the Statue of Liberty is a symbol of America responding to Giuliani's response.

Claim: America loves Mayor Giuliani for his response to the crisis.

The statue's embrace may be an obvious visual expression of the claim, but the transformation of the famous "I Love New York" button from a local to a national expression also underlines the embrace verbally.

Warrant: You embrace what you love physically, and you announce your love verbally.

The nation makes a tribute to the city by adopting its language and labels, just as the mayor himself did by appearing in a New York Fire Department cap throughout the crisis. Embracing people's words is—like embracing people themselves—a sign of affection and esteem.

Character: The statue shows massive strength, the mayor a modest but cocky and feisty spirit.

Though the two figures are not shown in their true proportions, their relative sizes emphasize the bulk of the statue and the strength of its limbs and hand. The relatively smaller mayor seems because of his size a proud boyish son of America; yet because of other aspects in his appearance (balding, wrinkles, and jowls) he seems a middle-aged man dressed in the formal uniform of social power expressing the capacity for exercising authority. He is being thanked for the mature exercise of power. ***Emotion: The statue shows maternal pride; the mayor's face expresses an "aw-shucks" gratitude combined with a stern, no-nonsense spirit.***

The statue's downward gaze (sad for the city, but fond of the mayor) combines with her embrace to express her emotion, whereas the mayor's scrunched-up face shows his conflicting emotions as a man reacting both to the ongoing effects of the terrorist attacks (witnessed by the smoke) and to the nation's gratitude (the embrace). Try covering first one half of his face and then the other: one side smiles, one frowns—the visual expression of his mixed emotions. He faces west toward most of the rest of the country, acknowledging its thanks and expressing his ongoing determination.

EXERCISES

1. Now it's your turn. The other examples Sheneman used to illustrate his argument are shown here. Choose one and make some notes on how it forms its visual and verbal arguments.
2. Find an editorial cartoon on a topic other than that of the terrorist attacks and their aftermath. Make some notes for a short analysis.

"I MADE A PURCHASE TO HELP STIMULATE THE ECONOMY."

NOW REQUIRING MORE VIGILANCE THAN EVER...

THE CITY THAT NEVER SLEEPS

ADVERTISEMENTS

"Promise, large promise, is the soul of advertisement." Samuel Johnson, a great English author of the eighteenth century, wrote those words over two hundred years ago, yet their argument remains a convincing one today in a culture saturated with advertising beyond even Johnson's imagination. Advertising's style—the ways in which large promises (or claims) about products are made—has changed considerably since those days, and even the hard sell of recent memory has given way to the kind of witty and indirect arguments made by the selections here. Ads nevertheless make claims both explicit and implicit. After studying a preliminary analysis of one example of an advertisement, you will be asked to find an ad of your own choice to analyze and clarify its claims.

People for the Ethical Treatment of Animals (PETA) has run the ad shown as part of its long-standing attack on the use of furs as clothing. PETA's choice here of supermodel Christy Turlington, her naked pose, and the slogan she is purported to announce—these elements and more make up interacting parts of a complicated and attention-getting argument. The overall argument consists of many claims, all supported by one of the most basic warrants of advertising: sex sells. What large promise does the overall argument make? Perhaps something to the effect that you can be beautiful, poised, witty, and fashionable without furs and at the same time ethically, socially (and perhaps politically) correct.

As we did with the editorial cartoons, let's make some notes on the argument's components by sorting them roughly into Toulmin's categories.

NOTES

Data: *A personal statement in words is enacted visually.*

Turlington's words say something to an audience about a choice, and that choice has been visibly made in front of that audience, thus proving her words are not empty ones. The violation of a normal social convention (being seen naked by the public) measures the strength of her conviction.

Claim: *Public nakedness shows more true decency than does wearing furs.*

Having made the choice, her action becomes one of defiance—she has proved she believes in a fundamental decency, one deeper than that defined by shallow social conventions or clothing fashions.

Warrant: *Sincere social protest is willing to risk violating social conventions.*

She has said what she would "rather" do. Acting on one's beliefs and convictions displays a sincerity, whereas conforming to social convention is often associated with hypocrisy, as is false modesty. Public nakedness may be seen by some as indecent and immoral, but wearing furs is seen by her as more indecent and immoral.

Backing: Social conventions can change as fashions do, and both may be changed by leaders of society and leaders of fashion.

Social standards of proper clothing have varied throughout history; moral decency is arguably transcendent and unchangeable. It is therefore more important and valuable than changeable styles. The model, who makes her living by being clothed in those changing styles, shows by her rejection of one clothing style that her moral identity is more important to her than her professional identity or social reputation as a modest woman. Her disrobing is a personal moral choice, not a self-interested or conformist one. In her finding ethical correctness superior to social correctness, Turlington invites comparison with the legendary Lady Godiva, who is said to have made a protest against injustice through nakedness.

Character: The model's body and face display beauty, dignity, and relaxed poise.

Her bold stare at the viewer is accompanied by what is perhaps the beginning of a sneer at (a) those less sophisticated people who find nakedness necessarily salacious, (b) those who would not be as socially daring in the name of what they believe to be right, and (c) those who are shocked more by nakedness than by the suffering of the animals trapped and killed to clothe that nakedness.

Emotion: The model feels calm, surprised at our surprise at her nakedness.

The comfortably crossed legs and hands create a sense of casual, natural ease, while the facial expression challenges those who might be shocked or made uncomfortable (a) were they in her naked presence or (b) were they naked themselves in her place. She displays no embarrassment about the naked human body and invites us to feel that there should be more embarrassment felt in wearing furs.

EXERCISE

Find an ad from your reading, one that you find striking in some way—amusing, off-putting, or puzzling, perhaps. Make some notes on an analysis of how the ad's verbal and visible parts act together to create the reactions you experience. Remember that, as with verbal arguments, the parts of a visual argument may not necessarily or automatically fall clearly into Toulmin's categories. Those divisions are meant only as aids for analysis—the process of breaking down into their constituent parts the causes of your visual experience. If you do not try to sort out the differences between, say, rational and emotional appeals, the danger is that you will fall back on a few general remarks to account for what is in fact a highly complex process. The idea is to try to do justice to that process in your own words, with the categories serving as an aid to organizing your insights.

HUMOROUS CARTOONS

One traditional definition for and defense of art is that it delights and instructs. Although comic cartoons are obviously more intended for delight than their editorial cousins, they may also be seen to make arguments. In fact, the wit and humor of comic cartoons are often created by the visual expression of competing or conflicting arguments, such as those expressed by the cover of your textbook and analyzed earlier. Let's look at another visual drama.

Something similar to the conflict within the cover art happens in the case of the Viking cartoon. The Viking should be familiar. Just as a lone palm tree and a tiny island provide an often-used cartoon symbol of isolation, the Viking, complete with traditional (at least in cartoons) horned helmet, crude sword, and spear, makes a long-standing symbol of primitive warrior fury. In fact, the word *berserk* was first used by their dismayed opponents to describe the Vikings' style of warfare.

The winners' stand, the altar on which athletic victory is worshiped, is another well-known symbol. Yet here the silver- and bronze-medal winners, the second- and third-place finishers, are conspicuous by their absence, and that of course is the basis of the joke, grisly though it may be.

In *Death in the Afternoon,* a book on bullfighting, Ernest Hemingway explained why in his view the Spanish custom was not exportable:

I am afraid, however, due to the danger of death it involves it would never have much success among the amateur sportsmen of America and

England who play games. We, in games, are not fascinated by death, its nearness and avoidance. We are fascinated by victory and we replace the avoidance of death by the avoidance of defeat.

Whether or not Hemingway's analysis strikes you as definitive, surely its distinctions are helpful in sorting out the basis of the cartoon, with its conflicting definitions of *competition* visually expressed. Let's make some notes about the contrasting values and assumptions on which those definitions are based.

NOTES

Data: The Viking is in the #1, or victor's, position on the stand. His well-used sword drips blood; his spear is much hacked.

The weapons and armor are startlingly out of place in the athletic setting, but the Viking looks unruffled, as if he thinks he belongs just where he is. The blood implies other, negative, data: The other competitors are not present because they have been killed!

Claim: True competition is a fight to the death and leaves no runners-up.

Unlike Hemingway, the Viking does not distinguish between avoidance of death and avoidance of defeat. To him every challenge is a challenge to battle. Finding himself in a modern context (the sports stadium and the events are implied by the stand), he competes in the only way he knows. Of course, his opponents were unarmed, but the more fools they!

Warrant: Battle is the most extreme struggle among men.

Another intruder, a figure with, say, a fishing pole, landing net, and wading boots in the #1 position would not be as funny, though fishing and other competitive ventures might also express the out-of-place idea. Because warfare enacts the most extreme conflict among contestants, it expresses the furthest (and hence the funniest) limit of the out-of-place theme.

Backing: The language of sports contains fossilized remnants of its origins in war: He is a "fierce" competitor with a "take no prisoners" style, and so on.

Sports announcers commonly use the emotional appeals inherent in the vocabulary of warfare to heighten the audience's excitement and to enhance the overall sense of importance of the events they are announcing. Coaches employ "strategy," quarterbacks carry out "aerial attacks," linemen "battle in the trenches." All in all, it's do or die for the old team, so let's cheer them on with fight songs!

Additional Claim: The crude and funny costume shows that the Viking's values and assumptions are out of date—modern competition is more civilized and less crude.

Here is the other side of the conflict between the definitions of competition. There is another way to be amused: The joke is on the Viking for being—like his weapons, dress, and beard—so primitive and crude.

We are flattered to be reminded that we have come a long way since the days of our barbaric ancestors and that our notions, like our competitions and our dress, are much more refined, tolerant of rivals, committed to fair play, and so on. The cartoon surprises because we take for granted our civilized superiority; it is amusing in part because it reminds us of that superiority by depicting a fantasy time-warp.

Character: His outer appearance shows his inner life—primitive, complacent, and aggressive.

The roughness of the clothing and weapons expresses a primitive character, as has been remarked. But the Viking's posture also contributes to our sense of him. He stands at a kind of formal attention, as if ready to accept the cheers of the crowd for his victory. Yet he is not flat-footed but rather is somewhat resilient and on his toes for further action. He seems ready to spring, perhaps at something his beady eyes have spotted in the middle distance over our shoulders—the last contestant! His head is cocked slightly as if he is pleased with his sense of his own character.

Emotion: The cartoonist invites us to feel shocked, amused, and superior.

We are invited to feel two senses of shock, first at the out-of-place historical conflict between primitive Viking and modern sports arena and second at the moral conflict between battle and sports. We are not invited to feel threatened by the Viking's aggressive posture—he is not looking at us—so we may be more easily amused at the conflicts depicted.

EXERCISES

1. Look at the other cartoons in this section (you might also look at the example at the end of the Minicasebook). Pick one and make some notes on an analysis of its argument.
2. Find a comical cartoon from your own reading, and make some notes on the way it works. Use Toulmin's categories by way of an outline.

"You see, Murphy's finger is coming from North Korea or someplace, but my finger comes up and hits Murphy's finger. That's how the Missile Defense system will work—if it works."

IV   Moving to Longer Arguments

Jonathan Swift, "A Modest Proposal"
Elizabeth Cady Stanton, "Address to the National Woman
    Suffrage Convention"
Martin Luther King, Jr., "Letter from Birmingham Jail"

INTRODUCTION

Because many introductory writing courses (and almost all students) eventually move on to the consideration of longer arguments, this
section provides material for that transition. It includes three classic essays by Jonathan Swift, Elizabeth Cady Stanton, and Martin Luther King,
Jr., for your enjoyment and analysis. You should be prepared by now to
analyze these longer works, because all big arguments are made up of
smaller ones. Don't forget to consider all sides of the Rhetorical Triangle—that is, take into account not only the reasoning involved but
also the appeals to character and emotion.

A MODEST PROPOSAL

Jonathan Swift

It is a melancholy object to those who walk through this great town
or travel in the country, when they see the streets, the roads, and cabin

doors, crowded with beggars of the female sex, followed by three, four, or six children, all in rags and importuning every passenger for an alms. These mothers, instead of being able to work for their honest livelihood, are forced to employ all their time in strolling to beg sustenance for their helpless infants, who, as they grow up, either turn thieves for want of work, or leave their dear native country to fight for the Pretender in Spain, or sell themselves to the Barbados.

I think it is agreed by all parties that this prodigious number of children in the arms, or on the backs, or at the heels of their mothers, and frequently of their fathers, is in the present deplorable state of the kingdom a very great additional grievance; and therefore whoever could find out a fair, cheap, and easy method of making these children sound, useful members of the commonwealth would deserve so well of the public as to have his statue set up for a preserver of the nation.

But my intention is very far from being confined to provide only for the children of professed beggars; it is of a much greater extent, and shall take in the whole number of infants at a certain age who are born of parents in effect as little able to support them as those who demand our charity in the streets.

As to my own part, having turned my thoughts for many years upon this important subject, and maturely weighed the several schemes of other projectors, I have always found them grossly mistaken in their computation. It is true, a child just dropped from its dam may be supported by her milk for a solar year, with little other nourishment; at most not above the value of two shillings, which the mother may certainly get, or the value in scraps, by her lawful occupation of begging; and it is exactly at one year old that I propose to provide for them in such a manner as instead of being a charge upon their parents or the parish, or wanting food and raiment for the rest of their lives, they shall on the contrary contribute to the feeding, and partly to the clothing, of many thousands.

There is likewise another great advantage in my scheme, that it will *5* prevent those voluntary abortions, and that horrid practice of women murdering their bastard children, alas, too frequent among us, sacrificing the poor innocent babes, I doubt, more to avoid the expense than the shame, which would move tears and pity in the most savage and inhuman breast.

The number of souls in this kingdom being usually reckoned one million and a half, of these I calculate there may be about two hundred thousand couples whose wives are breeders; from which number I subtract thirty thousand couples who are able to maintain their own children, although I apprehend there cannot be so many under the present distress of the kingdom; but this being granted, there will remain an hundred and seventy thousand breeders. I again subtract fifty thousand for those women who miscarry, or whose children die by accident or disease within the year. There only remain an hundred and twenty thousand children of poor parents annually born. The question therefore is, how this number shall be reared and provided for, which, as I have already said, under the present situation of affairs, is utterly impossible by all the methods hitherto proposed. For we can neither employ them in handicraft nor agriculture; we neither build houses (I mean in the country) nor cultivate land. They can very seldom pick up a livelihood by stealing till they arrive at six years old, except where they are of towardly parts; although I confess they learn the rudiments much earlier, during which time they can however be looked upon only as probationers, as I have been informed by a principal gentleman in the county of Cavan, who protested to me that he never knew above one or two instances under the age of six, even in a part of the kingdom so renowned for the quickest proficiency in that art.

I am assured by our merchants that a boy or a girl before twelve years old is no salable commodity; and even when they come to this age, they will not yield above three pounds, or three pounds and half a crown at most on the Exchange; which cannot turn to account either to the parents or the kingdom, the charge of nutriment and rags having been at least four times that value.

I shall now therefore humbly propose my own thoughts, which I hope will not be liable to the least objection.

I have been assured by a very knowing American of my acquaintance in London, that a young healthy child well nursed is at a year old a most delicious, nourishing, and wholesome food, whether stewed, roasted, baked, or boiled; and I make no doubt that it will equally serve in a fricassee or a ragout.

I do therefore humbly offer it to public consideration that of the hundred and twenty thousand children, already computed, twenty thousand may be reserved for breed, whereof only one fourth part to be males, which is more than we allow to sheep, black cattle, or swine; and my reason is that these children are seldom the fruits of marriage, a circumstance not much regarded by our savages, therefore one male will be sufficient to serve four females. That the remaining hundred thousand may at a year old be offered in sale to the persons of quality and fortune through the kingdom, always advising the mother to let them suck plentifully in the last month, so as to render them plump and fat for a good table. A child will make two dishes at an entertainment for friends; and when the family dines alone, the fore or hind quarter will make a reasonable dish, and seasoned with a little pepper or salt will be very good boiled on the fourth day, especially in winter. 10

I have reckoned upon a medium that a child just born will weigh twelve pounds, and in a solar year if tolerably nursed increaseth to twenty-eight pounds.

I grant this food will be somewhat dear, and therefore very proper for landlords, who, as they have already devoured most of the parents, seem to have the best title to the children.

Infant's flesh will be in season throughout the year, but more plentiful in March, and a little before and after. For we are told by a grave author, an eminent French physician, that fish being a prolific diet, there are more children born in Roman Catholic countries about nine months after Lent, than at any other season; therefore, reckoning a year after Lent, the markets will be more glutted than usual, because the number of popish infants is at least three to one in this kingdom; and therefore it will have one other collateral advantage, by lessening the number of Papists among us.

I have already computed the charge of nursing a beggar's child (in which list I reckon all cottagers, laborers, and four fifths of the farmers) to be about two shillings per annum, rags included; and I believe no gentleman would repine to give ten shillings for the carcass of a good fat child, which, as I have said, will make four dishes of excellent nutritive meat, when he hath only some particular friend or his own family to dine with him. Thus the squire will learn to be a good landlord, and grow popular among the tenants; the mother will have eight shillings net profit, and be fit for work till she produces another child.

Those who are more thrifty (as I must confess the times require) *15* may flay the carcass; the skin of which artificially dressed will make admirable gloves for ladies, and summer boots for fine gentlemen.

As to our city of Dublin, shambles may be appointed for this purpose in the most convenient parts of it, and butchers we may be assured will not be wanting; although I rather recommend buying the children alive, and dressing them hot from the knife as we do roasting pigs.

A very worthy person, a true lover of his country, and whose virtues I highly esteem, was lately pleased in discoursing on this matter to offer a refinement upon my scheme. He said that many gentlemen of his kingdom, having of late destroyed their deer, he conceived that the want of venison might be well supplied by the bodies of young lads and maidens, not exceeding fourteen years of age nor under twelve, so great a number of both sexes in every country being now ready to starve for want of work and service; and these to be disposed of by their parents, if alive, or otherwise by their nearest relations. But with due deference to so excellent a friend and so deserving a patriot, I cannot be altogether in his sentiments; for as to the males, my American acquaintance assured me from frequent experience that their flesh was generally tough and lean, like that of our schoolboys, by continual exercise, and their taste disagreeable; and to fatten them would not answer the charge. Then as to the females, it would, I think with humble submission, be a loss to the public, because they soon would become breeders themselves; and besides, it is not improbable that some scrupulous people might be apt to censure such a practice (although indeed very unjustly) as a little bordering upon cruelty; which, I confess, hath always been with me the strongest objection against any project, how well soever intended.

But in order to justify my friend, he confessed that this expedient was put into his head by the famous Psalmanazar, a native of the island Formosa, who came from thence to London above twenty years ago, and in conversation told my friend that in his country when any young person happened to be put to death, the executioner sold the carcass to the persons of quality as a prime dainty; and that in his time the body of a plump girl of fifteen, who was crucified for an attempt to poison the emperor, was sold to his Imperial Majesty's prime minister of state, and other great mandarins of the court, in joints from the gibbet, at four hundred crowns. Neither indeed can I deny that if the same use were made of several plump young girls in this town, who without one single groat to their fortunes cannot stir abroad without a chair, and appear at the playhouse and assemblies in foreign fineries which they never will play for, the kingdom would not be the worse.

Some persons of a desponding spirit are in great concern about that vast number of poor people who are aged, diseased, or maimed, and I have been desired to employ my thoughts what course may be taken to ease the nation of so grievous an encumbrance. But I am not in the least pain upon that matter, because it is very well known that they are every day dying and rotting by cold and famine, and filth and vermin, as fast as can be reasonably expected. And as to the younger laborers, they are now in almost as hopeful a condition. They cannot get work, and consequently pine away for want of nourishment to a degree that if any time they are accidentally hired to common labor, they have not strength to perform it; and thus the country and themselves are happily delivered from the evils to come.

I have too long digressed, and therefore shall return to my subject. 20 I think the advantages by the proposal which I have made are obvious and many, as well as of the highest importance.

For first, as I have already observed, it would greatly lessen the number of Papists, with whom we are yearly overrun, being the principal breeders of the nation as well as our most dangerous enemies; and who stay at home on purpose to deliver the kingdom to the Pretender, hoping to take their advantage by the absence of so many good Protestants, who have chosen rather to leave their country than to stay at home and pay tithes against their conscience to an Episcopal curate.

Secondly, the poorer tenants will have something valuable of their own, which by law may be made liable to distress, and help to pay their landlord's rent, their corn and cattle being already seized and money a thing unknown.

Thirdly, whereas the maintenance of an hundred thousand children, from two years old and upwards, cannot be computed at less than ten shillings a piece per annum, the nation's stock will be thereby increased fifty thousand pounds per annum, besides the profit of a new dish introduced to the tables of all gentlemen of fortune in the kingdom who have any refinement in taste. And the money will circulate among ourselves, the goods being entirely of our own growth and manufacture.

Fourthly, the constant breeders, besides the gain of eight shillings sterling per annum by the sale of their children, will be rid of the charge for maintaining them after the first year.

Fifthly, this food would likewise bring great custom to taverns, ²⁵ where the vintners will certainly be so prudent as to procure the best receipts for dressing it to perfection, and consequently have their houses frequented by all the fine gentlemen, who justly value themselves upon their knowledge in good eating; and a skillful cook, who understands how to oblige his guests, will contrive to make it as expensive as they please.

Sixthly, this would be a great inducement to marriage, which all wise nations have either encouraged by rewards or enforced by laws and penalties. It would increase the care and tenderness of mothers toward their children,when they were sure of a settlement for life to the poor babes, provided in some sort by the public, to their annual profit instead of expense. We should see an honest emulation among the married women, which of them could bring the fattest child to the market. Men would become as fond of their wives during the time of their pregnancy as they are now of their mares in foal, their cows in calf, or sows when they are ready to farrow; nor offer to beat or kick them (as is too frequent a practice) for fear of a miscarriage.

Many other advantages might be enumerated. For instance, the addition of some thousand carcasses in our exportation of barreled beef, the propagation of swine's flesh, and improvements in the art of making good bacon, so much wanted among us by the great destruction of pigs, too frequent at our tables, which are no way comparable in taste or magnificence to a well-grown, fat, yearling child, which roasted whole will make a considerable figure at a lord mayor's feast or any other public entertainment. But this and many others I omit, being studious of brevity.

Supposing that one thousand families in this city would be constant customers for infants' flesh, besides others who might have it at merry meetings, particularly weddings and christenings, I compute that Dublin would take off annually about twenty thousand carcasses, and the rest of the kingdom (where probably they will be sold somewhat cheaper) the remaining eighty thousand.

I can think of no one objection that will possibly be raised against this proposal, unless it should be urged that the number of people will be thereby much lessened in the kingdom. This I freely own, and it was indeed one principal design in offering it to the world. I desire the reader will observe, that I calculate my remedy for this one individual kingdom of Ireland and for no other that ever was, is, or I think ever can be upon earth. Therefore, let no man talk to me of other expedients: of taxing our absentees at five shillings a pound: of using neither clothes nor household furniture except what is of our own growth and manufacture: of utterly rejecting the materials and instruments that promote foreign luxury: of curing the expensiveness of pride, vanity, idleness, and gaming in our women: of introducing a vein of parsimony, prudence, and temperance: of learning to love our country, in the want of which we differ even from Laplanders and the inhabitants of Topinamboo: of quitting our animosities and factions, nor acting any longer like the Jews, who were murdering one another at the very moment their city was taken: of being a little cautious not to sell our country and conscience for nothing: of teaching landlords to have at least one degree of mercy toward their tenants: lastly, of putting a spirit of honesty, industry, and skill into our shopkeepers; who, if a resolution could now be taken to buy only our native goods, would immediately unite to cheat and exact upon us in the price, the measure, and the goodness, nor could ever yet be brought to make one fair proposal of just dealing, though often and earnestly invited to it.

Therefore, I repeat, let no man talk to me of these and the like expedients, till he hath at least some glimpse of hope that there will ever be some hearty and sincere attempt to put them in practice.   *30*

But as to myself, having been wearied out for many years with offering vain, idle, visionary thoughts, and at length utterly despairing of success, I fortunately fell upon this proposal, which, as it is wholly new, so it hath something solid and real, of no expense and little trouble, full in our own power, and whereby we can incur no danger in disobliging England. For this kind of commodity will not bear exportation, the flesh being of too tender a consistence to admit a long continuance in salt, although perhaps I could name a country which would be glad to eat up our whole nation without it.

After all, I am not so violently bent upon my own opinion as to reject any offer proposed by wise men, which shall be found equally innocent, cheap, easy, and effectual. But before something of that kind shall be advanced in contradiction to my scheme, and offering a better, I desire the author or authors will be pleased maturely to consider two points. First, as things now stand, how they will be able to find food and raiment for an hundred thousand useless mouths and backs. And secondly, there being a round million of creatures in human figure throughout this kingdom, whose sole subsistence put into a common stock would leave them in debt two millions of pounds sterling, adding those who are beggars by profession to the bulk of farmers, cottagers, and laborers, with their wives and children who are beggars in effect; I desire those politicians who dislike my overture, and may perhaps be so bold to attempt an answer, that they will first ask the parents of these mortals whether they would not at this day think it a great happiness to have been sold for food at a year old in this manner I prescribe, and thereby have avoided such a perpetual scene of misfortunes as they have since gone through by the oppression of landlords, the impossibility of paying rent without money or trade, the want of common sustenance, with neither house nor clothes to cover them from the inclemencies of the weather, and the most inevitable prospect of entailing the like or greater miseries upon their breed forever.

I profess, in the sincerity of my heart, that I have not the least personal interest in endeavoring to promote this necessary work, having no other motive than the public good of my country, by advancing our trade, providing for infants, relieving the poor, and giving some pleasure to the rich. I have no children by which I can propose to get a single penny; the youngest being nine years old, and my wife past childbearing.

ADDRESS TO THE NATIONAL WOMAN SUFFRAGE CONVENTION

Elizabeth Cady Stanton

A great idea of progress is near its consummation, when statesmen in the councils of the nation propose to frame it into statutes and constitutions; when Reverend Fathers recognize it by a new interpretation of their creeds and canons; when the Bar and Bench at its command set aside the legislation of centuries, and girls of twenty put their heels on the Cokes and Blackstones of the past.

Those who represent what is called "the Woman's Rights Movement," have argued their right to political equality from every standpoint of justice, religion, and logic, for the last twenty years. They have quoted the Constitution, the Declaration of Independence, the Bible, the opinions of great men and women in all ages; they have plead the theory of our government; suffrage a natural, inalienable right; shown from the lessons of history, that one class can not legislate for another; the disfranchised classes must ever be neglected and degraded; and that all privileges are but mockery to the citizen, until he has a voice in the making and administering of law. Such arguments have been made over and over in conventions and before the legislatures of the several States. Judges, lawyers, priests, and politicians have said again and again, that our logic was unanswerable, and although much nonsense has emanated from the male tongue and pen on this subject, no man has yet made a fair, argument on the other side. Knowing that we hold the Gibraltar rock of reason on this question, they resort to ridicule and petty objections. Compelled to follow our assailants, wherever they go, and fight them with their own weapons; when cornered with wit and sarcasm, some cry out, you have no logic on your platform, forgetting that we have no use for logic until they give us logicians at whom to hurl it, and if, for the pure love of it, we now and then rehearse the logic that is like a, b, c, to all of us, others cry out—the same old speeches we have heard these twenty years. It would be safe to say a hundred years, for they are the same our fathers used when battling old King George and the British Parliament for their right to representation, and a voice in the laws by which they were governed. There are no new arguments to be made on human rights, our work today is to apply to ourselves those so familiar to all; to teach man that woman is not an anomalous being, outside all laws and constitutions, but one whose rights are to be established by the same process of reason as that by which he demands his own.

When our Fathers made out their famous bill of impeachment against England, they specified eighteen grievances. When the women of this country surveyed the situation in their first convention, they found they had precisely that number, and quite similar in character; and reading over the old revolutionary arguments of Jefferson, Patrick Henry, Otis, and Adams, they found they applied remarkably well to their case. The same arguments made in this country for extending suffrage from time to time, to white men, native born citizens, without property and education, and to foreigners; the same used by John Bright in England, to extend it to a million new voters, and the same used by the great Republican party to enfranchise a million black men in the South, all these arguments we have to-day to offer for woman, and one, in addition, stronger than all besides, the difference in man and woman. Because man and woman are the complement of one another, we need woman's thought in national affairs to make a safe and stable government.

The Republican party to-day congratulates itself on having carried the Fifteenth Amendment of the Constitution, thus securing "manhood suffrage" and establishing an aristocracy of sex on this continent. As several bills to secure Woman's Suffrage in the District and the Territories have been already presented in both houses of Congress, and as by Mr. Julian's bill, the question of so amending the Constitution as to extend suffrage to all the women of the country has been presented to the nation for consideration, it is not only the right but the duty of every thoughtful woman to express her opinion on a Sixteenth Amendment. While I hail the late discussions in Congress and the various bills presented as so many signs of progress, I am especially gratified with those of Messrs. Julian and Pomeroy, which forbid any State to deny the right of suffrage to any of its citizens on account of sex or color.

This fundamental principle of our government—the equality of all 5 the citizens of the republic—should be incorporated in the Federal Constitution, there to remain forever. To leave this question to the States and partial acts of Congress, is to defer indefinitely its settlement, for what is done by this Congress may be repealed by the next; and politics in the several States differ so widely, that no harmonious action on any question can ever be secured, except as a strict party measure. Hence, we appeal to the party now in power, everywhere, to end this protracted debate on suffrage, and declare it the inalienable right of every citizen who is amenable to the laws of the land, who pays taxes and the penalty of crime. We have a splendid theory of a genuine republic, why not realize it and make our government homogeneous, from Maine to California. The Republican party has the power to do this, and now is its only opportunity. Woman's Suffrage, in 1872, may be as good a card for the Republicans as Gen. Grant was in the last election. It is said that the Republican party made him President, not because they thought him the most desirable man in the nation for that office, but they were afraid the Democrats would take him if they did not. We would suggest, there may be the same danger of Democrats taking up Woman Suffrage if they do not. God, in his providence, may have purified that party in the furnace of affliction. They have had the opportunity, safe from the turmoil of political life and the temptations of office, to study and apply the divine principles of justice and equality to life; for minorities are always in a position to carry principles to their logical results, while majorities are governed only by votes. You see my faith in Democrats is based on sound philosophy. In the next Congress, the Democratic party will gain thirty-four new members, hence the Republicans have had their last chance to do justice to woman. It will be no enviable record for the Fortieth Congress that in the darkest days of the republic it placed our free institutions in the care and keeping of every type of manhood, ignoring womanhood, all the elevating and purifying influences of the most virtuous and humane half of the American people. . . .

I urge a speedy adoption of a Sixteenth Amendment for the following reasons:

1. A government, based on the principle of caste and class, can not stand. The aristocratic idea, in any form, is opposed to the genius of our free institutions, to our own declaration of rights, and to the civilization of the age. All artificial distinctions, whether of family, blood, wealth, color, or sex, are equally oppressive to the subject classes, and equally destructive to national life and prosperity. Governments based on every form of aristocracy, on every degree and variety of inequality, have been tried in despotisms, monarchies, and republics, and all alike have perished. In the panorama of the past behold the mighty nations that have risen, one by one, but to fall. Behold their temples, thrones, and pyramids, their gorgeous palaces and stately monuments now crumbled all to dust. Behold every monarch in Europe at this very hour trembling on his throne. Behold the republics on this Western continent convulsed, distracted, divided, the hosts scattered, the leaders fallen, the scouts lost in the wilderness, the once inspired prophets blind and dumb, while on all sides the cry is echoed, "Republicanism is a failure," though that great principle of a government "by the people, of the people, for the people," has never been tried. Thus far, all nations have been built on caste and failed. Why, in this hour of reconstruction, with the experience of generations before us, make another experiment in the same direction? If serfdom, peasantry, and slavery have shattered kingdoms, deluged continents with blood, scattered republics like dust before the wind, and rent our own Union asunder, what kind of a government, think you, American statesmen, you can build, with the mothers of the race crouching at your feet, while iron-heeled peasants, serfs, and slaves, exalted by your hands, tread our inalienable rights into the dust? While all men, everywhere, are rejoicing in new-found liberties, shall woman alone be de-

nied the rights, privileges, and immunities of citizenship? While in England men are coming up from the coal mines of Cornwall, from the factories of Birmingham and Manchester, demanding the suffrage; while in frigid Russia the 22,000,000 newly-emancipated serfs are already claiming a voice in the government; while here, in our own land, slaves, but just rejoicing in the proclamation of emancipation, ignorant alike of its power and significance, have the ballot unasked, unsought, already laid at their feet—think you the daughters of Adams, Jefferson, and Patrick Henry, in whose veins flows the blood of two Revolutions, will forever linger round the campfires of an old barbarism, with no longings to join this grand army of freedom in its onward march to roll back the golden gates of a higher and better civilization? Of all kinds of aristocracy, that of sex is the most odious and unnatural; invading, as it does, our homes, desecrating our family altars, dividing those whom God has joined together, exalting the son above the mother who bore him, and subjugating, everywhere, moral power to brute force. Such a government would not be worth the blood and treasure so freely poured out in its long struggles for freedom. . . .

2. I urge a Sixteenth Amendment, because "manhood suffrage" or a man's government, is civil, religious, and social disorganization. The male element is a destructive force, stern, selfish, aggrandizing, loving war, violence, conquest, acquisition, breeding in the material and moral world alike discord, disorder, disease, and death. See what a record of blood and cruelty the pages of history reveal! Through what slavery, slaughter, and sacrifice, through what inquisitions and imprisonments, pains and persecutions, black codes and gloomy creeds, the soul of humanity has struggled for the centuries, while mercy has veiled her face and all hearts have been dead alike to love and hope! The male element has held high carnival thus far, it has fairly run riot from the beginning, overpowering the feminine element everywhere, crushing out all the diviner qualities in human nature, until we know but little of true manhood and womanhood, of the latter comparatively nothing, for it has scarce been recognized as a power until within the last century. Society is but the reflection of man himself, untempered by woman's thought, the hard iron rule we feel alike in the church, the state, and the home. No one need wonder at the disorganization, at the fragmentary condition of everything, when we remember that man, who represents but half a complete being, with but half an idea on every subject, has undertaken the absolute control of all sublunary matters.

People object to the demands of those whom they choose to call the strong-minded, because they say, "the right of suffrage will make the women masculine." That is just the difficulty in which we are involved to-day. Though disfranchised we have few women in the best sense, we have simply so many reflections, varieties, and dilutions of the masculine gender. The strong, natural characteristics of womanhood are repressed and ignored in dependence, for so long as man feeds woman she will try to please the giver and adapt herself to his condition. To keep a foothold in society woman must be as near like man as possible, reflect his ideas, opinions, virtues, motives, prejudices, and vices. She must respect his statutes, though they strip her of every inalienable right, and conflict with that higher law written by the finger of God on her own soul. She must believe his theology, though it pave the highways of hell with the skulls of new-born infants, and make God a monster of vengeance and hypocrisy. She must look at everything from its dollar and cent point of view, or she is a mere romancer. She must accept things as they are and make the best of them. To mourn over the miseries of others, the poverty of the poor, their hardships in jails, prisons, asylums, the horrors of war, cruelty, and brutality in every form, all this would be mere sentimentalizing. To protest against the intrigue, bribery, and corruption of public life, to desire that her sons might follow some business that did not involve lying, cheating, and a hard, grinding selfishness, would be arrant nonsense. In this way man has been moulding woman to his ideas by direct and positive influences, while she, if not a negation, has used indirect means to control him, and in most cases developed the very characteristics both in him and herself that needed repression. And now man himself stands appalled at the results of his own excesses, and mourns in bitterness that falsehood, selfishness and violence are the law of life. The need of this hour is not territory, gold mines, railroads, or specie payments, but a new evangel of womanhood, to exalt purity, virtue, morality, true religion, to lift man up into the higher realms of thought and action.

We ask woman's enfranchisement, as the first step toward the recognition of that essential element in government that can only secure the health, strength, and prosperity of the nation. Whatever is done to lift woman to her true position will help to usher in a new day of peace and perfection for the race. In speaking of the masculine element, I do not wish to be understood to say that all men are hard, selfish, and brutal, for many of the most beautiful spirits the world has known have been clothed with manhood; but I refer to those characteristics, though often marked in woman, that distinguish what is called the stronger sex. For example, the love of acquisition and conquest, the very pioneers of civilization, when expended on the earth, the sea, the elements, the riches and forces of Nature, are powers of destruction when used to subjugate one man to another or to sacrifice nations to ambition. Here that great conservator of woman's love, if permitted to assert itself, as it naturally would in freedom against oppression, violence, and war, would hold all these destructive forces in check, for woman knows the cost of life better than man does, and not with her consent would one drop of blood ever be shed, one life sacrificed in vain. With violence and disturbance in the natural world, we see a constant effort to maintain an equilibrium of forces. Nature, like a loving mother, is ever trying to keep land and

10

sea, mountain and valley, each in its place, to hush the angry winds and waves, balance the extremes of heat and cold, of rain and drought, that peace, harmony, and beauty may reign supreme. There is a striking analogy between matter and mind, and the present disorganization of society warns us, that in the dethronement of woman we have let loose the elements of violence and ruin that she only has the power to curb. If the civilization of the age calls for an extension of the suffrage, surely a government of the most virtuous, educated men and women would better represent the whole, and protect the interests of all than could the representation of either sex alone. But government gains no new element of strength in admitting all men to the ballot-box, for we have too much of the man-power there already. We see this in every department of legislation, and it is a common remark, that unless some new virtue is infused into our public life the nation is doomed to destruction. Will the foreign element, the dregs of China, Germany, England, Ireland, and Africa supply this needed force, or the nobler types of American womanhood who have taught our presidents, senators, and congressmen the rudiments of all they know?

3. I urge a Sixteenth Amendment because, when "manhood suffrage" is established from Maine to California, woman has reached the lowest depths of political degradation. So long as there is a disfranchised class in this country, and that class is women, a man's government is worse than a white man's government with suffrage limited by property and educational qualifications, because in proportion as you multiply the rulers, the condition of the politically ostracised is more hopeless and degraded. John Stuart Mill, in his work on "Liberty," shows that the condition of one disfranchised man in a nation is worse than when the whole nation is under one man, because in the latter case, if the one man is despotic, the nation can easily throw him off, but what can one man do with a nation of tyrants over him? If American women find it hard to bear the oppressions of their own Saxon fathers, the best orders of manhood, what may they not be called to endure when all the lower orders of foreigners now crowding our shores legislate for them and their daughters. Think of Patrick and Sambo and Hans and Yung Tung, who do not know the difference between a monarchy and a republic, who can not read the Declaration of Independence or Webster's spelling-book, making laws for Lucretia Mott, Ernestine L. Rose, and Anna E. Dickinson. Think of jurors and jailors drawn from these ranks to watch and try young girls for the crime of infanticide, to decide the moral code by which the mothers of this Republic shall be governed? This manhood suffrage is an appalling question, and it would be well for thinking women, who seem to consider it so magnanimous to hold their own claims in abeyance until all men are crowned with citizenship, to remember that the most ignorant men are ever the most hostile to the equality of women, as they have known them only in slavery and degradation.

Go to our courts of justice, our jails and prisons; go into the world of work; into the trades and professions; into the temples of science and learning, and see what is meted out everywhere to women—to those who have no advocates in our courts, no representatives in the councils of the nation. Shall we prolong and perpetuate such injustice, and by increasing this power risk worse oppressions for ourselves and daughters? It is an open, deliberate insult to American womanhood to be cast down under the iron-heeled peasantry of the Old World and the slaves of the New, as we shall be in the practical working of the Fifteenth Amendment, and the only atonement the Republican party can make is now to complete its work, by enfranchising the women of the nation. I have not forgotten their action four years ago, when Article XIV., Sec. 2, was amended* by invidiously introducing the word "male" into the Federal Constitution, where it had never been before, thus counting out of the basis of representation all men not permitted to vote, thereby making it the interest of every State to enfranchise its male citizens, and virtually declaring it no crime to disfranchise its women. As political sagacity moved our rulers thus to guard the interests of the negro for party purposes, common justice might have compelled them to show like respect for their own mothers, by counting woman too out of the basis of representation, that she might no longer swell the numbers to legislate adversely to her interests. And this desecration of the last will and testament of the fathers, this retrogressive legislation for woman, was in the face of the earnest protests of thousands of the best educated, most refined and cultivated women of the North.

Now, when the attention of the whole world is turned to this question of suffrage, and women themselves are throwing off the lethargy of ages, and in England, France, Germany, Switzerland, and Russia are holding their conventions, and their rulers are everywhere giving them a respectful hearing, shall American statesmen, claiming to be liberal, so amend their constitutions as to make their wives and mothers the political inferiors of unlettered and unwashed ditch-diggers, boot-blacks, butchers, and barbers, fresh from the slave plantations of the South, and the effete civilizations of the Old World? While poets and philosophers, statesmen and men of science are all alike pointing to woman as the new hope for the redemption of the race, shall the freest Government on the earth be the first to establish an aristocracy based on sex alone? to exalt ignorance above education, vice above virtue, brutality and barbarism above refinement and religion? Not since God first called light out of darkness and order out of chaos, was there ever made so base a proposi-

---

*The amendment as proposed by the Hon. Thaddeus Stevens, of Pennsylvania, extended the right of suffrage to "all citizens," which included both white and black women. At the bare thought of such an impending calamity, the more timid Republicans were filled with alarm, and the word "male" promptly inserted.

tion as "manhood suffrage" in this American Republic, after all the discussions we have had on human rights in the last century. On all the blackest pages of history there is no record of an act like this, in any nation, where native born citizens, having the same religion, speaking the same language, equal to their rulers in wealth, family, and education, have been politically ostracised by their own countrymen, outlawed with savages, and subjected to the government of outside barbarians. Remember the Fifteenth Amendment takes in a larger population than the 2,000,000 black men on the Southern plantation. It takes in all the foreigners daily landing in our eastern cities, the Chinese crowding our western shores, the inhabitants of Alaska, and all those western isles that will soon be ours. American statesmen may flatter themselves that by superior intelligence and political sagacity the higher orders of men will always govern, but when the ignorant foreign vote already holds the balance of power in all the large cities by sheer force of numbers, it is simply a question of impulse or passion, bribery or fraud, how our elections will be carried. When the highest offices in the gift of the people are bought and sold in Wall Street, it is a mere chance who will be our rulers. Whither is a nation tending when brains count for less than bullion, and clowns make laws for queens? It is a startling assertion, but nevertheless true, that in none of the nations of modern Europe are the higher classes of women politically so degraded as are the women of this Republic to-day. In the Old World, where the government is the aristocracy, where it is considered a mark of nobility to share its offices and powers, women of rank have certain hereditary rights which raise them above a majority of the men, certain honors and privileges not granted to serfs and peasants. There women are queens, hold subordinate offices, and vote on many questions. In our Southern States even, before the war, women were not degraded below the working population. They were not humiliated in seeing their coachmen, gardeners, and waiters go to the polls to legislate for them; but here, in this boasted Northern civilization, women of wealth and education, who pay taxes and obey the laws, who in morals and intellect are the peers of their proudest rulers, are thrust outside the pale of political consideration with minors, paupers, lunatics, traitors, idiots, with those guilty of bribery, larceny, and infamous crimes.

Would those gentlemen who are on all sides telling the women of the nation not to press their claims until the negro is safe beyond peradventure, be willing themselves to stand aside and trust all their interests to hands like these? The educated women of this nation feel as much interest in republican institutions, the preservation of the country, the good of the race, their own elevation and success, as any man possibly can, and we have the same distrust in man's power to legislate for us, that he has in woman's power to legislate wisely for herself.

A:\ King's Letter from Birmingham Jail --
a rhetorical analysis. htm
226 MOVING TO LONGER ARGUMENTS

LETTER FROM BIRMINGHAM JAIL

Martin Luther King, Jr.

April 16, 1963

My Dear Fellow Clergymen:

While confined here in the Birmingham city jail, I came across your recent statement calling my present activities "unwise and untimely." Seldom do I pause to answer criticism of my work and ideas. If I sought to answer all the criticisms that cross my desk, my secretaries would have little time for anything other than such correspondence in the course of the day, and I would have no time for constructive work. But since I feel that you are men of genuine good will and that your criticisms are sincerely set forth, I want to try to answer your statement in what I hope will be patient and reasonable terms.

I think I should indicate why I am here in Birmingham, since you have been influenced by the view which argues against "outsiders coming in." I have the honor of serving as president of the Southern Christian Leadership Conference, an organization operating in every southern state, with headquarters in Atlanta, Georgia. We have some eighty-five affiliated organizations across the South, and one of them is the Alabama Christian Movement for Human Rights. Frequently we share staff, educational and financial resources with our affiliates. Several months ago the affiliate here in Birmingham asked us to be on call to engage in a non-violent direct-action program if such were deemed necessary. We readily consented, and when the hour came we lived up to our promise. So I, along with several members of my staff, am here because I was invited here. I am here because I have organizational ties here.

But more basically, I am in Birmingham because injustice is here. Just as the prophets of the eighth century B.C. left their villages and carried their "thus saith the Lord" far beyond the boundaries of their home towns, and just as the Apostle Paul left his village of Tarsus and carried the gospel of Jesus Christ to the far corners of the Greco-Roman world, so am I compelled to carry the gospel of freedom beyond my own home town. Like Paul, I must constantly respond to the Macedonian call for aid.

Moreover, I am cognizant of the interrelatedness of all communities and states. I cannot sit idly by in Atlanta and not be concerned about what happens in Birmingham. Injustice anywhere is a threat to justice everywhere. We are caught in an inescapable network of mutuality, tied in a single garment of destiny. Whatever affects one directly, affects all indirectly. Never again can we afford to live with the narrow, provincial "outside agitator" idea. Anyone who lives inside the United States can never be considered an outsider anywhere within its bounds.

You deplore the demonstrations taking place in Birmingham. But your statement, I am sorry to say, fails to express a similar concern for the 5 conditions that brought about the demonstrations. I am sure that none of you would want to rest content with the superficial kind of social analysis that deals merely with effects and does not grapple with underlying causes. It is unfortunate that demonstrations are taking place in Birmingham, but it is even more unfortunate that the city's white power structure left the Negro community with no alternative.

In any nonviolent campaign there are four basic steps: collection of the facts to determine whether injustices exist; negotiation; self-purification; and direct action. We have gone through all these steps in Birmingham. There can be no gainsaying the fact that racial injustice engulfs this community. Birmingham is probably the most thoroughly segregated city in the United States. Its ugly record of brutality is widely known. Negroes have experienced grossly unjust treatment in the courts. There have been more unsolved bombings of Negro homes and churches in Birmingham than in any other city in the nation. These are the hard, brutal facts of the case. On the basis of these conditions, Negro leaders sought to negotiate with the city fathers. But the latter consistently refused to engage in good-faith negotiation.

Then, last September, came the opportunity to talk with leaders of Birmingham's economic community. In the course of the negotiations, certain promises were made by the merchants—for example, to remove the stores' humiliating racial signs. On the basis of these promises, the Reverend Fred Shuttlesworth and the leaders of the Alabama Christian Movement for Human Rights agreed to a moratorium on all demonstrations. As the weeks and months went by, we realized that we were the victims of a broken promise. A few signs, briefly removed, returned; the others remained.

As in so many past experiences, our hopes had been blasted, and the shadow of deep disappointment settled upon us. We had no alternative except to prepare for direct action, whereby we would present our very bodies as a means of laying our case before the conscience of the local and the national community. Mindful of the difficulties involved, we decided to undertake a process of self-purification. We began a series of workshops on nonviolence, and we repeatedly asked ourselves: "Are you able to accept blows without retaliating?" "Are you able to endure the ordeal of jail?" We decided to schedule our direct-action program for the Easter season, realizing that except for Christmas, this is the main shopping period of the year. Knowing that a strong economic-withdrawal program would be the by-product of direct action, we felt that this would be the best time to bring pressure to bear on the merchants for the needed change.

Then it occurred to us that Birmingham's mayoralty election was coming up in March, and we speedily decided to postpone action until after election day. When we discovered that the Commissioner of Public Safety, Eugene "Bull" Connor, had piled up enough votes to be in the run-off, we decided again to postpone action until the day after the run-off so that the demonstrations could not be used to cloud the issues. Like many others, we waited to see Mr. Connor defeated, and to this end we endured postponement after postponement. Having aided in this community need, we felt that our direct-action program could be delayed no longer.

You may well ask: "Why direct action? Why sit-ins, marches and *10* so forth? Isn't negotiation a better path?" You are quite right in calling for negotiation. Indeed, this is the very purpose of direct action. Nonviolent direct action seeks to create such a crisis and foster such a tension that a community which has constantly refused to negotiate is forced to confront the issue. It seeks so to dramatize the issue that it can no longer be ignored. My citing the creation of tension as part of the work of the nonviolent resister may sound rather shocking. But I must confess that I am not afraid of the word "tension." I have earnestly opposed violent tension, but there is a type of constructive, nonviolent tension which is necessary for growth. Just as Socrates felt that it was necessary to create a tension in the mind so that individuals could rise from the bondage of myths and half-truths to the unfettered realm of creative analysis and objective appraisal, so must we see the need for nonviolent gadflies to create the kind of tension in society that will help men rise from the dark depths of prejudice and racism to the majestic heights of understanding and brotherhood.

The purpose of our direct-action program is to create a situation so crisis-packed that it will inevitably open the door to negotiation. I therefore concur with you in your call for negotiation. Too long has our beloved Southland been bogged down in a tragic effort to live in monologue rather than dialogue.

One of the basic points in your statement is that the action that I and my associates have taken in Birmingham is untimely. Some have asked: "Why didn't you give the new city administration time to act?" The only answer that I can give to this query is that the new Birmingham administration must be prodded about as much as the outgoing one, before it will act. We are sadly mistaken if we feel that the election of Albert Boutwell as mayor will bring the millennium to Birmingham. While Mr. Boutwell is a much more gentle person than Mr. Connor, they are both segregationists, dedicated to maintenance of the status quo. I have hope that Mr. Boutwell will be reasonable enough to see the futility of massive resistance to desegregation. But he will not see this without pressure from devotees of civil rights. My friends, I must say to you that we have not made a single gain in civil rights without determined legal and nonviolent pressure. Lamentably, it is an historical fact that privileged groups seldom give up their privileges voluntarily. Individuals may see the moral light and voluntarily give up their unjust posture; but, as Reinhold Niebuhr has reminded us, groups tend to be more immoral than individuals.

We know through painful experience that freedom is never voluntarily given by the oppressor; it must be demanded by the oppressed.

Frankly, I have yet to engage in a direct-action campaign that was "well timed" in the view of those who have not suffered unduly from the disease of segregation. For years now I have heard the word "Wait!" It rings in the ear of every Negro with piercing familiarity. This "Wait" has almost always meant "Never." We must come to see, with one of our distinguished jurists, that "justice too long delayed is justice denied."

We have waited for more than 340 years for our constitutional and God-given rights. The nations of Asia and Africa are moving with jet-like speed toward gaining political independence, but we still creep at horse-and-buggy pace toward gaining a cup of coffee at a lunch counter. Perhaps it is easy for those who have never felt the stinging darts of segregation to say, "Wait." But when you have seen vicious mobs lynch your mothers and fathers at will and drown your sisters and brothers at whim; when you have seen hate-filled policemen curse, kick and even kill your black brothers and sisters; when you see the vast majority of your twenty million Negro brothers smothering in an airtight cage of poverty in the midst of an affluent society; when you suddenly find your tongue twisted and your speech stammering as you seek to explain to your six-year-old daughter why she can't go to the public amusement park that has just been advertised on television, and see tears welling up in her eyes when she is told that Funtown is closed to colored children, and see ominous clouds of inferiority beginning to form in her little mental sky, and see her beginning to distort her personality by developing an unconscious bitterness toward white people; when you have to concoct an answer for a five-year-old son who is asking: "Daddy, why do white people treat colored people so mean?"; when you take a cross-country drive and find it necessary to sleep night after night in the uncomfortable corners of your automobile because no motel will accept you; when you are humiliated day in and day out by nagging signs reading "white" and "colored"; when your first name becomes "nigger," your middle name becomes "boy" (however old you are) and your last name becomes "John," and your wife and mother are never given the respected title "Mrs."; when you are harried by day and haunted by night by the fact that you are a Negro, living constantly at tiptoe stance, never quite knowing what to expect next, and are plagued with inner fears and outer resentments; when you are forever fighting a degenerating sense of "nobodiness"—then you will understand why we find it difficult to wait. There comes a time when the cup of endurance runs over, and men are no longer willing to be plunged into the abyss of despair. I hope, sirs, you can understand our legitimate and unavoidable impatience.

You express a great deal of anxiety over our willingness to break   15
laws. This is certainly a legitimate concern. Since we so diligently urge people to obey the Supreme Court's decision of 1954 outlawing segregation in the public schools, at first glance it may seem rather paradoxical for us consciously to break laws. One may well ask: "How can you advocate breaking some laws and obeying others?" The answer lies in the fact that there are two types of laws: just and unjust. I would be the first

to advocate obeying just laws. One has not only a legal but a moral responsibility to obey just laws. Conversely, one has a moral responsibility to disobey unjust laws. I would agree with St. Augustine that "an unjust law is no law at all."

Now, what is the difference between the two? How does one determine whether a law is just or unjust? A just law is a man-made code that squares with the moral law or the law of God. An unjust law is a code that is out of harmony with the moral law. To put it in the terms of St. Thomas Aquinas: An unjust law is a human law that is not rooted in eternal law and natural law. Any law that uplifts human personality is just. Any law that degrades human personality is unjust. All segregation statutes are unjust because segregation distorts the soul and damages the personality. It gives the segregator a false sense of superiority and the segregated a false sense of inferiority. Segregation, to use the terminology of the Jewish philosopher Martin Buber, substitutes an "I-it" relationship for an "I-thou" relationship and ends up relegating persons to the status of things. Hence segregation is not only politically, economically and sociologically unsound, it is morally wrong and sinful. Paul Tillich has said that sin is separation. Is not segregation an existential expression of man's tragic separation, his awful estrangement, his terrible sinfulness? Thus it is that I can urge men to obey the 1954 decision of the Supreme Court, for it is morally right; and I can urge them to disobey segregation ordinances, for they are morally wrong.

Let us consider a more concrete example of just and unjust laws. An unjust law is a code that a numerical or power majority group compels a minority group to obey but does not make binding on itself. This is *difference* made legal. By the same token, a just law is a code that a majority compels a minority to follow and that it is willing to follow itself. This is *sameness* made legal.

Let me give another explanation. A law is unjust if it is inflicted on a minority that, as a result of being denied the right to vote, had no part in enacting or devising the law. Who can say that the legislature of Alabama which set up that state's segregation laws was democratically elected? Throughout Alabama all sorts of devious methods are used to prevent Negroes from becoming registered voters, and there are some counties in which, even though Negroes constitute a majority of the population, not a single Negro is registered. Can any law enacted under such circumstances be considered democratically structured?

Sometimes a law is just on its face and unjust in its application. For instance, I have been arrested on a charge of parading without a permit. Now, there is nothing wrong in having an ordinance which requires a permit for a parade. But such an ordinance becomes unjust when it is used to maintain segregation and to deny citizens the First-Amendment privilege of peaceful assembly and protest.

I hope you are able to see the distinction I am trying to point out. *20* In no sense do I advocate evading or defying the law, as would the rabid segregationist. That would lead to anarchy. One who breaks an unjust law must do so openly, lovingly, and with a willingness to accept the penalty. I submit that an individual who breaks a law that conscience tells him is unjust, and who willingly accepts the penalty of imprisonment in order to arouse the conscience of the community over its injustice, is in reality expressing the highest respect for law.

Of course, there is nothing new about this kind of civil disobedience. It was evidenced sublimely in the refusal of Shadrach, Meshach and Abednego to obey the laws of Nebuchadnezzar, on the ground that a higher moral law was at stake. It was practiced superbly by the early Christians, who were willing to face hungry lions and the excruciating pain of chopping blocks rather than submit to certain unjust laws of the Roman Empire. To a degree, academic freedom is a reality today because Socrates practiced civil disobedience. In our own nation, the Boston Tea Party represented a massive act of civil disobedience.

We should never forget that everything Adolf Hitler did in Germany was "legal" and everything the Hungarian freedom fighters did in Hungary was "illegal." It was "illegal" to aid and comfort a Jew in Hitler's Germany. Even so, I am sure that, had I lived in Germany at the time, I would have aided and comforted my Jewish brothers. If today I lived in a Communist country where certain principles dear to the Christian faith are suppressed, I would openly advocate disobeying that country's anti-religious laws.

I must make two honest confessions to you, my Christian and Jewish brothers. First, I must confess that over the past few years I have been gravely disappointed with the white moderate. I have almost reached the regrettable conclusion that the Negro's great stumbling block in his stride toward freedom is not the White Citizen's Counciler or the Ku Klux Klanner, but the white moderate, who is more devoted to "order" than to justice; who prefers a negative peace which is the absence of tension to a positive peace which is the presence of justice; who constantly says: "I agree with you in the goal you seek, but I cannot agree with your methods of direct action"; who paternalistically believes he can set the timetable for another man's freedom; who lives by a mythical concept of time and who constantly advises the Negro to wait for a "more convenient season." Shallow understanding from people of good will is more frustrating than absolute misunderstanding from people of ill will. Lukewarm acceptance is much more bewildering than outright rejection.

I had hoped that the white moderate would understand that law and order exist for the purpose of establishing justice and that when they fail in this purpose they become the dangerously structured dams that block the flow of social progress. I had hoped that the white moderate would understand that the present tension in the South is a necessary phase of the transition from an obnoxious negative peace, in which the Negro passively accepted his unjust plight, to a substantive and positive peace, in which all men will respect the dignity and worth of human personality. Actually, we who engage in nonviolent direct action are not the creators of tension. We merely bring to the surface the hidden tension that is already alive. We bring it out in the open, where it can be seen and dealt with. Like a boil that can never be cured so long as it is covered up but must be opened with all its ugliness to the natural medicines of air and light, injustice must be exposed, with all the tension its exposure creates, to the light of human conscience and the air of national opinion before it can be cured.

In your statement you assert that our actions, even though peace- ful, must be condemned because they precipitate violence. But is this a logical assertion? Isn't this like condemning a robbed man because his possession of money precipitated the evil act of robbery? Isn't this like condemning Socrates because his unswerving commitment to truth and his philosophical inquiries precipitated the act by the misguided populace in which they made him drink hemlock? Isn't this like condemning Jesus because his unique God-consciousness and never-ceasing devotion to God's will precipitated the evil act of crucifixion? We must come to see that, as the federal courts have consistently affirmed, it is wrong to urge an individual to cease his efforts to gain his basic constitutional rights because the quest may precipitate violence. Society must protect the robbed and punish the robber.

I had also hoped that the white moderate would reject the myth concerning time in relation to the struggle for freedom. I have just received a letter from a white brother in Texas. He writes: "All Christians know that the colored people will receive equal rights eventually, but it is possible that you are in too great a religious hurry. It has taken Christianity almost two thousand years to accomplish what it has. The teachings of Christ take time to come to earth." Such an attitude stems from a tragic misconception of time, from the strangely irrational notion that there is something in the very flow of time that will inevitably cure all ills. Actually, time itself is neutral; it can be used either destructively or constructively. More and more I feel that the people of ill will have used time much more effectively than have the people of good will. We will have to repent in this generation not merely for the hateful words and actions of the bad people but for the appalling silence of the good people. Human progress never rolls in on wheels of inevitability; it comes through the tireless efforts of men willing to be coworkers with God, and without this hard work, time itself becomes an ally of the forces of social stagnation. We must use time creatively, in the knowledge that the time is always ripe to do right. Now is the time to make real the promise of democracy and transform our pending national elegy into a creative psalm of brotherhood. Now is the time to lift our national policy from the quicksand of racial injustice to the solid rock of human dignity.

You speak of our activity in Birmingham as extreme. At first I was rather disappointed that fellow clergymen would see my nonviolent efforts as those of an extremist. I began thinking about the fact that I stand in the middle of two opposing forces in the Negro community. One is a force of complacency, made up in part of Negroes who, as a result of long years of oppression, are so drained of self-respect and a sense of "somebodiness" that they have adjusted to segregation; and in part of a few middle-class Negroes who, because of a degree of academic and economic security and because in some ways they profit by segregation, have become insensitive to the problems of masses. The other force is one of bitterness and hatred, and it comes perilously close to advocating violence. It is expressed in the various black nationalist groups that are springing up across the nation, the largest and best-known being Elijah Muhammad's Muslim movement. Nourished by the Negro's frustration over the continued existence of racial discrimination, this movement is made up of people who have lost faith in America, who have absolutely repudiated Christianity, and who have concluded that the white man is an incorrigible "devil."

I have tried to stand between these two forces, saying that we need emulate neither the "do-nothingism" of the complacent nor the hatred and despair of the black nationalist. For there is the more excellent way of love and nonviolent protest. I am grateful to God that, through the influence of the Negro church, the way of nonviolence became an integral part of our struggle.

If this philosophy had not emerged, by now many streets of the South would, I am convinced, be flowing with blood. And I am further convinced that if our white brothers dismiss as "rabble-rousers" and "outside agitators" those of us who employ nonviolent direct action, and if they refuse to support our nonviolent efforts, millions of Negroes will, out of frustration and despair, seek solace and security in black-nationalist ideologies—a development that would inevitably lead to a frightening racial nightmare.

Oppressed people cannot remain oppressed forever. The yearning *30* for freedom eventually manifests itself, and that is what has happened to the American Negro. Something within has reminded him of his birthright of freedom, and something without has reminded him that it can be gained. Consciously or unconsciously, he has been caught up by the *Zeitgeist,* and with his black brothers of Africa and his brown and yellow brothers of Asia, South America and the Caribbean, the United States Negro is moving with a sense of great urgency toward the promised land of racial justice. If one recognizes this vital urge that has engulfed the Negro community, one should readily understand why public demonstrations are taking place. The Negro has many pent-up resentments and latent frustrations, and he must release them. So let him march; let him make prayer pilgrimages to the city hall; let him go on freedom rides—and try to understand why he must do so. If his repressed emotions are not released in nonviolent ways, they will seek expression through violence; this is not a threat but a fact of history. So I have not said to my people: "Get rid of your discontent." Rather, I have tried to say that this normal and healthy discontent can be channeled into the creative outlet of nonviolent direct action. And now this approach is being termed extremist.

But though I was initially disappointed at being categorized as an extremist, as I continued to think about the matter I gradually gained a measure of satisfaction from the label. Was not Jesus an extremist for love: "Love your enemies, bless them that curse you, do good to them that hate you, and pray for them which despitefully use you, and persecute you." Was not Amos an extremist for justice: "Let justice roll down like waters and righteousness like an ever-flowing stream." Was not Paul an extremist for the Christian gospel: "I bear in my body the marks of the Lord Jesus." Was not Martin Luther an extremist: "Here I stand; I cannot do otherwise, so help me God." And John Bunyan: "I will stay in jail to the end of my days before I make a butchery of my conscience." And Abraham Lincoln: "This nation cannot survive half slave and half free." And Thomas Jefferson: "We hold these truths to be self-evident, that all men are created equal . . ." So the question is not whether we will be extremists, but what kind of extremists we will be. Will we be extremists for hate or for love? Will we be extremists for the preservation of injustice or for the extension of justice? In that dramatic scene on Calvary's hill three men were crucified. We must never forget that all three were crucified for the same crime—the crime of extremism. Two were extremists for immorality, and thus fell below their environment. The other, Jesus Christ, was an extremist for love, truth and goodness, and thereby rose above his environment. Perhaps the South, the nation and the world are in dire need of creative extremists.

I had hoped that the white moderate would see this need. Perhaps I was too optimistic; perhaps I expected too much. I suppose I should have realized that few members of the oppressor race can understand the deep groans and passionate yearnings of the oppressed race, and still fewer have the vision to see that injustice must be rooted out by strong, persistent and determined action. I am thankful, however, that some of our white brothers in the South have grasped the meaning of this social revolution and committed themselves to it. They are still all too few in quantity, but they are big in quality. Some—such as Ralph McGill, Lillian Smith, Harry Golden, James McBride Dabbs, Ann Braden and Sarah Patton Boyle—have written about our struggle in eloquent and prophetic terms. Others have marched with us down nameless streets of the South. They have languished in filthy, roach-infested jails, suffering the abuse and brutality of policemen who view them as "dirty nigger-lovers." Unlike so many of their moderate brothers and sisters, they have recognized the urgency of the moment and sensed the need for powerful "action" antidotes to combat the disease of segregation.

Let me take note of my other major disappointment. I have been so greatly disappointed with the white church and its leadership. Of course, there are some notable exceptions. I am not unmindful of the fact that each of you has taken some significant stands on this issue. I commend you, Reverend Stallings, for your Christian stand on this past Sunday, in welcoming Negroes to your worship service on a nonsegregated basis. I commend the Catholic leaders of this state for integrating Spring Hill College several years ago.

But despite these notable exceptions, I must honestly reiterate that I have been disappointed with the Church. I do not say this as one of those negative critics who can always find something wrong with the church. I say this as a minister of the gospel, who loves the church; who was nurtured in its bosom; who has been sustained by its spiritual blessings and who will remain true to it as long as the cord of life shall lengthen.

When I was suddenly catapulted into the leadership of the bus pro-test in Montgomery, Alabama, a few years ago, I felt we would be sup-ported by the white church. I felt that the white ministers, priests and rabbis of the South would be among our strongest allies. Instead, some have been outright opponents, refusing to understand the freedom movement and misrepresenting its leaders; all too many others have been more cautious than courageous and have remained silent behind the anesthetizing security of stained-glass windows.

In spite of my shattered dreams, I came to Birmingham with the hope that the white religious leadership of this community would see the justice of our cause and, with deep moral concern, would serve as the channel through which our just grievances could reach the power structure. I had hoped that each of you would understand. But again I have been disappointed.

I have heard numerous southern religious leaders admonish their worshipers to comply with a desegregation decision because it is the law, but I have longed to hear white ministers declare: "Follow this decree because integration is morally right and because the Negro is your brother." In the midst of blatant injustices inflicted upon the Negro, I have watched white churchmen stand on the sideline and mouth pious irrelevancies and sanctimonious trivialities. In the midst of a mighty struggle to rid our nation of racial and economic injustice, I have heard many ministers say: "Those are social issues, with which the gospel has no real concern." And I have watched many churches commit themselves to a completely other-worldly religion which makes a strange, un-Biblical distinction between body and soul, between the sacred and the secular.

I have traveled the length and breadth of Alabama, Mississippi and all the other southern states. On sweltering summer days and crisp autumn mornings I have looked at the South's beautiful churches with their lofty spires pointing heavenward. I have beheld the impressive outlines of her massive religious-education buildings. Over and over I have found myself saying: "What kind of people worship here? Who is their God? Where were their voices when the lips of Governor Barnett dripped with words of interposition and nullification? Where were they when

35

Governor Wallace gave a clarion call for defiance and hatred? Where were their voices of support when bruised and weary Negro men and women decided to rise from the dark dungeons of complacency to the bright hills of creative protest?"

Yes, these questions are still in my mind. In deep disappointment I have wept over the laxity of the church. But be assured that my tears have been tears of love. There can be no deep disappointment where there is not deep love. Yes, I love the church. How could I do otherwise? I am in the rather unique position of being the son, the grandson and the great-grandson of preachers. Yes, I see the church as the body of Christ. But, oh! How we have blemished and scarred that body through social neglect and through fear of being nonconformists.

There was a time when the church was very powerful—in the time when the early Christians rejoiced at being deemed worthy to suffer for what they believed. In those days the church was not merely a thermometer that recorded the ideas and principles of popular opinion; it was a thermostat that transformed the mores of society. Whenever the early Christians entered a town, the people in power became disturbed and immediately sought to convict the Christians for being "disturbers of the peace" and "outside agitators." But the Christians pressed on, in the conviction that they were "a colony of heaven," called to obey God rather than man. Small in number, they were big in commitment. They were too God-intoxicated to be "astronomically intimidated." By their effort and example they brought an end to such ancient evils as infanticide and gladiatorial contests.

Things are different now. So often the contemporary church is a weak, ineffectual voice with an uncertain sound. So often it is an arch-defender of the status quo. Far from being disturbed by the presence of the church, the power structure of the average community is consoled by the church's silent—and often even vocal—sanction of things as they are.

But the judgment of God is upon the church as never before. If today's church does not recapture the sacrificial spirit of the early church, it will lose its authenticity, forfeit the loyalty of millions, and be dismissed as an irrelevant social club with no meaning for the twentieth century. Every day I meet young people whose disappointment with the church has turned into outright disgust.

Perhaps I have once again been too optimistic. Is organized religion too inextricably bound to the status quo to save our nation and the world? Perhaps I must turn my faith to the inner spiritual church, the church within the church, as the true *ekklesia* and the hope of the world. But again I am thankful to God that some noble souls from the ranks of organized religion have broken loose from the paralyzing chains of conformity and joined us as active partners in the struggle for freedom. They have left their secure congregations and walked the streets of Albany, Georgia, with us. They have gone down the highways of the South on tortuous rides for freedom. Yes, they have gone to jail with us.

Some have been dismissed from their churches, have lost the support of their bishops and fellow ministers. But they have acted in the faith that right defeated is stronger than evil triumphant. Their witness has been the spiritual salt that has preserved the true meaning of the gospel in these troubled times. They have carved a tunnel of hope through the dark mountain of disappointment.

I hope the church as a whole will meet the challenge of this decisive hour. But even if the church does not come to the aid of justice, I have no despair about the future. I have no fear about the outcome of our struggle in Birmingham, even if our motives are at present misunderstood. We will reach the goal of freedom in Birmingham and all over the nation, because the goal of America is freedom. Abused and scorned though we may be, our destiny is tied up with America's destiny. Before the pilgrims landed at Plymouth, we were here. Before the pen of Jefferson etched the majestic words of the Declaration of Independence across the pages of history, we were here. For more than two centuries our forebears labored in this country without wages; they made cotton king; they built the homes of their masters while suffering gross injustice and shameful humiliation—and yet out of a bottomless vitality they continued to thrive and develop. If the inexpressible cruelties of slavery could not stop us, the opposition we now face will surely fail. We will win our freedom because the sacred heritage of our nation and the eternal will of God are embodied in our echoing demands.

Before closing I feel impelled to mention one other point in your 45 statement that has troubled me profoundly. You warmly commended the Birmingham police force for keeping "order" and "preventing violence." I doubt that you would have so warmly commended the police force if you had seen its dogs sinking their teeth into unarmed, nonviolent Negroes. I doubt that you would so quickly commend the policemen if you were to observe their ugly and inhumane treatment of Negroes here in the city jail; if you were to watch them push and curse old Negro women and young Negro girls; if you were to see them slap and kick old Negro men and young boys; if you were to observe them, as they did on two occasions, refuse to give us food because we wanted to sing our grace together. I cannot join you in your praise of the Birmingham police department.

It is true that the police have exercised a degree of discipline in handling the demonstrators. In this sense they have conducted themselves rather "nonviolently" in public. But for what purpose? To preserve the evil system of segregation. Over the past few years I have consistently preached that nonviolence demands that the means we use must be as pure as the ends we seek. I have tried to make clear that it is wrong to use immoral means to attain moral ends. But now I must affirm that it is just as wrong, or perhaps even more so, to use moral means to preserve immoral ends. Perhaps Mr. Connor and his policemen have been rather nonviolent in public, as was Chief Pritchett in Albany, Georgia, but they have used the moral means of nonviolence to maintain the immoral end of racial injustice. As T. S. Eliot has said: "The last temptation is the greatest treason: To do the right deed for the wrong reason."

I wish you had commended the Negro sit-inners and demonstrators of Birmingham for their sublime courage, their willingness to suffer and their amazing discipline in the midst of great provocation. One day the South will recognize its real heroes. They will be the James Merediths, with the noble sense of purpose that enables them to face jeering and hostile mobs, and with the agonizing loneliness that characterizes the life of the pioneer. They will be old, oppressed, battered Negro women, symbolized in a seventy-two-year-old woman in Montgomery, Alabama, who rose up with a sense of dignity and with her people decided not to ride segregated buses, and who responded with ungrammatical profundity to one who inquired about her weariness: "My feets is tired, but my soul is at rest." They will be the young high school and college students, the young ministers of the gospel and a host of their elders, courageously and nonviolently sitting in at lunch counters and willingly going to jail for conscience sake. One day the South will know that when these disinherited children of God sat down at lunch counters, they were in reality standing up for what is best in the American dream and for the most sacred values in our Judaeo-Christian heritage, thereby bringing our nation back to those great wells of democracy which were dug deep by the founding fathers in their formulation of the Constitution and the Declaration of Independence.

Never before have I written so long a letter. I'm afraid it is much too long to take your precious time. I can assure you that it would have been much shorter if I had been writing from a comfortable desk, but what else can one do when he is alone in a narrow jail cell, other than write long letters, think long thoughts and pray long prayers?

If I have said anything in this letter that overstates the truth and indicates an unreasonable impatience, I beg you to forgive me. If I have said anything that understates the truth and indicates my having a patience that allows me to settle for anything less than brotherhood, I beg God to forgive me.

I hope this letter finds you strong in the faith. I also hope that circumstances will soon make it possible for me to meet each of you, not as an integrationist or a civil-rights leader but as a fellow clergyman and a Christian brother. Let us all hope that the dark clouds of racial prejudice will soon pass away and the deep fog of misunderstanding will be lifted from our fear-drenched communities, and in some not too distant tomorrow the radiant stars of love and brotherhood will shine over our great nation with all their scintillating beauty.

Yours for the cause of Peace and Brotherhood,
Martin Luther King, Jr.

V   A Minicasebook on Censoring Rock and Rap

Fred Bronson, "A Selected Chronology of Musical
   Controversy"
Anna Quindlen, "Raised on Rock-and-Roll"
Frank Zappa, "On 'Junk Food for the Soul'"
Tipper Gore, "Curbing the Sexploitation Industry"
Brian K. Simmons, "The Effect of Censorship on Attitudes
   toward Popular Music"
Michael Kinsley, "Ice-T: The Issue Is Social Responsibility"
Barbara Ehrenreich, "Ice-T: The Issue Is Free Speech"
Sam Brownback, "Free Speech: Lyrics, Liberty, and License"
Douglas M. McLeod, William P. Eveland, Jr., and Amy I.
   Nathanson, "Support for Censorship of Violent and
   Misogynic Rap Lyrics"
Dan Moran, "Censorship Begins at Home"

INTRODUCTION

This section is designed to provide you with material on which to
base a longer argument in greater depth. The topic is one of today's most
controversial and important issues, and the material varies widely in
length, level, type of publication, and point of view. The selections range
from op-ed pieces to senatorial speeches and academic articles; they

include a satirical cartoon and a debate in a national magazine. The two professional academic articles are given complete with footnotes in professional form.

You can use the information here either alone or in conjunction with further research of the sort described in the Guide to Finding and Using Information at the end of the book. Good luck with your project!

A SELECTED CHRONOLOGY OF MUSICAL CONTROVERSY

Fred Bronson

FEBRUARY 1954

Rep. Ruth Thompson (R.-Mich.) introduces a bill in the House that would ban mailing any phonograph record or "other article capable of producing sound" that was "obscene, lewd, lascivious, or filthy." Punishment would include fines up to $5,000 and five years imprisonment.

OCTOBER 1954

WDIA in Memphis bans "Work With Me, Annie" and "Annie Had a Baby" by the Midnighters as well as "Honey Love" by the Drifters because of "offensive lyrics."

JANUARY 1957

Elvis Presley makes his third and final appearance on "The Ed Sullivan Show," but the camera operators are directed not to pan below the waist.

MARCH 1957

Cardinal Stritch, head of the Catholic archdiocese in Chicago, bans rock 'n' roll from schools because of its "tribal rhythms" and "encouragement to behave in a hedonistic manner."

JANUARY 1959

Link Wray's instrumental "Rumble" is dropped by many radio stations because the title refers to teenage gang violence. On "American

Bandstand," Dick Clark introduces Wray but does not mention the title of the song.

JANUARY 1962

In Buffalo, N.Y., Bishop Burke forbids students from dancing, singing about or listening to "The Twist" in any school or parish or at any youth event.

FEBRUARY 1962

The Radio Trade Practices Committee recommends that lyrics of all pop songs be screened by the NAB Code Committee "due to the proliferation of songs dealing with raw sex and violence beamed directly and singularly at children and teenagers."

FEBRUARY 1963

CBS tells Bob Dylan he cannot sing "Talking John Birch Society Blues," his take on the right-wing organization, on "The Ed Sullivan Show." Dylan refuses to appear.

FEBRUARY 1964

Gov. Matthew Welsh of Indiana deems "Louie Louie" by the Kingsmen to be pornographic and asks the state broadcasters association to ban the song.

FEBRUARY 1965

After splitting his pants during a London concert, P. J. Proby is banned from appearing on ABC-TV's "Shindig." *10*

JUNE 1965

Many American radio stations refuse to play the Rolling Stones' "(I Can't Get No) Satisfaction" because of "suggestive lyrics."

MARCH 1966

In an interview with London's *The Evening Standard,* John Lennon talks about Christianity and says of the Beatles, "We're more popular than Jesus Christ right now." As a result, burnings of Beatles records take place around the world.

JUNE 1966

The Beatles' "Yesterday And Today" album is released with "the butcher cover," featuring the Fab Four sitting with pieces of meat and decapitated baby dolls. The cover is withdrawn from stores and replaced by an innocuous photo of the Beatles.

JANUARY 1967

The Rolling Stones perform "Let's Spend The Night Together" on "The Ed Sullivan Show" after Jagger agrees to substitute the lyrics with "Let's spend some time together." Later, he claims to have sung the original words, but says he slurred them.

SEPTEMBER 1967

The Doors appear on "The Ed Sullivan Show." Jim Morrison is [15] asked to delete the lyric, "Girl we couldn't get much higher" from "Light My Fire," but doesn't.

SEPTEMBER 1968

One month after the Democratic convention, radio stations in Chicago ban the Rolling Stones' single "Street Fighting Man," fearful it might incite people to riot.

JANUARY 1969

Some 30,000 copies of John Lennon and Yoko Ono's "Two Virgins" album, featuring the couple nude on the cover, are seized by police at Newark airport in New Jersey. In Chicago, a record store displaying the cover is closed down by the vice squad.

FEBRUARY 1969

Protests greet the original Blind Faith LP cover of a nude 11-year-old girl holding a phallic-looking model airplane. Atco releases the album with two different covers so retailers can choose which they prefer to stock.

APRIL 1969

Detroit rockers MC5 agree to delete an expletive from the title song of their album "Kick Out The Jams." But Elektra drops the quintet after the members write another expletive on company letterhead and personally deliver the stationery to stores that refused to stock their album.

JULY 1969

Almost half of the Top 40 stations in the U.S. refuse to play the [20] Beatles' new single, "The Ballad Of John And Yoko," because of the lyric, "Christ, you know it ain't easy. . . ."

SEPTEMBER 1969

A two-page ad in the *Seattle Post-Intelligence* calls for criminal prosecution against "rock festivals and their drug-sex-rock-squalor culture." The spread, paid for by the city's Roman Catholic archdiocese, includes photos from local festivals with nudity and drug use blacked out.

OCTOBER 1970

President Richard Nixon tells radio broadcasters that rock lyrics should be screened and any songs suggesting drug use should be banned.

MARCH 1971

WNBC radio in New York bans "One Toke Over The Line" by Brewer & Shipley because of alleged drug references. Songwriter Tom Shipley compares pulling a record from the airwaves in the '70s to book-burning in the '30s.

APRIL 1971

The Illinois Crime Commission publishes a list of "drug-oriented rock records," including "Puff The Magic Dragon," "Yellow Submarine," "A Whiter Shade Of Pale" and "Hi-De-Ho (That Old Sweet Roll)."

APRIL 1973

On the syndicated "Soul Train," Curtis Mayfield is censored when [25] references to drugs are deleted from his song "Pusherman."

NOVEMBER 1975

In Tallahassee, Rev. Charles Boykin of the Lakeswood Baptist Church burns rock 'n' roll records, calling them the "devil's music."

DECEMBER 1976

In an interview on British television, the Sex Pistols land in hot water when bassist Glen Matlock utters an expletive. As a result, their U.K. tour collapses as most venues refuse to book the group. A month later, EMI drops the group from its roster. A&M signs the group and ends the deal nine days later without releasing any product.

MAY 1977

Virgin Records signs the Sex Pistols. The song "God Save The Queen" is banned from British radio because of "treasonous sentiments," but hits No. 2 on the chart anyway.

MAY 1985

The Parents' Music Resource Center (PMRC) is established by a group of mainly wives of Washington politicians, including co-chairs Susan Baker and Tipper Gore. Identifying five basic negative themes in rock music—free love/sex, sadomasochism, rebellion, the occult and drugs—the group fights for a rating system in order to alert parents to explicit lyrics.

FEBRUARY 1989

The City Council of New Iberia, La., passes an emergency ordinance requiring that materials that might fall under the state's definitions of obscenity be placed out of view of unmarried people under the age of 17. Violation carries a penalty of 60 days in jail and a $500 fine.

After Yusef Islam, once known as Cat Stevens, endorses the Ayatollah Khomeni's call for the execution of "Satanic Verses" author Salman Rushdie, radio stations around the U.S. drop Stevens from their playlists. KFI talk show host Tom Leykis holds a Cat Stevens record burning.

JANUARY 1990

A bill introduced in the Missouri legislature prohibits the sale of records that contain lyrics that are violent, sexually explicit, or perverse, unless they have an affixed parental advisory warning label and the lyrics printed on the album cover. Similar proposals follow in Maryland, Delaware, Florida and Kansas.

Police in Dade County, Fla., investigate incidents in which three retailers were caught in a sting set up by attorney Jack Thompson. Thompson says that the three stores sold unedited versions of 2 Live

30

Crew's album to a 16-year-old. As a result, the 52-store Spec's Music chain institutes an 18-to-purchase policy on stickered product.

RAISED ON ROCK-AND-ROLL

Anna Quindlen

Mister Ed is back on television, indicating that, as most middle-of-the-road antique shops suggest, Americans cannot discriminate between things worth saving and things that simply exist. *The Donna Reed Show* is on, too, and *My Three Sons,* and those dopey folks from *Gilligan's Island.* There's *Leave It to Beaver* and *The Beverly Hillbillies* and even *Lassie,* whose plaintive theme song leaves my husband all mushy around the edges.

Social historians say these images, and those of Howdy Doody and Pinky Lee and Lamb Chop and Annette have forever shaped my consciousness. But I have memories far stronger than that. I remember sitting cross-legged in front of the tube, one of the console sets with the ersatz lamé netting over the speakers, but I was not watching puppets or pratfalls. I was born in Philadelphia, a city where if you can't dance you might as well stay home, and I was raised on rock-and-roll. My earliest television memory is of *American Bandstand,* and the central question of my childhood was: Can you dance to it?

When I was fifteen and a wild devotee of Mitch Ryder and the Detroit Wheels, it sometimes crossed my mind that when I was thirty-four years old, decrepit, wrinkled as a prune and near death, I would have moved on to some nameless kind of dreadful show music, something akin to Muzak. I did not think about the fact that my parents were still listening to the music that had been popular when they were kids; I only thought that they played "Pennsylvania 6-5000" to torment me and keep my friends away from the house.

But I know now that I'm never going to stop loving rock-and-roll, all kinds of rock-and-roll: the Beatles, the Rolling Stones, Hall and Oates, Talking Heads, the Doors, the Supremes, Tina Turner, Elvis Costello, Elvis Presley. I even like really bad rock-and-roll, although I guess that's where my age shows; I don't have the tolerance for Bon Jovi that I once had for the Raspberries.

We have friends who, when their son was a baby, used to put a record on and say, "Drop your butt, Phillip." And Phillip did. That's what I love: drop-your-butt music. It's one of the few things left in my life that makes me feel good without even thinking about it. I can walk into any bookstore and find dozens of books about motherhood and love and human relations and so many other things that we once did through a combination of intuition and emotion. I even heard recently that some school is giving a course on kissing, which makes me wonder if I'm missing something. But rock-and-roll flows through my veins, not my brain. There's nothing else that feels the same to me as, say, the faint sound of the opening dum-doo-doo-doo-doo-doo of "My Girl" coming from a radio on a summer day. I feel the way I felt when I first heard it. I feel good, as James Brown says.

There are lots of people who don't feel this way about rock-and-roll. Some of them don't understand it, like the Senate wives who said that records should have rating stickers on them so that you would know whether the lyrics were dirty. The kids who hang out at Mr. Big's sub shop in my neighborhood thought this would make record shopping a lot easier, because you could choose albums by how bad the rating was. Most of the people who love rock-and-roll just thought the labeling idea was dumb. Lyrics, after all, are not the point of rock-and-roll, despite how beautifully people like Bruce Springsteen and Joni Mitchell write. Lyrics are the point only in the case of "Louie, Louie"; the words have never been deciphered, but it is widely understood that they are about sex. That's understandable, because rock-and-roll is a lot like sex: If you talk seriously about it, it takes a lot of the feeling away—and feeling is the point.

Some people over-analyze rock-and-roll, just as they over-analyze everything else. They say things like "Bruce Springsteen is the poet laureate of the American dream gone sour," when all I need to know about Bruce Springsteen is that the saxophone bridge on "Jungleland" makes the back of my neck feel exactly the same way I felt the first time a boy kissed me, only over and over and over again. People write about Prince's "psychedelic masturbatory fantasies," but when I think about Prince, I don't really think, I just feel—feel the moment when, driving to the beach, I first heard "Kiss" on the radio and started bopping up and down in my seat like a seventeen-year-old on a day trip.

I've got precious few things in my life anymore that just make me feel, that make me jump up and dance, that make me forget the schedule and the job and the mortgage payments and just let me thrash around inside my skin. I've got precious few things I haven't studied and considered and reconsidered and studied some more. I don't know a chord change from a snare drum, but I know what I like, and I like feeling this way sometimes. I love rock-and-roll because in a time of talk, talk, talk, it's about action.

Here's a test: Get hold of a two-year-old, a person who has never read a single word about how heavy-metal musicians should be put in jail or about Tina Turner's "throaty alto range." Put "I Heard It Through the Grapevine" on the stereo. Stand the two-year-old in front of the stereo. The two-year-old will begin to dance. The two-year-old will drop his butt. Enough said.

ON "JUNK FOOD FOR THE SOUL"
In Defense of Rock and Roll

Frank Zappa

THE NATURE OF MUSIC

> Music is the soul's primitive and primary speech . . . without articulate speech or reason. It is not only not reasonable, it is hostile to reason. . . . Civilization . . . is the taming or domestication of the soul's raw passions. . . . Rock music has one appeal only, a barbaric appeal, to sexual desire—not love, not eros, but sexual desire undeveloped and untutored . . .
>
> —*A. Bloom*

This is a puff pastry version of the belief that music is the work of the Devil: that the nasty ol' Devil plays his fiddle and people dance around and we don't want to see them twitching like that. In fact, if one wants to be a real artist in the United States today and comment on our culture, one would be very far off the track if one did something delicate or sublime. This is not a noble, delicate, sublime country. This is a mess run by criminals. Performers who are doing the crude, vulgar, repulsive things Bloom doesn't enjoy are only commenting on that fact.

In general, antirock propositions began when rock 'n' roll began, and most of these were racially motivated. In the fifties, petitions were circulated which said, "Don't allow your children to buy Negro records." The petitions referred to the "raw unbridled passion" of screaming people with dark skin who are going to drive our children wild. Some things never go out of fashion in certain ideological camps. They are like tenets of the faith.

Music's real effect on people is a new field of science called psychoacoustics—the way an organism deals with wiggling air molecules. Our ears decode the wiggling air molecules, and that gives us the information of a particular musical sound. Our brain says, "This is music, this is a structure," and we deal with it based on certain tools we have acquired.

I personally make music because I want to ask a question, and I want to get an answer. If that question and answer amuse me, then statistically, there are a certain number of other people out there who have the same amusement factor. If I present my work to them, they will be amused by it, and we will all have a good time.

I need to be amused because I get bored easily and being amused entertains me. If I could be easily amused, like many people who like beer and football, I would never do anything because everything that would be beautiful for my life would already be provided by American television.

But beer and television bore me, so what am I going to do? I am going to be alive for X number of years. I have to do something with my time besides sleep and eat. So, I devise little things to amuse myself. If I can amuse somebody else, great. And if I can amuse somebody else and earn a living while doing it, that is a true miracle in the twentieth century!

MUSIC AND THE DARK FORCES OF THE SOUL

> To Plato and Nietzsche, the history of music is a series of attempts to give form and beauty to the dark, chaotic, premonitory forces in the soul—to make them serve a higher purpose, an ideal, to given man's duties a fullness.
>
> —*A. Bloom*

This is a man who has fallen for rock's fabricated image of itself. This is the worst kind of ivory tower intellectualism. Anybody who talks about dark forces is right on the fringe of mumbo jumbo. Dark forces? What is this, another product from Lucasfilm? The passions! When was the last time you saw an American exhibit any form of passion other than the desire to shoot a guy on the freeway? Those are the forces of evil as far as I am concerned.

If there are dark forces hovering in the vicinity of the music business, they are mercantile forces. We meet the darkness when we meet the orchestra committees, when we get in touch with funding organizations, when we deal with people who give grants and when we get into the world of commerce that greets us when we arrive with our piece of art. Whether it's a rock 'n' roll record or a symphony, it's the same machinery lurking out there.

The reason a person writes a piece of music has got nothing to do with dark forces. I certainly don't have dark forces lurking around me when I'm writing. If someone is going to write a piece of music, in fact they are preoccupied with the boring labor and very hard work involved. That's what's really going on.

WHAT MAKES MUSIC CLASSICAL

> Rock music . . . has risen to its current heights in the education of the young on the ashes of classical music, and in an atmosphere in which there is no intellectual resistance to attempts to tap the rawest passions. . . . Cultivation of the soul uses the passions and satisfies them

sublimating them and giving them an artistic unity. . . . Bach's religious intentions and Beethoven's revolutionary and humane ones are clear enough examples.

—*A. Bloom*

This is such nonsense. All the people recognized as great classical   *10*
composers are recognized at this point for two reasons:

One, during the time these composers were alive and writing they had patrons who liked what they did and who therefore paid them money or gave them a place to live so that the composers would stay alive by writing dots on pieces of paper. If any of the compositions these men wrote had not been pleasing to a church, a duke, or a king, they would have been out of work and their music would not have survived.

There is a book called *Grove's Dictionary of Music and Musicians,* with thousands of names in it. You have never heard of most of the people in that book, nor have you heard their music. That doesn't mean they wrote awful music, it means they didn't have hits.

So basically, the people who are recognized as the geniuses of classical music had hits. And the person who determined whether or not it was a hit was a king, a duke, or the church or whoever paid the bill. The desire to get a sandwich or something to drink had a lot to do with it. And the content of what they wrote was to a degree determined by the musical predilections of the guy who was paying the bill.

Today, we have a similar situation in rock 'n' roll. We have kings, dukes, and popes: the A&R guy who spots a group or screens the tape when it comes in; the business affairs guy who writes the contract; the radio station programmers who choose what records get air play.

The other reason the classical greats survived is their works are played   *15*
over and over again by orchestras. The reasons they are played over and over again are: (1) all the musicians in the orchestra know how to play them because they learned them in the conservatory; (2) the orchestra management programs these pieces because the musicians already know them and therefore it costs less to rehearse them; (3) the composers are dead so the orchestras pay no royalties for the use of the music.

Today, survivability is based on the number of specimens in the market place—the sheer numbers of plastic objects. Many other compositions from this era will vanish, but Michael Jackson's *Thriller* album will survive because there are 30 million odd pieces of plastic out there. No matter what we may think of the content, a future generation may pick up that piece of plastic and say, "Oh, they were like this."

I suppose somewhere in the future there will be other men like Bloom certifying that the very narrow spectrum of rock 'n' roll which survives composes the great works of the later half of the twentieth century.

THE DIFFERENCE BETWEEN CLASSICAL MUSIC AND ROCK 'N' ROLL

> Rock music provides premature ecstasy and, in this respect, is like the drugs with which it is allied. . . . These are the three great lyrical themes: sex, hate and a smarmy, hypocritical version of brotherly love. . . . Nothing noble, sublime, profound, delicate, tasteful or even decent can find a place in such tableaux.
>
> —*A. Bloom*

Again, Bloom is not looking at what is really going on here. The ugliness in this society is not a product of unrefined art, but of unrefined commerce, wild superstition, and religious fanaticism.

The real difference between the classics and rock 'n' roll is mostly a matter of form. In order to say we have written a symphony, the design we put on a piece of paper has to conform to certain specifications. We have an exposition that lasts a certain amount of time, then modulation, development, and recapitulation. It's like a box, like an egg carton. We must fill all the little spaces in the egg carton with the right forms. If we do, we can call it a symphony because it conforms to the spaces in that box.

Compare that creative process to rock 'n' roll. If we want to have an AM hit record, we have another egg carton to fill. We have an intro, a couple of verses, a bridge, another verse, and then a fade out. All of which requires a "hook." That's a very rigid form. If we wander away from that form, our song's not going to go on the radio because it doesn't sound like it fits into their format.

Now, whether the person writing the song graduated from a conservatory or whether they came out of a garage, they know that in order to finish a piece they have to do certain things to make it fit into a certain form. In the classical period the sonata or a concerto or symphony had to be that certain size and shape or else the king was not going to like it. One could die. These were literally matters of life and death, but not in the way Bloom defines them.

THE ROCK BUSINESS

> The family spiritual void has left the field open to rock music. . . . The result is nothing less than parents' loss of control over their children's moral education at a time when no one else is seriously concerned with it. This has been achieved by an alliance between the strange young males who have the gift of divining the mob's emergent wishes— our versions of Thrasymachus, Socrates' rhetorical adversary—and the record-holding executives, the new robber barons, who mine gold out of rock.
>
> —*A. Bloom*

There is some truth to that, but how did we get to this point and what do we do about it?

We got here because teenagers are the most sought-after consumers. The whole idea of merchandising the prepubescent masturbational fantasy is not necessarily the work of the songwriter or the singer, but the work of the merchandiser who has elevated rock 'n' roll to the commercial enterprise it is.

In the beginning, rock 'n' roll was young kids singing to other kids about their girlfriends. That's all there was. The guys who make these records came from Manual Arts High School. They went into a recording studio, were given some wine, $25, and a bunch of records when their song came out as a single—which made them heroes at school. That was their career, not, "Well, we're not going to sing until we get a $125 thousand advance."

Today, rock 'n' roll is about getting a contract with a major company, and pretty much doing what the company tells you to do. The company promotes the image of rock 'n' roll as being wild and fun when in fact it's just a dismal business.

Record companies have people who claim to be experts on what the public really wants to hear. And they inflict their taste on the people who actually make the music. To be a big success, you need a really big company behind you because really big companies can make really big distribution deals.

Even people who are waiting to get into the business know it's a business. They spend a great deal of time planning what they will look like and getting a good publicity photo before they walk in the door with their tape. And the record companies tend to take the attitude that it doesn't make too much difference what the tape sounds like as long as the artists look right, because they can always hire a producer who will fix up the sound and make it the way they want it—so long as the people wear the right clothes and have the right hair.

RETAINING CLASSICAL MUSIC

Classical music is dead among the young. . . . Rock music is as unquestioned and unproblematic as the air the students breathe, and very few have any acquaintance at all with classical music. . . . Classical music is now a special taste, like Greek language or pre-Columbian archeology, not a common culture of reciprocal communication and psychological shorthand.

—A. Bloom

On this point, Bloom and I can agree, but how can a child be blamed for consuming only that which is presented to him? Most kids have never been in contact with anything other than this highly merchandised stuff.

When I testified in front of the Senate, I pointed out that if they don't like the idea of young people buying certain kinds of music, why don't they stick a few dollars back into the school system to have music appreciation? There are kids today who have never heard a string quartet; they have never heard a symphony orchestra. I argued that the money for music appreciation courses, in terms of social good and other benefits such as improved behavior or uplifting the spirit, is far less than the cost of another set of uniforms for the football team. But I frankly don't see people waving banners in the street saying more music appreciation in schools.

When I was in school, we could go into a room and they had records there. I could hear anything I wanted by going in there and putting on a record. I won't say I enjoyed everything that was played for me, but I was curious, and if I had never heard any of that music I wouldn't know about it. *30*

Once we're out of school, the time we can spend doing that type of research is limited because most of us are out looking for a job flipping hamburgers in the great tradition of the Reagan economic miracle. When all is said and done, that's the real source of America's barren and arid lives.

CURBING THE SEXPLOITATION INDUSTRY

Tipper Gore

I can't even count the times in the last three years, since I began to express my concern about violence and sexuality in rock music, that I have been called a prude, a censor, a music hater, even a book burner. So let me be perfectly clear: I detest censorship. I'm not advocating censorship but rather a candid and vigorous debate about the dangers posed for our children by what I call the "sexploitation industry."

We don't need to put a childproof cap on the world, but we do need to remind the nation that children live in it, too, and deserve respect and sensitive treatment.

When I launched this campaign in 1985 (long before my husband dreamed of running for president), I went to the source of the problem, sharing my concerns and proposals with the entertainment industry. Many producers were sympathetic. Some cooperated with my efforts. But others have been overtly hostile, accusing me of censorship and suggesting, unfairly, that my motives are political.

This resistance and hostility has convinced me of the need for a two-pronged campaign, with equal effort from the entertainment industry and concerned parents. Entertainment producers must take the first step, by labeling sexually explicit material.

But the industry cannot be expected to solve the problem on its *5* own. Parents should encourage producers to cooperate and praise them when they do. Producers need to know that parents are aware of the issue and are reading their advisory labels. Above all, they need to know that somebody out there cares, that the community at large is not apathetic about the deep and lasting damage being done to our children.

What's at issue is not the occasional sexy rock lyric. What troubles— indeed, outrages—me is far more vicious: a celebration of the most gruesome violence, coupled with the explicit message that sadomasochism is the essence of sex.

We're surrounded by examples—in rock lyrics, on television, at the movies and in rental videos. One major TV network recently aired a preview of a soap opera rape scene during a morning game show.

The newest craze in horror movies is something called the "teen slasher" film, and it typically depicts the killing, torture and sexual mutilation of women in sickening detail. Several rock groups now simulate sexual torture and murder during live performances. Others titillate youthful audiences with strippers confined in cages on stage and with half-naked dancers, who often act out sex with band members. Sexual brutality has become the common currency of America's youth culture and with it the pervasive degradation of women.

Why is this graphic violence dangerous? It's especially damaging for young children because they lack the moral judgment of adults. Many children are only dimly aware of the consequences of their actions, and, as parents know, they are excellent mimics. They often imitate violence they see on TV, without necessarily understanding what they are doing or what the consequences might be.

One 5-year-old boy from Boston recently got up from watching a *10* teen slasher film and stabbed a 2-year-old girl with a butcher knife. He didn't mean to kill her (and luckily he did not). He was just imitating the man in the video.

Nor does the danger end as children grow older. National health officials tell us that children younger than teen-agers are apt to react to excessive violence with suicide, satanism, drug and alcohol abuse. Even grown-ups are not immune. One series of studies by researchers at the University of Wisconsin found that men exposed to films in which women are beaten, butchered, maimed and raped were significantly desensitized to the violence. Not only did they express less sympathy for the victims, they even approved of lesser penalties in hypothetical rape trials.

Sadomasochistic pornography is a kind of poison. Like most poisons, it probably cannot be totally eliminated, but it certainly could be labeled for what it is and be kept away from those who are most vulnerable.

The largest record companies have agreed to this—in principle at least. In November 1985, the Recording Industry Association of America adopted my proposal to alert parents by having producers either put warning labels on records with explicitly sexual lyrics or display the lyrics on the outside of the record jackets. Since then, some companies have complied in good faith, although others have not complied at all.

This is where we parents must step in. We must let the industry know we're angry. We must press for uniform voluntary compliance with labeling guidelines. And we must take an active interest at home in what our children are watching and listening to. After all, we can hardly expect that the labels or printed lyrics alone will discourage young consumers.

Some parents may want to write to the record companies. Others 15 can give their support to groups like the Parent Teacher Association, which have endorsed the labeling idea. All of us can use our purchasing power. We have more power than we think, and we must use it. For the sake of our children, we simply can't afford to slip back into apathy.

My concern for the health and welfare of children has nothing to do with politics: It is addressed to conservatives and liberals alike. Some civil libertarians believe it is wrong even to raise these questions—just as some conservatives believe that the government should police popular American culture. I reject both these views. I have no desire to restrain artists or cast a "chill" over popular culture. But I believe parents have First Amendment rights, too.

The fate of the family, the dignity of women, the mental health of children—these concerns belong to everyone. We must protect our children with choice, not censorship. Let's start working in our communities to forge a moral consensus for the 1990s. Children need our help, and we must summon the courage to examine the culture that shapes their lives.

THE EFFECT OF CENSORSHIP ON ATTITUDES TOWARD POPULAR MUSIC

Brian K. Simmons

Recent years have seen a resurgence of interest in the content of popular music. Efforts by powerful activist groups such as the Parents' Music Resource Center, Congressional testimony by popular music artists and *2 Live Crew*'s obscenity trial have refocused national attention on the timeless problem of defining the limits of acceptable expression. With increased frequency, censorship of lyrics is being advocated as a solution.

There are many who feel that rather than curbing instances of undesirable content, censorship officials instead fuel the desire for controversial material. Anecdotal evidence seems to support such a contention. For example, when the Sex Pistols' "God Save the Queen" came under fire from the BBC, airplay on commercial radio stations and retail sales of the record increased dramatically (Frith). Furthermore, recording artist Frank Zappa warns that censoring objectionable popular music will only make the targeted audience want that music more. Zappa's intriguing notion provides the focus of this study.

There has been no basic empirical investigation of the relationship between the censorship of popular music and its perceived desirability. In this study, whether participants' knowledge of a popular album's censorship affected their desire to hear the material was evaluated experimentally in a field setting.

REVIEW OF LITERATURE

Controlling exposure to popular music through censorship is not a new idea. In surveying the history of the censorship of rock lyrics, McDonald notes that "an examination of the history of rock and roll reveals that the concerns of the Parents' Music Resource Center are certainly not new or original, since both individuals and organizations have long complained of the negative influence of rock and roll songs" (294). He further notes that numerous artists and songs have been the censorship targets of various entities. There has been no investigation of the effects of such actions.

The theoretical basis for examining the impacts of censorship can   5 be found in the literature of psychological reactance theory. Reactance theory holds that whenever a person's free choice is threatened the result is for him or her to want those choices even more (Brehm, *Theory of Psychological Reactance*). Thus, when freedom is lost (as when censoring an album prevents its purchase), the expected result would be reactance against the proscribing agent (the censor) and a measurable increase in the desire to possess the prohibited object (the censored album).

Reactance has been demonstrated in several social settings and over a wide span of ages (Brehm, *Psychological Reactance;* Brehm and Weintraub). The obstinate behavior of two-year-old children during this period is explained by their developing awareness of individual choice in the face of parental imposed limits on their behavior. Researchers also found evidence of reactance in adult consumer choices. Mazis and Mazis, Settle and Leslie examined the effects of a law which banned phosphates in all laundry detergents sold in two South Florida counties. The researchers discovered that consumers became more favorably disposed toward the detergents with phosphates only after the law was enacted. Similarly, a study by Broeder revealed that juries react favorably to information judges deemed inadmissible by valuing it more.

Adolescents (who comprise the largest audience for popular music) are especially vulnerable to psychological reactance. For example, when

Driscoll, Davis and Lipetz studied adolescent romantic relationships they found that a teen's desire and love for a member of the opposite sex was positively related to the extent the relationship was marked by parental interference.

Investigation into the effects of censorship on opinion change, however, has been negligible. As Cialdini notes, "although much data exist concerning our reactions to observing various kinds of potentially censorable material—media violence, pornography, radical political rhetoric—there is surprisingly little evidence on our reaction to the censoring of material" (239). The first empirical studies in this area were conducted by Ashmore, Ramchandra and Jones. In this experiment, college students were told that a controversial speech they were scheduled to hear had been censored by administrators at the college. Compared to control groups, participants' opinion about the position advocated in the scheduled speech became more favorable, while their estimation of the college administration became less favorable. These findings were interpreted in terms of psychological reactance.

Worchel and Arnold confirmed these findings in a slightly modified version of Ashmore et al.'s experiment. Worchel and Arnold note that "censorship whether by a positive, negative, or neutral source, enhances the desires of the potential audience to hear the communication and causes them to change their opinion in the direction of the censored communication. . . . The experiment yielded results suggesting that, in some cases, the audience may lower its opinion of a group if it takes on the role of censor" (374). Later, Worchel, Arnold and Baker found that when students learned about the banning of a speech favoring coed dorms, they were more in favor of the idea of coed dorms. Finally, Zellinger, Fromkin, Speller and Kohn (1974) demonstrated similar results using acts of censorship such as age restrictions. In their study, college students were shown advertisements for a novel which included a warning that the book was restricted to those 21 years of age and older. When the students were later asked to state their feelings toward the restricted book, they not only wanted to read it more than those in the control group, their estimated enjoyment of the book also rose.

METHODOLOGY

The extant research regarding the results of censoring information   10
is minimal. And, no known research has been conducted in the area of popular music censorship. However, recent developments seem to call for inquiry in this area. The present study sought to investigate the following null hypothesis: There is no statistically significant difference between a potential music listener's opinion toward an album when they know it is censored and when they do not.

A pretest-posttest with control group experiment was conducted involving 65 college students at a small Midwestern university. The pretest phase of the experiment began when two groups of randomly selected participants were given a slip of paper with the titles of nine rock albums arranged alphabetically by artist. Eight of the albums and artists were "legitimate," while one was fictitious. The subjects were then asked to rank order each of the albums according to which they would most like to hear. The statistical mean of each album was then calculated.

One week later, one-half the same subjects were told that in the previous session many students apparently were not familiar with each of the albums, and that they would be given some new information and asked to rank order the same ones again. This time, next to each album title and artist was a one-sentence description of the album's contents, e.g. "'Combat Rock' The Clash (This is the album containing 'Rock the Casbah' etc.)." The lone fictitious entry (the treatment) was "'By the Sword' by A.R.I. (This is the only album to have been declared legally obscene in Great Britain)." These descriptions were intended to serve as a point of reference for the subjects and to disguise the treatment. The other half of the pretest group was simply told the first set of rankings was lost and was asked to repeat their original rankings using the same information, and the statistical mean of each album was calculated.

Afterwards, a paired t-Test was used to analyze the statistical significance of the differences between the pretest and posttest means of the fictitious album. The assumption was that the new information about the fictitious album being declared legally obscene in Great Britain would cause the subjects to desire to hear the album more than before they knew of the censorship. Thus, the hypothesized relationship between a potential listener's opinion toward an album they know is censored and one that is not could be empirically tested.

RESULTS AND DISCUSSION

The experiment found that there was a statistical difference in the pretest and posttest means of the fictitious album as ranked by the group receiving the treatment. The album's pretest mean was 6.30303, while its posttest mean was 4.166667 ($t = 4.94, p > .05$). The difference in the album's mean as ranked by the control group was not statistically significant (4.261539 vs 4.907692, $t = 1.57, p > .05$). Hence the above stated null hypothesis was rejected.

The present study would seem to lend credence to the notion that the censoring of rock music can lead to an increased desire on the part of the listeners to hear the censored material. As noted above, one explanation for this is psychological reactance theory, which holds that people seek to re-establish freedoms forcibly taken from them.

The findings of this experiment contain several implications. First, the study indicates that those seeking to control people's access to rock music lyrics are actually making the problem worse by fostering a desire to hear the banned communication. This is especially true when the present study's findings are linked with previous research which found adolescents to be particularly susceptible to psychological reactance (Driscoll, Davis and Lipetz; Worchel and Arnold).

Second, the study lends some support to psychological reactance as an explanation for the phenomenon, rather than balance theory. Other researchers have suggested that if there is a "boomerang effect" when censoring materials it is the result of subjects seeking to reconcile their orientations toward the artist, the music, and the censor, as balance theory would hold. However, Worchel and Arnold reported that their experiment indicated that such was not the case, and that reactance theory was a better supported explanation for their discovery of a "boomerang effect." Similarly, the present study's findings can best be seen in light of reactance theory.

Third, the study would seem to indicate that the lyrical content of an album is possibly a factor in the subject's desire to hear a communication. Since the only knowledge subjects had of the fictitious album was that it had been declared legally obscene in Great Britain, it stands to reason that they were aware of the objectionable lyrical content, and that this was the driving reason behind their desire to hear the communication. However, this conclusion is tenuous at best as previous research suggests that listeners may not be attentive to lyrical content in any substantive way (Prinsky and Rosenbaum). Interestingly, if this is so then the entire premise on which banning objectionable lyrics stands is dubious.

The present study also has some limitations which must be noted. First, the method of revealing the subjects' desire to hear the communication is somewhat artificial. Asking the subjects to rank order an inclusive list of albums according to their desire to hear them is different than determining if they would actually purchase the album. Also, forcing the subjects to rank order the albums does not necessarily mean that the subject actually wants to hear a particular album. Third, there are other things which might also determine the subject's desire to hear the communication. Perhaps the fictitious album did not fall into the subjects' range of musical taste. Perhaps they had never heard of some of the albums even after additional information was given to them.

Future research is needed in this area. The present study, being one [20] of the first in the area, is exploratory in nature. The conclusions reached here are tentative. Minimally, further research with a greater degree of generalizability is called for. In addition, the notion that censoring rock lyrics causes listeners to have lower esteem for the censor needs to be empirically tested. Experiments need to be designed which will control the other factors which might influence a person's desire to hear a popular music selection (other than knowledge that it was censored). Finally, the entire line of inquiry needs to be evaluated in light of research suggesting that listeners do not attend to rock lyrics.

In conclusion, the present study sought to test the relationship between a potential music listener's knowledge of a censored song and his/her desire to hear that communication. It was found that there is a statistically significant relationship between the two. In other words, there does seem to be a "boomerang effect" associated with censoring popular music albums. Potential listeners do have an increased desire to hear the censored material after they know it has been censored. While this is not good news for those seeking to widen the scope of censored materials, it does provide some preliminary scientifically-grounded answers to an area previously dominated by mere conjecture.

WORKS CITED

Ashmore, R.D., V. Ramchandra, and R.A. Jones. "Censorship as an Attitude Change Induction." Presented at Eastern Psychological Association Convention, 1971.

Brehm, J.W. *A Theory of Psychological Reactance.* New York: Academic P, 1966. Brehm, S.S. "Psychological Reactance and the Attractiveness of Unattainable Objects: Sex Differences in Children's Responses to an Elimination of Freedom." *Sex Roles* 7 (1981): 937–49.

Brehm, S.S., and M. Weintraub. "Physical Barriers and Psychological Reactance: Two-year-olds' Responses to Threats to Freedom." *Journal of Personality and Social Psychology* 35 (1977): 830–36.

Broder, D. "The University of Chicago Jury Project." *Nebraska Law Review* 38 (1959): 744–60.

Cialdini, R.B. *Influence: Science and Practice,* 2nd ed. Glenview, IL: Scott Foresman, 1989.

Driscoll, R., K.E. Davis, and M.E. Lipetz. "Parental Influence and Romantic Love: The Romeo and Juliet Effect." *Journal of Personality and Social Psychology* 24 (1972): 1–10.

Frith, S. *Sound Effects: Youth, Leisure, and the Politics of Rock 'n' Roll.* New York: Pantheon, 1981.

Mazis, M.B. "Antipollution Measures and Psychological Reactance Theory: A Field Study." *Journal of Personality and Social Psychology* 31 (1975): 954–66.

Mazis, M.B., R.B. Settle, and D.C. Leslie. "Elimination of Phosphate Detergents and Psychological Reactance." *Journal of Marketing Research* 10 (1973): 390–95.

McDonald, J. "Censoring Rock Lyrics: A Historical Analysis of the Debate." *Youth & Society* 19 (1988): 294–313.

Prinsky, L.E., and J.L. Rosenbaum. "Leer-ics or Lyrics: Teenage Impressions of Rock 'n' roll." *Youth and Society* 18 (1987): 384–97.

Worchel, S., and S. Arnold. "The Effects of Censorship and Attractiveness of the Censor on Attitude Change." *Journal of Experimental Social Psychology* 9 (1973): 365–77.

Worchel, S., S. Arnold, and M. Baker. "The Effect of Censorship on Attitude Change: The Influence of Censor and Communicator Characteristics." *Journal of Applied Social Psychology* 5 (1975): 222–39.

Zappa, F. Statement to congress, U.S. Senate, 99th Congress, 1st Session, Committee on Commerce, Science and Transportation. *Record labeling.* Hearing, Sept. 19, 1985 (S. Hrg. 99/529). Washington D.C.: Government Printing Office, 1985.

Zellinger, D.A., H.L. Fromkin, D.E. Speller, and C.A. Kohn. *A Commodity Theory Analysis of the Effects of Age Restrictions on Pornographic Materials.* Paper No. 440, Lafayette, IN: Purdue U, Institute for Research in the Behavioral, Economic and Management Sciences, 1974.

ICE-T: THE ISSUE IS SOCIAL RESPONSIBILITY

Michael Kinsley

How did the company that publishes this magazine come to produce a record glorifying the murder of police?

> I got my 12-gauge sawed off
> I got my headlights turned off
> I'm 'bout to bust some shots off
> I'm 'bout to dust some cops off . . .
> Die, Die, Die Pig, Die!

So go the lyrics to *Cop Killer* by the rapper Ice-T on the album *Body Count.* The album is released by Warner Bros. Records, part of the Time Warner media and entertainment conglomerate.

In a *Wall Street Journal* op-ed piece laying out the company's position, Time Warner Co-CEO Gerald Levin makes two defenses. First, Ice-T's *Cop Killer* is misunderstood. "It doesn't incite or glorify violence . . . It's his fictionalized attempt to get inside a character's head . . . *Cop Killer* is no more a call for gunning down the police than *Frankie and Johnny* is a summons for jilted lovers to shoot one another." Instead of "finding ways to silence the messenger," we should be "heeding the anguished cry contained in his message."

This defense is self-contradictory. *Frankie and Johnny* does not pretend to have a political "message" that must be "heeded." If *Cop Killer* has a message, it is that the murder of policemen is a justified response to police brutality. And not in self-defense, but in premeditated acts of revenge against random cops. ("I know your family's grievin'—f____ 'em.")

Killing policemen is a good thing—that is the plain meaning of the words, and no "larger understanding" of black culture, the rage of the streets or anything else can explain it away. This is not Ella Fitzgerald telling a story in a song. As in much of today's popular music, the line between performer and performance is purposely blurred. These are po- 5 litical sermonettes clearly intended to endorse the sentiments being expressed. Tracy Morrow (Ice-T) himself has said, "I scared the police, and they need to be scared." That seems clear.

The company's second defense of *Cop Killer* is the classic one of free expression: "We stand for creative freedom. We believe that the worth of what an artist or journalist has to say does not depend on preapproval from a government official or a corporate censor."

Of course Ice-T has the right to say whatever he wants. But that doesn't require any company to provide him an outlet. And it doesn't relieve a company of responsibility for the messages it chooses to promote. Judgment is not "censorship." Many an "anguished cry" goes unrecorded. This one was recorded, and promoted, because a successful artist under contract wanted to record it. Nothing wrong with making money, but a company cannot take the money and run from the responsibility.

The founder of *Time,* Henry Luce, would snort at the notion that his company should provide a value-free forum for the exchange of ideas. In Luce's system, editors were supposed to make value judgments and promote the truth as they saw it. *Time* has moved far from its old Lucean rigidity—far enough to allow for dissenting essays like this one. That evolution is a good thing, as long as it's not a handy excuse for abandoning all standards.

No commercial enterprise need agree with every word that appears under its corporate imprimatur. If Time Warner now intends to be "a global force for encouraging the confrontation of ideas," that's swell. But a policy of allowing diverse viewpoints is not a moral free pass. Pro and con on national health care is one thing; pro and con on killing policemen is another.

A bit of sympathy is in order for Time Warner. It is indeed a "global 10 force" with media tentacles around the world. If it imposes rigorous standards and values from the top, it gets accused of corporate censorship. If it doesn't, it gets accused of moral irresponsibility. A dilemma. But someone should have thought of that before deciding to become a global force.

And another genuine dilemma. Whatever the actual merits of *Cop Killer,* if Time Warner withdraws the album now the company will be perceived as giving in to outside pressure. That is a disastrous precedent for a global conglomerate.

The Time-Warner merger of 1989 was supposed to produce corporate "synergy": the whole was supposed to be more than the sum of the parts. The *Cop Killer* controversy is an example of negative synergy. People get mad at *Cop Killer* and start boycotting the movie *Batman Returns.* A reviewer praises *Cop Killer* ("Tracy Morrow's poetry takes a switchblade and deftly slices life's jugular," etc.), and *Time* is accused of corruption instead of mere foolishness. Senior Time Warner executives find themselves under attack for—and defending—products of their company they neither honestly care for nor really understand, and doubtless weren't even aware of before controversy hit.

Anyway, it's absurd to discuss *Cop Killer* as part of the "confrontation of ideas"—or even as an authentic anguished cry of rage from the ghetto. *Cop Killer* is a cynical commercial concoction, designed to titillate its audience with imagery of violence. It merely exploits the authentic anguish of the inner city for further titillation. Tracy Morrow is in business for a buck, just like Time Warner. *Cop Killer* is an excellent joke on the white establishment, of which the company's anguished apologia ("Why can't we hear what rap is trying to tell us?") is the punch line.

ICE-T: THE ISSUE IS FREE SPEECH

Barbara Ehrenreich

Ice-T's song *Cop Killer* is as bad as they come. This is black anger—raw, rude and cruel—and one reason the song's so shocking is that in postliberal America, black anger is virtually taboo. You won't find it on TV, not on the *McLaughlin Group* or *Crossfire,* and certainly not in the placid features of Arsenio Hall or Bernard Shaw. It's been beaten back into the outlaw subcultures of rap and rock, where, precisely because it is taboo, it sells. And the nastier it is, the faster it moves off the shelves. As Ice-T asks in another song on the same album, "Goddamn what a brotha gotta do/ To get a message through/ To the red, white and blue?"

But there's a gross overreaction going on, building to a veritable paroxysm of white denial. A national boycott has been called, not just of the song or Ice-T, but of all Time Warner products. The President himself has denounced Time Warner as "wrong" and Ice-T as "sick." Ollie North's Freedom Alliance has started a petition drive aimed at bringing Time-Warner executives to trial for "sedition and anarchy."

Much of this is posturing and requires no more courage than it takes to stand up in a VFW hall and condemn communism or crack. Yes, *Cop Killer* is irresponsible and vile. But Ice-T is as right about some things as he is righteous about the rest. And ultimately, he's not even dangerous—least of all to the white power structure his songs condemn.

The "danger" implicit in all the uproar is of empty-headed, suggestible black kids, crouching by their boom boxes, waiting for the word. But what Ice-T's fans know and his detractors obviously don't is that *Cop Killer* is just one more entry in pop music's long history of macho hyperbole and violent boast. Flip to the classic-rock station, and you might catch the Rolling Stones announcing "the time is right for violent revolooshun!" from their 1968 hit *Street Fighting Man.* And where were the defenders of our law-enforcement officers when a white British group, the Clash, taunted its fans with lyrics: "When they kick open your front door/How you gonna come/With your hands on your head/Or on the trigger of your gun?"

"Die, Die, Die Pig" is strong speech, but the Constitution protects   5
strong speech, and it's doing so this year more aggressively than ever. The Supreme Court has just downgraded cross burnings to the level of bonfires and ruled that it's no crime to throw around verbal grenades like "nigger" and "kike." Where are the defenders of decorum and social stability when prime-time demagogues like Howard Stern deride African Americans as "spear chuckers"?

More to the point, young African Americans are not so naive and suggestible that they have to depend on a compact disc for their sociology lessons. To paraphrase another song from another era, you don't need a rap song to tell which way the wind is blowing. Black youths know that the police are likely to see them through a filter of stereotypes as miscreants and potential "cop killers." They are aware that a black youth is seven times as likely to be charged with a felony as a white youth who has committed the same offense, and is much more likely to be imprisoned.

They know, too, that in a shameful number of cases, it is the police themselves who indulge in "anarchy" and violence. The U.S. Justice Department has received 47,000 complaints of police brutality in the past six years, and Amnesty International has just issued a report on police brutality in Los Angeles, documenting 40 cases of "torture or cruel, inhuman or degrading treatment."

Menacing as it sounds, the fantasy in *Cop Killer* is the fantasy of the powerless and beaten down—the black man who's been hassled once too often ("A pig stopping me for nothin'!"), spread-eagled against a police car, pushed around. It's not a "responsible" fantasy (fantasies seldom are). It's not even a very creative one. In fact, the sad thing about *Cop Killer* is that it falls for the cheapest, more conventional image of rebellion that our culture offers: the lone gunman spraying fire from his AK-47. This is not "sedition"; it's the familiar, all-American, Hollywood-style pornography of violence.

Which is why Ice-T is right to say he's no more dangerous than George Bush's pal Arnold Schwarzenegger, who wasted an army of cops in *Terminator 2*. Images of extraordinary cruelty and violence are marketed every day, many of far less artistic merit than *Cop Killer*. This is our free market of ideas and images, and it shouldn't be any less free for a black man than for other purveyors of "irresponsible" sentiments, from David Duke to Andrew Dice Clay.

Just, please, don't dignify Ice-T's contribution with the word   10
sedition. The past masters of sedition—men like George Washington, Toussaint-Louverture, Fidel Castro or Mao Zedong, all of whom led and won armed insurrections—would be unimpressed by *Cop Killer* and probably saddened. They would shake their heads and mutter words like "infantile" and "adventurism." They might point out that the cops

are hardly a noble target, being, for the most part, honest working stiffs who've got stuck with the job of patrolling ghettos ravaged by economic decline and official neglect.

There is a difference, the true seditionist would argue, between a revolution and a gesture of macho defiance. Gestures are cheap. They feel good, they blow off some rage. But revolutions, violent or otherwise, are made by people who have learned how to count very slowly to ten.

FREE SPEECH: LYRICS, LIBERTY, AND LICENSE

Sam Brownback

Good afternoon. I want to thank the City Club of Cleveland for its hospitality, and the students who run the Youth Forum for the invitation, their top-notch administrative skills, and the opportunity to speak to you today.

I want to talk with you today about music and freedom, about lyrics, liberty and license. This is an issue that is important to me—as it is, I suspect, important to you. I can't think of a more fitting place for this discussion here, at a forum dedicated to upholding the principle of free speech, in Cleveland, the home of the Rock and Roll Hall of Fame.

As many of you know, I recently held a Senate hearing on the impact of violent music lyrics on young people. During this hearing, we heard a variety of witnesses testify on the effects of music lyrics that glorified rape, sexual torture, violence and murder. Some of these lyrics are almost unbelievably awful but they are backed by huge, powerful, prestigious corporations. I have grown more and more concerned about the content and the impact of these lyrics. And I have publicly criticized the entertainment executives who produce, promote, and profit from such music.

I am also the only Senator on the Commerce Committee to vote against a very popular bill that would coerce TV stations into labeling their programs.

I publicly opposed V-chip legislation. I have consistently voted against any sort of government involvement in regulating or rating music or television. 5

Some people don't think the two go together. They think that if you talk about some music lyrics being degrading and violent, then you must be in favor of censorship. Others think that if you vote against various government restrictions on television programs, or music content, you must approve of those programs and songs. Both views are mistaken.

And today, I'd like to talk about legislating in a way to maximize freedom, and agitating for civility and decency, and why the two not only can go together, but should—and indeed, if we are to preserve freedom, they must.

Most of you here have strong ideas about music. As indeed, you should. Music is powerful. It changes our mood, shapes our experience, affects our thoughts, alters our pulse, touches our lives. The rhythm, the beat, and the lyrics all impress us with their message. Thousands of years ago, the great philosopher Plato stated, "Musical training is a more potent instrument than any other, because rhythm and harmony find their way into the inward places of the soul, on which they mightily fasten."

As such, music lyrics have profound public consequences. In many ways, the music industry is more influential than anything that happens in Washington. After all, most people spend a lot more time listening to music than watching C-Span or reading the newspaper. They're more likely to recognize musicians than Supreme Court Justices. Most of us spend more time thinking about music than laws, bills, and policies. And that's probably a good thing.

And as many of you know, no one spends more time listening to music than young people. In fact, one recent study conducted by the Carnegie Foundation concluded that the average teenager listens to music around four hours a day. In contrast, less than an hour is spent on homework or reading, less than 20 minutes a day is spent talking to Mom, and less than five minutes is spent talking with Dad. If this is true, there are a lot of people who spend more time listening to shock-rock artist Marilyn Manson or Snoop Doggy Dogg than Mom or Dad. In fact, Marilyn Manson himself said: "Music is such a powerful medium now. The kids don't even know who the President is, but they know what's on MTV. I think if anyone like Hitler or Mussolini were alive now, they would have to be rock stars."

In short, because of the power of music, the time we spend listening to it, and the potency of its messages, music has a powerful public impact. It affects us, not only privately, but publicly. It helps shape our attitudes and assumptions, and thus, our decisions and behavior—all of which has a public dimension, and merits public debate.

Frankly, I believe there needs to be more public discourse over music. It is too important to ignore. Its influence reaches around the world. American rock and rap are popular exports. They are listened to by billions, in virtually every nation on earth. And for good or bad, our music shapes the way in which many people around the world view the U.S.— American music is the most pervasive (and loudest) ambassador we have. Unfortunately, its message is too often a destructive one.

Over the past few years, I have grown concerned about the popularity of some lyrics—lyrics which glorify violence and debase women. Some recent best-selling albums have included graphic descriptions of

10

murder, torture, and rape. Women are objectified, often in the most obscene and degrading ways. Songs such as Prodigy's single "Smack My Bitch Up" or "Don't Trust a Bitch" by the group, 'Mo Thugs, encourage animosity and even violence toward women. The alternative group Nine Inch Nails enjoyed both critical and commercial success with their song "Big Man with a Gun" which describes forcing a woman into oral sex and shooting her in the head at pointblank range.

Shock-rock bands such as Marilyn Manson or Cannibal Corpse go even further, with lyrics describing violence, rape, and torture. Consider just a few song titles by the group Cannibal Corpse; "Orgasm by Torture," or "Stripped, Raped and Strangled." As their titles indicate, the lyrics to these songs celebrate hideous crimes against women.

Many of you may already know the kind of lyrics I am talking about. If not, it is useful to read some of them—they won't be hard to find; they are quite popular. Then ask youself: what are the real-world effects of these lyrics? What do these lyrics celebrate, and what do they ridicule or denounce? What are the consequences of glorifying violence and glamorizing rape? Have record companies behaved responsibly when they produce music that debases women? You and your friends may come up with different answers. But they are good questions to think about. And I hope recording industry executives think about them as well.

It is a simple fact of human nature that what we hear and see, what we experience, affects our thoughts, our emotions, and our behavior. If it did not, commercials wouldn't exist, and anyone who ever spent a dollar on advertising would be a complete fool. But advertising is a multi-billion dollar business because it works. It creates an appetite for things we don't need, it motivates us to buy things we may not have otherwise. What we see and hear changes how we act.

Now think back to the music we have been talking about. How do these lyrics affect their fans? Different people will be affected in different ways. Some teens are more vulnerable than others. Young people who grow up in strong families, going to good schools, with adults who are committed to them, are probably going to be just fine. But let's consider what happens in some of America's inner cities, where many young men grow up without fathers, without good schools, surrounded by violence—how does this affect the way they think about, and treat women? Moreover, there have already been several studies done that have pointed to a loss of self-esteem among girls and young women. How does the fact that some of the best-selling albums feature songs that refer to them exclusively as "those bitches and sluts" affect them?

There are no easy answers to these questions. It is impossible to quantify the ways in which such lyrics affect us. But it is equally impossible to believe they have no effect at all.

Of course, most rock and rap do not have hyperviolent or perverse lyrics. In the grand scale of things, it is a small number of songs from an

15

even smaller number of bands that produce these sort of lyrics. They are the exception, not the rule.

It is also true that people will disagree over which music is offen-   *20* sive. Some people thought the Beach Boys were a problem, and some think the Spice Girls are. I do not happen to be one of them. There will always be songs about which reasonable people with good judgment will disagree.

But there should also be some things that we can all agree upon. And one of those things is that music which glorifies rape, violence and bigotry is wrong. It may be constitutionally protected. The huge entertainment corporations that produce, promote and profit from this sort of record may have a right to do so. But it is not the right thing to do.

So this past November, I held a hearing on the impact of music lyrics which glorified violence and debased women. We heard from a variety of witnesses—a parent, a representative from the American Academy of Pediatrics, a Stanford Professor, the head of the Recording Industry Association, and the head of the National Political Congress of Black Women, who has campaigned against gangsta rap. Should any of you want to see the record of the hearing, you may do so by logging on to my senate web site.

I held this hearing for two reasons: 1) to raise public awareness of some of these lyrics, so that potential consumers can make more informed judgments before they buy the music, 2) to examine, through hearing from witnesses from the medical and academic communities, the impact of such lyrics on youth attitudes and well-being.

It is a particularly important time to do so. Actual and virtual violence have dramatically increased over the last few decades. Over the last thirty years, violent juvenile crime has jumped over 500%. Teen suicide has tripled.

Crimes against women have increased. Casual teen drug use has   *25* jumped by almost 50 percent in the last four years alone.

There is also a sense that we have lost ground in ways that defy easy measurement. There is a feeling that we as a society have grown coarser, meaner, more alienated. Violence seems not only more widespread but less shocking. We have become more accustomed, and more tolerant, of tragedy, violence, and hate.

At the same time, there has been a marked increase in violence and misogyny in popular music. Now, this is not to say that music violence was the cause of real-life violence. Music is only one slice of the entertainment world, a small part of the popular culture. Whatever impact music has on our attitudes and behavior is bound to be complex and variant. But the best way, I believe—then and now—to determine what that impact is, what influence violent lyrics exert, is to encourage research, debate and discussion.

During the hearing, we did not call for censorship. We did not propose, consider, or tolerate any restriction of free speech. We did not ask

for legislation, regulation, litigation, or any other machination of government that would prohibit even the most racist, violent antiwoman
lyrics. When it comes to First Amendment issues, I vote as a libertarian.
I have voted against labels, against restrictions, against government med-
dling. But it is not enough to merely legislate in a mannner to protect
freedom. It is also necessary to agitate for the cultural conditions that safe-
guard freedom. Let me explain what I mean.

For free societies to endure, there must be a distinction between
what is allowed and what is honored. I believe that the First Amendment
assures the widest possible latitude in allowing various forms of speech—
including offensive, obnoxious speech. But the fact that certain forms of
speech should be allowed does not mean that they should be honored, or
given respectability. There are many forms of speech that should be thoroughly criticized, even as they are protected. Freedom of expression is
not immunity from criticism.

The proper response to offensive speech is criticism—not censor-   30
ship, and not apathy. Vigorous criticism of the perverse, hateful, and violent reflects a willingness on the part of citizens to take ideas seriously,
evaluate them accordingly, and engage them directly. A cultural predis-
position to care about ideas and to judge between them, while protecting the liberty of others, is the best bulwark of a free society. A citizenry
that evaluates ideas, that discerns the true from the false, that values reason over reaction, that affirms that which is edifying, and that refutes that
which is wrong is exactly the society most likely to value, to have, and
to keep free speech.

What we honor says as much about out national character as what
we allow. There is an old saying "Tell me what you love, and I'll tell you
who you are." The same can be said of societies, as well as individuals.
What we honor and esteem as a people reflects and affects our culture. We
grow to resemble what we honor, we become less like what we disparage.
What we choose to honor, then, forecasts our cultural condition.

That is important, because there are cultural conditions which make
democracy possible, markets open, and societies free. Democracy cannot
endure in a society that has lost respect for the law or an interest in self-
government. Societies become less free when they become more violent.
The more culturally chaotic we become, the more restrictions, laws and
regulations are imposed to maintain order.

Glorifying violence in popular music is dangerous, because a society that glorifies violence will grow more violent. Similarly, when
we refuse to criticize music that debases women, we send the message
that treating women as chattel is not something to be upset about. Record companies that promote violent music implicitly push the idea that
more people should listen to, purchase, and enjoy the sounds of slaughter. When MTV named Marilyn Manson the "best new artist of the
year" last year, they held Manson up as an example to be aspired and em-

ulated. Promoting violence as entertainment corrodes our nation from within.

This is not a new idea. Virtually all of the founding Fathers agreed—even assumed—that nations rise and fall based on what they honor and what they discourage. Samuel Adams, an outspoken free speech advocate, said the following: "A General dissolution of principles and manners will more surely overthrow the liberties of America than the whole force of the common enemy."

Unfortunately, in many circles, liberty is being redefined as "license"—the idea that anything goes, that all speech is morally equivalent. According to this view, we cannot judge or criticize speech no matter how offensive we may find it. After all, what is offensive to one person, the reasoning goes, may be acceptable, even enjoyable to someone else. Thus, the idea of honoring certain forms of speech and stigmatizing others become seen as infringements on liberty. This assumes that to have freedom of speech, you can't give a rip over what is said—and that tolerance is achieved by apathy. Their motto can be summed up in one word: "whatever." 35

This is dead wrong. A philosophy of "whatever" is poison to the body politic. Civility, decency, courtesy, compassion, and respect should not be matters of indifference to us. We should care about these things—care about them deeply. We should allow both honorable and offensive forms of speech. But just as certainly, we should honor that which is honorable, and criticize that which is not. If we, as a society, come to the place where we think anything goes, the first thing to go will be freedom.

The great southern author Walker Percy once stated that his greatest fear for our future was that of "seeing America, with all its great strength and beauty and freedom . . . gradually subside into decay through default and be defeated . . . from within by weariness, boredom, cynicism, greed and in the end, helplessness before its great problems."

I am optimistic about our future, but his point is an important one. America is at a place in history where our great enemies have been defeated.

Communism, with all of its shackles on the human spirit, has fallen. The Cold War is over. Our economy is strong, our incomes up, our expectations high. We are, in a sense, the only remaining world superpower.

Certainly, the future looks bright. But our continued success is not a historical certainty. It will be determined by the character of our nation—by the condition of our culture as much as our economy, or our policies. What we value, and what we disparage, are good predictors to what we soon shall be. 40

This is why I have both legislated in a libertarian manner, and agitated against hateful, racist, violent music lyrics. For those of us who are concerned about the loss of civility in society, and the glorification of hate, violence, and misogyny in popular music, our goal must be not to coerce, but to persuade. We should aim to change hearts and minds, rather than laws. Analyzing, evaluating, and sometimes criticizing lyrics is not only compatible with, but essential to, liberty.

May rock roll on, and freedom ring.

———

SUPPORT FOR CENSORSHIP OF VIOLENT AND MISOGYNIC RAP LYRICS
An Analysis of the Third-Person Effect

Douglas M. McLeod, William P. Eveland, Jr., Amy I. Nathanson

Recent calls for censorship of rap music have demonstrated the need to rest the perceptual and especially the behavioral components of Davison's third-person effect hypothesis. The hypothesis states that people perceive media content to have a greater impact on others than on themselves (perceptual component), and that these perceptions lead people to take actions, such as censorship, to prevent the impact (behavioral component). Results of a survey of college students ($N = 202$) using rap lyrics as the context revealed strong support for both components of the hypothesis. Limited support was found for the social distance corollary of the perceptual component, while the knowledge corollary of the perceptual component was not supported. A new target corollary to the perceptual component was proposed; it predicts that those groups seen as likely targets of a communication will produce larger third-person perceptions than will generalized others.

[Censors] are never worried about their own ability to differentiate between fantasy and reality, to resist being seized by uncontrollable urges to commit violent or immoral acts, or to remain decent, law-abiding human beings who do not wish to hurt or degrade others. But they are *very* worried about *your* ability to do so.

—*(Dority, 1991, p. 44)*

During the last decade or so in the United States, many people have expressed concern that rap music—especially rap with violent or misogynic lyrics—is harmful to not only the youth of society but also to society itself (Leo, 1993). Prominent politicians, including presidential candidates in the 1996 primary campaign, have called for record companies to engage in self-censorship to protect people from the negative effects of antisocial lyrics ("Time Warner," 1995). In response to such demands, some record company executives have cloaked themselves in the First Amendment (Bowman, 1992) and some have made concessions such as labeling or self-censorship (Dority, 1991; "Time Warner," 1995). The discourse surrounding this controversy is rarely based on research about the negative impact of rap music. Instead, it is founded primarily on perceptions of rap's powerful harmful effects on others. Research on the third-person effect suggests that individuals who advocate censorship believe in powerful effects on others but, ironically, not necessarily on themselves. In short, many people believe that they are able to resist negative media effects but that others are less capable (or willing) to do so and must be protected by censorship.

Formalized over a decade ago by public opinion researcher W. Phillips Davison, the third-person effect hypothesis states:

> People will tend to overestimate the influence that mass communications have on the attitudes and behavior of others. More specifically, individuals who are members of an audience that is exposed to a persuasive communication . . . will expect the communication to have a greater effect on others than themselves. And whether or not these individuals are among the *ostensible* audience for the message, the impact that they expect this communication to have on others may lead them to take some action. (Davison, 1983, p. 3)

The third-person effect hypothesis has two components: perceptual and behavioral. The perceptual component (or third-person *perceptions*), which has received frequent research attention and considerable empirical support, states that people will estimate the effects of media messages on themselves to be less than the effects on others. This first component of the third-person effect, however, is at most an interesting perceptual phenomenon. The perceptual tendency predicted by the third-person effect becomes more meaningful if it is linked with real-world consequences as hypothesized by Davison.

The behavioral component, which has typically been ignored by theorists and rarely tested by researchers (Mutz, 1994), proposes that these perceptions of media impact will lead to behavior intended to protect the public from perceived negative effects. Other studies have suggested that third-person perceptions held by public officials can lead them to take policy actions to quell public outcries (Cook et al., 1983). Although third-person perceptions may have many implications for public policy, the present study examines one behavioral component— expressed support for censorship of allegedly harmful media content.

The purpose of this analysis, which is part of a larger study of third-person effect, is to replicate findings on third-person perceptions and to add to the small but growing pool of evidence on the behavioral   *5* component. This study examines the relationship between third-person perceptions in the context of violent and misogynic rap lyrics and support for censorship of this content.

LITERATURE REVIEW AND HYPOTHESES

Evidence of Third-Person Effects:
The Perceptual Component

The past decade has brought about numerous tests of the perceptual component of the third-person effect hypothesis using several different methodologies, including sample surveys and experiments. Researchers have examined third-person perceptions from media content such as libelous newspaper articles, pornography, the television movie *Amerika,* product advertisements, public service announcements, and various forms of political communication.

According to Perloff (1993), 13 of the 14 studies on the third-person effect at that time found support for the perceptual component of the hypothesis. Recent research has continued to demonstrate support (e.g., Gunther & Hua, 1996; Lee & Yang, 1996; Price, Tewksbury, & Huang, 1996). In the initial formulation, Davison (1983) suggested that third-person perceptions were caused by the overestimation of effects on others but relatively accurate estimates of effects on self. For the most part, the literature indicates that people do in fact overestimate the effects of media content on others (Cohen et al., 1988; Gunther, 1991; Gunther & Thorson, 1992; Perloff et al., 1992; Price et al., 1996). This is consistent with the literature on pluralistic ignorance showing that people are typically inaccurate in their perceptions of the climate of opinion (e.g., Miller & Prentice, 1994; O'Gorman, 1986; Toch & Klofas, 1984). However, the evidence on whether people can accurately assess media effects on themselves is mixed, with some studies finding underestimates of effects on self (Cohen et al., 1988), some finding relatively accurate estimates (Gunther, 1991; Perloff et al., 1992), and some finding overestimates (Gunther & Thorson, 1992).

One condition for the perceptual effect is that the media impact must be perceived to be negative by respondents (Gunther & Mundy, 1993). This condition is especially important because it supports assertions (e.g., Gunther & Mundy, 1993; Gunther & Thorson, 1992) that third-person perceptions are a special case of the "it can't happen to me" syndrome, identified in social psychology under terms such as "unrealistic optimism" (Weinstein, 1980). In fact, messages believed to produce positive effects may cause a "reverse third-person effect" (Gunther & Thorson, 1992). Both third-person perceptions and reverse third-person perceptions can be explained by a general tendency for people to fall prey to some form of self-serving bias (e.g., Brown, 1986; Zuckerman, 1979), which leads people to compare themselves favorably to others for ego enhancement reasons.[1]

We expected to replicate previous findings of the perceptual component of the third-person effect. Using antisocial messages in the form of either violent or misogynic rap lyrics, in which we presume respondents to perceive negative effects, we predicted the following:

H1: Perceived effects of antisocial rap lyrics on others will be greater than perceived effects on self.

Davison (1983) noted, "In the view of those trying to evaluate the effects of a communication, its greatest impact will not be on 'me' or 'you,' but on 'them'—the third persons" (p. 3). Consistent with Davison's intuition, Cohen et al. (1988) found that the size of the third-person perception differential increased as the social distance between self and other increased. That is, respondents assessed increasingly larger media impact as the "other" was changed from "other Stanford students" to "other Californians" to "public opinion at large."

Since this initial research, several studies have addressed the social distance corollary of the third-person perception. Gunther (1991) found that University of Minnesota students perceived greater effects on "other Minnesota residents" than on "other University of Minnesota students," which is consistent with the social distance corollary. However, Cohen and Davis (1991), using "people from your home state," "people from your region of the country," and "people in the U.S. in general" as the comparison groups in their study, found no support for increased third-person perceptions for more socially distant groups.

Despite Cohen and Davis's (1991) null findings, we expected to find an effect of social distance on the strength of third-person perceptions. Because individuals are likely to believe they are more similar to members of their own social group than to members of other social groups (Brewer & Kramer, 1985), it is possible that the size of the third-person effect will increase as the social distance between self and other increases. We expected that respondents would perceive the social distance between themselves and other groups to increase as they moved from students at their own university (due to similarities in age, geography, and academic interests) to youths from New York and Los Angeles (due to age similarities) to the "average person," an analog to Cohen et al.'s (1988) "public opinion at large" or Cohen and Davis's (1991) "people in the U.S. in general." Therefore, our predictions are informed by the social distance corollary as follows:

H2: The size of the third-person perception will increase as the social distance of the comparison group increases.

Finally, research hints that third-person perceptions are linked to perceived knowledge about the content area (Lasorsa, 1989). However, measures of actual knowledge have been found to be unrelated to third-person perceptions (Lasorsa, 1989; Price & Tewksbury, 1994). The logic behind this knowledge corollary is that perceptions of oneself as more knowledgeable about a topic should lead to perceptions that one is better able to defend against negative media effects and thus is less easily influenced than novices. Therefore, we predicted that students who perceived themselves to be more knowledgeable about rap music would be particularly susceptible to third-person perceptions.

> H3: Perceived knowledge of rap music will be positively associated with third-person perceptions.

Evidence of Third-Person Effects: The Behavioral Component

The behavioral component states that third-person perceptions will lead to actions to redress negative media effects, such as censorship (or support for censorship) or public policy change (Davison, 1983). Despite the fact that most studies have tested this hypothesis as third-person perceptions (not simply perceived effects on self or others), few have explained why this is the appropriate test. We assert that the reason one would expect the third-person effect differential to be a stronger predictor of censorship attitudes than either of the perceived effects on self or perceived effects on other components is based on the nature of people who support or engage in censorship.

Salmon (1989, p. 38) has noted that social interventions that "do not consider the person's capacity to make an informed decision" are instances of "strong paternalism." In our view, censorship of media content is the epitome of strong paternalism in social intervention because it inherently assumes that people are not capable of screening content for themselves and, if they are exposed, they (or society) will be harmed in some way. We believe that censorship is based on this paternalistic foundation.

It has been argued that censorship is supported by people in order to protect relatively "helpless" others (e.g., Dority, 1991; Frohnmayer, 1994). Censorship advocates do not see a need for censorship for themselves because they either are smart enough to resist negative effects or can simply avoid harmful media content when necessary. In the view of a censor, it is those who are not "smart enough" or "wholesome" enough to do the right thing who need the protection that censorship provides. This seems to set up a necessary comparison of self and other. Indeed, Frohnmayer (1994, p. 47) discusses censorship as being closely linked to "the urge to be ethically pure, morally superior," especially in times of social stress. Similarly, Dority (1991) states, "The censor's most visible and striking characteristic is a flagrantly displayed belief in his or her own moral and spiritual superiority" (p. 44). Davison (1983) himself notes, "Insofar as faith and morals are concerned, at least, it is difficult to find a censor who will admit to having been adversely affected by the information whose dissemination is to be prohibited. . . . It is the general public that must be protected" (p. 14). In all of these comments about the characteristics of censors it is clear that there is a comparison with oth-

15

ers, since superiority is an inherently relative concept. Thus it should not be simple perceived effects of media content on others but the perceived effects of media on others relative to oneself that spurs people to support censorship.

The paternalistic perception of superiority may be another manifestation of the illusion of control (Langer, 1975) or general self-serving bias (Brown, 1986), of which, as we noted above, the third-person effect may be a special case. That is, censors believe that the content is not dangerous to themselves personally (because they are immune to influence) but that others lack the self-control, knowledge, intelligence, goodness, and so on to protect themselves from harmful media content. Just as third-person perceptions may be founded on a need to maintain an illusion of control or superiority over others, Frohnmayer (1994) notes that censorship is also "an issue of control, of power over what others will or will not have the opportunity to experience" (p. 47). It may be, then, that this illusion of control that generates third-person perceptions could also lead people to want to take control over others, meaning that the link between third-person perceptions and behaviors is spurious. Unfortunately, we will not be able to test the possibility of spuriousness in the present study.

Gunther (1995) argues that people consider the level of media impact on themselves—whatever the level that happens to be—to be acceptable. Their judgment of an unacceptable level of influence is made by comparison to the acceptable (presumably inconsequential) impact on themselves. The more unacceptable the impact on others—that is, the greater relative to themselves—the more likely they are to support censorship to protect others. This interpretation is consistent with our paternalism argument. Essentially, people feel that the level of effect media have upon themselves is acceptable, but any deviation from this level toward greater effects is harmful. The greater the deviation from effects on themselves, the greater the need for censorship.

In summary, it is not simply the perceived impact of media content on oneself or on others that should lead to support for censorship. Instead, support for censorship should be most prevalent among those who hold the paternalistic or morally superior perception that they are relatively immune to the negative effects of media content compared to the masses (the third-person perception).[2]

Only a few studies have directly tested the behavioral component of the third-person effect hypothesis (Mutz, 1994), and only very recently have researchers tested the relationship between third-person perceptions and the desire for censorship. Thompson, Chaffee, and Oshagan (1990) found that perceptions of the negative effects of pornography on others were *negatively* associated with desire for censorship, but they did not fully interpret what they admitted was an unexpected finding. Although this finding would seem contrary to the third-person effect hypothesis, their research did not actually test the relationship between third-person perceptions and desire for censorship. As we have noted, the desire for censorship should be related to the *difference* between perceived effects on

20

self and perceived effects on others (i.e., third-person perceptions), so Thompson et al.'s finding should not be interpreted as evidence against the behavioral component of the third-person effect hypothesis.

Rucinski and Salmon (1990), however, did test the behavioral component of the third-person effect by examining the relationship between third-person perceptions and support for independent monitoring of political media content. Although their dependent variable is not truly censorship of the offensive media content, the finding is applicable. They found that neither perceived effects on self nor third-person perceptions had an impact on support for monitoring. Perceived effects on others did have a small positive effect. This finding is inconsistent with the behavioral component of the third-person effect hypothesis.

Two published studies provide evidence supporting the relationship between third-person perceptions and desire for censorship. Gunther's (1995) national study of pornography indicated that the size of third-person perceptions was positively related to favoring restrictions on pornographic material, although perceived effects on self also made a strong contribution. The relationship between third-person perceptions and regulation of pornography was even stronger when Gunther excluded participants who did not demonstrate the third-person perception for pornographic content.

Similarly, Rojas, Shah, and Faber (1996) demonstrated that third-person perceptions were positively associated with the desire to censor violence on television, and pornography, and support for censorship in general. In addition, they found that a measure of hypothetical censorship behaviors was also strongly predicted by third-person perceptions.[3]

The present research was designed to provide an additional test of the relationship between the perceptual and behavioral components of the third-person effect hypothesis and to clarify whether it is perceived effects on self, perceived effects on others, or the third-person perception that is most strongly related to censorship attitudes. Following Davison (1983), Gunther (1995), and Rojas et al. (1996), we predicted:

> H4: Third-person perceptions about the effects of rap will be positively associated with support for censorship of rap.

METHOD

Questionnaires were administered to 202 students in two introductory mass communication courses at the University of Delaware.[4] These courses draw students from a wide variety of academic majors (62% of the respondents were from majors other than communication); however, the sample was disproportionately female (70%). The mean age of respondents in this sample was just over 20 years old.

Respondents were randomly given one of two versions of a nine-page questionnaire, which were identical except for the third page.[5] This page presented the stimulus material—rap lyrics adapted from actual songs. One set of lyrics constituted the violent rap stimulus; the other constituted the misogynic rap stimulus. The different stimuli were used to provide more than one context for third-person effects. The violent stimulus portrays the life of a "gangsta" who is not afraid to use a gun to settle his problems. In the misogynic stimulus, a man uses a woman for sex but is embarrassed to be seen with her in public; he clearly treats her as little more than temporary sexual gratification.

Lyrics were chosen that celebrated values considered by the authors to be antisocial. In order to test whether our respondents also considered the lyrics antisocial (thus enabling a third-person perception), respondents were asked to rate their perceptions of the lyrics on an 11-point scale ranging from 0 (*very antisocial*) to 10 (*very prosocial*). Both sets of lyrics were considered antisocial by respondents ($M = 1.98$ and $M = 2.4$ for violent and misogynic lyrics, respectively).

Respondents were instructed to read the lyrics carefully and encouraged to refer back to them as they filled out the remainder of the questionnaire. Following the lyrics and the social desirability question were the items used to create four scales for the third-person perceptions measures. Respondents were asked to estimate the effects of "listening to songs with these types of lyrics" on the knowledge, attitudes, and behaviors of each of the following referent groups: "you," "other University of Delaware students," "people your age in cities like New York and Los Angeles," and "the average person."[6]

The instrument used to measure third-person perceptions was an 11-point scale ranging from 0 (*no effect*) to 10 (*a great deal of effects*). Perceived effects on knowledge, attitudes, and behaviors were summed to create the scales for each referent group (effects on self Cronbach's $\alpha = .79$, effects on the Delaware students $\alpha = .82$, effects on New York/Los Angeles youth $\alpha = .85$, effects on the average person $\alpha = .85$). These four scales are used in the analyses displayed in Table 1. Difference scores between self and each of the three comparison groups were also computed to represent third-person perceptions. The reliabilities for the self versus Delaware students, self versus average person, and self versus New York/Los Angeles youth were .61, .60, and .74, respectively.[7]

The next set of measures was seven items used to create the support for censorship scale ($\alpha = .87$). Subjects were asked to think again about the song lyrics as they responded to the seven (5-point) Likert-type items. The seven statements dealt with support for industry self-censorship, banning airplay during hours when children might be listening, support for federal or local laws, and banning sale of the content.

A single item was used to measure perceived knowledge of rap music. Subjects were asked how knowledgeable they were about each of several types of music using an 11-point scale ranging from 0 (*not at all*) to 10 (*a great deal*).

Due to their expected relationship to censorship attitudes and third-person perceptions, three additional variables (gender, conservatism, and liking of rap) were measured and used as controls in the regression

30

Table 1

*t Tests of Differences between Perceived Effects on Self and Delaware Students,
New York/Los Angeles Youth, and the Average Person*

	Self	versus	Comparison Group		
			Delaware Students	New York/ Los Angeles Youth	Average Person
Violent rap (*df* = 98−100)	5.56		8.96	15.14	8.74
Misogynic rap (*df* = 98)	3.26		8.17	12.75	7.46
Total (*df* = 197−199)	4.43		8.58	13.95	8.10

Note: Mean figures for the self reported here are based on the comparison with the largest number of cases possible. Significance tests are based on the actual number of cases in the analysis. All differences between self and the three comparison groups (for the total sample as well as for the violent rap and misogynic rap subsamples) are significant at the $p \le .01$ level.

analysis. Conservatism was created by summing responses to two items asking about respondent's political orientations on social and economic issues ($r = .53$). For both items, 7-point scales ranging from *very liberal* to *very conservative* were used to measure responses. Two items also were used to measure liking of rap. The first indicator in the scale was part of a set of items that asked respondents to rank order by preference nine different music types, one of which was rap. Rankings for this item were reversed so that higher values represented greater preference for rap compared to other musical genres. The second indicator was part of a group of items that asked respondents how much they liked each of the nine music types using an 11-point scale ranging from 0 (*not at all*) to 10 (*a great deal*). These two items ($r = .79$) were standardized and then summed to create the liking of rap variable.

To test Hypotheses 1 and 2, *t* tests of the size of the difference between perceived effects on self and perceived effects on others were conducted. Hypothesis 3 was tested using bivariate correlation analysis. Hypothesis 4 was tested using a regression technique called the "diamond model" as advocated by Whitt (1983) for dealing with hypotheses that predict an effect for a difference score variable (third-person perceptions in this case) above and beyond the effects of its components (perceived effects on self and perceived effects on others). For the regression analyses in Table 2, the final block of variables entered into the equation contain the self plus other variable and the third-person perception variable for each of the three comparison groups. According to Whitt (1983), when these two variables are entered simultaneously into a regression equation, a significant effect for the difference score variable should be interpreted as support for the hypothesis.

Table 2

Hierarchical Multiple Regression Model Predicting
Attitudes toward Censorship of Rap Lyrics

	Comparison Group		
Independent Variable	Delaware Students	New York/ Los Angeles Youth	Average Person
Block 1			
Gender (female)			
$\beta1$	.11	.11	.11
$\beta2$	.11	.12	.10
Conservatism			
$\beta1$	.27**	.27**	.27**
$\beta2$	.24**	.23**	.24**
R^2 (%)	7.5**	7.5**	7.5**
Block 2			
Social desirability			
$\beta1$	−.10	−.10	−.10
$\beta2$	−.03	.00	−.05
Incremental R^2 (%)	0.9	0.9	0.9
Block 3			
Liking of rap			
$\beta1$	−.13	−.13	−.13
$\beta2$	−.11	−.11	−.10
Knowledge of rap			
$\beta1$	−.02	−.02	−.02
$\beta2$	−.05	−.06	−.03
Incremental R^2 (%)	1.8	1.8	1.8
Block 4			
Self + other perceptions			
$\beta2$	.04	.07	.05
Third-person perceptions			
$\beta2$	.17*	.22**	.15*
Incremental R^2 (%)	2.8*	5.6**	2.3
Final R^2 (%)	13.0*	15.8**	12.5

Note: $N = 189$. $\beta1$ = standardized beta upon entry of block into equation (thus controlling for previous and current blocks); $\beta2$ = standardized beta from full model (final beta controlling for all variables in the model).
*$p < .05$; **$p < .01$.

RESULTS

Hypotheses 1–3: The Perceptual Component

Hypothesis 1 predicted that the perceived effects of the rap lyrics on others would be greater than perceived effects on self. Table 1 presents the results of *t* tests that demonstrate strong support for this hypothesis. Overall, the third-person perception differentials were significant for comparisons of self to other Delaware students, self to youth from New York and Los Angeles, and self to the average person. In addition, separating out the perceptual difference by condition (violent vs. misogynic rap) revealed that both conditions induced a perceptual third-person effect (Table 1).

Hypothesis 2 stated that the size of third-person perceptions should increase as comparisons were made with referent groups more socially distant from the perceiver. There was only limited support for this hypothesis (Table 1). The group that was expected to be most socially distant, the average person, did not produce the greatest third-person perception. Instead, youth from New York and Los Angeles demonstrated the largest perceptual difference from self, significantly greater than the difference between self and other Delaware students, which was not significantly less than the difference between self and the average person.

Hypothesis 3 predicted a positive association between perceived knowledge of rap and third-person perceptions. Our results failed to support this hypothesis; in none of the three tests (Delaware students, New York/Los Angeles youth, or average person) was there a significant relationship between third-person perceptions and perceived knowledge of rap. The nonsignificant correlations ranged from $-.03$ (average person) to $+.09$ (Delaware students). Although inconsistent with our hypothesis, these findings are consistent with studies that have tested the relationship between *actual* knowledge and third-person perceptions.

Hypothesis 4: The Behavioral Component

Hypothesis 4 linked third-person perceptions with support for censorship of the presumably harmful content of rap music. To test this hypothesis, we used the diamond model in a multiple regression analysis (Whitt, 1983). The first block of the regression equation entered gender and conservatism as predictor variables, revealing that conservatives were more likely to support censorship of antisocial rap lyrics, but revealing no significant effect for gender.[8] Second, because previous research had indicated that "perceived harm" is an important predictor of willingness to support government regulations of media content (Rucinski & Salmon, 1990), our measure of perceived social desirability of the "message" in the rap lyrics was entered into the regression equation next. The effect of social desirability on support for censorship was not significant. Our third control block included perceived knowledge of rap as well as our index of liking of rap. Both of these variables were significantly related to opposition to censorship at the zero–order level; however, both were reduced to nonsignificance after controls for the first two regression blocks.

The final block of the regression equation in Table 2 provided the test for Hypothesis 4. Here, both perceived effects on self and perceived effects on others (combined into two–item indices) and third–person perceptions (two–item difference scores) were entered into the equation simultaneously. The evidence indicates that for each of the three comparison groups, third–person perceptions were significantly related to censorship attitudes, while self and other perceptions were in no case significantly related to support for censorship. The strongest relationship between third–person perceptions and support for censorship comes from the New York / Los Angeles comparison group, although all three comparison groups produced similar regression coefficients. Thus our data indicated strong support for Hypothesis 4 in each of three separate tests.[9]

DISCUSSION

The results of this study provide solid support for both the perceptual and behavioral components of the third–person effect hypothesis. Consistent with past research, our respondents perceived others to be more influenced by negative media messages than themselves. In addition, this perception was strongly related to support for censorship, even after controlling for other important variables. The study provided less support for the knowledge and social distance corollaries of the perceptual component of the third–person effect hypothesis. However, our findings may shed some light on these areas of third–person effect research and lead to more fruitful research in the future.

The present study makes several contributions to the literature on third–person effects. Using a unique material (rap music), it replicated findings on the third–person perception. The supposed impact of antisocial rap lyrics is currently a hotly debated topic in news media, political discussions, and on the presidential campaign trail. Antisocial rap provides, then, a socially relevant context in which to study third–person effects.

The current political climate makes tests of the link between the perceptual and behavioral components of the hypothesis important. Politicians from both the Left and the Right have recently called for (at least) industry self–censorship of rap music in order to protect the masses. The present study adds to the small body of literature (required to add relevance to third–person perceptions) by assessing the relationship between these perceptions and support for censorship. In so doing, it investigates one plausible cause for the desire to censor media content. If it is the case (as research seems to indicate) that third–person perceptions are based on an overestimation of effects on others, the desire for censorship caused by third-person perceptions is built on a flawed foundation. Any censorship that results from misperceptions may in fact be unnecessary censorship.

The present study, like any single research effort, has its limitations. For instance, our test of the behavioral component actually used an attitudinal measure as the dependent variable. That is, we were unable to measure censorship behaviors directly, and therefore we were forced to rely on self-report measures of support for censorship. This may not be a severe limitation, however, since public policy, such as restrictions on objectionable media content, is often based on public opinion.

Another limitation of this study is our inability to make strong causal inferences. Our cross-sectional data and limited number of controls restrict a conclusion of association between third-person perceptions and support for censorship. Future research might attempt to experimentally manipulate third-person perceptions in much the way the climate of opinion has been manipulated in studies of impersonal influence (Mutz, 1992). This would strengthen inferences about the direction of causality.

Finally, our homogeneous and gender-biased student sample may have provided greater third-person perceptions than those of the population. Davison (1983) suggests that third-person perceptions are greater among those who believe they are "experts" in a particular domain, and enrollment in a course in mass communication may have led our respondents to consider themselves experts in the domain of media effects. This sample issue is one common to many third-person effect studies (e.g., Cohen et al., 1988; Gunther, 1991; Mutz, 1989; Perloff, 1989).

These limitations, however, do not cast serious doubt on the major 45 findings of the study, which help to move third-person effect research forward. Regarding our first hypothesis, our results indicated a consistent pattern of perceiving three groups of others (other Delaware students, New York and Los Angeles youth, and the average person) to be more influenced by both violent and antisocial rap lyrics than oneself. This finding adds to the substantial research demonstrating a perceptual third-person effect for negative media messages.

The social distance corollary (H2) predicted that the size of the perceptual bias will increase as the referent group becomes more socially distant from the perceiver. We operationalized social distance by assuming a priori that respondents would believe that other students at their university would be the most similar, people in their age group in New York and Los Angeles would be a little less similar, and people in the average person group would be the least similar. The social distance corollary held with the exception of the average person comparison group, which was perceived as similar to the other Delaware students group.

The most likely explanation of this finding is that the respondents considered the average person to be older than themselves, generally outside the target audience of rap music and hence less likely to be influenced.

By contrast, the youth of large urban cities may be considered a prime target for rap, and therefore more likely to be influenced by it. We suggest that future research take into account "target groups" in studies of the third-person effect.

The results of this study reveal that there may be two separate perceptual evaluations that regulate the size of the third-person perception—perceived social distance and perceived likelihood of exposure to the content (the target corollary). In this study, the effect of the target corollary seemed to be more powerful than the impact of social distance. However, it may also be that perceived social distance was not specified correctly in our a priori assumptions. This indicates the need for future research to directly measure perceived social distance to test these assumptions.

The results of this test of the social distance corollary point to the importance of considering the relationship of the third-person comparison group to the target market of the media content. Although the target market corollary seemed to outweigh the social distance corollary in our test, there are some questions about how important the target market consideration is with regard to judgments about effects on self. Perceived effects on self (more or less part of the target audience in this study) were seen as being less than the impact on the average person (somewhat outside the target audience). This may reflect the fact that the social distance corollary was not completely overrun by the target market corollary. It may also be that respondents do not consider target markets when they make judgments about themselves—instead, they see themselves as unlikely to be influenced by media content despite their membership in its target market. This explanation has some support in our data; while we do not have direct measures of exposure, the zero-order correlations between perceived effects on self and knowledge of rap ($r = .03$) and liking of rap ($r = .13$) are nonsignificant. Research examining the link between exposure and perceived effects on self, however, has generally found significant results (Rucinski & Salmon, 1990).

Clearly, the social distance corollary and the target corollary merit further research. Such research should also investigate an alternative interpretation of the target corollary. Conceivably, respondents could be passing judgment on the typical education level of members of the third-person comparison groups and making the assumption that less educated people are more susceptible to negative media influence (a possibility that is consistent with paternalistic notions that may account for linkages between third-person perceptions and the desire for censorship). Future research could measure perceived educational levels, perceived social distance (i.e., dissimilarity), and the perceived likelihood of exposure to the stimulus genre (e.g., rap music) of each of the comparison groups in order to investigate the various explanations for these results.

Our results did not support the knowledge corollary predicted by the third hypothesis. Although some research has indicated that perceived knowledge of a content domain leads to greater third-person perceptions (Lasorsa, 1989), our results indicated no significant effect. This finding is similar to those of Lasorsa (1989) and Price and Tewksbury (1994), who found that actual knowledge was not related to third-person effects. It is possible that respondents in our study had no incentive to exaggerate their knowledge of rap music (as is likely for Lasorsa's measure of perceived political knowledge), and therefore their perceptions in fact were an accurate representation of their actual knowledge. It is possible that the knowledge corollary may only hold in situations where perceived knowledge is an overestimate of actual knowledge.

Finally, our data provide strong support for the behavioral component of the third-person effect (H4), which states that perceiving others as more influenced by media content than oneself is related to support for taking actions to protect others. In several tests comparing the impact of the third-person perception with additive indices of perceived effects on self and perceived effects on others, the third-person perception was consistently a significant predictor while the additive index was in no case significant. The impact of third-person perceptions on support for censorship was strong despite controls for several correlates of censorship (gender, conservatism, social desirability of the content, and knowledge of and liking of the content, in question).

Findings of a strong relationship between third-person perceptions and support for censorship provide insight into the real-world impact of third-person perceptions. Whereas some might question the importance of a perceptual error, regardless of its consistency, few media researchers would dispute the importance of a perceptual bias that leads to support for censorship. By providing correlational evidence for the behavioral component of the third-person effect hypothesis, we have bared the "teeth" of the third-person effect.

It is possible that the effects of third-person perceptions go beyond support for censorship. Future third-person research should attempt to link third-person perceptions to more broad public opinion processes. For instance, are those who exhibit third-person perceptions more likely to participate in the public opinion formation and change processes (regarding censorship or otherwise) as radio talk show callers or protestors? Are those who hold third-person perceptions consistently more likely to hold strong attitudes on public issues, whatever the valence? Future third-person effect research may benefit most from links to more broad public opinion research and to psychological research on the concept of pluralistic ignorance.

Researchers from both social science and legal perspectives should *55* further explore the impact of third-person perceptions on attitudes toward media censorship. In a time when the political climate is replete with calls for censorship of not only rap lyrics but also other forms of media content, this research is all the more important.

APPENDIX

Social Desirability

On a scale from 0 to 10, circle the number that indicates how you rate the message in the lyrics in terms of its antisocial/prosocial content.

Liking of Rap

Please rank the following types of music in order of your preference: country (e.g., Garth Brooks, Clint Black, Mary Chapin Carpenter, etc.), classic rock (e.g., Led Zeppelin, Rolling Stones, Aerosmith, etc.), heavy metal (e.g., Metallica, AC/DC, Megadeath, etc.), rap/hip-hop (e.g., Public Enemy, Salt 'N' Pepa, Snoop Doggy Dogg, etc.), alternative (e.g., Pearl Jam, Nine-Inch Nails, Nirvana, etc.), classical (e.g., Bach, Beethoven, Mozart, etc.), jazz (e.g., Miles Davis, Wynton Marsalis, Pat Metheny, etc.), reggae (e.g., Bob Marley, Peter Tosh, UB40, etc.), pop (e.g., Whitney Houston, Madonna, Phil Collins, etc.).

On a scale from 0 to 10, 0 being *not at all* and 10 being *a great deal,* circle the number that indicates how much you *like* each of the following types of music. . . .

Knowledge of Rap

On a scale from 0 to 10, 0 being *not at all* and 10 being *a great deal,* circle the number that indicates how *knowledgeable* you are about the artists and lyrics of each of the following types of music. . . .

Perceived Effects of Rap

(a) Overall, how much do you think *you* would learn from listen- 60 ing to songs with these types of lyrics? (b) Overall, how much would you say *your* attitudes would be influenced by listening to songs with these types of lyrics? (c) Overall, how much would you say that *your* behavior would be affected by listening to songs with these types of lyrics? (These same three questions were asked with other University of Delaware students, people your age in New York and Los Angeles, and the average person as the referent groups).

Support for Censorship

(a) Songs with these types of lyrics should be banned from radio play during hours when children might be listening. (b) Songs with these types of lyrics should be banned from radio play during any time of the day. (c) Songs with these types of lyrics should be required to carry a parental advisory label to warn consumers about the possible negative effects of their content. (d) Songs with these types of lyrics should be banned from MTV and other music video programs. (e) Songs with these types of lyrics should be self-censored by record companies. (f) Songs with these types of lyrics should be removed from music store shelves by local ordinance. (g) Sale of albums with songs containing these types of lyrics should be banned by federal law.

Conservatism

The terms "liberal" and "conservative" may mean different things to people depending on the kind of issue one is considering. (a) In terms of economic issues, would you say you are very liberal, liberal, somewhat liberal, neutral, somewhat conservative, conservative, very conservative? (b) Now, thinking in terms of social issues, would you say you are very liberal, liberal, somewhat liberal, neutral, somewhat conservative, conservative, very conservative?

NOTES

1. The motivational interpretation for the third-person effect has not gone un-challenged, however (see Perloff, 1993). The same can be said for attribution biases (e.g., Perloff & Fetzer, 1986) and pluralistic ignorance (e.g., Mullen, 1983) research paradigms in psychology, on which the third-person effect motivational explanation is based. We agree with Tetlock and Levi (1982), however, that the debate over motivational versus cognitive explanations is not fruitful until the theories have been developed enough to provide a critical test. It is most likely, we think (see also Perloff, 1993), that both motivational and cognitive biases occur simultaneously, as demonstrated by Sherman, Presson, and Chassin (1984) in a study of the causes of pluralistic ignorance. However, the motivational bias is stressed here because the bulk of evidence and theory in the third-person effect literature supports a motivational interpretation.
2. Although it may seem counterintuitive to predict that the causal force in the third-person effect is not absolute perceived effects on self or perceived effects on others but instead the difference between them, the third-person effect is not the only hypothesis that proposes that perceived differences between self and others may be the basis for holding political opinions or taking political actions. Relative deprivation theory has been applied to political science in order to explain why some people engage in protest activities (e.g., Barnes, Farah, & Heunks, 1979; Barnes & Kaase, 1979). This theory predicts that it is not absolute deprivation (in terms of one's life as a whole or standard of living) but the perceived deprivation by comparison to expectations or comparable reference groups that leads people to engage in political protest.
3. Three recent conference papers present somewhat contradictory evidence on this point, however. Lee and Yang (1996) found a significant relationship between third-person perceptions and support for censorship of sexually explicit television content in Korea, and Gunther and Hua (1996) found similar support for censorship among those evidencing greater third-person perception across a range of television content types in Singapore. However, Price et al. (1996) reported no significant relationship between third-person perceptions and support for censorship of a potentially offensive advertisement beyond the zero-order level. However, the relationship was at least in the predicted direction in this study.

4. A question at the end of the questionnaire asked respondents if they had ever heard of the third-person effect. Of the few who reported knowing about the third-person effect, none was able to correctly answer an open-ended follow-up question about the nature of the hypothesis. For that reason, all subjects were retained for the analysis.

5. Question wordings are included in the appendix.

6. Several studies (Gunther, 1991, 1995; Price & Tewksbury, 1994; Tiedge, Silverblatt, Havice, & Rosenfeld, 1991) have found that there are no effects for the ordering of the self versus other questions. Price and Tewksbury (1994) also demonstrated that the observed third-person perceptual bias was not due to a contrast effect (i.e., making comparisons regardless of the order). Therefore, we made no attempt to randomize the order of the comparison groups.

7. Although the reliability of a difference score cannot be tested directly via Cronbach's alpha, Cohen and Cohen (1983) provide a formula to calculate it. The reliability of a difference score is calculated by subtracting the correlation between the two components of the difference score from the average of their reliabilities, then dividing by one minus the correlation between the component scores.

8. One of the anonymous reviewers of this manuscript suggested that the relationship between political ideology and censorship might be nonlinear, such that not only strong conservatives but also strong liberals (e.g., feminists) might support censorship. However, analyses using power polynomials (see Cohen & Cohen, 1983) to test for a quadratic (inverted U) effect of conservatism on censorship attitudes revealed no significant deviation from linearity of this form in our data. Despite this, it should be noted that support for censorship is not necessarily limited to the conservative end of the ideological continuum and may be based instead on the group whose speech is going to be censored (see Sullivan, Pierson, & Marcus, 1983).

9. One of the anonymous reviewers of this manuscript suggested that another analytical strategy, the Taylor model, would be a more stringent test of our hypothesis. Taylor (1973) argues that in order to test a hypothesis of effects of a difference score above and beyond its components' combined effects while avoiding linear dependence, the two components should be entered individually into the regression equation (unlike the diamond model, which combines them into an index). Then, instead of using the difference score as a predictor, the absolute size of the difference score and a pair of dummy variables (representing the possible directions of the difference score: positive, negative, and no difference) should be entered into the equation as an indirect representation of the difference score. The results of this analytical technique for the present data produced null findings for H4. In none of the three regressions did either the size of the difference between self and other or the direction of the difference between self and other significantly predict support for censorship. Examination of the final beta coefficients for self and other (separately) also showed null findings in two of the three tests. Only for the Delaware students comparison group did perceived impact on self (negatively) and others (positively) significantly predict support for censorship. We do not believe, however, that the results of this analytical strategy are meaningful. Although the Taylor model does avoid the linear dependence problem that prevents the test of the difference score and its two components

in the same regression equation (because they are correlated at 1.0), even Taylor himself notes that severe multicollinearity remains a problem in this model (Taylor, 1973). Our data reveal evidence to support this assertion. In addition to indirect indications of multicollinearity, such as regression co-efficients that are reversed in sign for their zero-order counterparts and large beta weights that do not attain statistical significance (e.g., $\beta = .20$), more direct tests, such as the multiple correlation between predictor variables (as large as .95 in the New York/Los Angeles regression model) and the variance inflation factor (see Neter, Kutner, Nachtsheim, & Wasserman, 1996) all indicated high levels of multicollinearity in our regression equations. It is for this reason that we have chosen to interpret the results of the diamond model only—we believe that the low levels of multicollinearity in this model reveal the true relationships betwen the independent and dependent variables. However, we leave it to the reader to decide which strategy seems more appropriate.

REFERENCES

Barnes, S. H., Farah, B. G., & Heunks, F. (1979). Personal dissatisfaction. In S. Barnes & M. Kaase (Eds.), *Political action* (pp. 381–407). Beverly Hills, CA: Sage.

Barnes, S. H., & Kaase, M. (1979). Introduction. In S. Barnes & M. Kaase (Eds.), *Political action* (pp. 13–26). Beverly Hills, CA: Sage.

Bowman, J. (1992, July). Plain brown rappers. *National Review*, pp. 36–38, 53.

Brewer, M. B., & Kramer, R. M. (1985). The psychology of intergroup attitudes and behavior. *Annual Review of Psychology, 36,* 219–243.

Brown, J. D. (1986). Evaluations of self and others: Self-enhancement biases in social judgments. *Social Cognition, 4,* 353–376.

Cohen, J., & Cohen, P. (1983). *Applied multiple regression/correlation analysis for the behavioral sciences* (2nd ed.). Hillsdale, NJ: Lawrence Erlbaum.

Cohen, J., & Davis, R. G. (1991). Third-person effects and the differential impact in negative political advertising. *Journalism Quarterly, 68,* 680–688.

Cohen, J., Mutz, D., Price, V., & Gunther, A. (1988). Perceived impact of defamation: An experiment on third-person effects. *Public Opinion Quarterly, 52,* 161–173.

Cook, F. L., Tyler, T., Goetz, E. G., Gordon, M. T., Protess, D., Leff, D. R., & Molotch, H. L. (1983). Media and agenda setting: Effects on the public, interest group leaders, policy makers, and policy. *Public Opinion Quarterly, 47,* 16–35.

Davison, W. P. (1983). The third-person effect in communication. *Public Opinion Quarterly, 47,* 1–15.

Dority, B. (1991, January/February). Profile of a censor. *The Humanist,* pp. 43–44.

Frohnmayer, J. (1994). *Out of tune: Listening to the First Amendment*. The Freedom Forum First Amendment Center, Vanderbilt University.

Gunther, A. (1991). What we think others think: Cause and consequence in the third-person effect. *Communication Research, 18,* 355–372.

Gunther, A. (1995). Overrating the X-rating: The third-person perception and support for censorship of pornography. *Journal of Communication, 45*(1), 27–38.

Gunther, A. C., & Hua, A. P. (1996, May). *Public perceptions of television influence and opinions about censorship in Singapore.* Paper presented at the annual meeting of the International Communication Association, Chicago.

Gunther, A. C., & Mundy, P. (1993). Biased optimism and the third-person effect. *Journalism Quarterly, 70,* 58–67.

Gunther, A. C., & Thorson, E. (1992). Perceived persuasive effects of product commercials and public service announcements: Third-person effects in new domains. *Communication Research, 19,* 574–596.

Langer, E. J. (1975). The illusion of control. *Journal of Personality and Social Psychology, 32,* 311–328.

Lasorsa, D. L. (1989). Real and perceived effects of "Amerika." *Journalism Quarterly, 66,* 373–378, 529.

Lee, C., & Yang, S. (1996, August). *Third-person perceptions and support for censorship of sexually explicit visual content: A Korean case.* Paper presented at the annual meeting of the Association for Education in Journalism and Mass Communication, Anaheim, CA.

Leo, J. (1993, December 20). At a cultural crossroads. *U.S. News & World Report,* p. 14.

Miller, D. T., & Prentice, D. A. (1994). Collective errors and errors about the collective. *Personality and Social Psychology Bulletin, 20,* 541–550.

Mullen, B. (1983). Egocentric biases in estimates of consensus. *Journal of Social Psychology, 121,* 31–38.

Mutz, D. C. (1989). The influence of perceptions of media influence: Third person effects and the public expression of opinions. *International Journal of Public Opinion Research, 1,* 3–23.

Mutz, D. C. (1992). Impersonal influence: Effects of representations of public opinion on political attitudes. *Political Behavior, 14,* 89–122.

Mutz, D. C. (1994). The political effects of perceptions of mass opinion. *Research in Micropolitics, 4,* 143–167.

Neter, J., Kutner, M. H., Nachtsheim, C. J., & Wasserman, W. (1996). *Applied linear regression models* (3rd ed.). Chicago: Irwin.

O'Gorman, H. J. (1986). The discovery of pluralistic ignorance: An ironic lesson. *Journal of the History of the Behavioral Sciences, 22,* 333–347.

Perloff, L. S., & Fetzer, B. K. (1986). Self-other judgments and perceived vulnerability to victimization. *Journal of Personality and Social Psychology, 50,* 502–510.

Perloff, R. M. (1989). Ego-involvement and the third person effect of televised news coverage. *Communication Research, 16,* 236–262.

Perloff, R. M. (1993). Third-person effect research 1983–1992: A review and synthesis. *International Journal of Public Opinion Research, 5,* 167–184.

Perloff, R. M., Neuendorf, K., Giles, D., Change, T. K., & Jeffres, L. W. (1992). Perceptions of "Amerika." *Mass Communication Review, 19*(3), 42–48.

Price, V., & Tewksbury, D. (1994, November). *The roles of question order, contrast, and knowledge in the third-person effect.* Paper presented at the annual conference of the Midwest Association for Public Opinion Research, Chicago.

Price, V., Tewksbury, D., & Huang, L. N. (1996, May). *Denying the Holocaust: Third-person effects and decisions to publish a controversial advertisement.* Paper presented at the annual meeting of the American Association for Public Opinion Research, Salt Lake City, UT.

Rojas, H., Shah, D. V., & Faber, R. J. (1996). For the good of others: Censorship and the third-person effect. *International Journal of Public Opinion Research, 8,* 163–186.

Rucinski, D., & Salmon, C. T. (1990). The "other" as the vulnerable voter: A study of the third-person effect in the 1988 U.S. presidential campaign. *International Journal of Public Opinion Research, 2,* 345–368.

Salmon, C. T. (1989). Campaigns for social "improvement": An overview of values, rationales, and impacts. In C. T. Salmon (Ed.), *Information campaigns: Balancing social values and social change* (pp. 19–53). Newbury Park, CA: Sage.

Sherman, S. J., Presson, C. C., & Chassin, L. (1984). Mechanisms underlying the false consensus effect: The special role of threats to the self. *Personality and Social Psychology Bulletin, 10,* 127–138.

Sullivan, J. L., Pierson, J., & Marcus, G. E. (1983). *Political tolerance and American democracy.* Chicago: University of Chicago Press.

Taylor, H. F. (1973). Linear models of consistency: Some extensions of Blalock's strategy. *American Journal of Sociology, 78,* 1192–1215.

Tetlock, P. E., & Levi, A. (1982). Attribution bias: On the inconclusiveness of the cognition-motivation debate. *Journal of Experimental Social Psychology, 18,* 68–88.

Thompson, M. E., Chaffee, S. H., & Oshagan, H. H. (1990). Regulating pornography: A public dilemma. *Journal of Communication, 40*(3), 73–83.

Tiedge, J. T., Silverblatt, A., Havice, M. J., & Rosenfeld, R. (1991). Discrepancy between perceived first-person and perceived third-person mass media effects. *Journalism Quarterly, 68,* 141–154.

Time Warner abandons raps—and a bit more. (1995, October 9). *U.S. News & World Report,* p. 18.

Toch, H., & Klofas, J. (1984). Pluralistic ignorance, revisited. In G. M. Stephenson & J. H. Davis (Eds.), *Progress in applied social psychology* (Vol. 2, pp. 129–159). New York: John Wiley & Sons.

Weinstein, N. D. (1980). Unrealistic optimism about future life events. *Journal of Personality and Social Psychology, 39,* 806–820.

Whitt, H. P. (1983). Status inconsistency: A body of negative evidence or a statistical artifact? *Social Forces, 62,* 201–233.

Zuckerman, M. (1979). Attribution of success and failure revisited: The motivational bias is alive and well in attribution theory. *Journal of Personality, 47,* 245–287.

CENSORSHIP BEGINS AT HOME

Dan Moran

VI   A Guide to Finding and Using Information

Conducting research in a college or university library, or on the Internet, may at first seem like a daunting task: The sheer number of sources available to you can appear overwhelming. However, taking the time to learn what kinds of research materials your library and the Internet provide and how to use them will ultimately lend depth as well as validity to your argumentative essays.

When they hear the word *library,* most people naturally think first of books. But a library contains numerous other sources, such as academic and scientific journals, magazines, newspapers, government publications, dissertation **abstracts, indexes,** and **bibliographies.** Most libraries today also have a wide array of sources available online, including various reference works, often on searchable databases. Any of these sources may prove invaluable to your research. Books can provide a thorough treatment of some particular issue, and articles in journals and newspapers can provide up-to-the-minute information on the same subject. This current information is especially important in disciplines where new experiments and research are almost constantly altering past findings and conclusions.

Nothing will be more helpful to your discovery of the library's resources than the assistance of trained research librarians. These members of the library's staff are usually located at the reference desk. Before you begin searching for sources for a particular paper, consult a research librarian to help you identify the sources that are best suited for the level of research necessary for the assignment. Never be embarrassed to ask the reference librarians anything about the library or its workings: Their job is to assist you, and their expertise is wasted unless it is used.

Some material in this chapter is adapted from Ebest, et al., *Writing from A to Z* (McGraw-Hill, 2003; 4th edition).

As you uncover the wealth of resources available in and through the library and on the Internet, keep in mind that the purpose of research is to expand and support your argument, not to replace it with a series of statistics or quotations. The sample paper at the end of this chapter illustrates the appropriate use of the material you find in your research.

LOCATING INFORMATION IN THE LIBRARY AND ON THE INTERNET

One of the first steps in writing an essay or a research paper is to find an appropriate topic, one that is neither too broad nor too narrow. If you have only a general subject in mind but not a specific topic, looking in the library catalog and browsing books in the relevant shelves (commonly called "stacks") can help.

For a general overview of a broad topic, articles in encyclopedias can also be helpful, and they often end with a list of recommended books. However, because the information in encyclopedias is often general and always dated, you should use it only to help you find appropriate sources for your paper, not as a source itself.

Increasingly, the Internet itself can help you find an appropriate topic, gain a general overview of it, and even narrow the topic so that it is appropriate and manageable. Browsing "top stories" on the home pages of Internet sites sich as excite.com, msn.com, and aol.com will help you identify current issues. After you've found a topic that interests you, doing general searches using **key words** related to the topic will enable you to survey the topic's coverage on the Web.

Vast resources are available to you on the Internet and at the library. Library staff can help you make the most of both, and your teacher may require specific numbers of each kind of resource, but you might want to keep the capabilities and limitations of each type in mind. The books and periodicals in the library have gone through a screening process for accuracy and reliability. The publishers decided that the works were worth publishing, and the library decided that they were worth buying. The online databases and references available to you at the library have also been carefully selected, but the library cannot vouch for every article or link you find using electronic resources. And when you surf the Internet, you're essentially on your own, as you alone must decide whether a Web site is credible.

Electronic and print resources each offer advantages and disadvantages. The printed page is static, whereas electronic—hypertext—documents are interactive and searchable. Therefore, searching for a particular word or phrase in an Internet document is much faster than searching through a print document line by line. But reading an entire book on-screen is difficult, and without special Web tools or hardware, you cannot underline or annotate electronic documents. Given these capabilities and limitations, whenever possible, use the Internet to locate a particular piece of information in a large document, and use printed books when you need to study an entire work. If printing electronic documents, whether whole articles or parts of books, is an option for you, it's one way to take advantage of both mediums.

Relatively few books are available on the Internet, but the full texts of most periodical articles are available electronically through databases such as Lexis-Nexis, ProQuest, and InfoTrac, which are subscription-based services. Fortunately, many college and university libraries (as well as some public libraries) subscribe to these services, so that they are free, or relatively low-cost, to library users.

If the book you are looking for is checked out of the library, or the periodical you need isn't part of the library's holdings in any format, you may be able to obtain material through an "interlibrary loan" agreement, if your library has one with another library. Increasingly, college and university libraries are linked electronically, making interlibrary loans quick and easy to do.

Using the print and electronic resources at your library and the electronic sources available on the Internet, and possibly even obtaining materials through interlibrary loan can take a lot of time, especially if you carefully evaluate the reliability of the sources you're considering, a topic covered in more detail later in Part VI. Allowing yourself sufficient time to conduct research and work with your sources is crucial to the successful completion of research-based writing projects.

LOCATING BOOKS

The Library Catalog

The library catalog is a record of all the library's books, classified alphabetically by their authors, titles, and subjects. It may be available electronically at computer terminals in the library, and possibly on the Internet, or it may be available in centrally located card files, called a card catalog. The format of each library's online catalog is slightly different, but if you know the title or author of a specific book you want, simply look for it in the author or title listings in the computer or in the author or title section of the card catalog. For example, if you wanted to find a copy of *Walden* by Henry David Thoreau, you would type in the book title or the author's last name to reach a computer screen resembling the one at the top of page 296; or you would look for the title in the W section of the card catalog or for the author in the T section to locate a card resembling the one below.

The call number on the first line of the computer screen and in the upper left corner of the card is the book's "address" within the library. If

Call No.:   P3541 Thor

Author: Thoreau, Henry David, 1817–1862.

Main Title: Walden : or Life in the woods / by Henry David

                Thoreau; with an introduction by Harold Smith.

Publisher: New York : Random House, 1983.

```
P3541    Thoreau, Henry David

Thor          Walden.  With an introduction

         by Harold Smith.  New York:

         Random House, 1983.
```

you go to the shelf that houses the book with this call number, you will be able to locate unless it has been checked out. Computerized catalogs often provide information about the loan status of a book.

　　When you go through the library catalog, always have a piece of paper handy on which to record call numbers, and be sure to copy them completely and accurately. You may waste time looking for PZ4014 because you forgot that the proper number of your book is PZ4014(t). The extra seconds you spend writing down call numbers could save you minutes when searching the stacks.

The subject catalog is slightly different from the author and title catalogs. It allows you to look up a particular subject (which can be a person, event, or issue) and find a list of books in the library that address the topic. For example, if you were researching animal rights, you would look under "animal rights" to find a number of computer entries or cards identifying books on the topic.

If the library catalog provides no works dealing with your specific topic, try looking under related topics before stopping your search. If, for example, you were researching a paper on some aspect of artificial intelligence, you might find under the main heading, "Artificial Intelligence," a cross-reference entry for "Artificial Intelligence—Computers" or a card that reads "See Also: Computers." In addition to using these cross-references, try to think of other headings, such as "Robotics," to be sure you do not overlook what might be an important source. You might find it helpful to consult the *Library of Congress Subject Headings* (LCSH), usually located near the catalog. This reference book shows the particular wording that most libraries use to name subjects; for example, "Flying Saucers," not "UFOs," is the subject heading for information about unidentified flying objects. For each subject heading, LCSH also lists subtopics and related subjects.

Online Catalogs and Databases

Some libraries subscribe to large databases that are used throughout the United States and Canada. The chief virtue of a database is that it usually provides up-to-date listings for specific articles and books concerning topics in different fields and disciplines. If you would like to search a database, your library may allow you to do so yourself, or a reference librarian may do it for you. Because online computer time can be expensive, your library may charge a fee for this service. Some of the more popular online databases are

> Bibliographical Retrieval Services (BRS)
> Dialog (a compendium of databases)
> Educational Resources Information Center (ERIC)
> Research Libraries Information Network (RLIN)
> Online Computer Library Center (OCLC)
> ProQuest
> Lexis-Nexis

Remember that if you find or are given a book title from a database, you will then have to look it up in the library catalog to find out whether your library owns the book and where it is shelved.

Search Engines, Metasearch Engines, and Subject Directories

The overwhelming amount of information available electronically may be most efficiently explored by the sorting and retrieval power of search engines and subject directories. Although they differ slightly, each works when prompted by the key words you enter to produce a list of links that may be appropriate. Some of the most popular of these tools are

Search Engines

Google	<www.google.com>
Alta Vista	<www.altavista.com>
All The Web	<www.alltheweb.com>
HotBot	<www.hotbot.com>
Excite	<www.excite.com>
Lycos	<www.lycos.com>

Metasearch Engines

MetaCrawler	<www.metacrawler.com>
Ixquick	<www.ixquick.com>

Subject Directories

Yahoo!	<www.yahoo.com>
Dmoz	<www.dmoz.org>

Please see "Evaluating The Reliability of Online Sources", on page 302, for information about evaluating Internet sources.

Call Numbers and the Stacks

Libraries use one of two systems to assign call numbers to books. The first is the older Dewey Decimal System, which uses numbers to classify books according to their categories:

000–099	General Works
100–199	Philosophy
200–299	Religion
300–399	Social Sciences
400–499	Language
500–599	Natural Science
600–699	Technology
700–799	Fine Arts
800–899	Literature
900–999	History and Geography

These divisions are further subdivided by groups of ten to classify works more narrowly within their broader fields. For example, 800–899 indicates literature in general, and the numbers 810–819 indicate American literature. Many public libraries still use this system to classify their books.

The Library of Congress system begins with letters to classify books within 21 general categories:

A	General Works
B	Philosophy, Psychology, and Religion
C	Auxiliary Sciences of History
D	History (General)
E,F	American History (North and South)

G   Geography, Anthropology, and Recreation
H   Social Sciences
J   Political Science and Official Documents
K   Law
L   Education
M   Music
N   Visual Arts
P   Language and Literature
Q   Science
R   Medicine
S   Agriculture
T   Technology
U   Military Science
V   Naval Science
W   Bibliography and Library Science

As with the Dewey Decimal System, these categories are further sub-divided according to more specific topics. Most university libraries now classify their books according to the Library of Congress system; however, some of those libraries still classify their older holdings by the Dewey Decimal System.

Once you have compiled your list of call numbers, you are ready to search your library's stacks. Simply go to the shelf that houses works on the subject depicted by your book's call number. For example, if your call number was PN1899.W5, you might find it on a shelf marked PN1860–2000. Larger, multifloor libraries often feature maps near elevators or staircases. Consult these to save time.

After you find your book, it is a good idea to scan its "home shelf" for other books on the same topic. Since the library uses a classification system based on subjects, books concerning the same subject will be housed together. This check will show you the range of titles the library offers on your topic. It will also provide a rough idea of the extent to which people have written about your topic; for example, the number of books on the death penalty will be considerably larger than the number of books on the death of Socrates. You also may find some titles you overlooked when searching the library catalog. Finally, if the book you seek has been slightly misplaced, you may find it near its proper position.

Recalls and Interlibrary Loans

If the book you want has been lent to another patron, many libraries allow you to recall the book and then borrow it for a designated length of time. If you want a book not owned by your library, you may acquire the book by requesting an interlibrary loan in which your library will try to borrow the book from another library and then lend it to you. Both recalls and interlibrary loans are performed by the library's staff; consult the circulation librarian for specific details.

LOCATING ARTICLES IN PERIODICALS

A periodical is any newspaper, magazine, or academic journal published on a regular basis. Most libraries subscribe to a number of periodicals, which they keep on their periodical shelves for a predetermined length of time. After this time is up, the periodicals are bound in covers (usually marked according to volume number) and housed in a different part of the library. Almost any research project must feature periodicals, because they are the primary sources for current information and opinions.

When searching for periodicals, proceed in the same manner as you would when searching for books: Keep a list handy to which you add complete citations as you research your topic, and, after compiling your initial list, search the library's periodical stacks for the articles. After finding roughly ten citations, search for the articles. Keep in mind, however, that your library may not subscribe to all the periodicals you need; if this happens, you may want to talk to your circulation librarian about an interlibrary loan.

Indexes

Because the library catalog lists only books, you will need to consult periodical indexes, which are usually located in the periodical section of the library, to find articles about your topic. These indexes may be published as printed volumes, on CD-ROMs, or online (online indexes can usually be accessed from a computer terminal in the library). In general, one volume of a printed index covers only one year of articles, but online and CD-ROM indexes usually contain bibliographic listings for several years and may include abstracts of articles as well. In fact, many online indexes include not only abstracts of articles but the complete articles themselves. Your research librarian can help you locate and use specific indexes or collections of periodicals.

THE READERS' GUIDE TO PERIODICAL LITERATURE Available in print, on CD-ROM, and online, the *Readers' Guide to Periodical Literature* is the most widely consulted periodical index. It lists all the articles in nearly 200 general-interest magazines and the *New York Times*.

To use the *Readers' Guide,* simply look up your subject, which will be listed alphabetically. For example, if you were researching the ethics of genetic engineering, you might find the following entry:

> **Engineering, Genetic**
> Change for the Better? [scientists debate
> virtues of gen. eng.] W. Waltz. il *Scientific
> Quarterly* 11:17–22 Nov 7 '92

This entry tells you that the article "Change for the Better?" was written by W. Waltz, is illustrated (il), and appears on pages 17 through 22 of

Scientific Quarterly, volume 11, which is dated November 7, 1992. The bracketed passage is a summary of the article. The *Readers' Guide* features such summaries only when the title of the article does not connote in some way the subject of the article.

Your library may have other periodical indexes in addition to *Readers' Guide.* The InfoTrac series of indexes, available online and on CD-ROM, covers general-interest magazines and scholarly journals, a number of major newspapers, and U.S. legislative documents. University Microfilms (UMI) also publishes electronic indexes, including the Pro-Quest series, for general-interest magazines and newspapers. These indexes use a format similar to the one employed by the *Readers' Guide.*

NEWSPAPER INDEXES   For background information and overviews, magazine articles are usually better sources than newspaper articles. But for a detailed chronicle of events as they develop, newspaper articles are better. Some widely circulating newspapers, such as the *New York Times* and *Wall Street Journal,* provide their own indexes, arranged by subject. NewsBank is a monthly index to newspapers from over 500 cities in the United States. Texts of the indexed articles are available on microfiche.

INDEXES TO SCHOLARLY JOURNALS   Articles in the journals of various academic disciplines are listed in specialized indexes, which may be available as databases on CD-ROM and online as well as in print. Some of the most common indexes are

> *Social Sciences Index* for fields such as anthropology, psychology, sociology, economics, and political science
>
> *Education Index* for all areas of educational theory and child development
>
> *Humanities Index* for an interdisciplinary variety of topics, including history, classics, folklore, religion, philosophy, and the arts
>
> *Index Medicus* (print) and *Medline* (electronic) for biomedical literature, nursing, and dentistry
>
> *MLA International Bibliography* for books and articles on literature, modern languages, linguistics, and folklore
>
> *PAIS [Public Affairs Information Service] International in Print* for social and economic issues and international relations

Abstracts

An abstract is a short summary of the main points of a book or article. Collections of abstracts allow you to "skim" a number of articles in one sitting without having to look for the articles themselves. Although you will eventually have to read a number of articles carefully, reading abstracts can save you time by helping you narrow your search to articles that pertain directly to your topic. Abstracts are especially helpful to those researching a scientific issue, for they frequently summarize the findings of experiments and research. Some of the most popular collections are

> *Biological Abstracts*
> *Book Review Digest*
> *Chemical Abstracts*
> *Historical Abstracts*
> *Physics Abstracts*
> *Women's Studies Abstracts*

Government Documents

Many university libraries are listed as United States Government Depositories. Every time any branch of the government releases a publication (such as the results of a study, the findings of a congressional committee, or an analysis of information from the last census), a copy of that publication is sent to each of these libraries. Even if your library is not a government depository, it should still own the current indexes to these publications and should be able to acquire the ones you need through interlibrary loan. You can access many government publications online through FedWorld at <www.fedworld.gov/> or the Library of Congress at <www.loc.gov>.

Finding Your Periodicals

Once you have compiled your list of citations, and if abstracts or full articles are not available in electronic format, find out whether your library subscribes to the periodicals you need by consulting the library's Union List of Serials, an alphabetical listing of all your library's periodical holdings. Next look on the periodical shelves to see how long your library keeps its periodicals before binding them. If the articles you need are already bound, find out where your library keeps its bound periodicals, and locate your article there. Some periodicals may be kept on microfiche; ask your research librarian for details.

EVALUATING THE RELIABILITY OF ONLINE SOURCES

Your credibility as a writer and the strength of your argument depend on the reliability of all the sources, print and electronic, that you use; but you need to take extra care to protect your credibility and to ensure your argument's integrity when using Internet sources. Specifically, when conducting research on the Internet, you must carefully evaluate each source before you consider using and citing the information it presents. Why? Because almost anyone anywhere with Internet access and storage space on a server can build and "publish" a Web site. While this openness results in the astonishing diversity of content that we find on the Internet, it also means that a lot of subjective, opinionated, misleading, and simply false or inaccurate material resides on the Web.

URLs

Begin your assessment of an online source by looking at its site's URL (Uniform Resource Locator, also known as the Web site's address). The last few letters of the URL indicate what kind of site you've found by identifying what kind of entity hosts the site on its server:

.com	A site for commercial purposes, hosted on a commercial server. Anyone anywhere in the world can register for a domain name with this top-level domain designation.
.net	This designation was originally for organizations directly involved with the Internet. Increasingly, however, it is being used by businesses and individuals when their desired name under .com has already been registered. As with .com, anyone can register a name in the .net domain and the sites are hosted on commercial servers.
.org	This domain designation is for miscellaneous organizations, including, and usually, nonprofits. The sites, however, are often hosted by commercial servers.
.gov	Sites with this designation are for and hosted by U.S. federal, and occasionally state, government entities.
.mil	U.S. military sites.
.edu	This domain was originally designated for four-year accredited colleges and universities, but some two-year institutions of higher learning have been able to register under this domain.
Country Codes	Established by the International Standards Organization, these domain designations are for sites hosted in individual countries other than the United States Examples include .uk (for the United Kingdom); .au (for Australia); and .de (for Germany).

In general, for academic researchers, sites hosted by governments, colleges and universities, and well-established news and information organizations such as CNN, the *New York Times*, and PBS (Public Broadcasting System) will be more reliable than lesser-known or strictly commercial sites that, motivated by the need to make a profit, present biased or misleading information. Also of questionable reliability are personal Web pages, especially ones not hosted on a college or university server, and definitely ones whose creators don't have academic credentials or are not verifiably affiliated with a reputable organization. The inclusion of a tilde (~) in a URL usually means that a page is on a personal site.

Other Indicators of Reliability

You can judge the reliability of Internet sources based on various other indicators, some readily apparent, some less apparent or even hidden.

The appearance of a page is worth noticing. How much care went into designing the site? How carefully written is the site's content? Look at grammar and spelling; are they correct? Look for typos or other signs of carelessness. A carelessly done or unprofessional-looking page is less credible than one that looks carefully or professionally done. Similarly, a page or site that is difficult to navigate can be a warning sign.

Since the Internet is a means to continually publishing the most current information available, and Web pages are easy to update, the currency of a page's information is important. Even if the currency of specific content on the site isn't important (if, for instance, it is a historical document), a researcher wants to rely on sites that are regularly maintained. Do the links on the page work? Do they link to other carefully created, well-maintained sites? Look for a "last updated" statement on the page. If such a statement isn't in sight, you might be able to get last updated information using your browser by going to the file menu and selecting "properties."

If you can, find out who authored the material on the site. If you can't find a "created by" line on the page, backtrack through the site the page is on and follow up on links. Sometimes you can find out who authored (or sponsors) a page by checking for a copyright line at the bottom of the page. If you can identify the author of the page, use the author's name as a new search term to find additional information about her or him or other documents on the Web or in print that the person has authored. An established author who has print publications will likely be taken more seriously as a source than someone who expresses his views only on a self-produced Web site.

The credibility of a page's author (and/or sponsor); the kind of information on a page; the purpose of a page and the type of server the page's site is hosted on; and the verifiability of the information on a page are the main indicators of an Internet source's credibility. Some search engines, like Google (<www.google.com>), include information about how frequently Web sites are visited, and some subject directories (Librarians' Index to the Internet, for instance, <www.lii.org>), provide mini-reviews of sites as well as scores to indicate the sites' quality. Ultimately, though, you must use your common sense and critical reading skills to determine whether a Web site contains information that is valid and useful to your research.

TAKING NOTES

Some sources are so useful that you'll want to take many notes; others may be worth only a sentence or two of general summary; still others may turn out not to be useful at all. Before you start taking notes, skim the table of contents or the subheads (on a Web site, look for a link to the site map). This quick look may tell you that the source isn't one you can use. If, however, it does seem to contain relevant information, read through it. Then take notes, which can be your responses to the source as well as a report of what the source says. It is particularly valuable to jot down your first reaction to a source because it can help shape your presentation of the material in your paper; in addition, it is easier to remember this way. Just be sure to indicate somehow which notes are your own evaluations. You can write your notes on index cards; you can type your notes—or keep just the bibliographical information—on a computer; or you can annotate photocopies and highlight key passages. Or you can use some combination of techniques. Many writers like to photocopy or print out articles so that they can refer to them throughout the drafting process, as they sharpen the focus of the paper and build their argument. Although every writer has a different system for taking research notes, there are two basic guidelines to follow as you develop a system for yourself:

- Be organized.
- Summarize and paraphrase instead of copying long quotations.

Be Organized

Use a new page or a new index card for each new note or piece of information so that you can easily rearrange your notes as you draft your paper. (Make sure you identify the source on each note.) Arranging the information in different ways can give you a feel for the different ways your paper could be organized. For example, what you may at first regard as a piece of evidence for your "backing," you may later decide to treat as a separate "claim."

Keep all your notes together. As you conduct your research, you may find an argument that sounds similar or flatly contradictory to one you previously encountered. Having all your notes in one place will make it easy to cross-reference arguments and facts.

Record the complete bibliographical information for each source you consult. It is much easier to delete information about sources you don't end up using than to try to retrace your steps and find missing information about sources you do use. Some writers keep bibliographical notes on 3×5 cards and content notes on 4×6 cards so that the two kinds can be easily differentiated. Those who keep their notes on computer make a separate file for their source notes, which they can alphabetize with a simple command (if the entries begin with the author's last name). If you choose to keep the source information on note cards (one source per card) or to photocopy it directly from the sources, you can arrange the cards or photocopies in alphabetical order when it's time to type the references or list of works cited for your paper.

Summarize, Paraphrase, and Quote

Before you begin making notes about a source, read through the article or chapter. Then make a note that summarizes it. Next, consider whether any particularly important or useful ideas are expressed in the work; if so, **paraphrase** them. Writing a paraphrase requires using your own words to express an idea in a source. Make a note of a quotation only if the idea needs to be expressed in the exact words of the source. Figures 1, 2, and 3 are examples of a summary note, a paraphrase note, and a quotation note based on the following paragraphs. (Notice that the source, including the page number, is indicated at the top of each note.)

> Human actions bring about scarcities of renewable resources in three principal ways. First, people can reduce the quantity or degrade the quality of these resources faster than they are renewed. This phenomenon is often referred to as the consumption of the resource's "capital": the capital generates "income" that can be tapped for human consumption. A sustainable economy can therefore be defined as one that leaves the capital intact and undamaged so that future generations can enjoy undiminished income. Thus, if topsoil creation in a region of farmland is 0.25 millimeter per year, then average soil loss should not exceed that amount.
>
> The second source of scarcity is population growth. Over time, for instance, a given flow of water might have to be divided among a greater number of people. The final cause is change in the distribution of a resource within a society. Such a shift can concentrate supply in the hands of a few, subjecting the rest to extreme scarcity.
>
> —Thomas Homer-Dixon, Jeffrey Boutwell, and George Rathjens, "Environmental Change and Violent Conflict," *Scientific American* Feb. 1993: 38–45.

"Environmental Change," Homer-Dixon, Boutwell, and Rathjens, p. 40

The major human causes of shortages of renewable resources are (1) overconsumption, (2) overpopulation, and (3) unequal distribution.

Figure 1. Summary Note

"Environmental Change," Homer-Dixon,
Boutwell, and Rathjens, p. 40

There are three major causes of shortages of
human resources. (1) People consume the resources or
dilute their quality faster than the resources can
regenerate. (In this regard, a sustainable economy is one
that uses resources only as fast as they can be renewed.)
(2) Population increases put excessive demand on
the supply of resources. (3) A few people take control
of the resources and restrict distribution of them.

Figure 2. Paraphrase Note

"Environmental Change," Homer-Dixon,
Boutwell, and Rathjens, p. 40

Homer-Dixon, Boutwell, and Rathjens use financial terms
to describe resource consumption. Depleting resources
faster than they can be renewed is "the consumption
of the resource's 'capital.'" Accordingly, a sustainable
economy is one that "leaves the capital intact and
undamaged so that future generations can enjoy
undiminished income."

Figure 3. Quotation Note

USING YOUR NOTES

Your paper should not be a "quotation dump" in which you string
together a large number of quotations without any interpretation or remarks. Instead it should express your own ideas and opinions, which you
have developed and refined in the course of your research. The appropriate use of quotations is as *evidence that supports the claim or warrant at*

hand. If you are relying on a warrant with the backing of expert testimony or statistics, quoting that material will strengthen your argument's ethos by showing your reader that your opinion is an informed one.

Always integrate quotations gracefully into your text; don't just drop them in. Quoted material should flow into your prose. Compare these two treatments of a quotation:

> Incorrect: Samuel Johnson also praised London. "When a man is tired of London, he is tired of life."
>
> Correct: As Samuel Johnson once remarked, "When a man is tired of London, he is tired of life" (Boswell 231).

Notice how the quotation in the second example is part of the sentence. A common way to incorporate quotations is to use phrases such as "once remarked," "as one expert has said," "as one critic has observed," and "as one study has found."

Notice also that the second example leaves no doubt about who said the quoted words and indicates where they can be found. The parenthetical reference between the end quotation marks and the period identifies the author and the page number of the work where the quotation can be found. The full bibliographical information for the source is at the end of the paper under the author's name in the list of works cited.

Plagiarism

Plagiarism means taking someone else's words or ideas and passing them off as your own. However minor or innocent such an act might seem to you, any attempt to deceive one's audience violates the spirit of the objective pursuit of truth and the principles of academic honesty. Institutions of higher learning always expect you to act as part of this great tradition, and the penalties for plagiarism are stiff, ranging from an F to expulsion.

The most obvious kind of plagiarism is to use someone's exact words as if they were your own—for example, to repeat Samuel Johnson's aphorism, "When a man is tired of London, he is tired of life," without acknowledging that the words are Johnson's. But there are other forms of plagiarism, such as writing, "When a man is tired of Manhattan, he is tired of life." To avoid plagiarism, you would need to add a phrase like "to paraphrase Samuel Johnson."

Another kind of plagiarism occurs when a paraphrase does not acknowledge the source. Here is an example:

> Original Passage: "Anyone who knows the frantic temper of the present schools will understand the transvaluation of values that would be effected by [the abolition of grades]. For most of the students, the competitive grade has become the essence. The naive teacher points to the beauty and the ingenuity of the research; the shrewd student asks if he is re-

Example of
Plagiarism:

sponsible for that on the final exam."—Paul
Goodman, p. 34
If grades were abolished, our entire set of educational values would be upset. Many students see
their grades as the essence of academic success;
while their teachers may concern themselves only
with their subject matter, the students want to
know what they will need to know to pass an
exam.

Although only a few exact words from the original appear in the example (*values, essence*) the exact idea is repeated without any credit to Paul
Goodman. An example of quoting without plagiarizing would be

Correctly
Quoted:

Paul Goodman has argued that abolishing grades
would result in a "transvaluation of values" concerning education as a whole. Many students view
their grades as the "essence" of education and are
more concerned with what they need to know for
exams than with the "beauty and ingenuity" of
their subject matters (Goodman 34).

When in doubt, provide a citation, and remember that online sources require the same careful citation that print sources do. These precautions
will save you the embarrassment of being accused of academic dishonesty.

DOCUMENTING SOURCES

The most obvious purpose of parenthetical references is to tell your
readers the source of information or a quotation. The parenthetical references are keyed to a list at the end of the paper. There are several systems
for citing references. This text explains the MLA (Modern Language Association) and APA (American Psychological Association) systems. You
can find out more about these documentation styles at <http://www.
mla.org> and <http://www.apastyle.org>.

The MLA System

The MLA format for identifying sources is used primarily by scholars in English, foreign languages, and other humanities disciplines. The
parenthetical references in the text, which identify the author and usually the pages, refer to a list of works cited, which are arranged alphabetically by author.

PARENTHETICAL REFERENCES Parenthetical references include the author's last name and the page number of the source; for
example,

```
(Goodman 34)
```

as shown on page 309 at the end of the correctly quoted version of the passage by Paul Goodman.

If the author's name is mentioned in the sentence, only the page number is needed in the parenthetical reference immediately after the author's name.

If you are discussing an entire work, you do not need to include page numbers in the parenthetical reference.

If you consulted more than one work by the same author, include a shortened version of the title in your citation (underline titles of books; enclose titles of essays and articles in quotation marks):

```
(Goodman, Growing Up 34)
```

If the work has two or three authors, use all their names:

```
(Goodman and Strong 143-44)
```

If the work has more than three authors, use the first name and *et al.*:

```
(Goodman et al. 134)
```

If the work, such as a brief newspaper article, is not signed, identify it with a short version of the title:

```
("Education" 44)
```

If a statement has two or more sources, separate them with a semicolon:

```
(Goodman 34; Strong 98-99)
```

If you consulted sources by authors with the same last name, differentiate them by including their first initials or first names in the parenthetical references:

```
(Paul Goodman 34; Percival Goodman 178-79)
```

LIST OF WORKS CITED   The complete information about the works identified in the parenthetical references comes on a separate page, titled "Works Cited," at the end of the paper. The entries are double-spaced, and the second and subsequent lines of each entry are indented half an inch (five spaces if you are using a typewriter).

The formats for common and not-so-common sources can be found in the 5th edition of the *MLA Handbook for Writers of Research Papers* (New York: Modern Language Association of America, 1999). Every writer of research papers should consult that handbook when preparing his or her final draft. However, here are examples of formats for most of the kinds of sources you are likely to use.

Books

Book by a Single Author

> Willeford, Charles. <u>New Hope for the Dead</u>. New York:
> Ballantine, 1985.

Book by Two or Three Authors

> Killiam, James, and Robert Cole. <u>Medical Ethics in</u>
> <u>America</u>. Boston: Globe, 1991.
>
> Olds, Sally B., Marcia L. London, and Patricia E.
> Ladewig. <u>Maternal Newborn Nursing</u>. 3rd ed. Menlo
> Park: Addison-Wesley, 1988.

Book by More Than Three Authors

> Barker, Francis, et al. <u>1642: Literature and Power</u>
> <u>in the Seventeenth Century</u>. Essex: U of Essex,
> 1981.

Two or More Books by the Same Author

> Sullivan, Michael. <u>The Arts of China</u>. Berkeley:
> U of California P, 1967.
>
> ---. <u>The Birth of Landscape Painting in China</u>.
> Berkeley: U of California P, 1961.
>
> ---. <u>The Meeting of Eastern and Western Art</u>.
> Berkeley: U of California P, 1989.

Book by a Corporate Author

> Editors, Inc. <u>How to Write Effective Prose</u>. New York:
> Editors, 1990.

Edited Book

> Peil, Manfred, ed. <u>Modern Views on Classic Films</u>.
> Los Angeles: Smithdon, 1992.

Book with an Author and an Editor

> Donne, John. <u>Poetical Works</u>. Ed. H. J. C. Grierson.
> 2 vols. Oxford: Oxford UP, 1912.

Book without an Author or an Editor

> Merriam-Webster Dictionary of English Usage.
> Springfield: Merriam-Webster, 1989.

Translated Book

> Trebelli, Salvatore. My Life on Stage. Trans. Erin
> Cairns. New York: Musicland, 1972.

Book Edition Other Than the First

> de Man, Paul. Blindness and Insight: Essays in the
> Rhetoric of Contemporary Criticism. 2nd ed.
> Minneapolis: U of Minnesota P, 1983.

Republished Book

> Mitchell, Juliet. Woman's Estate. 1971. New York:
> Vintage, 1973.

Multivolume Series

> Chambers, E. K. The Elizabethan Stage. 5 vols.
> Oxford: Clarendon, 1923.

Volume in a Multivolume Series

> Twichett, Denis, and Michael Lowe, eds. The Ch'in and
> Han Empires, 221 B.C.-A.D. 220. New York:
> Cambridge UP, 1986. Vol. 1 of The Cambridge
> History of China. 15 vols. to date. 1978-.

Book in a Series

> Bruner, Charlotte H., ed. The Heinemann Book of
> African Women's Writing. Heinemann African
> Writers Series. London: Heinemann, 1993.

Parts of Books

Selection in an Anthology or Compilation

> Neary, Adam. "The Impossibility of Utopia." Essays in
> Modern Political Theory. Ed. Lenore Kingsmore.
> New York: Political, 1982. 176-92.

Signed Article in an Encyclopedia

> Ruoff, A. Lavonne Brown. "Native American Prose and
> Poetry." Benét Reader Encyclopedia of American
> Literature. Ed. George Perkins, Barbara Perkins,
> and Phillip Leininger. New York: Harper, 1991.

Unsigned Article in an Encyclopedia

> "Coffee." Encyclopaedia Britannica. 1992 ed.

Introduction, Preface, Foreword, or Afterword

> Sirr, Lauren. Preface. School Certification and Its
> Critics. Chicago: Copper, 1982. v-xii.

Periodicals

Newspaper Article

> Donner, Matthew. "The Plight of the Intern." New York
> Times 1 Apr. 1990, sec. 2: 1+.

Article in a Monthly Magazine

> Pinho, Genero. "Revitalizing Traditional Opera."
> Opera Monthly Feb. 1991: 77-89.

Article in a Journal Paginated by Year or Volume

> Gale, Richard P. "The Environmental Movement and the
> Left: Antagonists or Allies?" Sociological
> Inquiry 53 (1983): 179-99.

Article in a Journal Paginated by Issue

> Stevenson, Warren. "'The Tyger' as Artefact." Blake
> Studies 2.1 (1969-70): 9.

Unsigned Article or Editorial

> "Finally a Solution." Editorial. Nation 16 Dec.
> 1988: 12.

Review

> Cather, Willa. Rev. of The Awakening, by Kate Chopin.
> Pittsburgh Leader 8 July 1899: 6.

Other Sources

Unpublished Dissertation

> Yount, Neala Schleuning. "'America: Song We Sang Without Knowing'--Meridel Le Sueur's America." Diss. U of Minnesota, 1978.

Government Document

> United States. General Accounting Office. <u>Siting of Hazardous Waste Landfills and Their Correlation with Racial and Economic Status of Surrounding Communities</u>. Washington: GPO, 1983.

Lecture, Speech, or Address

> Freudenberg, Nicholas. "The Grass Roots Environmental Movement: Not in Our Backyards." Annual meeting of American Assoc. for the Advancement of Science. New Orleans. 15 Feb. 1990.

Film

> <u>12 Monkeys</u>. Dir. Terry Gilliam. Perf. Bruce Willis, Brad Pitt, and Madeline Stowe. Universal, 1995.

Television or Radio Program

> "Satanic Cults and Children." <u>Geraldo</u>. CBS. WCBS, New York. 19 Nov. 1987.

Recording

> Barber, Samuel. "Adagio for Strings," op. 11. Perf. Smithsonian Chamber Players. Cond. Kenneth Slowik. <u>Metamorphosis</u>. BMG, 1995.

Live Performance

> <u>The Tempest</u>. By William Shakespeare. Dir. Carey Perloff. Perf. David Strathairn, Graham Beckel, David Patrick Kelly, and Vera Farmiga. Geary Theater, San Francisco. 30 Jan. 1996.

Work of Art

> Vermeer, Jan. <u>Young Woman with a Water Jug</u>.
>
>> Metropolitan Museum of Art, New York.

Court Decision

> Brown v. Board of Ed. 347 US 483. 1954.

Interview, Unpublished Letter, E-mail, or Other Personal Communication

> Moreno, Gloria. Personal interview. 29 Mar. 1999.
>
> Meredith, Lloyd. E-mail to the author. 14 Jan. 1999.

Current MLA Guidelines for Documenting Electronic Sources

The 5th edition of the *MLA Handbook for Writers of Research Papers* includes extensive guidelines for documenting electronic sources. The MLA's Web site also provides information about documenting electronic sources. To find this information, go to <www.mla.org> and click on the "MLA Style" link to get to the link labeled "Frequently Asked Questions About MLA Style."

The following is a list of the basic requirements for citing an Internet or electronic source according to MLA style:

1. Author or editor name, followed by a period.
2. The title of the article or short work (such as a short story or poem) enclosed by quotation marks.
3. The name of the book, journal, or other longer work in italics.
4. Publication information, followed by a period:
   City, publisher, and date for books
   Volume and year for journals
   Date of a magazine
   Date and description of government documents.
5. The date on which you accessed the information (no period).
6. The URL, placed within angle brackets, followed by a period.

Selected models follow.

Online Reference Database or Scholarly Project

> <u>Victorian Women Writers Project</u>. Ed. Perry Willett.
>
>> 22 Feb. 1999. Indiana U. 26 Feb. 1999
>>
>> <http://www.indiana.edu/~letrs/vwwp>.

Book

> James, Henry. <u>Daisy Miller</u>. New York: Harper, 1892.
> 10 Mar. 1999 <http://eldred.ne.mediaone.net/
> hjj/dm/daisy0.html>.

Part of an Online Book

> Brooke, Rupert. "Seaside." <u>Collected Poems</u>. 1916.
> <u>Project Bartleby</u>. Ed. Steven van Leeuwen. 2000.
> Columbia U. 2 Sept. 2001 <http://www.bartleby.
> com/232/108.html>.

Online Book within a Scholarly Project

> Alcott, Louisa May. <u>Flower Fables</u>. Boston, 1855. <u>The</u>
> <u>Electronic Text Center</u>. Ed. David Seaman. 2000.
> Alderman Lib., U. of Virginia. 22 April 2001
> <http://etext.lib.virginia.edu/toc/modeng/
> public/AlcFlow.html>.

Article in a Scholarly Journal

> Haviland, Beverly. "The Return of the Alien: Henry
> James in New York, 1904." <u>The Henry James Review</u>
> 16.3 (1993). 26 Feb. 1999 <http://musc.jbu.edu/
> journals/henry_james_review>.

Article in a Newspaper

> Ginsburg, Elizabeth. "Greener Golf Courses,
> Ecologically, That Is." <u>New York Times on the</u>
> <u>Web</u> 25 Nov. 2001. 3 Dec. 2001 <http://www.nyt.
> com/2001/11/25/garden/255CUTT.html>.

Article in a Magazine

> Peyser, Marc. "Home of the Gray." <u>Newsweek</u> 1 Mar.
> 1999. 25 Feb. 1999 <http://newsweek.com/
> nw-srv/printed/us/front.htm>.

Review

> Anderson, Karen. Rev. of "Red Hook," by Gabriel
>
> Cohen. <u>January Magazine</u> 30 Nov. 2001. 3 Dec.
>
> 2001 <http://www.januarymagazine.com/crfiction.
>
> redhook.html>.

Article from an Online Encyclopedia

> "Toni Morrison." Encyclopaedia Britannica Online.
>
> 1994-1999. Encyclopaedia Britannica,
>
> 4 Mar. 1999 <http://members.cb.com/bol/
>
> topic?eu=55183&setn=#s_top>.

CD-ROM

> <u>The Civil War: A Newspaper Perspective</u>. Nashville;
>
> Folio, 1990. CD-ROM. Accessible Archives, 1994.

The APA System

The chief alternative to the MLA system for documenting sources is the system used by the APA, described in the *Publication Manual of the American Psychological Association,* 5th edition (Washington, DC: APA, 2001). This system is used primarily in psychology, sociology, and other social science disciplines. The main differences from MLA style are that the parenthetical references show the date of publication and that the list of works cited is called "References" and has the date as the second element of the entries.

PARENTHETICAL REFERENCES As with the MLA style, the APA style requires short parenthetical references within the text. Unlike with the MLA style, these references include the date of publication, but page numbers are included only for direct quotations. Here is an example of a parenthetical reference in APA style (note that the author's name does not appear in the parentheses here, because the name appears in the text):

> Paul Goodman (1962, p. 34) argued that abolishing
>
> grades would have revolutionary consequences,
>
> because "the competitive grade has become the
>
> essence" for most students.

If you do not mention the author's name in the text, include it in the parenthetical reference:

> (Goodman, 1962, p. 34)

If your sources include two works by an author in the same year, differentiate them by putting a letter after the date, both in the parenthetical reference and in the reference list:

(Goodman, 1962a)

If your sources include two authors with the same last name, use their initials in the parenthetical citations:

(P. S. Goodman, 1962)

If a work has two authors, use an ampersand between their names in the parenthetical reference:

(Goodman & Strong, 1962)

If the work, such as a brief newspaper article, is not signed, refer to it by the first few words of the title, starting with the first important word (underline book titles; enclose article and essay titles in quotation marks):

("Education," 1962, p. 34)

If you cite two or more works by the same author in one parenthetical reference, follow the author's name with the years in chronological order, separated by commas:

(Goodman, 1962, 1972)

If you cite two or more sources in one parenthetical reference, give them in alphabetical order and separate them with semicolons:

(Goodman, 1962; Strong, 1958)

Personal communications, such as letters, e-mail messages, and telephone conversations, do not need to be included in the list of references. They can simply be identified in the parenthetical reference in the text:

(Goodman, personal communication, January 8, 1970)

LIST OF REFERENCES   The MLA and APA requirements for the list of works cited are different on several counts. The first is that APA titles this page "References" rather than "Works Cited."

Notice also that MLA gives authors' first names, whereas APA shows only initials. APA style reverses last name and initials on all authors of a multiauthor work, not just the first author, as MLA does. Additionally, in APA style, only the first word of titles and subtitles of books and magazine articles is capitalized. However, APA style for the title of periodicals is like MLA style; namely, all important words are capitalized. Unlike the MLA, the APA includes the state abbreviation for cities of publication that are "not well known."

In APA style, as in MLA style, the first line of each entry is flush with the left margin and subsequent lines are indented five to seven spaces. If your word processing program makes creating these "hanging indents" difficult, paragraph style (first line indented, subsequent lines flush left) is acceptable. Finally, titles of books, periodicals, movies, and so on are italicized in APA style, unless your word processor can only do underlining.

Books

Book by a Single Author

Anderson, B. (1992). <u>Modern sport psychology</u>. New York: Jacobson Press.

Book by Two or More Authors

Bennet, M., & Juran, S. (1989). <u>Inventing culture</u>. Boston: Globe.

Book by a Corporate Author

National Association of Anglers. (1990). <u>The ten best bass rivers in America: A guide</u>. Seattle: Nature Press.

Edited Book

Kagan, J., & Coles, R. (Eds.). (1972). <u>Twelve to sixteen: Early adolescence</u>. New York: Norton.

Book without an Author or an Editor

<u>Merriam-Webster dictionary of English usage</u>. (1989). Springfield, MA: Merriam-Webster.

Translated Book

Segouin, J. (1976). <u>Selling the sunset</u> (S. Moccio, Trans.). New York: Brookson. (Original work published 1974)

Book Edition Other Than the First

Bennett, W. L. (1988). <u>News: The politics of illusion</u> (2nd ed.). New York: Longman.

Separately Titled Volume in a Multivolume Work

      Schultz, J. (Ed.). (1982). The history of thought: Vol. 11. The Elizabethan world. New York: Edgeboro.

Parts of Books

Selection in an Anthology or Compilation

      Tobias, A. L. (1988). Bulimia: An overview. In K. Clark, R. Parr, & W. Castelli (Eds.), Evaluation and management of eating disorders (pp. 142-150). Champaign, IL: Life Enhancement Publications.

Article in an Encyclopedia

      Haseltine, W. A. (1992). AIDS. In Encyclopedia Americana (Vol. 1, pp. 334-336). Danbury, CT: Grolier.

Periodicals

Article in a Daily Newspaper

      Keane, V. (1990, July 21). More trouble for the troublemakers. New York Newsday, p. A21.

Article in a Magazine

      Dahlin, R. (1996, April 1). Laughing halfway to the bank. Publishers Weekly, 42-46.

Article in a Journal Paginated by Volume or Year

      Crisp, A. H., Palmer, R. L., & Kalucy, R. S. (1976). How common is anorexia nervosa? A prevalence study. British Journal of Psychiatry, 128, 549-554.

Article in a Journal Paginated by Issue

      Hansen, G. B. (1988). Layoffs, plant closings, and worker displacement in America: Serious problems that need a national solution. Journal of Social Issues, 44(4), 153-171.

Two or More Articles by Same Author in Same Year

Steinberg, L. (1987a). The impact of puberty on family relations: Effects of pubertal status and pubertal timing. Developmental Psychology, 23, 451-460.

Steinberg, L. (1987b). Recent research on the family at adolescence: The extent and nature of sex differences. Journal of Youth and Adolescence, 16, 191-197.

Unsigned Article or Editorial

Fortune Global Service 500: The 50 largest retail companies. (1991, August 26). Fortune, 37, 179.

Review

Giles, J. (1996, January 22). A cold, bleak Caribbean [Review of the book The autobiography of my mother]. Newsweek, 62.

Other Sources

Unpublished Dissertation

Hall, C. (1993). Social networks and availability factors: Mobilizing adherents for social movement participation. Unpublished doctoral dissertation, Purdue University, Lafayette, IN.

Government Document

U.S. Department of Justice. (1991). Criminal victimization, 1990 (Special Report No. NCJ-122743). Washington, DC: Bureau of Justice Statistics.

Research Report or Monograph

Robertson, M. J., Ropers, R., & Boyer, R. (1985). The homeless of Los Angeles County: An empirical evaluation (Document No. 4). Los Angeles:

University of California, Los Angeles, Basic Shelter
Research Project, School of Public Health.

Unpublished Paper Presented at a Meeting

Allgeier, E. (1986, August). <u>Coercive versus
consensual sexual interactions</u>. Paper presented at
the annual meeting of the American Psychological
Association, Washington, DC.

Film or Videotape

Stein, P. L. (Producer), & Levy, P. R.
(Director). (1994). <u>Neighborhoods: The hidden cities
of San Francisco</u> [Videotape]. San Francisco: KQED.

Court Decision

Brown v. Board of Educ., 347 U.S. 483 (1954).

Current APA Guidelines for Documenting Electronic Sources

In general, provide the author, date, and title information as you
would for a print source. After the title, add a brief description of the
type of online document (enclosed in square brackets). At the end of
the citation, provide a retrieval statement that includes the date the information was retrieved and the URL or, if no URL is available, the
name of the site or database. Unlike in MLA style, in APA style URLs
are not enclosed within angle brackets. The APA provides extensive
guidelines for documenting electronic sources at <http://www.apastyle.
org/elecref.html>.

Web Site

James, L. (1998, October 9). Highlights of
the results. <u>Driving Road Rage Survey</u> [Web page].
Retrieved December 10, 1998 from the World Wide Web:
http://www.aloha.net/~dyc/surveys/highlights.html

Chapter or Section in an Internet Document

Sound Partners for Community Health (2001,
November 30). The high cost of dying. In <u>Issues: End
of Life Decisions</u>. Retrieved December 2, 2001 from

http://www.soundpartners.org/information1981/
information_show.htm?attrib_id=1123&doc_id=23912

Article from Online Journal

Kraut, R., Lundmark, V., Patterson, M.,
Kiesler, S., Mukopadhyay, T., & Scherlis, W. (1998,
September). Internet paradox: A social technology
that reduces social involvement and psychological
well-being? American Psychologist, 53, 1017-1031.
Retrieved October 31, 1998 from the World Wide Web:
http://www.apa.org/journals/amp/amp5391017.html

Newspaper Article Online

Young, J. R. (1998, November). Gender and
electoral politics: Scholar's book rides the
historical coattails of family values. The Chronicle
of Higher Education, p. A14 [Newspaper article
online]. Retrieved Nobember 14, 1998 from the World
Wide Web: http://chronicle.com/weekly/v45/i11/
11a01401.htm

Online Posting (Listserv/Mailing List or Usenet/Discussion List)

Kenyon, E. (1998, July 22). Safety and the
lone researcher 2#. Biog-Methods Archives [Online
discussion list archive]. Retrieved November 2, 1998
from the World Wide Web: http://www.mailbase.ac.uk/
lists/biog-methods/1998-07/0002.html

*U.S. Government Report Available on a Government Agency Web Site,
No Publication Date Indicated*

United States Department of the Interior.
(n.d.). School Construction and Operations, Trust
Reform, Public Safety, and Water and Land Claims
Settlements Lead BIA FY2002 Budget Request. Retrieved
December 2, 2001 from http://www.doi.gov/news/
schconst.htm

Paper Presented at a Symposium, Abstract Retrieved from a University Web Site

> Considine, J. A. (1996). <u>Emerging Indigenous Crops of Australia</u>. Paper presented at the Third National Symposium of New Crops. Retrieved November 29, 2001 from http://www.hort.purdue.edu/newcrop/ proceedings1996/v3-toc.html

CD-ROMs and Portable Databases

> Steinhausen, H. C., & Vollrath, M. (1993). The self-image of adolescent patients with eating disorders. [CD-ROM]. <u>International Journal of Eating Disorders, 13</u>(2), 221-227. Abstract from: SilverPlatter File: PsycLIT Item: 80-33985

SAMPLE RESEARCH PAPER: MLA AND APA FORMATS

The sample research paper on pages 325–344 illustrates MLA style and makes a cogent argument for transracial adoption. Page 345 is a cut-away that shows the same paper set in APA style.

Sample Paper Format: MLA Style

Kimberley Waibel

Professor Moekle

Writing 39C

May 2, 2002

In the Best Interest of the Child?

Transracial adoption has historically followed a pattern
much like that of a roller coaster; one year it is favored, the
next year it is opposed. While the roller coaster has taken many
twists and turns, the motor propelling it has never changed.
Like many things, transracial adoption's past has been the
result of the racial views and prejudices of the judicial
system, the adoption agencies, and special interest groups.
This is evident when one looks closely at the court rulings and
social service practices that have been the driving force in
transracial adoption practices. Also obvious are discrepancies
in agency procedures and legal decisions. Consequently, minority
children available for adoption have suffered at the hands of
those who are charged with protecting them. The present system
has failed our children and we must do something to change it.
In order to bring transracial adoption's roller coaster ride to
an end, we must understand its past and the dynamics surrounding
it. We begin in one of the most racially volatile eras in U.S.
history--the 1940s.

The end of World War II came at a time when prevailing
social attitudes were steeped in racism. Many Blacks worked as
domestic help in the homes of wealthy and middle-class White
families. Bathrooms and drinking fountains were separated Black

1

Waibel 2

from White, and communities were far from culturally mixed.
Minorities in general were having a difficult time being accepted
as equals in the eyes of the White society. This is the climate
in which transracial adoption surfaced in this country. It began
with the end of the war, which left many children all over the
world without parents and without homes (Simon and Alstein,
Adoption, Race, and Identity 1-2). In addition, many of the
American troops created illegitimate children in the countries
to which they had been deployed (Bagley 135). As a result,
many American families began to adopt children from foreign
countries. Known as intercountry adoption, this practice was,
and still is, very controversial. Yet it was through the efforts
of the practitioners of intercountry adoption that transracial
adoption, within our own country, came to be recognized as
a feasible solution to the predicament adoption agencies
faced concerning minority children. In 1948, in Minneapolis,
Minnesota, a Black social worker named Laura Gaskin placed a
Black child with a White adoptive family (Hermann 150). Thus,
transracial adoption was born.

The atmosphere of the forties and fifties no doubt gave rise
to fierce opposition regarding interracial adoption. The families
who ventured into the unknown realm of transracial adoption were
likely condemned by their families, friends, and communities.
These families were torn apart by the legal system as well. In
1955, a case known as In re Adoption of a Minor was decided in
the District of Columbia. The case involved an illegitimate
child born to a White couple, the birth mother and her new

husband, a Black man. With the mother's permission, the Black man filed a petition to adopt the child. The court refused, citing that the child would lose the social status of a White man by virtue of the fact that his father of record would be Black (Simon and Alstein, A.R.I. 40). While the court of appeals reversed the district court's ruling, the district court's ruling represents the deeply rooted prejudices of this time period.

In 1958, the Child Welfare League of America published its Standards for Adoption Service (SAS). In it were guidelines upon which, had it been published only three years earlier, the D.C. district court could have based its decision. The SAS explicitly promoted inracial (same-race) adoption as the only acceptable form of adoption. Under the subtitle "Matching," the CWLA held that "Physical resemblances should not be a determining factor in the selection of a home, with the possible exception of such racial characteristics as color" (Simon and Alstein, A.R.I. 4). Concurrently, the rate of transracial adoption diminished, and while specific statistics are unavailable, it is safe to assume that the position stated by the CWLA influenced many adoption agencies against practicing transracial adoption. Fortunately, the sexual revolution and the Civil Rights Movement were soon to follow, forcing the CWLA to reevaluate its position.

The sexual revolution brought about many changes in society, not the least of which was the increased availability of contraception and abortion. However, such services were primarily available to middle- and upper-class White people, due

5

Waibel 4

to the cost of things like birth control pills and doctors'
visits. What resulted was not a total reduction in the number of
children available for adoption, but a reduction in the number
of White children available for adoption (Simon and Alstein,
A.R.I. 2). Furthermore, the historical treatment of minorities
by adoption agencies was one that seemed to either exclude or
discourage participation. Statistics show that many more White
families were accepted as adoptive parents than minority
families (Simon and Alstein, Transracial Adoptees and Their
Families 9). These factors left adoption agencies facing an
interesting predicament. Should they continue to promote
inracial adoption, thereby leaving hundreds of children without
homes? Or should they place minority children with White
families that could give them stability and happiness? The
sexual revolution left these questions to be answered by the
agencies.

At the same time, Martin Luther King, Jr., was leading the
nation's Civil Rights Movement, which promoted racial harmony
and the full integration of Black people into society. This
allowed the adoption agencies to feel that transracial adoption
could be acceptable and would further the cause of racial
integration. Consequently, in the late 1960s, the CWLA reversed
its earlier position, now stating that "...families who have the
capacity to adopt a child whose racial background is different
from their own...should be encouraged to consider such a child"
(McRoy 149). Also interesting is that the National Association
for the Advancement of Colored People (NAACP) and the National

Waibel 5

Urban League both made statements endorsing transracial adoption
as a reasonable alternative to traditional adoption (McRoy 149).
As a result, the frequency of transracial adoptions increased
nationwide, and between 1967 and 1972, while different sources
cite very different statistics, approximately 5,000 to 10,000
transracial adoptions occurred across the country (McRoy 150).

In 1972, a new influence made its voice heard. In a national
conference, the National Association of Black Social Workers
(NABSW) presented a viewpoint ardently opposed to transracial
adoption. The 5,000 member association passed a resolution
against transracial adoption, stating that "Black children
in white homes are cut off from the healthy development of
themselves as Black people" (McRoy 150). Furthermore the NABSW
went so far as to call transracial adoption a form of genocide
(Simon and Alstein, <u>A.R.I.</u> 15). Support for the NABSW came from
African-American separatists who surfaced in response to the
Civil Rights Movement. These separatists reinforced the NABSW's
position by stating that the adoption of Black children by White
families would be detrimental to the African American community
as a whole (Hayes 305). As a result, the CWLA again reversed its
position, restating the importance of inracial placements in
order to facilitate a child's integration into its adoptive
family (McRoy 150). Following the announcements made by the
NABSW and the CWLA, the rate of transracial adoptions decreased
dramatically. In 1975, the last year the federal government
collected information on adoption statistics, the number of
transracial adoptions was 831, as reported by the Department

Waibel 6

of Health, Education and Welfare. This is much lower than the record high in 1971, when 2,574 transracial adoptions were recorded (Simon and Alstein, <u>Transracial Adoptees and Their Families</u> 5). It is important to remember that minorities still constituted the bulk of the adoptable population. We can conclude that, while 831 children were adopted, many more were left without families.

Until this point in transracial adoption's history, the U.S. Supreme Court had refused to get involved, on the basis that such cases were domestic issues (Simon and Alstein, <u>A.R.I.</u> 48). In 1977, Drummond vs. Fulton County came before the Supreme Court. A White couple from Georgia had been the foster parents of a three-year-old boy since he was one month old. The agency denied the petition to adopt the child when he was one year old, and the Fifth Circuit Court of Appeals upheld the agency's decision on the grounds that there were racial differences between the parents and the child (Simon and Alstein, <u>A.R.I.</u> 42). The U.S. Supreme Court, staying true to its history of rejecting domestic cases, refused to hear the case, stating, "It is obvious that race did enter into the decision of the Department" (Simon and Alstein, <u>A.R.I.</u> 42). However, the Court declared its confidence that race was not the only factor in the department's decision. While this assertion may have been true, the Court unknowingly established a precedent that allowed race to be a factor, although not the only one, in cases concerning adoption. This started the resurgence of opposition to transracial adoption. More fuel was added to the opposition's

fire in 1978, when the Indian Child Welfare Act was passed. The
act was passed to ensure that Indian children removed from their
biological parents would be placed with families that were
representative of the American Indian's culture and heritage
(McRoy 150). By providing that a minority group deserved special
consideration during adoption proceedings with regard to their
culture, the federal government advanced the anti-transracial
adoption movement. However, the opposition's influence on
adoption law and standards did not last long. This was due
to the changing racial attitudes in society approaching the
eighties. While far from totally equal, Black people were, at
this point, seen as social equals and had been integrated into
society for some time. Therefore, the NABSW had a much harder
time promoting their views to a society that, as a whole, no
longer believed in separation of the races.

In 1984, a landmark case was decided. Surprisingly, the
Supreme Court overlooked tradition and got involved in the case
known as Palmore vs. Sidoti. A married White couple got divorced
and the mother was awarded custody of their three-year-old
daughter. When the mother became involved with a Black man, the
father sought custody of his daughter. When the mother and her
boyfriend married, the state court revoked the mother's custody
and awarded custody to the father. The court stated that "a
racially mixed household would have a detrimental effect on
the child if she remained there" (Landrith). The U.S. Supreme
Court, in a unanimous decision, reversed the lower court's
decision based on the Fourteenth Amendment's Equal Protection

Waibel 8

Clause, which states that "No state shall...deny to any person within its jurisdiction the equal protection of the laws" (Grolier's). Four years later, in 1988, the CWLA's Standards for Adoption Services presented a much diluted position concerning transracial adoption. While still maintaining inracial adoption to be the best alternative, the 1988 SAS states, "If aggressive, ongoing recruitment efforts are unsuccessful in finding families of the same ethnicity or culture, other families should be considered" (Simon and Alstein, A.R.I. 32). As of the most recent research, the CWLA's position has not changed, despite the fact that the NABSW renews its vehement position against transracial adoption yearly.

Despite the recent legal efforts to abolish race as a determinant in adoption, transracial adoption is still not a completely accepted practice. Other factors still influence whether or not minority children are adopted by White families. First of all, there is a prevailing attitude that transracial adoption is not an ideal, nor is it an equal alternative to inracial adoption. When children are placed transracially, it is seen as a subordinate decision; "second best" (Simon and Alstein, A.R.I. 32). Such an attitude creates a situation in which adoption agencies go to extreme measures to find same-race homes for a child, allowing the child to spend additional time in foster or institutional care. The older the child gets, the more developed his identity is, the more difficult it is for him to integrate into an adoptive family. However, one of the biggest influences on the state of transracial adoption today

10

Waibel 9

lies in the ambiguity of the views of not only the adoption agencies, but the federal government as well. State by state, the guidelines regarding transracial adoption have differed greatly throughout its history. This is evident when one looks at the individual states' statistics. From 28 agencies in California, 62 children were placed transracially in 1974, as compared to the 37 children placed transracially from 27 agencies in Michigan (Simon and Alstein, Transracial Adoption 32). Even in the present day, courts in individual states decide transracial adoption cases differently. Michigan, Maryland, and Pennsylvania have all been involved in cases where children were removed from custody based solely on their race, Matter of "Male" Chiang, Queen vs. Queen, and McLaughlin vs. Pernsley, respectively (Simon and Alstein, A.R.I. 49-50). Oftentimes a lower court will rule in favor of the adoption agency removing a child placed transracially, and a higher court will reverse the ruling. This inconsistency in decision making is detrimental to the children, as they will often be shuffled from one place to the other, back and forth from adoptive parents to foster care, and back again.

This discrepancy doesn't exist solely at the state level. In 1972, the same year the NABSW came out against transracial adoptions, the U.S. Supreme Court declared all antimiscegenation (interracial marriage) laws unconstitutional. The Court, essentially, has upheld that race is not a determinant for who can and cannot be a family. Yet, the Court has failed to extend this judgment to rulings against transracial adoption. The

Waibel 10

adoption agencies, however, are the most ambiguous with regard
to transracial adoption. Agencies will place Black children in
White foster homes, often for years at a time, but not allow
those same families to adopt their foster children. In 1989, in
Napa Valley, California, several White families were recruited
to provide temporary (45 days) foster care for Black infants
born addicted to drugs. Several years later, when the families
tried to adopt their foster children, the department of social
services began removing the children and placing them with Black
foster parents (Simon and Alstein, A.R.I. 54). Not only are
such actions detrimental to the foster child, but they create
emotional strains for the foster family as well. People fall
in love with the children they care for, and when one is taken
away, whether by accident or purposefully, it is devastating to
all parties involved.

Social service organizations, funded by the government and
our tax dollars, have been denying adoptable children homes in
this manner since the 1940s without the public's knowledge.
Essentially, transracial adoption has been an issue ignored by
much of the popular media, preventing the general public from
forming any kind of opinion on the subject. Unfortunately, this
leaves this issue to be decided by special interest groups like
the NABSW who use their influence to frame adoption standards
through the CWLA. The views of such groups have proven to be
physically and emotionally harmful to the children whom they are
trying to protect. While adoption agencies try to search for a
racial match for a child, that child spends unnecessary time in

Waibel 11

foster or institutional care. In addition, adoption agencies have actually lowered their applicant requirements in order to make an inracial placement. A young Black boy in Ohio was killed by his adoptive Black parents after social workers failed to acknowledge potential warning signs about the couple's qualifications (Hermann 155). The present structure has failed our children and will continue to do so if it is left alone. What is needed is a major restructuring of the adoption system as we know it. Within a new system, all kinds of changes can be made in order to find the most loving and suitable home for orphaned children. However, it is impossible for each individual state to come up with its own system without there being discrepancies across state lines. A federal agency needs to be formed in order to regulate, investigate, and assist the adoption agencies in this country. Such an agency would serve as an umbrella organization to which all adoption agencies, public or private, would answer. Hopefully, this restructuring would also include the passage of a law banning any restrictions based on the race of the child or the adoptive parent. In the words of the NABSW, "Human beings are products of their environment and develop their sense of values, attitudes, and self-concept within their family structure" (McRoy 150). Restructuring the adoption system will give minority children a better chance of finding what the NABSW says they need most, a family.

    As has been shown, the adoption services available in this country are sorely inadequate. Rectifying this situation will

Waibel 12

not only take a lot of manpower, but it will require that
federal funds be allocated in order to meet the demands of
creating and operating a new system. In addition, this proposal
is, in fact, a long-term solution and we will obviously need to
implement short-term solutions as well. While the government is
busy trying to change the adoption situation, children are still
going to require adoption and foster services, and some short-
term objectives will create an atmosphere in which adoption and
foster care can still flourish.

Recent laws have fortunately eased the trials of parents
and children seeking to finalize interracial adoptions. The
Howard M. Metzenbaum Multiethnic Placement Act of 1994 (MEPA)
prohibits adoption and foster care placement agencies from
delaying or preventing placements due to racial differences
between the child and the would-be parents (National Adoption
Information Clearinghouse [NAIC]). In addition, a 1996 law
amending this act, the Interethnic Adoption Provisions (IEP),
strengthened the power of the government to enforce MEPA.
In addition to addressing bias by adoption and foster care
agencies, these laws are intended to shorten the time that
a child must wait for placement (NAIC). Both laws are a
significant step in the right direction.

Nevertheless, it may be some time before there are
statistically significant changes to the current state of
affairs. Change could best be promoted were the Department
of Health and Human Services to add a fifth division to its
department, the Office of Adoption and Foster Care. In the

15

beginning, this organization would be charged with the reformation of the adoption system, and would later oversee and govern the new system. In order for this office to regulate adoption fairly, it is important that all adoption agencies be required by law to follow the policies established by the office. To assure the public that their local agencies are legal, the office needs to establish a membership of agencies which can promote themselves as such. Nonmembership agencies would be subject to investigation from the office and would eventually die out due to lack of funding, as all public funds would be directed through the office to its membership.

Adoption agencies are not the only players in the adoption game, however, and other useful organizations need to be targeted for membership as well. Interim-care facilities, such as group homes like Orangewood Children's Home in Orange, California, provide children with a positive environment in which to grow while they are separated from their natural parents, or while they are waiting for a foster or adoptive family. Such organizations are integral to the adoption process and would benefit from the government membership system. Such a system of membership not only allows for fair regulation, but reassures those who seek out such services that the agency they have chosen will follow certain procedures in order to ensure a quick and successful adoption.

Secondly, the new office must sit down to establish a set of rules and procedures that agencies must follow. Covered in this set of rules would be things such as placing a ceiling over

Waibel 14

adoption fees, limiting the amount of time a child spends in foster or group care, and speeding up the paperwork process involved in adoption. These three subjects are universal concerns with regard to adoption, transracial or not. Transracial adoption, however, needs to be an issue of utmost concern to this office, and at the top of this list would be a rule stating that race cannot be an impediment to the adoption process, nor will race be a factor when determining the appropriateness of a family for a particular child. The important thing here is that race not be used as an excuse for why a child is without a family.

Social workers need to stop looking at transracial adoption as a second-rate alternative and start treating it as an equally valuable alternative to inracial adoption. In a study done by William Feigelman and Arnold R. Silverman of Nassau Community College, they found that "[transracially adopted] children's adjustments were generally similar to those of White in-racially adopted children" (600). In fact, little proof has been given to support the opposition's claims that transracially adopted children are maladjusted and have identity problems. We can conclude, then, that transracial adoption can and should be practiced with no more possible risk than any other type of adoption. From this point on, the Office of Adoption and Foster Care would be charged with overseeing and investigating the actions of adoption agencies. It would create a system of regulation that safeguards the children and the parents, rather than special interest groups and politicians.

While maintaining the adoption system, the office would also offer a wide variety of support and educational services for adopted and foster children and their families. Such services would include: regular group meetings for adopted children, regular meetings for adoptive parents, workshops on special-needs adoption, including transracial adoption and adoption of children with disabilities, and a widespread media campaign to promote the uniqueness of families formed through adoption as well as to recruit prospective families. In addition, the office needs to actively recruit minorities as prospective adoptive parents, not to promote inracial adoption, but to create as diverse a database of prospective parents as possible. This is achieved by setting up agencies in primarily minority areas staffed by a multi-ethnic group of people as has been previously recommended (McRoy 156-157). Not only does this create a more heterogeneous group from which to choose, but it also allays the fears of anti-transracial adoption groups that minorities will continue to be excluded from the adoption process.

The benefits of this restructuring will certainly outweigh   20
its costs. The government already pays for a vast majority of the country's social workers; thus the main budgetary increase would come from staffing the new office. Since the office would be a part of the already-established Department of Health and Human Services, it is possible that some staff members from other areas could be utilized here as well. Adoption has always been a state's issue; thus each individual state has a budget set aside for adoption services. Since the federal government would be

Waibel 16

relieving the states of many of their responsibilities regarding adoption, it would be fair for the states to be required to hand the money they set aside for adoption services over to the government. Not only does this relieve some of the federal government's budgetary tensions, but it allows for a smaller increase in taxes on the public, due to the fact that they are already paying for these services. The only difference is that the money goes to the federal government instead of the state government. However, there will have to be either an increase in taxes or a decrease in spending to help pay for this restructuring. The increase in taxes could be achieved by increasing property taxes on property worth over $500,000. Other revenue could be acquired by increasing interest rates on luxury loans over $500,000. Spending can be cut in every department with regard to the perks that agency officials receive. While the amount that this would generate is unknown, it is conceivable that this office could be maintained with minimal tax increases and spending decreases. However it is done, we have, in the end, ensured a future for abandoned children, something that has no price tag.

Unfortunately, this is a long-term process, and there are a few things we can do in the meantime in order to keep transracial adoption alive. First, all of the small organizations that have been formed over the years that promote transracial adoption, such as Parents to Adopt Minority Youngsters (PAMY), Families for Interracial Adoption, and Opportunity, need to come together to form a single advocacy group. This group should then create a database of transracial adoptees and their families and invite them to become part of the organization. Then they need to hire a professional lobbyist to give them a voice in Washington, D.C. Combining these groups of people would prove to be fruitful in expediting the implementation of the preceding proposal.

The second thing that is essential in promoting transracial adoption is the widespread involvement of the media. The media is so important to the cause of transracial adoption, and it has already proven to be a very powerful force. On September 9, 1992, the state of Texas removed a Black boy from his White foster parents, Lana and Phillip Jenkins. In October of that same year, the Jenkinses appeared on The Phil Donahue Show. The show aired a tape of the Jenkinses' son, Christopher, being taken away from his parents kicking and screaming. As a result, the Jenkinses received calls and letters in support of their cause, and the national attention was beneficial because, on January 15, 1993, the Jenkinses got Christopher back. Through the media, the state of Texas was forced to change its laws to allow transracial adoption. James Myart, the attorney for the Jenkinses, told Phil Donahue that "It was the national attention brought by you [Donahue], quite frankly, that got the people in the state of Texas, and throughout this country, to rally in support of this White family and this Black child" (Donahue 15 March 1994). More media attention like this is needed to get the general public involved in this issue so they can pressure their representatives in Washington to do something about it.

Waibel 18

While the most ideal of all situations is for all children
to be born into a family that could provide them with the love
and support they need to grow into a productive adult, this is
not likely to ever be the case. Thus we must provide those
children who don't have the benefits of a loving family with the
resources to find one. The adoption system we presently use is
inefficient and inconsistent. The very children it strives to
protect are the ones who suffer the most. Minority children have
suffered the most because of the controversies and conflicting
viewpoints regarding transracial adoption. The very title
"transracial adoption" places a stigma upon the practice, making
it sound like placing a minority child in a White family is the
process of stepping over a specific line, of crossing a set
boundary. This is not the case. Transracial adoption is not
about color or political agendas; it is about love. With the
help of the media, the public, and the federal government, it is
possible to put the love back into the adoption process for all
of the adoptable children.

Works Cited

Austin, Judy, ed. Adoption: The Inside Story. New York: Barn Owl
    Books, 1985.

Bagley, Christopher, Loretta Young, and Anne Scully. International
    and Transracial Adoptions. Brookfield, Vermont: Ashgate
    Publishing Company, 1993.

Brophy, Beth. "The Unhappy Politics of Interracial Adoption."
    U.S. News and World Report 13 Nov. 1989: 72-74.

Day, Dawn. The Adoption of Black Children. London: Souvenir Press
    Ltd., 1984.

Feigelman, William, and Arnold R. Silverman. "The Long-Term Effects
    of Transracial Adoption." Social Service Review 58 (1984):
    588-602.

Hayes, Peter. "Transracial Adoption: Politics and Ideology." Child
    Welfare 72 (1993): 301-310.

Hermann, Valerie Phillips. "Transracial Adoption: 'Child-Saving'
    or 'Child-Snatching'?" National Black Law Journal 13
    (1993): 147-164.

Kallgren, Carl A., and Pamela J. Caudill. "Current Transracial
    Adoption Practices: Racial Dissonance or Racial Awareness?"
    Psychological Reports 72 (1993): 551-558.

Landrith, James A. The Multiracial Activist. 30 Nov. 2001
    <http://www.multiracial.com>.

McRoy, Ruth G. "An Organizational Dilemma: The Case of Transracial
    Adoptions." The Journal of Applied Behavioral Science 25.2
    (1989): 145-160.

Waibel 20

National Adoption Information Clearinghouse. 30 Nov. 2001
        <http://www.calib.com/naic/index.htm>.
The Phil Donahue Show. NBC. KNBC, Los Angeles, 15 Mar. 1994.
Rosenthal, Donna. "Did Cultures Clash over 'Schindler's'?" Los
        Angeles Times 22 Jan. 1994: F1, F9.
Simon, Rita James, and Howard Alstein. Transracial Adoption. New
        York: John Wiley and Sons, Inc., 1977.
---. Transracial Adoptees and Their Families. New York: Praeger
        Publishers, 1987.
---. Adoption, Race, and Identity. New York: Praeger Publishers,
        1992.
Wheeler, David L. "Black Children, White Parents." The Chronicle of
        Higher Education 15 Sept. 1993: A9, A16.
Zastrow, Charles H. Outcome of Black Children-White Parents
        Transracial Adoptions. San Francisco: R&E Research
        Associates, Inc., 1977.

Sample Paper Format: APA Style

In the Best Interest of the Child?   4

References

Austin, J. (Ed.). (1985). Adoption: The inside story.
New York: Barn Owl Books.

Bagley, C., Young, L., & Scully, A. (1993).
International and transracial adoptions. Vermont: Ashgate.

Brophy, B. (1989, November 13). The unhappy politics
of interracial adoption. U.S. News & World Report, 45,
72-74.

In the Best Interest of the Child?   3

a feasible solution to the predicament adoption agencies
faced concerning minority children. In 1948, in
Minneapolis, Minnesota, a Black social worker named Laura
Gaskin placed a Black child with a white adoptive family

at least
1"

at least
1"

In the Best Interest of the Child?   2

center title

In the Best Interest of the Child?

5 spaces

Transracial adoption has historically followed a
pattern much like that of a roller coaster; one year it is
favored, the next year it is opposed. Athough the roller
coaster has taken many twists and turns, the motor
propelling it has never changed. Like many things,

5 spaces

In the Best Interest of the Child?   1

at least
1"

Running head: IN THE BEST INTEREST OF THE CHILD?

In the Best Interest of the Child?
Kimberly Waibel
Rutgers University

center title, name, school

GLOSSARY

ad hominem Latin for "to the man"; personal attack on an opponent instead of on the opponent's arguments

ad populum Latin for "to the people"; an argument that appeals to general sentiments or prejudices

allusion A reference to a person or fact (for example, the American Revolution) that the audience is expected to know without explanation

analogy A comparison for purposes of explanation, usually between something concrete and something abstract

analysis The breaking down of complete matters into simpler ones

appeal A traditional name for the method by which the arguer hopes to convince the reader; for example, the appeal to reason

argument Language organized and used to convince others

assertion A declaration of belief

assumption Ideas or values that the writer takes as givens

audience The imagined readers of your argument

authority A reliable, expert source of support

backing The authority or evidence on which a warrant is based

begging the question An attempt to assume in advance what needs to be proved

bibliography A list of works on a subject

claim The conclusion your argument is attempting to prove

cliché An expression so worn out as to convey little meaning

connotation The associations inspired by a word; its flavor or spirit, as opposed to the strict meaning, its denotation

data Facts that prompt you to make your argument

deductive reasoning Reasoning from general principles to particular conclusions

demonstration The provision of reasons and evidence to support assertions

denotation The literal, dictionary definition of a word

diction Word choice: "high" diction is formal, "low" diction informal

enthymeme A syllogism whose parts are not all clearly stated

equivocate To deliberately use ambiguous words to confuse the issue

ethos The qualities of character, intelligence, and morality that an arguer conveys through the manner of argument

grounds A term in Toulmin's system that is equivalent to *data*

hyperbole A statement exaggerated for effect

hypothesis A conditionally held theory to aid in exploring the meaning of what you seek to explain

inductive reasoning The type of reasoning that proceeds from particular facts to general explanations

inference The intuitive act of recognizing an implication

irony Intentionally saying one thing to convey another

logos The traditional name for the appeal to reason or logic

metaphor A comparison that illustrates meaning through figurative language, for example, "Babe Ruth was the Sultan of Swat."

non sequitur A statement that does not follow from a previous statement

paradox An apparent contradiction that contains a deeper meaning, for example, "nothing is so invisible as the obvious"

paraphrase Restating a point in your own words

pathos The traditional name for the appeal to emotion or feeling

persona The implied character created by the writer to speak for him or her; for example, at a given time a writer's persona may seem to be a joker, but the writer is a *person* whose complex identity may not be reduced to a role played at a particular time

persuasion The act of seeking to convince others

plagiarism Using someone else's words or ideas without giving proper credit

point of view The attitude with which a writer approaches the subject

post hoc, ergo propter hoc Latin for "after this, therefore because of this"; the false assumption that, because one event happened after another, the first somehow caused the second

premise The underlying assumption from which one begins to make a point

qualifier A restriction or modification in the extent of an argued claim

rebuttal The part of an argument that allows for exceptions without having to give up the claim as generally true

red herring A false or misleading issue designed to disguise the real issue

refutation The process of meeting and overcoming the arguments of your opponent

rhetoric Traditionally, the art and study of persuasion; now loosely used to suggest an emphasis on manner at the expense of matter

rhetorical question A question asked figuratively, for effect, rather than literally, for information

simile Using *like* or *as* in acknowledgment that one is using figurative language: "In the world of baseball, Babe Ruth was like a giant."

syllogism A classical method of deductive reasoning in which two premises considered together lead with certainty to a conclusion

syntax Word order

thesis The central idea of an argument or essay

tone The way a writer "sounds"; the writer's attitude

Toulmin system The method of reasoned argument invented by Stephen Toulmin and emphasized in the appeals to reason analyzed in this book

transition A link between points or sections in writing

trope A name for "figure of speech"

warrant The underlying generalization (explicit or implicit) that the writer expects the reader to share and that connects the data with the claim

writing process A general term for the stages involved from prewriting through the production of a final draft

CREDITS

CLEVELAND AMORY, "The Trials of Animals," *The New York Times,* September 17, 1989, Copyright © 1989 The New York Times Co. Reprinted by permission.

ROBERT ATWAN, "A Meditation on Barbie Dolls." Used with permission from the author.

JAMES BARSZCZ, "Can You Be Educated from a Distance?" Reprinted with permission from the author.

SARA BIRD, "The Q Gene," *The New York Times,* May 1, 1994. Copyright © 1994 The New York Times Co. Reprinted by permission.

DICK BOLAND, "Serving Time the Old-Fashioned Way," March 4, 1998. Reprinted by permission from Dick Boland and Creators Syndicate.

LINDA BOWLES, "Big Brother's Two-Minute Hate," May 13, 1998. Reprinted with permission from Linda Bowles and Creators Syndicate.

FRED BRONSON, "A Selected Chronology of Musical Controversy," *Billboard,* March 26, 1994. Copyright © BPI Communications, Inc. Used with permission.

SAM BROWNBACK, "Free Speech: Lyrics, Liberty, and License," May 15, 1998. *Vital Speeches,* City News Publishing Co. Reprinted by permission.

RHONDA BURNS, "Downsizing the Middle Class." Used with permission from the author.

STEPHEN CHAPMAN, "Public Servants Often Behave Like Masters," March 11, 1998. Reprinted with permission from Stephen Chapman and Creators Syndicate.

MONA CHAREN, "Reparations Question Won't Go Away," June 22, 2001. Reprinted with permission from Creators Syndicate; "Living Together: Test Run for Loneliness," March 23, 1999. Reprinted with permission from Mona Charen and Creators Syndicate.

LINDA CHAVEZ, "Scientists Keep Crossing the Line on Cloning," November 27, 2001. Reprinted by permission of Linda Chavez and Creators Syndicate.

SALLY CHEN, "Smoking Is Bad for Everyone So It Should Be Illegal." Used with permission from the author.

CHUCK D., "'Free' Music Can Free the Artist," *New York Times,* April 29, 2000. Copyright © 2000 by the New York Times Co. Reprinted by permission.

MATTHEW E. CONOLLY, "Euthanasia Is Not the Answer." Used by permission of the author.

E. J. DIONNE, "Tough Call on Cell Phones." Copyright © 2001 The Washington Post. Reprinted with permission.

HELEN DODGE, "Special Crimes Need Special Laws." Used by permission of the author.

BARBARA EHRENREICH, "Ice-T: The Issue Is Free Speech," *Time,* July 20, 1992. Copyright © 1992 Time Inc. Reprinted by permission.

MAUREEN FARSAN, "Shouting Fire in a Virtual Theater." Reprinted with permission from the author.

DON FEDER, "An Amendment Is Not the Way to Honor the Flag." Reprinted with permission from Don Feder and Creators Syndicate.

SAMUEL FRANCIS, "'Hate Crime' Laws Change the Law," June 27, 1998. Copyright © 1998 Tribune Media Services, Inc. All rights reserved. Reprinted with permission.

MAGGIE GALLAGHER, "It's the Final Step in Killing Marriage." Copyright © 2001 Maggie Gallagher. Distributed by Universal Press Syndicate. Reprinted with permission. All rights reserved.

HENRY LOUIS GATES, JR., "Whose Canon Is It, Anyway? Its Not Just Anglo-Saxon." Copyright © 1991 by Henry Louis Gates, Jr. Originally published in *The New York Times.* Reprinted by permission of the author.

INDEX